# THE SEARCH FOR POLITICAL SPACE: GLOBALIZATION, SOCIAL MOVEMENTS, AND THE URBAN POLITICAL EXPERIENCE

In *The Search for Political Space* Warren Magnusson argues that the emergent political spaces of the twenty-first century will be more like local municipalities than sovereign states. These ambivalent spaces point beyond themselves and disrupt the dominant discourse of sovereignty.

In an effort to rethink the boundaries and horizons of contemporary politics, the author focuses on the practical experiences of recent social movements in relation to municipal government. Using examples from Britain, the United States, and Canada, he proposes that, although constrained by the state, the market, and the modern social disciplines, municipal politics offers a place where ordinary people can engage locally with global issues. The discussion ranges over such topics as socialist economics, municipal foreign policy, feminist direct action intergovernmental fiscal struggles, environmental activism, the politics of identity, and the practices of local democracy. From various perspectives, Magnusson addresses the underlying question: how can people use the space afforded by the municipality to transcend the political limits of the state?

*The Search for Political Space* is a valuable contribution to the study of urban politics within the context of political theory, and the issues and arguments it raises are fundamental to discussions of the future of politics in the twenty-first century.

WARREN MAGNUSSON is Professor of Political Science, University of Victoria.

STUDIES IN COMPARATIVE POLITICAL ECONOMY AND PUBLIC POLICY

Editors: MICHAEL HOWLETT, DAVID LAYCOCK, and STEPHEN MCBRIDE, *Simon Fraser University*

Editorial Advisory Board

ISABEL BAKKER, *Political Science, York University*

COLIN BENNETT, *Political Science, University of Victoria*

WALLACE CLEMENT, *Sociology, Carleton University*

WILLIAM COLEMAN, *Political Science, McMaster University*

BARRY EICHENGREEN, *Economics, University of California (Berkeley)*

WYNN GRANT, *Political Science, University of Warwick*

JOHN HOLMES, *Geography, Queen's University*

JANE JENSEN, *Political Science, Université de Montréal*

WILLIAM LAFFERTY, *Project for an Alternative Future, Oslo*

GORDON LAXER, *Sociology, University of Alberta*

RONALD MANZER, *Political Science, University of Toronto*

JOHN RAVENHILL, *Political Science, Australia National University*

PETER TAYLOR-GOOBY, *Social Work, University of Kent*

MARGARET WEIR, *Brookings Institution, Washington, D.C.*

WARREN MAGNUSSON

# The Search for Political Space

## Globalization, Social Movements, and the Urban Political Experience

UNIVERSITY OF TORONTO PRESS
Toronto Buffalo London

© University of Toronto Press Incorporated 1996
Toronto Buffalo London
Printed in Canada

ISBN 0-8020-5959-7 (cloth)
ISBN 0-8020-6889-8 (paper)

Printed on acid-free paper

---

**Canadian Cataloguing in Publication Data**

Magnusson, Warren, 1947–
The search for political space : globalization,
social movements, and the urban political experience

Includes index.
ISBN 0-8020-5959-7 (bound) ISBN 0-8020-6889-8 (pbk.)

1. Municipal government. 2. Right and left
(Political science). I. Title.

JS78.M3 1996 320.8'5 C96-930833-7

---

University of Toronto Press acknowledges the financial assistance to its publishing program of the Canada Council and the Ontario Arts Council.

# Contents

# Acknowledgments

This book grows out of two intellectual projects – a critique of the state-centricity of contemporary political thought and an empiricial study of the nature and effects of municipal radicalism. Originally, I meant to keep these projects separate, but they have coalesced gradually since I began working on them in the late 1980s. I like to think that my empirical work has grounded my theoretical reflections, and vice versa.

Much of this book has appeared in some previous form, but only the most assiduous follower of my work could have seen more than a fraction of it. Chapters 3 to 6 and 10 to 12 are very near to their originals; the others have been thoroughly revised or are based on previously unpublished papers. Obviously, the Introduction and Conclusion and the connecting passages are new. As for the rest:

Chapter 1 began as a revision of 'Decentring the State, or Looking for Politics,' in W.K. Carroll, ed., *Organizing Dissent: Contemporary Social Movements in Theory and Practice* (Toronto: Garamond Press, 1992), 69–80. It also incorporates material from 'Critical Social Movements,' in A.-G. Gagnon and J.P. Bickerton, eds., *Canadian Politics: An Introduction to the Discipline*, 1st ed. (Peterborough, ON: Broadview Press, 1990), 525–41.

Chapter 2 began as a revision of 'The Reification of Political Community,' in R.B.J. Walker and S.H. Mendlovitz, eds., *Contending Sovereignties: Redefining Political Community* (Boulder: Lynne Rienner, 1990), 45–60. Copyright © 1990 by Lynne Rienner Publishers. Used with permission of the publisher. I have also incorporated material from 'Social Movements and the State: Presentation and Representation,' in G. Albo, D. Langille, and L. Panitch, eds., *A Different Kind of State? Popular Power and Democratic Administration* (Toronto: Oxford University Press, 1993),

122–30. The latter paper was originally presented at a Workshop on Democratic Administration at York University in April 1991.

Chapter 3 is little altered from 'De-Centring the State,' in J.P. Bickerton and A.-G. Gagnon, eds., *Canadian Politics*, 2nd ed. (Toronto: Broadview Press, 1994), 567–86.

Chapter 4 was originally published as 'The Constitution of Movements vs. the Constitution of the State: Rediscovering the Local as a Site for Global Politics,' in Henri Lustiger-Thaler, ed., *Political Arrangements: Power and the City* (Montreal: Black Rose Books, 1992), 69–93. It is little changed here. An earlier version of the paper was presented at a joint session of the Socialist Studies Society and the Canadian Sociology and Anthropology Association in Charlottetown, P.E.I., in May 1992.

Chapter 5 is a slightly extended version of an article published as 'Metropolitan Change and Political Disruption: The New Left, the New Right, and the Postwar Orthodoxy,' in Frances Frisken, ed., *The Changing Canadian Metropolis: A Public Policy Perspective* (Berkeley: Institute of Governmental Studies Press, University of California, and Toronto: Canadian Urban Institute, 1994), vol. 2, pp. 541–60. An earlier version of this paper was presented at a conference in North York on the Changing Canadian Metropolis, in October 1990. Both the conference and the book were sponsored by the Canada Mortgage and Housing Corporation.

Chapter 6 is based on a well-travelled and often modified paper, ultimately published in much the same form as here under the title 'Power and Politics in the Global City,' in Janice Caulfield and John Wanna, eds., *Power and Politics in the City: Brisbane in Transition* (South Melbourne: Macmillan of Australia, 1995), pp. 18–33. This paper was given in its earliest version at the Department of Political Science at York University in January 1990, then later at the Great Lakes Economic Development Conference in Chicago in September that year, and finally at the Conference on Power and Policy in Brisbane at Griffith University, Queensland, in October 1992.

Chapter 7 has appeared in no previous form.

Chapter 8 is based loosely on a series of papers delivered in 1989, the first ('Libertarian Municipalism and the Reification of Political Space') at the International Conference on the Welfare State and Civil Society at the University of Ottawa in January, the second ('Radical Municipalities: A Comparative Perspective') at the Canadian Political Association Annual Meeting at Université Laval in June, and the third ('Radical Municipalities in North America') at the American Political Science Association Annual Meeting in Atlanta in August.

Chapter 9 derives from a paper ('Restructuring the Local State: Fiscal Struggles in Britain and British Columbia in the 1980s') delivered at a joint session of the Canadian Political Science Association and the Canadian Historical Association at their annual meetings at the University of Victoria in May 1990.

Chapter 10 is a slightly extended version of a paper co-written with Leslie Kenny, and published as 'In Transition: The Women's House Saving Action,' in *Canadian Review of Sociology and Anthropology* 30, no. 3 (1993), 359–76. It was originally delivered under a different title ('In and Against the State') to the Canadian Political Science Association Annual Meeting in Charlottetown, P.E.I., in June 1992.

Chapter 11 was published as 'Dissidence and Insurgency: Municipal Foreign Policy in the 1980s,' in Henri Lustiger-Thaler and Daniel Salée, eds., *Artful Practices: The Political Economy of Everyday Life* (Montreal: Black Rose Books, 1994), 162–88. Considerably longer versions of this paper were delivered at the Fourth International Karl Polanyi Conference at Concordia University, in November 1992, and at the American Political Science Association Annual Meeting in Washington in September 1993.

Chapter 12 was published originally in *Millennium: Journal of International Studies* 23, no. 3 (Winter 1994), 621–45.

In terms of financial support, my main debt is to the Social Sciences and Humanities Research Council of Canada – and hence to the Canadian people – for providing research grants in 1987–90 and again since 1994. Without this assistance I would not have been able to do any of the primary research that informs my analysis. The University of Victoria has also provided small research grants and conference travel funding, and this help has been crucial. York University, the University of Ottawa, Griffith University, the University of Liverpool, and the Canada Mortgage and Housing Corporation have provided welcome support that enabled me to attend particular conferences. The CMHC was particularly generous with respect to Chapter 5.

SSHRCC funding enabled me to conduct interviews with officials, politicians, community activists, journalists, and urban analysts in a number of different cities on both sides of the Atlantic. My thanks go to Judy Abdo, Chris Adamson, Larry Agran, Liz Amer, Jacques Aubry, Eve Bach, Fred Barker, Maurice Barnes, Jan Barnsley, John Benington, Gideon Ben-Tovim, Clive Betts, David Blunkett, Sam Boskey, John Brauer, Kathleen Burgess De Vries, Jon Caulfield, Laura Chase, Mary

Chesworth, Dave Clark, Peter Clavelle, James Conn, Jeremy Corbyn, Lea Cousineau, Richard Crowson, John Darwin, Libby Davies, Penny Deleray, Jacques Desmarais, Megan Ellis, David Finkel, Gillian Freedman, Richard Gilbert, Ann Fagan Ginger, Michael Goldrick, Sue Goss, Geoff Green, Lucy de Groot, Greg Guma, John Gyford, H. Lee Halterman, Pierre Hamel, Pierre J. Hamel, Mike Harcourt, Ken Hawkins, Margaret Hodge, Roger Hollander, Thomas Hutton, Chuck Iverson, Peter Kilfoyle, Helen Jackson, Anne Johnston, Trevor Jones, Mark E. Kann, Thomas J. Kent, Usman Khan, Robert Kraushaar, Jack Layton, Dan Leckie, Don Lennox, Steve Lord, Peggy Lyons, Rachel Magnusson, Diane Martin, Neil Mayer, John McDonnell, Ruth Midgley, Robert Mier, Richard Minns, David Moberg, Emma Morgan, Vicki Morris, Salin Muwakkil, James Nixon, Conn O'Ryan, Pierre Paquette, Michael Parkinson, Dolores Press, Lisa Price, Jim Quail, Bob Quick, Harry Rankin, Vicki Roberts, Damaris Rose, Marvin Rotrand, Joel Rubenzhal, François Saillant, Bernie Sanders, Jenny Sands, Mukesh Savani, Gus Schultz, Marion Scott, John Sewell, Erik Shragge, John Shutt, Kram Sidiq, Al Silbowitz, Myer Simiaticki, Nancy Skinner, Douglas Smith, Alfred Stocks, Peter Totterdill, Marie-Odile Trépanier, Beth Wagstaff, Michael Ward, Les Weatheritt, Chris Webb, Pauline Weinstein, Gerda Wekerle, Alan Wigfield, Fred Wilson, Valerie Wise, and Dennis Zane. Leslie Kenny also spoke on our behalf with Bonnie Agnew, Shashi Assanad, Nancy Drewitt, Gail Edinger, Jeff Fox, Jerry Fordyce, Anne Kloppenborg, Gardia Koolwine, Lee Lakeman, Betty Lough, Monica Matsi, Parvin Parvoti, Ajax Quinby, Vicky Randall, Judy Rogers, Esther Shannon, Muggs Sigurgeirson, Greda Smith, Mercy Thomas, and Frances Wasserlein. I hope I have not forgotten anyone, because everyone was remarkably open and helpful.

Thanks again to the SSHRCC, I was able to employ a number of valuable research assistants from time to time, both in Victoria and in the study cities. All of these assistants were efficient and helpful. I am grateful to Barbara Arneil, Peter Cozens, Diane Crossley, Aquiles Garro-Jimenez, Thomas Graham, Sandra Kahale, Leslie Kenny, Yvon Lacoste, Michael Lancaster, Evan Leeson, Marie-France Lefort, Sharon Lord, David MacDonald, Peter McLaverty, John Meredith, Patricia Murphy, Rod Neufeld, Marc Piche, Ruth Rogers, Fred Rose, Catherine Ross, Sharon Walls, and Jerry Wedmedyk for their work and their insights – as well as to all those people who facilitated their work.

A number of academics outside Victoria were especially helpful to me when I was attempting to find out more about the patterns of local politics elsewhere. I am indebted to Larry Bennett, Terry Fowler, John

Gyford, Thomas Kent, Jacques Léveillée, Michael Parkinson, Patrick Seyd, Jim Sharpe, Derek Shearer, and others in this respect. I owe particular thanks to Pierre Clavel, who inspired me with his own work and graciously shared various research facilities with me. In a project like this, one is gratified to discover that the notion of an international scholarly community is more than a pretty illusion.

Intellectually, I owe my greatest debt to Rob Walker, whose influence is apparent throughout this book, but especially in Part One. The first three essays were written in consequence of a joint paper we wrote, which in turn drew heavily on analyses he had developed in the context of his work with the Committee for a Just World Peace. The two of us have taught political theory together at the University of Victoria for more than fifteen years, and have shared much in that time. He has taught me and many others to think in new ways about politics and the state.

Bill Carroll, Allene and Norman Magnusson, Bruce Milne, Michael M'Gonigle, Leo Panitch, and Judith Stamps also deserve particular thanks, for their ideas and criticism and for the stimulus they offered. Leslie Kenny did most of the interviews in connection with Chapter 10, and also co-wrote the conference paper and article on which this chapter is based. It would have been impossible for me to pursue this line of research without her assistance I am truly grateful for the opportunity to have worked with such a bright and creative student.

At the University of Toronto Press, Virgil Duff has been a patient and supportive editor. Caroline Andrew and Dennis Judd made very useful suggestions for improving the manuscript. Matthew Kudelka proved to be an efficient and sensitive copy editor.

My colleagues in the Department of Political Science at the University of Victoria – especially Colin Bennett, Terry Morley, Norman Ruff, and Jeremy Wilson – have shared many burdens, as have our departmental staff – Doris Lam, Laurel Barnes, and Erin Kuyvenhoven – who have worked cheerfully and efficiently through some difficult times. The department has provided a friendly and stimulating environment for both teaching and research. I have learned a great deal from my students over the years, and I am especially grateful to those in the Interdisciplinary Program in Contemporary Social and Political Thought, who keep pressing me forward into new intellectual domains. I hope this book will answer their questions about what I do when I am left to my own devices.

WARREN MAGNUSSON

# THE SEARCH FOR POLITICAL SPACE

# Introduction: Elusive Spaces

> The famous sovereignty of political bodies has always been an illusion, which, moreover, can be maintained only by the instruments of violence, that is, with essentially nonpolitical means. Under human conditions, which are determined by the fact that not man but men live on the earth, freedom and sovereignty are so little identical that they cannot even exist simultaneously. Where men wish to be sovereign, as individuals or as organized groups, they must submit to the oppression of the will, be this the individual will with which I force myself, or the 'general will' of an organized group. If men wish to be free, it is precisely sovereignty that they must renounce.[1]

When Hannah Arendt wrote these words thirty-five years ago, she was little concerned about distinguishing between men and women. Her interest was in the way that freedom – political freedom – had been lost, not just in the Nazi Germany that she had fled but in the Western civilization that she treasured. In a way, her work was a long meditation on the loss of that freedom and the conditions for its recovery.[2] Steeped in the thought of her ambiguous mentor, Martin Heidegger, and caught between the many currents of critique among the exiled German intelligentsia, Arendt found the political reflections of the eighteenth-century American revolutionaries revealing.[3] From them, and from the experiences of later revolutionaries who had created fragile spaces of freedom, she drew her own ideas about the possibility of and the human necessity for a politics that could shatter the illusion of sovereignty. She knew how hard such a politics was, and how easily it could collapse under the demand for total control. That demand for control – that insistence on the unity that would resolve all differences – was at the heart of the illusion of sovereignty and the violence it produced everywhere.

As far as I know, Arendt was never interested in municipal government. In this, she was typical of most political theorists and political scientists. However, she was one source of inspiration for the New Left activists of the 1960s and 1970s, who shared her concerns about the sovereignties of the state, capitalism, and bourgeois culture. These concerns extended to the practices of the Old Left, which was (so it seemed) organized on its own sovereignty principles in socialist parties and labour unions. Escaping the sovereignty principle meant affirming the possibility of popular democratic action within public spaces that were not ordered from above. Such 'free' spaces, where people could present themselves to one another and engage in actions that respected one another's autonomy, were akin to the ones Arendt had envisioned. The search for such spaces marked the politics of the New Left in the 1960s and the new social movements of the 1970s and 1980s, and inspired new political coalitions like the European Greens. Throughout these decades, there was a profound sense among progressive activists that the spaces that had been reserved for people to participate in their own government were entirely inadequate to their ostensible purpose, even in the most open of liberal democracies. In the face of sovereignty, democracy was an illusion.

In the mid-1990s the sense of despair about the lack of political space has become acute. This is reflected in the resurgence of fascism and right-wing populism on both sides of the Atlantic. One hears less now than a decade ago about libertarian capitalism and libertarian socialism, and more about the fundamentalist politics of identity, which has taken its most sickening forms in the hills of Bosnia-Herzegovina and the villages of Rwanda and Burundi. The evident failure of liberal and social democratic politicians from Bill Clinton downward has heightened anxieties everywhere and contributed to the sense that a more open, egalitarian, and humane politics is nearly impossible.

Nevertheless, the world keeps surprising us, not least in the constant innovations of the young, who keep inventing political spaces of their own. This book seeks to understand those spaces – especially the ones in the dark corners of municipal politics – where people can act freely and effectively. I hope that I have managed to hold the balance that Arendt sought between a clear-eyed analysis of the difficulties of politics and a proper sense of the possibilities of creative political action. Like old soldiers refighting the last war, we may come to despair simply because we cannot see that the times have changed and that the space for action is different.

To talk of the search for political space is difficult, because space is such an elusive concept. Most of us know that Einstein discovered the relativity of space and time, and so vanquished for good the notions of absolute space that had informed Newtonian physics. Many people have sensed that the models of space and time that we use for social and political analysis reflect the old Newtonian assumptions.[4] Historical and anthropological research seems to confirm that premodern people had different ways of thinking about time and space, but such alternatives have been pushed to the margins in our own era.[5] That there are other conceptions of space and time suggests that currently dominant ways of thinking are not simply a result of the human brain's organization. Thus, we have to consider the possibility that our Newtonian assumptions freeze contemporary political and social understanding in a way that prevents us from dealing with our problems effectively.

Geographers have long held that the uncritical understanding of space in social theory has led to profound distortions. They complain that time has been privileged in relation to space, and hence that history has been invoked over geography in developing the most influential social theories.[6] Historians, of course, see things differently, and complain that social theory – including economic and political theory – tends to abstract from history, and hence from the effects of time. The leading disciplines of the social sciences – political science, sociology, and economics – are all criticized for the way that they abstract from space *and* time, geography *and* history, and pose their findings in an imaginary world that can never be.[7] In truth, these findings (and the theories that inform them) are based on unstated and unexamined assumptions about the nature of space and time – assumptions that mirror the ideas that Einstein discredited at the beginning of this century.

This apparent lag in social theory is the source of growing concern, but there is no agreement about what would be involved in bringing our thinking up to date. How does one 'think socially' in four-dimensional (or *n*-dimensional) terms, so that the intimate relationship between space and time becomes apparent?[8] How does one reformulate traditional theories of social causation in light of the discoveries of quantum physics, which emphasize the uncertainty of our observations and the apparent absence of causation at the subatomic level?[9] Do the recent developments in chaos theory provide a clue to understanding the breakdown and reorganization of social systems?[10] These are only some of the questions that nag at the edges of social science (see Chapter 12 for further reflections on this subject). In many ways they mirror the challenges that come from postmodernist or poststructuralist thinking. While these challenges are extremely various and have emerged in many different academic disciplines, they have in common a conviction that there can be no secure foundations for our thinking.[11] This may be another way of saying that there is no absolute space – and hence that there can be no rightful sovereignty.

Many people find such challenges profoundly disturbing and are apt to blame the postmodernists for disrupting the critical spaces from which modern intellectuals have done their work. One of the signs of modernity is to be self-critical and to question one's own intellectual assumptions. However, critics have always held out the hope that there is a secure space (sovereign centre?) just over the intellectual horizon, from which it will be possible to make accurate judgments and produce true knowledge. It is this hope that the postmodernists seem to have dashed by insisting that all knowledge is necessarily local and particular – relative if you will – and that there is no absolute standpoint from which to judge the truth. The fact that this epistemological position accords reasonably well with the insights of twentieth-century philosophy is no comfort to those who complain that the practical certainties they require have been destroyed by nihilistic criticisms.[12]

As will become clear, I have little sympathy for those who live in terror of relativism.[13] I think that I am much more likely to die in an earthquake or be run over by a bus than to have my life destroyed by the recognition that I am not God and that I will never fully understand the world I live in. (As I recall, I noticed I wasn't God when I was quite young.) An understanding of the relativity of our own moral and political judgments ought to lead to a kind of modesty, rather than to a nihilistic abandonment of morality and politics. Since I cannot imagine how large numbers of people could live together without morality and politics, I expect that both morality and politics will be produced regardless of what philosophers or critics have to say. If both are developed under conditions that encourage recognition of the limits of anyone's judgment, and of the relativity of people's values, and of the timeful character of political action, that will not be a bad thing. We live not in a distant future, or in another country, but here and now; our responsibilities have to be understood in terms of particular people with wants, needs, aspirations, and values that can only be understood within context. To be disappointed that we cannot live in the absolute, with absolute knowledge, is rather silly. If intellectuals have a particular responsibility, it is not to decry relativism and tell people that they are lost without absolutes, but rather to explain that the search for absolutes is an evasion of our moral and political responsibilities. Just as in daily life we have to make choices without benefit of certainty, and to take responsibility for our actions nonetheless, so in public affairs or social life we have to take charge and be accountable without ever knowing for certain that what we do will seem right or good to our descendants or even to our neighbours. Neither philosophy nor science nor religion can guarantee that anyone is right.

It is in this tentative but responsible spirit that we have to approach the problem of rethinking the space – and time – for contemporary politics. There are many reasons for believing that we have to give up on the idea that there is an absolutely determined, singular space in which politics has to occur. We probably also have to abandon the notion that our history is all of a piece – in other words, that everyone in the world is living in the same time (I explore this thought further in Chapter 3.) And we have to accept that space and time are relative to each other, at least in the sense that particular conceptions of the one involve assumptions about the other. These are difficult moves to make. What begins to emerge when we loosen our Newtonian conceptions is the possibility, if not the necessity, of understanding our world in terms of a multiplicity of incommensurable realities. The world – and hence politics – is not one thing only, but many things simultaneously. These many things are related to one another in ways that we can only dimly perceive. There are patterns, perhaps even 'laws' of political development, but to know them is not to have the means of predicting outcomes. On the contrary, it appears that the future is inherently open-ended. As I emphasize in Chapter 1, we cannot locate ourselves in relation to just one world and just one history; instead we have to come to terms with the multiplicity of worlds and histories – spaces and times – that make up the political conditions we face.[14] This is a lesson that many are just beginning to learn in the wake of the Cold War.

Later in this book – particularly in Parts Two and Three – I will be dealing less with philosophical issues than with the *practical* search for political space, especially as it occurs in a municipal context. This reflects my conviction that the important issues are ultimately practical, and that the political possibilities of the present – the 'timeful spaces' we can enter – have to be understood in terms of the concrete activities in which people are engaged. The most interesting and innovative of these activities run up against old, formulaic answers to the question of political space – answers that tell us where our politics has to be and hence *what* it has to be. Generally, these answers can be traced to the beginnings of modernity. Unfortunately, they ignore or misconstrue most of what is going on politically. There is a huge gap (if I may be forgiven a crude spatial metaphor) between the politics that engages people practically and the politics that is described in most contemporary writings. (I explore this theme in Chapter 2.) The what, where, why, and how of the politics that most affects us are usually pushed aside in favour of an analysis that focuses on what people have long thought 'politics' has to be about. To the extent that we analyse the various fields of political practice outside the framework of politics as traditionally conceived, we tend to apply analytical tools that are designed for other purposes. The result is that good political analysis is driven out by bad psychology and even worse moralizing. In this book I attempt to focus on the ongoing effort to discover, explore, and rearticulate timeful political spaces, without prejudging these efforts in terms of the conventional assumptions of political science or its rivals.

I am especially interested in the municipality as a political space, because it has so long been offered to ordinary people as a place where they can participate in the business of the state. Since the modern system of representative government began to develop in the seventeenth century, analysts have recognized that there is inevitably a gap between the rulers and the ruled. Indeed, the representative system was designed to sustain that gap and thus ensure responsible government rather than mob rule. John Stuart Mill and other nineteenth-century analysts recognized that it was essential in an increasingly democratic culture to allow for popular participation without disrupting the good order of the state. Local self-government was the obvious means, and it has been on offer ever since in the liberal democracies. From the beginning, however, the terms were set in favour of the state. The municipality, which supposedly derived from the state and had only such powers as the state permitted, was recognized as the only appropriate form of the local polity. If people wanted local self-government, they would have to take it in municipal form. (I consider the class implications of this in Chapter 6.) This they have done to a degree in all the liberal democracies, but there is general recognition now that the municipality as such is inadequate as a political space. Not only are people demanding the right to participate in wider public decisions, but they also are complaining that municipal government gives them little control over immediate local issues. There is a disjuncture between the political spaces that are being claimed democratically and the ones that are offered to people as sites for public participation.

It is this disjuncture that commands my attention in this book. I approach it from two directions. First, I am interested in the nature of the state and the municipal spaces it provides to people for local self-government. I believe that far too little attention has been paid to the municipality in analyses of the state and that one can only get a proper sense of the character of the modern state by examining its organization and operations in the context of municipal government. I also believe that political science must decentre the state as its object of study if it is to make sense of government and politics. What I mean by this will soon become clear (Chapters 1 and 2 are especially important in this respect); I will mention now that at the heart of this approach is a recognition that the state is a contingent feature of political organization and, moreover, only one dimension of the political arrangements that we now confront. To choose the most obvious example, the market is at least as important a feature of contemporary political arrangements as the state. It is a grave error to attribute politics to the state and economics to the market and to attempt to analyse the latter as a natural rather than a political phenomenon. As Aristotle and Plato recognized, politics in its highest sense is not just about who should hold what office, but also about what sort of offices there should be, and, most generally, what sort of arrangements we should have for our life together as human beings. The state is but one aspect of our arrangements; as political analysts and political actors, we must attend to things as a whole.

This leads me to a second angle of approach. If politics is about the way people organize their affairs – and about the way their affairs are organized for them – then we have to look carefully at what happens in the places where people actually live. This means attending to the politics of everyday life, and also to the ways in which people move out of their everyday routines to make wider political claims. Shifts of the latter sort are typically understood as *social* movements (a term that I retain in the analysis that follows: see Chapters 2 and 10 especially), but the activities concerned are really political. We are talking here of movements that take people out of their daily routines and away from their ordinary conceptions of themselves as passive subjects.[15] These movements involve people in active citizenship and thus lay claim to a political space that may or may not conform to the spaces allowed by the existing system of government. Thus, there are always political challenges coming from the ruled and the excluded, and these challenges first appear as localized movements. In terms of the possibilities for political change, the critical space appears where new things emerge out of otherwise ordered routines, at the juncture of localities and movements. It follows, then, that we must attend carefully to the relationship between this critical space and the one originally afforded to ordinary people for their participation in government – the municipality. To the extent that the state makes other spaces available for popular participation, it is in imitation of this original.

The municipality is designed to provide an enclosure for popular politics, and so to render that politics safe for the state, the market, and the other forms of government to which we are subject. The state in turn encompasses these enclosures and formally centres politics upon itself. It creates its own vortex, which pulls the media, the movements, the parties, the pressure groups, and the political scientists toward it. To understand these processes of enclosure and centring is crucial. However, it is equally important to recognize that efforts to structure political space in this way have never been – and probably never can be – fully successful. (I explore this matter most concretely in Chapters 7 to 11.) The possibility of creating political space in a different dimension is always there. Although I would certainly not argue that the municipality is the only place where interesting things are happening politically, I would say that what happens in this space is especially significant. The municipality is identified with the local community, it is understood as an organization of civil society, and it is intended to provide ordinary people with a place to participate in the business of the state. Thus, the political space of the municipality is ambiguous or – in the currently fashionable term – liminal.[16] (See Chapter 4 for a fuller explanation of this idea.) It is of the people, but not; of the state, but not; of society, but not; of the locality, but not. How this space is used is of great significance, for, as I shall argue later (in Chapter 12), the political space of the municipality is much more akin to the political space of the world in which we live than is the artificial construct of the state. If the municipality really is beneath notice – as it is for most of those who hold themselves out as political analysts – then politics itself is beneath notice. This is hardly a satisfactory conclusion for those who pretend to be political scientists.

For various practical reasons – including both my linguistic limitations and my prior training – I take the practices of local government and urban politics in the advanced industrial countries of the English-speaking world as the starting point for my empirical investigations. As it happens, I never stray far from this starting point, because I find that so many of the dilemmas and opportunities of contemporary politics appear vividly in that context. Moreover, I take the widespread resistance to this starting point as a sign that closer attention is required. It seems that everyone knows that local government is not that important, and that urban politics is really just a metaphor for something else, like the politics of race. However, it is not clear why or how everyone knows this, since most of the people who know it never think about it. As Straussian political philosophers have argued, what is passed over quickly and without apparent thought is what has to be hidden for one reason or another, often to disguise the fact that no one knows the reasons or cares to disclose them.[17] Foucault and a host of other critical analysts have made the related point that to understand things we have to focus on what those things displace or repress.[18] Clearly, in the context of the modern state system, local government has been displaced and repressed as a locus for serious politics. We have to ask why this is, and what its implications are for the contemporary search for political space. How can democrats so quickly dismiss the level of government that is supposed to provide for popular participation in the day-to-day management of public affairs? Is it that they think that popular participation is a sham, or that the day-to-day presence of government in our lives is of little importance? Or do they suppose that the merely local is necessarily of little significance because it is confined to a particular space? Do people have a certain spatial hierarchy in mind when they think about politics, such that the important business is at the top (at the level of nation-states) and the trivialities are at the bottom? Are they working within what Lyotard would call a 'metanarrative' that makes nations or states the heroes or heroines of history? Or is there some other subject of history (the individual? the working class? women? the oppressed peoples of the world?) that focuses people's attention and obliges them to put in the shade what they 'know' is unimportant? There seem to be some assumptions at work that need to be re-examined in light of ongoing political experience.

As will become apparent in the pages that follow, it is my view that the most problematic assumptions are bound up with the doctrine of sovereignty – a doctrine that is, in many ways, the constitutive ideology of political science (and hence of the other social sciences). The discipline of political science has been a practice of inquiry trailing in the wake of sovereignty. Political science is, as its early practitioners insisted, the 'science of the state.'[19] As new forms of political organization took shape in the modern era, it became apparent that sovereignty would be one of the organizing principles of the new world order. In each country there would be a central authority beyond which there could be no appeal, and the rulers would extend mutual recognition to one another. The claims of universal religion, clan loyalty, tribal identity, and regional solidarity were to give way to the power of the state. As Max Weber pointed out, the modern state claimed a monopoly on the legitimate use of violence, and it enforced that monopoly with armed might.[20] However, as he realized, the power of the state was not simply a matter of organized violence. This power came also from the *ideal* of the *Rechtstaat* – a state of law and order in which the highest aspirations of human civilization could be realized.[21] That ideal found expression in the great national revolutions, from the American onward, which established a paradigm for politics at its highest and most serious. The earliest political scientists, who began to identify themselves as such about a hundred years ago, were rarely enamoured of violent revolution; nonetheless, they understood high or serious politics as a matter of state- or nation-building. They saw politics as a unique and potentially noble vocation whose bounds were determined by the requirements of statehood. This has remained the predominant view – as revealed by our nervous jokes about politicians who puff themselves up with dreams of statesmanship.

Even so, there has been a lingering hope that the need for sovereignty will ultimately be overcome, and that one day, somehow, people will be able to govern themselves without resorting to the organized violence of the state.[22] This hope has been anchored in a faith that people will ultimately recognize the unity of the human species and act in accordance with principles of justice that give everyone a fair opportunity to live a fulfilling life. Whether this unity is to be secured by a world government, a common culture, a global economy, or a shared religion, or some combination of these has never been clear, but the aspiration for transcendence nonetheless can be sensed in even the most realistic dialogues. One might suggest, in fact, that the ideal of the *Rechtstaat* implies its own transcendence, in so far as believers are impelled by the logic of their own convictions to seek as a goal for the whole world the justice that they have imagined for their own state. It is no accident, then, that a forceful idealism has followed in the train of the conquerors, with missionaries bringing Christian civilization to the savages, magistrates introducing European justice to the ignorant, and businessmen promoting the ethics of the free market among the corrupt, the subservient, and the other-worldly.

In many ways, the dialectic of sovereignty repeats the dilemmas of Christianity and the other monotheistic religions (as I indicate in Chapter 1). On the one hand, there is the hope of transcendence – of a heaven on earth once evil is finally overcome. On the other hand, there is the conviction that human beings cannot overcome their wickedness and are condemned to a world in which their ideals can be only imperfectly realized. This polarity between heaven and earth – between a world yet to come and the here and now – is expressed in the relationship between the idealized notions of one world and the practical realities of the state system. As in Augustinian theology, the ideal is invoked to confirm the harsh reality.[23] Machiavelli, for one, complained about the way that this theodicy worked to produce a politics of hopelessness. Much of his work was designed to recover the value of the merely local and particular, in face of the demand that everything be judged in terms of its transcendent meaning.[24] In this respect, his work anticipates much of the thinking associated with Foucault, Derrida, and other postmodern critics. He draws our attention to a world in which absolute truths are absent, loyalties and identities are constantly shifting, and sovereignty is a dream (or a nightmare) rather than a fixed reality. He is thus a theorist of groundless politics (or politics without foundations), and he frightens us with his apparent indifference to traditional moral questions. This indifference is linked, in ways we still find puzzling, to passionate political commitments that apparently override concerns about individual well-being. Machiavelli is many things, but he is certainly no advocate of political passivity. On the contrary, he insists that in a world without sovereignty – God's or anyone else's – intense political activity is required to sustain anything of value to human beings.

This view – that the timeful spaces for politics are not just *there* in a reassuring hierarchical grid, but instead must be created by ongoing human action – is one that recurs at the margins of political thought.[25] However, it is constantly displaced by claims to sovereign truth, which conceal or legitimate claims to sovereign power. God may not be present on earth, but there are plenty of people who claim to speak with His voice. Moreover, the Augustinian ideology of the state system legitimates the claim that each state is a moral universe, with a sovereign beyond whom there is no appeal. The fixing of politics and morality within impermeable borders certainly offers a kind of security: a release from ambiguity and hence from the vexations of personal responsibility. In many ways it is similar to the old idea that the father is head of the household. And, like *that* old idea, it seems not only antique but unrealistic. To identify a sovereign or a patriarch or any other ultimate authority is not to resolve our moral or political dilemmas. It is simply to insist on a particular process for resolving those dilemmas. As we have discovered in families, the process is usually unworkable, because the people concerned are not and cannot be contained within the household. Thus we are faced, whether we like it or not, with moral and political situations that cannot be resolved by appeals to sovereign authority. However much we would like to run to Daddy or run to the state to solve our problems, we find a vacuum there, precisely where ultimate authority is supposed to reside. Daddy and the state keep throwing the problems back at us.

This has become particularly obvious since 1989. Many of the states established in the wake of European imperialism have collapsed in on themselves, and people have moved in waves across electronically fenced borders and over the sea itself. Even in the most powerful states there are wild zones where the police and soldiers can do little to protect people from the gangs that exercise effective control. The desperate efforts of the U.S. government to maintain its southern border are signs of a much more dramatic collapse in Bogotá and Port-au-Prince, Kigali and Kabul, Pnomh Penh and Mogadishu. The spatial solution to the problems of the world – the solution promised by the state system – has evidently failed hundreds of millions if not billions of people.[26] This obviously raises some difficult questions. Why should so many be pushed outside the fortress-states into a wilderness where there is no security – where survival depends on the most desperate measures? Isn't the state system supposed to provide for security? If it cannot, why not? Why should those who have been excluded from the system show respect for the carefully constructed borders, freedoms, property, and other privileges of those who live within it? In what sense is a system secure when it is threatened by movements that it cannot control?

Of course, it is unlikely that this book will be read by anyone who is not within one of the state-fortresses that offer illusions of security. As such, it must speak to the concerns of the privileged – to the people behind the gates at Newport Beach or Ca-na-da. Those concerns are bound up with the realities outside. There is a sense – no doubt often confused, but nonetheless real – that even the strongest state-fortresses are no longer secure and that life within them has less and less to offer. In the new world order that emerged after 1945 – the democratized and liberalized state system – the people of the privileged countries were promised not only physical security but also economic prosperity and personal opportunity. Each state was supposed to be a realm of freedom, connected with other states in a world of enterprise and exchange. A person born in Western Europe or North America expected security 'from cradle to grave' – that is, the right to an appropriate education, the chance to work at a decent job, a guarantee of an adequate income and health care, and the right to move about and see the world in safety. This was the promise of the welfare state, but it is a promise that has been fading for the last twenty years.[27] We are told now that the state cannot guarantee our jobs or pensions, that it cannot ensure that we can walk the streets safely or sleep safely in our homes, that in future security will be increasingly in our own hands – just as it is in the wild lands outside the state-fortresses. Such talk, however exaggerated, is a sign that the leaders of states no longer have confidence that they can deliver the security that the system is supposed to provide. If even the strong states cannot deliver to the people who are supposed to be the main beneficiaries of the state system, what hold can that system have on the popular imagination? In particular, how can the spaces for 'high' politics, as defined by the system, be sustained indefinitely?

To pose these questions is not to suggest that the state is about to wither away. On the contrary, it is to suggest that the 'either/or' of the doctrine of state sovereignty is profoundly misleading. There is no more reason to suppose that states are about to disappear than to think that capitalism or bureaucracy or patriarchy is on its way out. While we may not like these contemporary phenomena, they seem rather persistent and it is not at all clear what it would mean for them to disappear. What ought to be apparent, however, is that the world is not just the outcome of a single one of these systems, and that politics is more complex and challenging than any monological reading of the human condition could suggest. The state system that has developed in the modern era involves a massive political effort, marked by both force and propaganda, to fix politics in a particular form, to centre politics upon the sovereign institutions of the state. If we allow our own political understanding to be fixed in the same way, the opportunities and dangers of the present are likely to be profoundly misconceived, and we are likely to find ourselves acting to an old script that relegates most of us to the crowd scenes.

This may be a roundabout way of saying that, as a venue for popular activity, the city deserves our political attention as much as or more than the state. The city is the very milieu of modern life, and there is no indication that our ostensibly postmodern future will involve an abandonment of the urban in favour of the rural. On the contrary, postmodernity seems to involve a speeding up, an intensification, a spreading out of the urban experience; the life of fragmented identities, instantaneous connections, and constant movement is becoming the norm everywhere. Postmodernity may involve a new spatial order, but that order is a child of the city and not of the state.[28]

Max Weber was not merely a theorist of the nation-state, or a simple apologist for it. One of his crucial insights was into the forms of what he called 'nonlegitimate domination' – forms that had emerged in medieval Europe, where rulers lacked the power to establish effective sovereignty over the nascent bourgeoisie of the towns and cities.[29] If city air did not always make men free (as the medieval proverb suggested), the 'disorder' of the city – which is to say the order it generated apart from the edicts of the sovereign, the nobility, and the prelates of the church – certainly liberated people from many constraints. As Weber recognized, this civic space of economy, society, culture, personal religion, and politics was never captured completely by the power of the emergent modern state. In fact, it developed beside the state as its significant other, and was reconceived in the eighteenth century as 'civil society' or later just 'society.' That society should be nurtured and protected by the state, that the state should serve society, that indeed society was the rationale for the state – these became the commonplace ideas of modern liberalism. Thus, the paradoxical truth has been that the dominant conceptions of the *Rechtstaat* (or perfect state) have also been models of the good city. This is not always apparent, because those models are usually implicit.[30] Much is said about models of law, principles of justice, and forms of governmental organization, but it is assumed without comment that people will go on raising their children, doing business, building roads, running hospitals, and all the other things that need to be done. This implicit order will, it is assumed, arise 'naturally,' and the *Rechtstaat* will somehow give it form and substance.

The theorists of sovereignty[31] suppose that to give form to society is a matter of imposing a particular spatial order. In the ideal at least, a state contains its cities and constitutes an economy, a society, and a culture. (I discuss this further in Chapter 2.) Thus, a state that fails to contain its cities, and constitutes no culture, society, or economy of its own, is really an imperfect state and scarcely deserves to exist. The sovereignty principle is based on the idea that cities can in the end be controlled – that they can be subjected to the disciplines of the state and be made to conform to the wishes of the sovereign. That this is not so ought to have become apparent by now, but that truth is often lost in the illusions of sovereignty. A city creates its own spatial order – or, more accurately, people create their own spatial order through civic organization – and this process of creation is not subject to regulation from any single centre. The order or disorder of the city constantly challenges and disrupts the order of the state or the state system.

There have of course been many intuitions to this effect, brushed aside by most political scientists but developed by social theorists who have approached politics from outside the spaces defined by the disciplines of sovereignty. A remarkable example of this has been provided in recent years by feminists. Although women have long questioned the institutions and practices that have been designed to control them,[32] it is only in the last few decades that this has resulted in a body of theory that seriously challenges the foundations of contemporary political thought. Central to this process has been the idea that 'the personal is the political.'[33] One way of understanding this is to suggest that personal relations – especially between men and women or parents and children – have to be understood on the same model as relations between governments and citizens or between contending parties. It follows that questions of power and authority, and liberty and equality, and dictatorship and self-government, have to be explored not only in the distant realm of the state, but also in immediate, day-to-day human relations. Injustice and oppression are not simply contained in the laws or policies of governments; in fact they are deeply embedded in personal psychology. Thus, the field for political action is not confined to the matters we have left to governments; rather, it extends to the whole of human life. If feminists are correct in their analysis, this larger field is structured by gender. The main axis of politics is thus the relationship between men and women, and it is within the spaces defined by this relationship that the most important political activities are likely to occur.

Some feminist analyses are marked by the claim that there is ultimately only *one* axis of politics – that everything follows from the practices of patriarchy and the resistances of women to the rule of the fathers. In many ways this mimics traditional Marxist analyses that seek to reduce politics to the relation between classes. However, both these forms of idealism reflect a basic assumption of sovereignty, which is that politics must have a single centre or axis of struggle. Truer to the 'disorder' of women,[34] workers, and the city itself is the postmodernist insight that politics occurs in many venues and on many axes. To seek to put everything under the same sign is to obscure most of what is happening. This truth is reflected in the actual diversity of social movements in the contemporary city. Every attempt to fix politics in a particular form is quickly disrupted by a new movement that challenges the assumptions that went before. Thus, the contemporary struggles within feminism over the issue of who women are and who gets to speak for them are in no way peculiar.[35] Such struggles reflect the proliferation of identities and political concerns in the context of civic life. (Leslie Kenny and I take up this issue in relation to feminism in Chapter 10.)

According to the conventional accounts, it was the experience of the New Left in the late 1960s that provided the original milieu for feminist rethinking.[36] This is significant, because the New Left was characterized by a 'turning away' – from the state, from electoral politics, and even from the conventional forms of revolutionary politics that focused on an overthrow of the government. As it developed from the late 1950s onward, New Left politics on both sides of the Atlantic located itself especially in the spheres of culture and education and set its face against bureaucratic administration.[37] Although bureaucracy was sometimes identified with the state, it was more often understood as a pervasive cultural practice that mechanized human life wherever it appeared. It followed, then, that a liberatory politics had to claim for itself a space that defied the institutionalized divisions between public and private, and foreign and domestic. The New Left was in many respects un-Marxist or anti-Marxist; even so, it echoed the insights of an earlier revolutionary tradition in which the state was understood as a superstructure based on something else. To Marxists and other old socialists, that something else was obviously capitalism; the New Left, however, was inclined to consider other possibilities. In this context, pacifism, environmentalism, and feminism became important currents of thought and helped to broaden and complicate people's conceptions of the appropriate spaces for political action. Hence, by the 1970s many could arrive at the conclusion that 'the local is the global, and the global is the local.' (See Chapter 11 especially in this regard.)

This practical redefinition of political space has profound implications, for it signals a refusal to respect the carefully constructed boundaries of the state system. (In Part Three, I look at a number of instances of boundary-challenging in the context of recent municipal politics.) Whether these boundaries are the ones that separate one country from another, distinguish matters of local or national jurisdiction, protect private property, or buttress parental authority, they all have been questioned in one way or another by social movements that can trace their contemporary origins to the ferment of the New Left. These movements originate in the disorder of the city – the manifold resistances to non-legitimate domination.[38] The political practices they generate illustrate the fact that politics cannot be fixed on the axis that connects the citizen with the state, or indeed on any other single axis.[39]

I began working seriously on this book in 1988. I intended it originally to be a more strictly empirical study of 'radical municipalism' in the three countries most familiar to me: Canada, Britain, and the United States. (My original intentions are still visible in Parts Two and Three.) I had been struck by the way that the Labour Left in Britain had been able to mobilize its strength in local government to challenge the policies associated with Thatcherism.[40] (On this theme, see especially Chapters 8 and 9, but also Chapter 11.) While the Conservatives at the centre were busy dismantling the welfare state, privatizing industry, deregulating capital, and rearming the country for a new round of the Cold War, the Labour councils, which controlled most of the major cities in Britain, were moving in exactly the opposite direction. They were trying to revive and reinterpret old traditions of municipal socialism and thus to deepen and extend the socialist experiment that Thatcher wanted to end. They also challenged her foreign policy, opposed nuclear arms and nuclear energy, and began to articulate concerns about race, gender, and the environment that were associated with the new social movements. Given the weakness of the Labour Party nationally, it was not hard to believe that the *real* opposition to the Conservatives was not in Parliament but among the local authorities, where an increasingly radical Labour Party exercised its influence. This was remarkable, given the ideological assumptions of the British left. The Labour activists still believed that socialism depended on decisive national action and regarded their own activities at the local level in terms of national mobilization. Indeed, many of them believed, in traditional Marxist fashion, that the decisive struggles would be the ones organized around the workplace and that community-based action was inevitably secondary to what happened on the labour front. Thus, there was particular enthusiasm in the winter of 1984–5, when the coal miners were on strike and the local authorities promised to open a 'second front' by defying the government's fiscal regulations (the consequences of which action I discuss in Chapter 9).

It appeared to me that this Labour insurgency was similar to the defiance offered to the Reagan administration by various 'radical ghettos' in the United States.[41] (See Chapter 8.) Obviously, the centre of political gravity was further to the right in the United States than it was in Britain. There was no national party that could carry forward the hope for socialism. Nevertheless, there was obviously more – and more effective – radicalism in the United States than European (or European-influenced) socialists liked to admit. It was a variegated, localized radicalism, usually with weak connections to organized labour. However, its connections with environmentalism, feminism, the civil rights movement, and the antiwar movement were generally strong, and on a wide range of issues the American radicals often gave the lead to their European counterparts. What is more, the fragmentation of the American state, the sheer size of the country, and the strength of the old traditions of local, populist initiative gave American radicalism a character more sympathetic to local communities as significant venues for political action. The Americans were not expecting a national revolution that made struggles at the local level redundant, nor were they attempting to squeeze their radical activities into the framework of a single political party. It seemed to me that the efforts of American radicals, which came together in particular places like Berkeley and Santa Monica, were more significant than most analysts recognized.

In Canada, I began thinking about all this from what was not always a comfortable distance. British Columbia was the site of Canada's most muscular neoconservatism in the 1980s, and I had coedited two books on this experience and the political responses to it.[42] As I discuss in Chapters 5 and 8, there had been an upsurge of progressive political activity in the 1970s and early 1980s in various Canadian cities, including those in British Columbia.[43] What I noticed was that civic progressives in Canada, radicals in the United States, and local socialists in Britain tended to share a common language of political change. As I saw it, they were all searching for political space in the context of the contemporary crisis in social democracy. Everywhere there was an emphasis on democratization, and this carried forward the themes of the 1960s. Leaders talked about breaking free from the old bureaucratic models of social change – about giving ordinary people the chance to develop and run public programs that they wanted. There was a heightened sensitivity to questions of race and gender, as well as a new radical environmentalism. To the extent that people focused on the economy, the emphasis was on questions of organization, management, and planning; comparatively little attention was paid to the issues of productivity that had been so important to socialists in the past. (However, see Chapter 6 for recent changes in emphasis.) This was a radicalism that carried forward the optimism of the 1960s into the dark times of neoconservatism. What I sensed in the 1980s was that many radicals had been driven – sometimes against their better judgment – to explore the political space offered by urban politics and municipal government, in the hope that this would connect them with a wider popular base and give them a place within the state to contest the logic of contemporary capitalism. This turn to the local was rarely informed by a theory of local politics; it was more of a practical response to disappointments with postwar liberalism and social democracy. Despite this, the themes of popular participation and local control – themes that had animated traditional discussions of municipal government – kept reappearing in different guises. The activists concerned usually had a confused sense that what they were doing was new, and yet was somehow a repetition of what people had tried many times before.

In my earlier comparative and theoretical work on local government, I had argued that the systems of municipal government, which had developed hand in hand with the institutions of representative democracy, were actually designed to *contain* democracy.[44] This was not immediately obvious, since the rhetoric of local government put so much emphasis on the need to provide for popular participation. However, the participation had to take particular forms if it was to be acceptable. Leaders had to be properly elected, or appointed on merit; also, the form of democracy could not be allowed to degenerate into mass meetings of the sort that had characterized ancient Athens. It seemed to me that, despite all the talk about democracy, there was a strong animus *against* direct popular participation in government that had shaped even socialist thinking about municipal institutions. At the same time, it was quite obvious that people in the business of designing institutions of government had firm ideas about what should be done at the local level. There was a vast literature setting out the appropriate functions of local government, recommending organizational models, and specifying the levels of service to be achieved. Generally, people's conceptions of local democracy were driven by ideas about the things local governments should do and the way those governments should be organized. Democracy was tacked onto a predetermined administrative agenda. The capitalist economy established the parameters for action in ways that most people hardly noticed. Even socialists were usually unaware that they were modelling their alternatives on what worked under capitalist conditions.

In this context, I found the prospect of an alternative politics at the local level quite exciting. It seemed to me that the radicals of the new generation were exploring and testing means of local action to an extent that had not been seen for almost half a century. (Compare Chapter 7 on this earlier phase of municipal radicalism.) Their agenda was not just to work into practice the socialist ideas that had crystallized in the 1930s and 1940s, but rather to expand the radical repertoire. These were people who thought that progressive politics had to be reinvented under the new conditions of the postwar era. Like the neoconservatives, they sensed that the statist, social democratic agenda that had dominated politics in the 'developed' countries after the Second World War had been largely exhausted. (I explore the relationship between the New Left and the New Right more fully in Chapter 5.) A new politics of some sort was required. Many (perhaps most) of the people concerned put their political energy into wider social movements, but there was a pervasive sense that people had to come together somewhere, somehow, if major social change was to be achieved. This coming together was quite commonly conceived in traditional terms – as unification at the national level. However, many of the activists believed that unities had to be established at the local level if the conditions for progressive politics were to be maintained, and this led them into the unfamiliar terrain of municipal politics.

On entering the municipal field, people soon discovered that they were in a highly ambiguous political space. The municipality was obviously a part of the state's local administrative apparatus, and as such it was clearly a subordinate unit within the hierarchy of sovereignty. (I address the political implications of this most directly in Chapters 9 and 11.) Yet at the same time, every major city was an important node in a global network of cities that was not subject to effective regulation by the state system. Significantly, Thatcher's program was to liberate the City – Europe's financial centre, the City of London – from control of the state, while bringing the local authorities to heel. In so far as local authorities could claim to represent the cities – and hence the dynamism of the new world order – they could pose as political rivals to national governments. Thatcher understood this well enough. She was also aware that the boundary between the state and civil society was rather blurry at the municipal level. Municipalities had been conceived originally as corporations belonging to the local business class, with a mission to promote their cities within the global economy. (See Chapter 6.) They still appeared to many people to be essentially economic rather than governmental bodies, and seemed as such to be entitled (according to the doctrines of *laissez-faire*) to a certain autonomy in relation to the central state. On the other hand, municipalities also functioned as mediators and disciplinary authorities in the context of local social relations. To the extent that there was an effort to redeem the city as a community (or community of communities), that effort was likely to pass through the institutions of municipal government, even if it was not centred there. Under conditions of globalization, such an effort was likely to connect a city with its counterparts elsewhere in the world. Thus, the boundaries that contained the municipality politically were always breaking down. People engaged in municipal politics were drawn into wider fields of activity in which sovereignty was at best irrelevant and at worst an obstacle to effective action.

In its vitality, urban politics always passes beyond itself, sometimes flowing in the channels of the state but usually spilling over the boundaries that contain it geographically and functionally. Rarely, if ever, is urban politics contained within the municipal field, which can never offer any final resolutions. (Compare Chapters 4 and 12.) The institutional weight of the state grounds the municipal authorities in questions of land use and local administration.[45] Nevertheless, urban politics takes people beyond these questions, especially when it is invested with the hopes and aspirations of vital social movements. This is what seems to have been happening in many cities in the 1980s, when national politics was exceedingly bleak to many activists. Although it would be wrong to imply that there have been many dramatic successes in the effort to revive the municipalities as venues for creative political action, it would be equally wrong to suppose that this effort has been insignificant. Even if we were to conclude once again that the most promising fields for creative politics were elsewhere, we would have to define those fields in relation to the experiences of urban politics and local government. Among political theorists especially, the refusal to deal with the urban and the local has been an excuse for not addressing some obvious realities. What is more, that refusal has been a means for reasserting assumptions about the necessity of sovereignty without justifying them. To put it simply, urban politics would not be as vexed as it is if sovereignty actually worked the way it is assumed to do. The truth is that nation-states are beginning to appear more and more like local authorities that have to operate in a world where sovereignty is just a dream. If we want to understand this political condition, we are well advised to attend to the realities of urban politics.

I engage with those realities most concretely in Parts Two and Three of this book, which derive from my research on radical municipalism. Some of the description I offer is quite detailed, and its analytical purpose may not be apparent to those who skip lightly over the theoretical reflections in Part One. My purpose throughout this book is to relate the practical search for political space in the municipal context to the wider issues that I have broached in this introduction. Those issues relate to the effects of the state-centric (or 'sovereignty') thinking that still dominates contemporary politics. In Part One, I attempt to develop a critique of this thinking that is both relevant to an understanding of the urban, and intelligible to an audience not yet convinced that the urban is a crucial focus for political analysis. In these opening essays I do not argue every point in detail; rather, I try to set out my main ideas in a relatively brief compass. My intention is not to establish a single, unassailable thesis but to indicate some of the reasons for decentring the state in our political thinking and adopting a more open and self-critical approach to questions about the space and time for political action. Some will follow me to my conclusion that the municipality is an especially significant space for political action. Others will focus instead on the idea that critical social movements are at the edge of political innovation. I will have achieved my objective if I convince readers that we must approach these questions afresh.

Part One derives from a series of articles I wrote in the wake of a controversy among the academic left in Canada over a paper that Rob Walker and I presented in 1987 on the need to decentre the state.[46] In that paper we developed a particular critique of the state-centricity of the Canadian left and argued that current attitudes were the result of an ongoing attachment to bourgeois and ultimately Christian conceptions of politics. The controversy that this analysis produced was confined to small academic circles, but it was still vigorous enough to generate a number of invitations for me to explain our ideas to undergraduate audiences. It was in this context that I drafted the originals of Chapters

1, 2, and 3. I have left one of these papers (written in 1993) intact; it appears here as Chapter 3. The other two, which I drafted earlier, I have revised extensively for this book, mostly by expanding and qualifying my arguments. The results are Chapters 1 and 2, which present the ideas on which this book is based in the most general terms. Chapter 3 picks up on these ideas and poses them again in a particular context – one that for me is very close to home. Then, in Chapter 4, I relate the main arguments specifically to the question of the municipality. It is there that I come as close as I ever do to articulating a normative theory of local government and urban politics. When preparing this book, I restrained the urge to tinker with the formulations I offer in Chapter 4, which I drafted in 1992. Canada was then in the midst of a debate over the ill-fated Charlottetown Accord, and I was responding to a request to consider the role of the municipality in an ideal constitutional order. I took the opportunity to explain why I rejected the view that municipalities ought to replace states as our central political organizations. For reasons that I have already intimated here, I argued against any repetition of the sovereignty solution on a smaller scale, and in favour of an approach to municipal politics that would challenge the constrictions of sovereignty in a variety of ways.

In Part One I set out my theoretical position. In Parts Two and Three I again pose the question of the municipality, but in terms more familiar to students of urban politics. In Chapter 5, I situate the question in relation to the Canadian postwar experience, using the latter as an exemplar for more general trends. Then in Chapter 6, I look more particularly at recent entrepreneurialism in municipal government from a comparative and historical perspective. These essays were originally prepared for interdisciplinary (and in the latter case international) audiences of urbanists. Although I have added to them slightly, I have left the analysis intact for publication here. Chapters 4, 5, and 6 all discuss current limitations on municipal government *and* the possibility of an urban politics that transcends those limitations. In my own mind, the three analyses complement each other, in that they converge on the same conclusion from different starting points. However, readers may notice differences that highlight the complexity of the issues. In Chapters 7 and 8 (written specifically for this volume), I examine the experience of municipal radicalism in two historical periods (roughly from the 1880s to the 1930s and from the 1960s to the present); in doing so, I explore with some insistence the possibility of a critically effective politics in the municipal context. My reflections in Chapter 8 are based on my own primary research. In both these chapters, I am attempting to explain more concretely the political possibilities that arise in the municipal context.

In Part Three, I examine in greater detail some of the challenges that have recently been posed to the constrictive space of local government. In Chapter 9, I look at fiscal struggles – claims on the part of municipalities to tax and spend as they please, regardless of restrictions imposed by the state – and consider what they suggest about the capacity of local authorities to resist the impositions of sovereignty. In Chapter 10, I come at the question of sovereignty from a different direction, looking at the attempts of the women's movement to maintain an institution of its own within the local state. And, finally, in Chapter 11, I look more generally at recent municipal efforts to connect the local with the global in ways that defy state sovereignty. These three essays were written independently and are not intended to be a summary of the recent experience of municipal radicalism. However, they illustrate even more concretely the potential that people have been able to uncover in a political space that is often disregarded.

Thus, the movement of the book is toward an ever more specific demonstration of the political possibilities that I outline in Part One. (Those who want grounding for the discussion in Part One may prefer to read Parts Two and Three first. Practically all the chapters can be read independently; the order in which they are considered depends on the reader's interests and preferences. However, it is well to remember that the theoretical analysis and empirical investigations here are interdependent.) Lest readers become too comfortable with a particular conception of political space, in Chapter 12 I pose yet again the theoretical issues, in the context of an article originally written for a special issue of an international relations journal on the topic of social movements. I reprint the article intact, because it takes up the issue of sovereignty from a different starting point – the space of world politics – and arrives once again at the urban. There are differences between the analysis in this chapter and the earlier formulations in Part One. To me, these differences are matters of emphasis, but they may seem more significant to other readers who want the accounts in Chapters 4 and 12 to dovetail exactly. I return to this matter in the Conclusion, but for the moment let me just say that the purpose of this book is to open up certain questions about the space for political action, rather than to impose my own answers with authorial sovereignty.

# PART ONE

# Looking for Politics

Although the search for political space is practical, there is no practice without an implicit theory. My purpose in Part One is to bring some of our key operating assumptions to the surface and to expose these assumptions to a critique that induces new thinking about the places where we can act politically. In Chapter 1, I offer some general reflections on the state-centricity of contemporary political thought and explore both the effects of this bias and the metaphysical assumptions that underpin it. In a preliminary way I make the argument for a different conception of politics – one that problematizes centring practices, recognizes the multiplicity of political spaces, and puts what is normally excluded in the foreground of our political vision. In Chapter 2, I explore in more detail the contemporary reification of political community in the form of the liberal-democratic nation-state. I take issue with the arguments that naturalize the sovereign state and the sovereign individual as the poles of our political existence, and that consequently obscure and devalue localities and social movements as forms of political community. I argue for a shift in analytic and practical focus to the juncture between localities and movements. In Chapter 3, I approach this juncture from a particular example – the internationally publicized battle over the Clayoquot Sound wilderness area on the southwest coast of Vancouver Island. This leads to a more serious exploration of the contemporary effects of sovereignty/liberalism as a form of political closure, and of the possibilities for critical social movements in this context. Particular emphasis is placed on the necessary relationship between the local and the global – a theme that I develop in a slightly different way in Chapter 4. In the latter I begin with some reflections on the dizzying effects of aboriginal claims to sovereignty in Canada and elsewhere. I explore the implications of recognizing political spaces that defy sovereignty as normally understood and that point beyond themselves to a different terrain. I suggest that the municipality can be conceived in these terms and caution against the desire among localists to reproduce the state on a smaller scale. I argue that truly creative politics defies enclosure and that the emergent potential of the municipality is a function of its expansiveness.

# 1

# Decentring the State

The people working here are committed to the environment, and they don't have any political ... we're not a partisan organization.

Sharon Chow for the Sierra Club of Western Canada.[1]

This is a curious statement coming from a professional politician working for a pressure group. It is also typical. The Sierra Club is one of the world's biggest and most powerful environmental organizations. It was founded in the United States almost a hundred years ago and has more than 400,000 members. It is actively engaged in a variety of environmental campaigns in North America and elsewhere. Its resources for research are considerable; it employs a battery of lawyers and lobbyists in the United States; and it has extensive relations with the media. Although it is a comparatively conservative organization, and never uses tactics of civil disobedience, it engages in extensive public relations campaigns, lobbies every level of government, and challenges environmental malpractice in the courts. These are not the club's only activities – it also organizes wilderness outings and provides information on outdoor activities to its members – but it has from the beginning been essentially a political organization. It was founded to promote conservation by educating the public, lobbying for better legislation, and working for proper enforcement of existing environmental laws. Any government or corporation that has had to deal with the Sierra Club would be quick to point out that it is about as partisan a group as any in its field, and that its posture of political neutrality is really just a convenient front.

Even so, the club still appears to many of its members – and evidently to its officers – as an organization outside politics. This reflects the widespread assumption that politics *proper* is related to the business of gaining and exercising state power. If the club refuses to endorse candidates for public office, keeps its focus strictly on environmental issues, and tries not to be drawn into wider political controversies, its leaders can argue that they are staying clear of politics. The logic of such self-effacement is familiar. To back the losers in an election is dangerous for an organization that wants to influence the victors, and in any case neutrality makes it easier to mobilize people with different party affiliations. Why would the organization get involved in issues unrelated to its mandate if those issues are likely to prove divisive? And, of course, there are tax advantages to be gained by avoiding what the government regards as political activity: organizations that stay clean in this respect can apply for charitable status and get tax breaks for their donors. The result is a sort of politics of denial – political activists pretend that their public-spirited activities are not really political. In this pretense, politics is viewed as the sordid part of public activity – the part associated with the struggle for power and its forceful exercise.

The foul odour of politics in people's nostrils comes in part from their experience of it in other contexts. We talk of the politics in our workplaces, families, and networks of friends – and we are rarely saying anything flattering. Obviously, the struggle for power and influence is not confined to government, let alone to political parties. The fact that politics in the state seems to reproduce the nastiest features of the politics of everyday life does not help its image. This helps to explain the fact that, when people do become active – that is, when they identify conditions of life they want to change and begin to engage with others in pursuing such change – they often deny that their activity is political. This is a way of saying, 'What I am doing is public-spirited. I am not out for personal advancement or power over others. I just think this is right, and I am working to achieve it.' Our culture makes such claims deeply suspect, and it demands of the politically active constant proofs of public-spiritedness and self-sacrifice. Thus, the insistence by activists in the Sierra Club and other organizations that their activities are not *really* political makes both psychological and political sense.

Given the contemporary mood, it is hard to convince sceptics that the sordidness of political struggle is the underside of an activity that takes people into a domain of selflessness and public spirit. However, it should be clear that the search for political space is not just an effort to assert self-interest or to impose domination. It is also a moral search – a quest for a place where people can act on their values and pursue their ideals. It thus involves an effort to become human in the fullest sense. In this effort we are inevitably confronted with the facts of human difference: not everyone is so passionate about the environment, or so careless about their material comforts; not everyone is egalitarian, compassionate, or religious; and we all come out of different cultural traditions that are differently interpreted. Inevitably, politics is a matter of artful negotiation and compromise, and its claim to a peculiar dignity is keyed to the virtue of moderation.[2] In the most benign political processes we are compelled to deal seriously with other people's ideals and interests, and this can teach us profound lessons in respect for one another.

Our nervousness about such claims is a reflection of our own doubts. In part we are seeking an excuse for our own inaction and irresponsibility, but most of us are genuinely confused about the locus of politics in its best sense. We feel that it is supposed to be centred in the state, and that Bill Clinton, or Newt Gingrich, or the Prince (or Princess?) of Wales ought to be the bearer of our hopes and dreams and the artist of human reconciliation. Needless to say, this is a drift of sentiment that brings us up short and leaves us in a mood of cynical despair. The opposing populist sentiment is one that takes us back into ourselves, where we seek something clean and pure – perhaps in an environmental club like the Sierra, or in a theatrical ensemble like the Raging Grannies.[3] And yet these latter activities often seem ineffectual, in that they merely flutter at the edges of the power constituted by the state. The state is supposed to make our idealism effective by giving us the means to rule ourselves – democratically, liberally, lawfully. Unfortunately, these means are never where they are supposed to be. They keep floating away into the routines of bureaucracy, the arcane movements of global capital, the slow majesty of the courts, and the deceits of politicians. The bright promise of democratic politics shines like the Holy Grail, forever beyond our grasp.

This religious imagery is not accidental: our problems in identifying politics are bound up with religious confusions. Given the Christian context in which our current political institutions emerged, it is not surprising that these institutions are invested with hopes and aspirations that are intelligible only in terms of Christian doctrines of sin and redemption. As I indicate below, these doctrines are connected with metaphysical assumptions that many of us bring to bear quite unconsciously. To think our way through the political possibilities of the present era requires more than a gesture of tolerance toward the polytheistic and nontheistic religions of Asia, Africa, and the Americas. We need to come to terms with a world of genuine pluralism, a world which is threatened both by the post-Christian totalitarianism of Western liberalism and by the many reactions to it – reactions that inevitably produce conflicts that cut through the boundaries between states and cultures.[4] These conflicts keep reappearing at the centre of our politics, yet they are neither within nor outside the states where our politics are supposed to be. Similarly, the universalistic aspirations expressed by movements like socialism, liberalism, feminism, and environmentalism are somehow there and not there, contained and uncontained within spaces where we look for political redemption. The political effects of this are troubling and confusing, and there is no way that we can position ourselves with certainty in respect to our opportunities.

In fact, certainties are the main obstacles to creative thinking, and the certainty of certainties in Western political thought is the state itself. The state has become the uncontested fixture of the Western political imagination. The eternal presence of the state is confirmed by our daily routines, trumpeted on television, written into our history, and impressed on our consciousness in a way that makes anarchists doubt their own sanity. If we are to understand the world more completely and to identify the various spaces where we act, we must do a great deal of difficult decentring. Most obviously, this means decentring the state. However, as I indicate below, similar moves are required in relation to the metaphysical assumptions that have underpinned both Christianity and Western liberalism as well as the revolutionary movements that have challenged them. In the next three chapters we will be looking more closely at the reification of political community under modern liberalism, the challenges implicit in critical social movements, and the potential of the municipality as a locus for creative politics. But to begin, it is worth thinking in more general terms about the challenges we confront.

## The Deceptions of Social Science

Most of the readers of this book will have been schooled in the social sciences, probably the science of politics, which originated about a hundred years ago as the science of the state. Writing in the mid-1930s, Frederick Watkins declared:

> Among contemporary social scientists it is a virtually unquestioned assumption that the state forms the basic concept of political science. A typical example of

the current opinion is to be found in the writings of [the nineteenth-century Swiss theorist] Bluntschli, who defines political science as 'the science which is concerned with the state, which endeavors to understand and comprehend the state in its fundamental conditions, in its essential nature, its various forms of manifestation, its development.'[5]

Anticipating the effort after the Second World War to redefine the discipline, Watkins went on to say that

the chains by which mankind is bound are forged not only by the state but by an infinity of lesser associations as well. This leads irresistibly to the conclusion that the proper scope of political science is not the study of the state or of any other specific institutional complex, but the investigation of all associations insofar as they can be shown to exemplify the problem of power. (p. 83)

However, this insight did little to change the focus of political science. Theorists like David Easton[6] reconceptualized the state as a political system but kept the focus where it had been in the past – namely, on the way governments dealt with the pressures from their social environment and made authoritative allocations of value.

The state-centricity of political science is certainly understandable. After all, it is in the state – more specifically, in the various institutions centred on parliaments, congresses, and national assemblies – that the supreme laws are made. The state claims ultimate authority, not only over individual citizens but also over churches, business corporations, universities, and any other organizations that happen to intrude on its territory. In the eighteenth century the new political economists came to understand these organizations as occupying a space apart from the state, which came to be described as civil society. From a political perspective, bodies of this sort could be analysed as intermediary organizations between the state and citizenry, and hence as part of a hierarchy of authority, the apex of which was in the state. Whether the image was of a circle with a centre or a pyramid with a peak, it seemed logical to conceive of the state as the point from which sovereign authority was exercised. That Europe (and eventually the world) was divided into sovereign states, which resisted one another's intrusions and tried to organize their affairs independently, seemed to confirm the truth of the image. Each state was a neat little container with its own laws, its own government, its own economy, its own society, and its own culture, and thus its own politics. At the centre of each modern state was some sort of sovereign authority – no longer a king simply, but perhaps a parliament like Britain's or an even more complex set of institutions like the ones created by the U.S. Constitution. Politics – serious politics, at least – seemed to focus on these centres, and if anything, democratization intensified this focus. What could be more natural than this, since, as Aristotle indicated, politics was supposed to be about the organization of complete communities? In the real world, there were no more complete communities than states.

Political scientists have never been so naïve as to think that the most important political events are played out in parliaments. On the contrary, they have recognized that cabinets and bureaucracies, political parties and pressure groups, and even courts and armies are important political venues. Nonetheless, the politics of these outlying organizations have usually been understood in relation to the state's central authority – the imaginary place where final decisions are made about law and public policy. Thus, the organization of the state has become the central question of political theory, in both its explanatory and normative guises. On the conceptual periphery have been the subordinate theories of public administration (dealing with the implementation of public policy) and the superordinate theories of international relations (dealing with matters between states, not subject to legal resolution). These theories take for granted that politics and government are structured by the state system and so need to be understood through an analysis of the state.

Despite interdisciplinary jealousies, sociologists and economists have largely accepted these assumptions by political scientists. Given a terrain of study in civil society, sociologists and others have turned their attention to whatever is beyond the immediate control of the state. This has led to a certain intellectual stroppiness, since it is obvious that societies and economies are organized on principles only partly defined by states. At the same time, there has been a tendency to bring the state back in, by reconceiving it as an organization within society. Lo and behold, the state reappears in the very guise that political scientists have given it – as the ultimate legal authority and hence as the centre for political activity. Moreover, the boundaries given to societies turn out to be the same as the ones given to states. Even economists are inclined to take those boundaries for granted. States have made this convenient and almost inevitable, because they have collected social and economic statistics for their own populations and imposed legal uniformities within their own territories. As a result, social and economic phenomena are most immediately intelligible in state-centric terms. The data make it easy to talk about the American gross national product, German monetary policy, Japanese trade unions, the French women's movement, Austrian Catholicism, South African racism, and host of other phenomena. It is even possible to introduce a global dimension by comparing phenomena cross-nationally. This has provided for plenty of work for social scientists, who are nominally separated into departments of economics, sociology, and political science, but who are all studying what fits into the epistemological framework created by the state system. State authorities have kindly provided the necessary resources.

Of course, this state-centricity has been challenged quite vigorously, from the very inception of the social sciences as we know them. Marxists, for instance, have been particularly insistent that capitalism is a mode of production involving many states, and that it cannot be understood as if it were contained within a single state. Other analysts, from critics steeped in the traditions of the universal religions to neoclassical economists and theorists of symbolic interactionism, also have tried to decentre the state in their thinking. In fact, it might be argued that practically all serious social theory tries to decentre the state, in the sense that it recognizes the state system as only one phenomenon among the many that have to be understood in terms of global processes or structures. The grand theories of the social sciences are typically framed in terms that defy containment within particular states. It is true that these theories often relocate the centre of politics in some particular culture (Europe or the West or modernity) or in the struggles of a particular subject of history (the individual, the working class, or whatever). Such moves involve their own illusions; even so, they place politics on a wider terrain than the state and in a qualitatively different space. This space might be defined by people's struggles to throw off the shackles of tradition, realize their freedom, express their particular identities, create new forms of society, economy, and government, or pursue any other objectives that theorists might ascribe to popular activities.

However, it takes more than a leap of theoretical imagination to displace the state from the centre of our political thinking. The decentring moves that we can trace through the works of the great theorists have had remarkably little effect on the way people think about social, political, and economic phenomena. This applies not only to ordinary people and to workaday social scientists, but also to the great theorists themselves. When we look through the work of Marx or Weber or Durkheim, we find great minds at work, ranging far and wide over the globe and into the darkest crannies of everyday life; but all these thinkers keep circling back to the problem of the state as if it were the inevitable centre of their political analysis. One can sense their problem. How *can* a person be relevant politically without addressing the state? Isn't the ultimate question one of revolution or reform? Doesn't economics reduce itself to a policy issue: Was Adam Smith right? Or was it Marshall or Schumpeter, Keynes or Friedmann, Robert Reich or Jeffrey Sachs? And isn't sociology what informs social policy? Isn't Foucault ultimately an analyst of prisons, disciplines, and deviant sexualities? How can a great theorist avoid being read – and avoiding reading himself or herself – as a theorist of the state, when the state is the given of everyday political practice and the touchstone of political relevancy? It is no accident that Marx is remembered less as an analyst of capitalism than as a theorist of statist revolution.

The tyranny of the preconstituted fact is nowhere more evident than in this context. It is not just that states produce the statistical data that serve them. They also produce historical narratives and daily dramas that are intelligible only in relation to a community of fate. These tales are reproduced daily in the media, taught as facts in the schools, and absorbed into academic discourse as a background to intellectual inquiry. Even the greatest intellectuals have to work with the precoded facts of their culture, which are already marked as data about, say, French history, American experience, German identity, British common sense, and so on. These facts cannot be simply decoded, and the intellectuals who work with them often project the imagined experience of their own state onto the world as a whole. How much of American political science is just an extension of the belief that everyone is an American or on the way to becoming one? How much of European thought is merely a result of imperial rivalries? Is German sociology or French philosophy more than a meditation on a parochial experience? Is British empiricism more than a reaction to French arrogance? One hopes constantly for transcendent insights from the great thinkers of the metropolitan powers, but one is brought up short by the spells of the *lycées* and the *Gymnasien* – or the solemn certainties of Oxbridge and the Ivy League. In each of these parochialisms we can see the intellectual shadow of a particular state.

## The Entrapment of Politics

According to the conventional accounts, it was in the context of the creation of the modern state – in Europe, roughly from the sixteenth century onward – that politics came to be recognized (or recognized more clearly) as a distinct activity. It is not that rulership and contests for power had never been known: quite the contrary. However, in Europe at least, rulership had not been constituted in an impersonal domain of its own, separate from the family, business, and religion. Nor had rulers made their claims to sovereignty effective in relation to the other domains, or even to one another. It was only in the sixteenth century that rulers were able to recover and reshape the ideas of Roman *imperium*, and to give effect to an idea of the state as an entity sufficient unto itself – as not tied to any dynasty, as independent of other states and supreme in relation to the other domains of human life.[7] The term 'sovereignty' was coined by Jean Bodin to express the new reality.[8] At first it referred to the person of the king; gradually it was reinterpreted as an abstract principle and linked with a new notion of citizenship inspired by the practices of the early Roman Republic and the ancient Greek polities. As such, it pointed toward the possibility of *popular* sovereignty – of rulership by the citizens themselves within each state.[9] This was the aspiration of the liberal democrats of the eighteenth and nineteenth centuries; it was finally achieved in a certain way in the twentieth century.

Most of the readers of this book have grown up in a liberal democracy that offers extraordinary privileges to its citizens. The apparatus of the state protects businessmen and tourists in their ventures abroad – and springs their children from Thai jails when youthful enthusiasm for drugs and fast money gets the better of common sense. The state guards its borders to keep the poor from migrating in search of work, and to defend its citizens' access to the natural resources and means of production contained within. The state also guarantees the other rights of citizenship; these include not only the right to participate in government – by voting for the legislators, running for public office, and voicing opinions before governors and fellow citizens – but also the right to receive those services such as education, health care, and income support, that enable people to take advantage of the economic and social opportunities within the state. One need only watch the images from the world's latest disaster area to recognize that there is much to support the view that statelessness is a condition of horrible insecurity – as Hobbes tried to indicate 350 years ago.[10]

For us, the lucky ones, the state is a domain of opportunity. It is a protected space where we can live out our lives, a source for services we need, and a place where we can be citizens in the fullest sense. At least in principle, those who live in the privileged states are free to participate in politics. We can be passive in relation to it, hoping that others will do what is necessary to protect our interests. Or we can take an active part in governing ourselves. Although we may look down on politics as a sordid activity full of manipulation and deceit, we also see it as a space where we can pursue our highest ideals. From this perspective, politics is the crown of citizenship, and as such it seems necessarily oriented toward the state. At its best the state appears as a benign container for politics, set apart from other states and from the society it governs. People can leave behind what they are in society, and enter the domain of the state as equal citizens who are equally subject to its laws and equally entitled to participate in the process of their revision. At least in the abstract, in its formal constitutions the state recognizes human equality, human dignity, and human freedom. Thus, the activity of constituting a new state in accordance with the right principles – Nelson Mandela's activity, or George Washington's – seems particularly fine and noble. Those with a classical bent can see themselves in the spirit of Lycurgus or Solon.

However, in one of his brilliant early essays,[11] Karl Marx pointed out that the abstract recognition of human dignity in modern constitutions served to conceal the concrete realities of life. Marx devoted his life to uncovering the realities of capitalism and came to understand it as a fundamentally exploitative mode of production that justified itself in terms of the abstract freedoms it offered. These abstract freedoms were embodied in the modern state – in the laws it ostensibly produced and the rights it ostensibly granted. Marx hoped and believed that working people ultimately would come to *see* these freedoms as abstractions, and take control of the concrete conditions of their lives – that is, take control of the means of production and organize themselves as associated producers in a new mode of production that would free everyone from unnecessary toil and enable everyone to express his or her individuality. For this to happen, he thought, those who depended for their living on the sale of their labour would have to come to understand themselves as workers rather than citizens, and pursue their interests as a class in relation to the dominant bourgeoisie. Politics of this sort – the politics of class struggle – could know no boundaries. It had to involve every aspect of life and transcend the divisions between one state and the next – divisions that meant little in an international capitalist system.

It is surely one of the great ironies of history that Marx's name came to be associated, in the century after his death, with an exceptionally nasty form of statist absolutism. However, the connections are not arbitrary.

The Marxist parties that developed after his death in 1883 worked within the context of an evolving state system that tended to contain politics in the privileged spaces afforded for citizenship. In the most advanced capitalist countries, such as Britain and the United States, these spaces were privileged indeed, not only by virtue of the power implicit in the *Pax Britannica* (and later the *Pax Americana*), but also by virtue of the rules of citizenship that had been vindicated by the advance of modern liberalism. Although full citizenship was long restricted to propertied white males, the prospect of universal citizenship was there almost from the beginning, and the demand for it became a logical focus of struggles from below. Once formally achieved – as it was for whites in the 1920s and for others in the 1960s – such citizenship afforded the opportunity to pursue reforms that would alter the conditions of life in civil society. From this developed the welfare state. The successful liberal-democratic states at the apex of the international capitalist system offered a model to be emulated elsewhere, or to be attacked from without – in either case by statist means.

The Bolshevik Revolution of 1917 is usually cited as the first great effort to break out of the system. By design or necessity, the Bolsheviks created a state against capitalism and against the existing state system, deploying the means of state power to secure the boundaries of the Soviet Union and establish hegemony over the society within it. This provided a model that inspired many nationalist revolutionaries outside the West, who hoped to create their own states against Western imperialism. The successes of Japan after the Meiji Restoration (1868) and of Germany after its unification (1871) were also inspiring, in terms not only of the military and economic advance that came with successful state-building, but also of the cultural vindication and rise in social welfare that resulted. It is significant that even Gandhi – perhaps the least statist of the twentieth-century revolutionary leaders – was ultimately seen by his own movement as the founder of a new state. In the twentieth century it has seemed to most people that effective oppositional politics necessarily passed through the state system, which had somehow to be used against itself to challenge the oppressive relations that it secured.

Those who have had greatest reason to reject modern, statist politics have thus affirmed that politics. Although movements outside the West (and even within it) have mobilized ethnic nationalism, traditional cultures and religions, and antiracist and anti-imperialist feelings, they have not succeeded in escaping the hegemonic forms of Western statism. Often these forms have been reproduced in horrific versions; but despite that, the tendency is to regard the state as a bulwark against internal barbarism and external domination. When the state implodes, people try to re-create it, and the world community remains on edge until the proper forms have been restored. National sovereignty and constitutional government exist as pleasant facades for concealing unpleasant realities in many parts of the world. Not all of this unpleasantness is *over there*, where only the aid workers and journalists go. Increasingly, it is visible from the White House, from Wall Street, and from the other centres of Western power. However, the dangers of undisciplined social protest at the gates of the great palaces have at least until recently been offset by a system of parties and pressure groups that channels political activity through the state and thus disciplines it.

It is testimony to the power of the Western state system that its forms have been so widely reproduced in the context of decolonization. The state, like the 'free market,' appears as an inevitable mode of organization, to be renounced only at the cost of expulsion from civilization. Many movements have arisen, within and outside the West, to challenge the practices associated with statism, but most of them have been drawn into the vortex of statist politics. The history of socialism in the twentieth century has been exemplary in this respect, marked as it has been by the predominant belief that the path to the future (be it communist or social democratic) lay *through* the state.[12] There is little reason to think that other movements will be less susceptible to the state's charms. State-centrism is just as apparent in the politics of environmentalism, feminism, and cultural renewal as in the politics of socialism itself.

## The Metaphysic of Unity and the Logic of Identity

One is tempted to explain the power of the state system simply in terms of the political economy of advanced capitalism and the historical legacy of Western imperialism.[13] However, an explanation that ends at that point is liable to obscure the ideological underpinnings of the system. Western culture is monotheistic, and the triumph of the West in the world has been marked by the spread – or, should we say, imposition? – of its monotheistic assumptions. Militant Islam, which so frightens Western commentators, is the mirror image not only of militant Christianity but also of the militant liberalism that rearticulates Christianity in secular terms. These monotheistic movements pose a particular political problem that the state system is supposed to resolve. Each variant of

Christianity, or Islam, or 'secular humanism' (as liberalism is sometimes called), makes a claim to universal truth that puts it at odds with all rivals. Even those who would like to be left alone, and have no militant universalism of their own to offer, are liable to be regarded as dangerous enemies. The state system is supposed to restrain the raging militancy of the monotheistic religions by allowing each state to determine its own religious identity. However, the translation of Christianity into secular humanism has rendered this solution unstable. Liberals regard the state system and the market economy as expressions of universal human rights, and so endow the institutions that restrain religious militancy with their own religious quality. Those who refuse these institutions are regarded as enemies of human rights and, hence, as inhuman beings. Under the pressures of conflict, some of the people concerned live up to their billing.

It is important to identify the assumptions at the core of monotheism, because they are so often obscured by more superficial ideological conflicts. Generally, monotheism depends on a metaphysic of unity. Monotheists who retain a belief in the Deity think of the world as a manifestation of God's will or nature. For them, this world has an inner logic or inner unity, which is an effect of God. We humans may never be able to understand this transcendental logic; even so, the incoherences that appear to us are illusory. Accordingly, the purpose of science is to help us understand as best we can the laws of nature, which necessarily reflect the Oneness or unity of God. Faith helps us understand what would otherwise be beyond us, and the chief article of faith is the belief that everything coheres in the will or nature of God: that somehow things all fit together, and everything can be understood in the same terms. Many suppose that in repudiating God, they are repudiating the metaphysical assumptions that are involved in a faith in God. This is simply not so. In this post-Christian era, we in the West continue to live with notions of good and evil, sin, guilt, repentance, and redemption that we take from the Christian and earlier Judaic past. These notions are as visible in secular movements such as feminism and environmentalism – agitated as they are by thoughts of uncleanliness and sexual misbehaviour – as in more obviously religious movements such as neo-conservatism. What is more, we continue to invoke metaphysical assumptions about the ultimate unity of things, which come out of a belief in the One God who is the source of everything. Thus, we seek not only the laws of nature that explain the physical world we encounter, but the laws of nature that govern our own behaviour. We want to know the final cause of things, the ultimate end of human existence, and the path – the *one* path – that we can take to redeem ourselves. The search for the one politics that can make good of the mess we have created – that can redeem our sins – is the secularized version of the search for the one way to God. It invokes the same metaphysical assumptions.

Theodor Adorno related these metaphysical assumptions to what he called the logic of identity.[14] This is a logic which assumes that what is most fundamental about any thing is its ultimate identity or essence. According to this view, the essence of each thing is distinct: what it *is*, is inside it and is completely independent of what is outside it. On the other hand, all things have an underlying identity, which is nature itself. The purpose of science is to decode and represent this nature to us humans, and hence to identify each object in its essence. This means putting everything in its proper place. In working through this logic, we establish a hierarchy – or, more accurately, a series of hierarchical dualisms, such as the ones that distinguish reality from the imagination or the natural from the unnatural. We put ourselves at the top, but we assume that there is a base or foundation of everything [God?], which can be uncovered by science and logic [revelation?]. We may be deluded into mistaking appearances for reality, but reason – rightly guided by our faith in the ultimate unity of all things – should enable us to see through this veil and get at the real truth. Then we will know what every thing and every person has to be in order to be true to its own essence. This is the totalitarian vision promised by true science.

Subsequent critics have pointed out that this way of thinking was sexist in origin: it was the men who were supposed to get at the real truth of things; women were mired in their emotions and could not see through to reality.[15] It was also racist in origin: the whites were the ones who were supposed to have figured out how things really were, and who developed the science to see through the myths of other peoples.[16] And of course, as Marx understood, it was a way of thinking that expressed the view of the dominant class, which claimed to understand how things really were – and so could see very clearly that it was impossible to pay workers better wages.[17] All of this should at least give us pause, for it suggests how the logic of identity or the metaphysic of unity can be deployed ideologically. Marx tried to invert the conventional logic – to show that the proletariat, not the bourgeoisie, was in a position to see things as they really were, and that the proletariat, not the bourgeoisie, was in the vanguard of history.[18] Similar operations have been performed by those who have identified patriarchy rather than capitalism as the underlying reality: it is said that patriarchy can best be understood from the standpoint of women, and that women are the ones who must lead in developing the theories and practices that will overcome patriarchy.[19] Others have claimed that neither capitalism nor patriarchy is as fundamental as the human domination of the natural world. According to this reading, the human predicament is largely a consequence of an exploitative relation to nature, in which both men and women, and both workers and capitalists, are involved: to change this fundamental reality requires a different set of theories and practices.[20]

Unfortunately, each of these inversions depends on the logic of identity and the metaphysic of unity. In each case there is an attempt to identify a fundamental reality, to suggest that all else is appearance, and to push forward a theory that privileges one set of political practices. This can lead to a kind of totalitarian thinking. In the actual practices of the social movements that have produced these theoretical inversions, there is a struggle between this totalitarianism and the critical spirit that arises from holding different analyses simultaneously. This latter spirit can be an effect of accepting more than one of the fundamental critiques of existing thought, or of holding these critiques in relation to practices that do not appear simply good or bad. On the other hand, a totalitarian reversal is likely to reproduce the fixed identities that people have already been assigned. These identities may be understood biologically – as effects of skin colour, or genitalia, or ethnic or family origin; or they may be measured by ideological commitment – as interpreted by religious fervour, political activity, sexual practices, or even habits of garbage disposal. In any case, preferred origins and orientations are identified, and this puts people who lack the marks of political correctness under suspicion among those who seek a reversal of the existing order.

In Adorno's time, Fascists, Nazis, and their various imitators put the logic of identity and the metaphysic of unity to particularly virulent uses. We see today a recrudescence of these forms of politics in Europe, South Asia Central Africa, and elsewhere. However, the phenomenon is apparent in other guises as well. Already, in Hitler's time, international communism had begun to degenerate into a front for Russian national socialism. Despite or because of this, the Russian model was imitated in East Asia and parts of Africa and Latin America. This collapse of a universalist humanism into a particularist fundamentalism seems paradigmatic, in the sense that we can observe the same tendencies in movements like environmentalism and feminism. In the latter case there has recently been a shift from a universalist, emancipatory feminism toward a particularist, disciplinary feminism oriented toward regulatory controls on sexual expression. In the former case the disciplinary emphasis was always more pronounced, and has helped to establish an environmentalist discourse that legitimates acts of violence and a philosophy of antihumanism. On the other hand, both feminist and environmentalist fundamentalism – like socialist fundamentalism before them – have proved to be rather weak in relation to nationalist and religious fundamentalism. This reflects the fact that the latter are more accepting of traditional social and economic relations (especially the family and the market), and thus, in a way, are more inclusive in their appeal to ordinary people. In the play of fundamentalist identity politics, the conservative or right-wing movements always seem to win. Each generation of progressives tends to forget this.

It is salutary to recall, once again, that the modern state system emerged in the seventeenth century as a relatively civilized *solution* to the problem of rival fundamentalisms. That the solution has now become part of the problem should not lead us to suppose that a return to fundamentalism is the answer. The state system establishes a fixed hierarchy of identities that puts citizenship at the top. People are supposed to accept this hierarchy for the sake of peace, even if their religious beliefs tell them that the claims of citizenship are as nothing in relation to the claims of righteousness. In principle, sovereignty can be adapted to deal with all sorts of religious and semireligious conflicts; in practice it depends on the creation of strong national loyalties. Hence the intimate relationship between nationalism and statism.[21] The state system becomes most problematic when particular nationalisms overreach themselves and thus destabilize the system, or, alternatively, when the hierarchy of identities in a particular territory can no longer be secured. Both sets of problems are apparent today. As such, they illustrate the basic dilemma of the state system: it offers a centre (or a hierarchy of centres) that cannot hold.

## Toward the Multiplicity of the Political

That there must be a centre – that we are lost without one – is a monotheistic prejudice. Or, rather, it is a monotheistic solution to the problem of monotheism. Sometimes this is conceived in mechanical terms: there must be sovereignty, a monopoly of the legitimate means of coercion in each state, and the states must be in a balance of power with one another. Sometimes the conception is more idealistic: there is a community of nations held together by common values, and committed to resolving their disputes by peaceful means. In either case there is the supposition or demand that something must hold the system together, lest there be the most horrible anarchy. This ultimately Hobbesian view is based on the belief that we can somehow expunge politics from the centre of human affairs and replace it with some sort of fixture. However that fixture is conceived – as a mechanical device, a set of unquestionable values, an ordination of God, or whatever – it serves the same purpose: it orders political conflict so that the centre remains secure. Whatever else this achieves, it devalues politics as a human activity. Once disciplined, politics appears as a sometimes sordid but always subordinate activity that serves ideals established by other means. Without discipline, politics is what threatens the centre that must hold.

This Augustinian conception of the state system as providing the discipline necessary for good politics can no longer be sustained. Whether the world order that began to take shape in the sixteenth century is better or worse than what went before is a moot point. We can no longer just take that order for granted or assume that its principles are immutable.[22] Clearly, the state system developed in a particular context, one that was marked not only by deadly conflict between rival Christianities but also by the competition between distinct European imperialisms. Statism and capitalism evolved hand in hand, as did secularism, scientism, liberalism, and humanism. The system imposed on the world came out of a particular European experience, and it is by no means clear that it can survive a more genuine multiculturalism.[23] It presupposed relations between master and man, man and woman, people and the environment, humans and God, that have since been subjected to severe questioning. These questions cannot be silenced by appealing to a cultural unity that underpins the state system: that unity is not there. Instead, at the centre, is a confused and confusing politics that will not go away, no matter how much we wish it would. To see that is to recognize that fundamentalism is not just a problem *out there*, to be destroyed by force or isolated by skillful diplomacy. It is, rather, a problem *within* every political practice, and one that can only be met by bringing the outside in. The internalization of what is alien is necessary for opening a movement to the reality that it is only one among many and that it will destroy itself if it seeks hegemony.

Marx's narrative is a tale of the hubris of capital, in which the master ultimately becomes the man. It has been a powerful narrative that has ordered much progressive thinking in this century. A different and apparently opposing story – one that tells of the hubris of Bolshevism, in which the Communist becomes the Capitalist – has been all but universally accepted since 1989. The temptation is to use this second story to erase the first, thereby restoring to the bourgeoisie its nineteenth-century conception of itself as the bearer of human dreams.[24] A more critical understanding arises from holding these two narratives together as expressions of different but equally instructive truths. Both tales are cautionary, in that they draw our attention to the arrogance of those who believe that they have exhausted the possibilities of human life in their own practices. With such cautions in mind, we can approach the universalist claims of both the secular and the religious monotheists in a different way. Once we bring the outside in, these universal visions appear as quite particular accounts of specific experiences, which generate partial understandings of human possibility. There may be some similarities in these accounts, but they are ultimately incommensurable. This means that they must exist in an uncertain relationship with other visions that are rooted in other experiences. This is a relationship that must be negotiated politically, since there is no overarching vision that puts every movement in its place.

The differences between feminist politics, socialist politics, and environmentalist politics – to take three powerful examples from the contemporary politics of social movements in the West – are not illusory. Each of these politics orients itself toward a different dimension of the human situation, offers a critique specific to that dimension, and points toward a transformational politics located in a specific space and time. The space–time of capitalism is to be understood in terms of the succession of different modes of production and the internal dynamics of each mode. Hence, we can see ourselves at a particular moment – and a particular place – in the development of the capitalist system, and understand tactics of resistance and strategies for transformation accordingly. The space–time of patriarchy is different: the origins of patriarchy seem more remote and obscure, the history of it longer and more complex, the venues and forms of struggle against it quite different from the ones that emerge from an analysis of capitalism.[25] To be effective, feminist politics has to define its own terrain, work out its own history, specify the practices appropriate to its object, and resist the efforts of others to force feminism into alien political spaces. The same is true for environmentalism, which necessarily shifts our attention to the space–time of life on earth and forces us to engage in a politics that transcends merely human concerns. The distinctiveness of each of these transformational movements is crucial for their success, and there is certainly nothing to be gained by forcing them all onto the same political terrain.

This means that we must overcome the demand for a universal politics to replace the politics of states. On the left, that demand has been particularly insistent, as a continuing legacy of Marxist politics. The collapse of the left's socialist centre, which has been as apparent in the West as in the East since 1989, has been accompanied by a nostalgic yearning for the politics of the recent past. Without that centre, the space for progressive politics has become confused and increasingly confusing. However, this decentring of the left was already evident thirty years ago: in a sense, history has caught up with itself, and what was once evident only to the few is now apparent to virtually everyone. One implication of this is that the categories of left and right, progressive and conservative, radical and reformist no longer have such fixed meanings (or, for some, any meanings at all). If such categories reappear in the analysis here, it is not on the assumption that they can be filled with simple or true meanings. On the contrary, it is assumed that these categories are inevitably confused and contested – but just as inevitably part of any meaningful analysis of broad political trends. We cannot escape our recent history so easily, and that is a history that puts the institutions and practices of modern civilization at issue. The politics of the left responds to the understanding that many of the practices to which we have become attached are oppressive, exploitative, and destructive. At its best, therefore, it is a profoundly critical politics that articulates various transformational ideals in relation to one another and poses them all in relation to existing cultural achievements.

From this perspective, a 'left' politics is a less comfortable, more political politics than conservative politics. It is a politics in which human differences are taken seriously and the various critiques of what we are and what we do come to the forefront of practice. Thus, the search for political space appears as something especially of the left – as something particularly important for realizing the possibilities of a progressive politics. For those who see little wrong with the world, the existing political spaces may be perfectly satisfactory. However, a critical politics necessarily involves a search for political space. Sometimes this is mistaken as a search for a place where everyone and everything can be reduced to some new order. This is the monotheistic impulse, and it is present in otherwise critical social movements, which attempt to hegemonize political space. On the other hand, the critical spirit keeps breaking through and re-posing the problem as one of relations between otherwise autonomous movements with distinctive and powerful critiques. The 'space of spaces' that appears when these movements are lively is the one most conducive to a progressive politics. It is one that necessarily decentres the state as the focus of political activity.

In this way we are drawn inexorably to the problem of location – a problem that we might approach through the question of political community. If states are not the best localities for politics, where can we live our political lives?

# 2

# The Reification of Liberal Community

Political community has long been conceived as an enclosure, be it in the form of a tribe, a polis, or an empire. In the first of the canonical texts of Western political philosophy, the polis is presented as the ideal enclosure – indeed, as the enclosure that makes politics possible.[1] Aristotle's view was that the *polis* – often described, misleadingly, as a city-*state* – was a uniquely suitable space for citizenship. As he conceived it, citizenship involved a relationship between people who were free and equal, and who thus (being masterless but not undisciplined) had to deliberate with one another about their goals and objectives and the means for achieving them. Citizenship was the golden mean between what Aristotle perceived as the barbaric indiscipline of the northern tribes on the one hand, and the unmanly subservience of the subjects of the Persian Empire on the other. Although we might now dispute Aristotle's understanding of the cultures surrounding him, and condemn him for his racism, sexism, and class prejudice,[2] the central claim that he makes is still compelling. This is that a properly political – one is tempted to say civilized – relationship between people is one that recognizes their freedom and equality and fosters the mutual respect necessary for calm deliberation and a free exchange of ideas. Neither the selfishness that refuses any responsibility to others, nor the subservience that releases others from their own responsibilities, is really compatible with the ethic of citizenship. Citizenship, and hence politics as it should be, is something that must be produced in the mean between these extremes.

After a long sojourn in the Orthodox (later Islamic) East, Aristotle was reappropriated by Western Christianity as an exemplar of its own traditions. In the context of Western imperialism – and hence of many confrontations with 'barbarian' tribes and subjects of Oriental despotisms – the idea took hold that the West could distinguish itself from other civilizations not only by its Christianity and its economic dynamism, but also by its peculiarly political traditions. Somehow the spirit of ancient Greece had moved itself first to Italy, then to the Low Countries, France, and England, and finally across the Atlantic to the English settlements in America. In this Western venue the polis was reconceived as a republic: on a large scale, part Roman and part Greek, ancient but modern, classical but Christian. [3] The doctrines of constitutional government, the rule of law, individual rights, and state sovereignty slowly congealed.[4] Slowly but surely the republic was democratized, in the imagination and later in practice. In the democratic republic the status of noncitizenship was gradually erased: all subjects were included in a regime whose disciplines had been taught and whose promises had been offered. Such an inclusive regime had long been regarded as dangerous if not impossible; but in the new, democratic, republican vision the possibility of such a regime was taken as a proof of the superiority of Western civilization. If all the world was redeemed and became like the West, then all the world could have a democratic politics on the Western model.

It was not until the latter part of the twentieth century that the full implications of this vision were realized. The Western powers had not only to allow their colonies to become independent, but also to recognize the independence of their subject peoples. They had to admit other powers to statehood, recognize their nominal sovereignty, and establish international organizations that gestured toward the equality of nations. At the same time, they had to enfranchise the non-Western peoples within their own national borders and begin making good on the idea that women as well as men could be citizens. Although these processes are by no means complete, they have gone far enough to establish the ideal of the liberal-democratic state as the norm, not just in the West but elsewhere in the world. If one's regime does not conform to these principles, the suspicion lingers that it is inherently barbaric or that it fails to give people the freedom they must have to be fully human. One may wish to put the same question marks beside these presumptions as one would want to attach to Aristotle's judgments. Nevertheless, the neo-Aristotelian challenge of the expansionist West is difficult to avoid. If the liberal-democratic state is not the mean between the extremes of barbarism and subservience, then what is?

**Between Liberalism and Nationalism**

Most contemporary theorists of democracy take the state and the nation for granted; in doing so they beg many of the questions that need to be answered about the kinds of political community we require. Until the nineteenth century these questions were addressed more explicitly within the republican tradition, and we can find some interesting answers in the works of Harrington, Montesquieu, Rousseau, Madison, de Tocqueville, Mill, and others. From about Mill's time onward, however, the answers get more and more formulaic until the questions themselves begin to disappear. One aspect of this erasure is the disappearance of local government as a focus for serious theoretical inquiry. In most English and American treatises on democracy one searches in vain for any serious discussion of local government, local politics, or local democracy.[5] The authors nevertheless seem to take for granted some system of local government – something like the one they know. Local government is supposed to be necessary for efficient and responsive public administration, citizen participation in public affairs, and an appropriate separation of powers. But – with some notable exceptions[6] – the authors regard any explanation of these matters as superfluous, and pass the reader off to de Tocqueville and Mill[7] for expressions of democratic hope, and to Madison for cautions about the dangers of democratic extremism.[8]

One is left with the impression that something is being hidden. If so, what is it? The answer becomes apparent if we ask what contemporary democratic theory would be like if the locality had been placed at the centre of analysis. The locality, in the sense of the place where people live their day-to-day lives, is an obvious analogue to the ancient polis. As the venue for everyday life, it is the site for face-to-face contact, immediate economic and social relations, immediately shared experience and interests. The locality is on the scale that the Greeks imagined was necessary for politics: not so large as to be beyond the scope of ordinary citizens, yet not so small as to be absorbed into familial and neighbourly relations. It is of a scale that permits and demands politics to be a collective activity involving relations among equals. From this perspective – the perspective of the original classics of Western political philosophy – the locality appears to have political primacy, in the sense that it demands recognition as the optimal political community.[9] This is especially true if we assume that a good political community is one which engages ordinary people in the activity of self-government and does not relegate them to the status of spectators.

Of course, there is an argument for enlarging the scale of political community, to ensure self-sufficiency in economic, military, or cultural terms.[10] Certainly the modern locality, caught in a web of wider social relations, is not sufficient unto itself, even for the most parochial of its inhabitants. In this light the state can be presented as the inevitable modern enclosure for politics. Hence, Ernest Gellner:

> The agrarian phase of human history is the period during which, so to speak, the very existence of the state is an option. Moreover, the form of the state is highly variable. During the hunting-gathering stage, the option was not available. By contrast, in the post-agrarian, industrial age there is, once again, no option; but now the presence, not the absence of the state is inescapable.[11]

Gellner explains this ultimately in terms of the educational requirements of industrial society: localities are not big enough to have their own graduate schools, and so they must be contained within states.[12] Others have put it differently, but the claim is always similar: we have no alternative to the state today because only states are large enough to have effective armies, manage economies, provide services efficiently, and/or [fill in the blanks]. Contemporary political theorists rarely think it necessary to explore the smaller-scale options for achieving these state goals: the mere assertion of the state's necessity is enough to set the audience nodding in approval and allow the theorist to get on to more interesting questions.

The assumption of inevitability in contemporary discourse about the state seems curious when we consider the mounting evidence regarding the insufficiency of states as political communities. This is not just a matter of states being too large for politics in Aristotle's sense. Although that is obviously an important issue, there is also the matter of states being too *small* to enclose the most pressing political problems: the control of military violence, management of the economy, redistribution of resources, protection of the biosphere, and so on. These are transnational if not global problems that demand transnational if not global solutions. The state's capacity to act autonomously on these matters has been diminishing dramatically since the 1960s, and this has encouraged the development of a myriad of ad hoc international institutions.[13] Inadequate and unsatisfactory as these institutions may be, they are certainly a sign that states themselves are beginning to suffer from the inadequacies attributed to local governments. In the circumstances, the claim that the state provides the inevitably necessary framework for dealing with the modern world seems quite unwarranted, and even a bit bizarre.

Of course, the implicit argument is not really that the state is self-sufficient. It is rather that the state is big enough to create order within its own bounds: to light a candle in the dark night of international relations. The dark night itself is to be negotiated by the arts of war and diplomacy rather than by politics. The 'realist' theorists of international relations insist that these arts cannot really be considered under the same rubric as politics, because they are practised under conditions in which no form of solidarity can be assumed.[14] Politics proper happens in a civilized domain, one in which people can count on others to keep their violence and deceit within bounds. There are enforceable norms of conduct within this domain, because people have a community of interest and sentiment that sustains an authority with a monopoly over the legitimate means of coercion. Thus, the space *within* the state is the domain in which we can hope to achieve the ideals articulated in the grand tradition of Western political thought.[15] Outside, nothing is secure; inside are liberty, equality, and fraternity, democracy, order and progress, conservatism and radicalism, liberalism and socialism, even reform and revolution. The state keeps the barbarians out – or, more accurately, keeps them locked up in states of their own. (Whether the barbarians do less harm or more under this arrangement is a moot point.)

In any case, this argument ignores the great range in the scale and power of states. The smallest – the microstates of the Pacific, the Caribbean, and the Indian Ocean – have little military capacity, and are actually locality-based: they are really local governments that have been granted a putative statehood by the magic of international recognition. At the other end of the scale are those great empires, now described as states, that have the advantages and disadvantages which flow from imperial power. In Anglo-American thought the paradigmatic states have been Britain and the United States, the hegemonic powers of the nineteenth and twentieth centuries. A convenient mental leap allows statehood and hegemony to be identified with each other, so that the self-sufficiency of the hegemon is attributed to the state per se. The other states that enter into the mainstream of political theory as implicit models all are potentially hegemonic (or at least counterhegemonic): Germany, France, Russia, China, India, Japan.[16] These are the states that appear to be worlds unto themselves, culturally, economically, and politically. The rest of the world is in fact a non-place in the theory of the state, and this leads to a kind of analytical schizophrenia. This has become apparent in Canadian debates about independence and national unity. The main argument for Quebec sovereignty seems to be that, since neither Canada nor Quebec can really be sovereign, the Québécois might as well take the trappings of statehood for themselves and enjoy the psychic rewards of sending their own delegates to international conferences.[17] Similar claims have been advanced by Scots, Catalan, and other nationalists in Europe.

For some, the state is simply the political form of the nation, nations being conceived as the givens of human existence. However, it is obvious that nations are not given: if they were, states would not go to the trouble they do in trying to create a sense of national identity. The presumption is that the state will work as a political unit only if its citizens identify strongly with one another and thus with their country. Since the state is usually organized on a scale that transcends the immediate locality, a sense of community has to emerge from something other than daily interactions. This might involve ties of kinship or religion: political relationships have often been established on such bases. The problem is that relationships of this sort tend to stretch from one locality to the next without filling any of the territory up. Different tribes and sects are liable to inhabit the same area, and they have to be induced to accept the same political order. An imperial authority of some sort may bring this about, but the theory of the state suggests that the preferred situation is one in which people accept the territorial unit as a natural community. Thus, the state demands nationhood as a condition of its own existence, and nation-building is regarded as the most glorious of statesmanlike activities. The trouble is that people are quite recalcitrant in this respect, and form attachments to nations that cannot become states or that make a mess of the state system in the regions where it has been established. In the 1990s we have been witnessing the effects of this in the Balkans and the Caucasus.

The assumption that small states are vulnerable, and that they are incapable of the sort of cultural, social, and economic autonomy that large states enjoy, leads to the idea that the locality must surrender itself to the nation whenever the nation demands. This is the other side of the coin of sovereignty. Outwardly, the state retains its autonomy in an anarchic system of international relations; inwardly, it establishes itself as the supreme authority. This principle of sovereignty is quite consistent with federalism or the separation of powers, since the assumption is that in a crisis the centre can reorder its relations with the periphery. Local or regional autonomy is contingent on state security. In countries like Canada, which are threatened with dissolution, the presumption is that only big, populous regions can be taken seriously as potential successor states. Regarding the Cree in northern Quebec and the Inuit in the Arctic, no one really takes their claims to national independence seriously.[18] At the same time, provinces like Alberta and British Columbia are serious contenders for statehood, even though in cultural terms they are barely distinguishable from the rest of English-speaking Canada.[19] Apparently, a proper state is one that has a certain weight in terms of population and resources. The Inuit and the Cree are just not weighty enough from this point of view.

The obverse of these mostly implicit arguments for weighty states is the explicit attack on the locality as an appropriate political community. This attack appears mostly in the literature on public administration, rather than in political theory or theories of the state.[20] It has an interesting ideological guise. It is clothed in nineteenth-century rhetoric about the necessity of local self-government, but its thrust is to demolish any claims by localities to political autonomy. Instead, means are offered, on the one hand, for more efficient, effective, responsive, and responsible administration of local affairs; and, on the other, for more active citizen participation in affairs of state and a more appropriate geographical division of powers within the state. The locality is deconstructed as a set of autonomous individuals involved in complex social relations of varying geographic scales.[21] Communal loyalties are presented as archaic revivals manipulated by self-interested politicians. The exigencies of the state and the market are accepted as given, and boundary rationalization is conceived as an adaptation to these exigencies. In the end, localities disappear in these analyses except as constructs of the state and the market – and the claims of localities to political primacy disappear as well.

In a curious inversion, the locality (rather than the state) is thus presented as an *artificial* community. Since everyday life lacks definite boundaries, to impose boundaries for purposes of local administration – establish a political container and say, 'This is the locality' – does indeed seem artificial. We use services from hither and yon, and there is no natural area within which all our immediate needs can be met. Communal loyalties spread over the region and beyond, but they contract toward the neighbourhood and the block. There is no agreed order of priority among these loyalties. Thus, the container chosen for local government and politics is apparently arbitrary or artificial, in terms of both objective and subjective measures of community identity.[22] As we have noted, one might say the same of the state and of the national community it is supposed to contain. Only by strenuous effort can governments render communities natural and inevitable which would otherwise seem highly questionable. Those of us who live in states that are threatened by separatist movements are perhaps better able than others to understand the fragility and artificiality of state-centric communities.

There are powerful ideological forces that tend to fix the state and the market as components of the natural environment. Capitalism has won out, we are told; the state is inevitable; there it is, just the way it is; stop whining and be happy. Both the state and the market can be understood as fulfilling the requirements of the abstract individual – that self-contained, distinct, and autonomous person, who exists only in the imagination of liberal theorists. The abstract individual requires the freedom of the market, and the market is in principle global. The free market is thus a natural necessity, and one that provides the ground for individuality and hence for political community. The kind of political community required by 'individuals' – that is, by people formed in and through market relations – is one that is relatively extensive, and that can secure a wider space for market freedom while protecting personal safety and private property. Such a community is a state, which is safer, more secure, and more civilized if it can mobilize a national identity to sustain itself. Nationalism thus can be a support to liberalism, provided that it does not turn over into a kind of statism that destroys the ground for a liberal community. In this context, local government and local politics appear to be practical necessities, but no more than that. They allow for the more effective provision of services and for the inclusion of the citizenry as informed consumers. However, the natural political community is on a different scale, one that transcends the locality and establishes the abstract relations necessary for modern individuality. As natural requirements of the 'individual,' the state and the market appear to be elemental necessities, as fixed as coastlines and river basins but much more important as parameters for political organization.

Although there are still some adherents to the idea that the rational boundaries of local government are given by the land and the sea – and although environmentalists have revived such notions in recent years[23] – the predominant theories of local government organization are still ostensibly market-centred or state-centred. Many people believe that the differences between these approaches are fundamental. Public choice is the paradigmatic market-centred theory, for it sees the problem of local government organization as involving a relationship between producers and consumers of public goods.[24] This theory points toward a multiplicity of producers in competition with one another, with various forms of consumer organization to purchase the goods. This organizational proliferation is opposed by theorists who assert the need for state control over markets in public and private goods.[25] Their preference is for a hierarchy of authorities from centre to locality, each with comprehensive jurisdiction within its own sphere and each subordinated to the one above. The ideological quarrel between market-centred and state-centred theorists thus reflects a familiar difference of opinion about the appropriate relationship between the state and civil society. Although the issues at stake are important enough, the arguments on both sides tend to obscure the common assumptions of the protagonists. Both take the state and the market for granted as the grounds for political organization. The market-centred theorists take as natural a global economy organized and protected by state action. For their part, the state-centred theorists accept as natural the patterns of life created by market relations, and attempt to adapt the state to these realities. Thus, the organizational possibilities are enclosed in a circle.[26]

The localities that make sense either in terms of the state or in terms of the market are inherently unstable. The requirements of state administration are constantly changing as new services are developed, new technologies are introduced, and new ideas about means and ends are articulated. The market is even less stable: people move, adopt new fashions, acquire new goods and new tastes. Thus, the local boundaries defined by the state or the market are likely to become obsolete as soon as they are established. This instability seems to contrast with the fixity of the state, the market, and the individual abstractly conceived. In nationalist ideology, the state is the political embodiment of the nation and is responsible for protecting and developing it. This involves creating a national market, defining and protecting national rights of citizenship, and providing the public goods and services essential to one nation. Since nation-building requires intense loyalties, the state is accorded a monopoly on the symbols of patriotism, which it invokes against internal and external challenges. This monopoly of patriotic symbolism is the ideological counterpart of the monopolies of political authority and legitimate violence that are implicit in the principles of state sovereignty. In the ideology of liberalism, freedom is conceived in terms of individual autonomy, and that autonomy is measured in relation to the state. The market thus appears as a domain of individual freedom, and individual self-expression is measured in terms of consumer choice. Consumer sovereignty becomes the counterpoint to state sovereignty, and the two sovereignties overwhelm the locality as a place where politics can be imagined.

The state and the market are conceived as complementary forms of order, which between them secure the conditions for individual freedom. Thus, civilization is supposed to develop between the Scylla of barbarism and the Charybdis of subservience. Unfortunately, the market and the state appear to allow for and even encourage forms of barbarism and subservience. In so far as the market frees the individual from social responsibilities and allows the successful to use their market power to subvert the interests of others, it clearly encourages a kind of barbarism. This form of barbarism has attracted increasing attention in the context of the class struggle that seems to have shattered the Keynesian welfare state. It is a complement and in many ways an encouragement to the forms of barbarism associated directly with the state. Neoconservatism and neoliberalism have provided ideological support for freeing the market and hence capital from many state controls. In turn, the state has been strengthened as an apparatus for labour discipline. As it alienates itself from the many in the service of the few, the neoconservative state undercuts the rationale for citizenship and leaves itself open to corruption and violence. The effects of this are especially evident in those parts of the world where neither the state nor the legally recognized market has much to offer ordinary people. Such areas are within the West as well as outside it.

To be included in the state and the market – as most people in the West and a substantial number elsewhere evidently are – is evidently an important privilege. The individual so positioned has both the rights of the citizen and the powers of the consumer. However, these rights and powers are dependent on forms of subservience. It is a condition of citizenship that one acknowledges practically the primacy of the state in the hierarchy of one's communal loyalties. Moreover, citizenship requires obedience to increasingly detailed regulations about one's personal behaviour. The state is not indifferent to what its citizens are like. Similarly, the market requires that the people who serve it adhere to the demands of consumers. Thus, by participating in consumer sovereignty, people who are otherwise producers take part in their own subjugation to the tyranny of market demand. People have to produce themselves for the market in a form that the market requires, and this means abiding by rules of conduct that are in many ways stricter than the ones the state itself would care to enforce. The double effect of the state and the market is to constrain people's lives within narrow routines. Barbarism is for some the only escape.

**Localities beyond Enclosure**

The limitations of liberalism and nationalism have not gone unnoticed, and there has been a good deal of thinking in the late twentieth century about how to enrich democracy. Some imagine that this is essentially a matter of empowering consumers: of strengthening the market in relation to the state and providing for more choice in public services.[27] Others have a more realistic view of the capacities of the ordinary consumer, and think in terms of organizing the unorganized to make their voices heard in the boardrooms where decisions are made. This involves the creation of new bodies to represent the clients of public agencies or the consumers of particular goods and services.[28] In many ways these organizations are conceived as the demand-side counterparts of supply-side unions, in that they represent those whose numbers are great but whose market power as individuals is limited. Neighbourhoods can be conceived in much the same terms, as places where people enjoy certain things (and suffer certain threats) in common, but as individuals often lack the means to enforce their preferences. In this context, local control can be seen as a means for enforcing consumer sovereignty – for making the state and the market responsive to what people actually want.[29] The decentralist, populist thrust of such a demand makes sense in terms of the alienation of the state and the market from popular democratic control. Faced as we are with institutions and practices that are simply *there* – beyond question or control and effectively naturalized as elements of our daily environment – it is not surprising that we often think in terms of appropriating as much power as we can within the limits that have been established. Thus, there is a strong impetus toward a type of democratic reform that reconstitutes the public in terms of competing groups of consumers.

There is not much room in this vision for the locality as a venue for politics, because politics has been written out of the equation. The key political decisions are already embedded in the state and the market. Consumer sovereignty is not intended to challenge those decisions: it is supposed to operate within the framework established. Much the same might be said about ideas of industrial democracy and worker participation.[30] At one time these notions were posed in an ostensibly challenging way, keyed as they were to the hope that power could be shifted from the boardroom to the shop floor. By some accounts Yugoslavia was a model of industrial organization.[31] There has been less said about this in recent years, and not only because the Yugoslavs have been giving us lessons on how *not* to deal with ethnic conflicts. Those conflicts were exacerbated by the weakness of the Yugoslav economy – a weakness which exposed the fact that the workers' councils there were tacked onto an economic system that worked on a different basis.[32] The successful capitalist economies are of course more productive; however, their productivity in terms of output per worker evidently depends on their capacity to shed labour as required. Marx understood this well, which is why he was sceptical about theories like Mill's, which suggested that capitalist enterprises could be transformed into industrial democracies. Recent experience in the West as well as in Yugoslavia seems to suggest that worker participation in industrial management can only be allowed to the extent that it is consistent with the needs of capitalist enterprise. Those needs are determined by the requirements for profit. Thus, even the powerful unions that people were writing about twenty years ago have been exposed as the weak bodies that they are.

This leads some to the idea that there is an electronic fix to the problems of empowerment. If only we could wire everyone up, so that we could deliberate and vote together in electronic town halls, then perhaps we could control the conditions of our lives. We might call this the New Age illusion, in which we imagine the world away and reconceive ourselves as personalities on television. But how would this new decision forum relate to the institutions of public government or supposedly private production? Would it simply provide for the sort of capricious intervention in the daily activities of politicians and public servants that has characterized referendum democracy in California? If not, what would its purpose be? [33] There certainly is reason to think that electronic referenda are likely to be geared to political and governmental requirements that have already been established by other means. This has been the case with referendum democracy in the past. A political community established in cyberspace is likely to reproduce the existing forms of political organization, and thus to extend the state and the market into a new domain. This would just reproduce the problems that electronic democracy was supposed to solve. Different possibilities will only emerge if existing relations of power are challenged more directly.

This brings us back to the question of locality, for the presumption is that contemporary representative democracy is flawed by virtue of the fact that power is alienated from the ordinary people. We, the people, are *here*, in our local communities, but the powers that govern our lives are *there*, somewhere else. If Mohammed will not come to the Mountain, then the Mountain will come to Mohammed; if the powers of the state and the market cannot be vested in local communities, then the local communities will appear *en masse* where those powers can be exercised. Theories of electronic democracy express this hope for a resolution in which the state and the locality become one and the market is corrected in terms of the requirements of everyday life. Older theories of *soviet* democracy – that is, of a form of state based on local, popular assemblies, which would hold the higher authorities to strict account – express a similar hope for a magical resolution to the problem of distant power.[34] However, experience in West and East suggests that these institutional forms just offer illusions to the desperate and opportunities to the manipulative. More honest and thoughtful responses to the problem of democracy put the question of process at the centre. Given that democracy is a means for us to do things for ourselves and to exercise some control over the things that are done to us, then it has to be related to particular purposes.[35] We have to think about how we provide for education, health care, or policing democratically. And we have to think about how we relate these activities to one another, not least in terms of deciding what resources are to be devoted to these different purposes. But when we look at the fine details it becomes clear that there are no simple answers to the question of how we democratize education, or how we democratize decision-making about education. All kinds of democratic practices, from the holding of public meetings and the conducting of referenda to the election of representatives and the empowerment of individual clients, may be appropriate in different circumstances. It makes little sense to reduce democracy to a single activity like voting. Life is too complicated to be enclosed in a voting booth, even if the booth is in one's own home.

Theories of consumer control and industrial democracy at least have the advantage of relating democratic practice to the activities of daily life. As such, they point toward the need for a critical relationship to both the state and the market. The recent predominance of neoconservatism has allowed for a release of critical energy in relation to the state, so that it has become an element of popular faith that governments are necessarily bureaucratic, inefficient, and insensitive. Politicians are refigured as dishonest entrepreneurs, not up to the rigours of the market and unfortunately free from its disciplines. By contrast, the market is treated with uncritical reverence, as an institution that constantly corrects itself and the people who abuse it. Two centuries of critical analysis seem to have been dismantled with the Berlin Wall. It is easy to become cynical in this context, but the practices that give rise to popular alienation and anomy are still there. These practices are not simply effects of the state, and they are incomprehensible in the terms posed by neoconservatives. There is still much more vitality in the critiques developed by the New Left, who recognized that they were dealing with an ensemble of oppressive and barbarizing practices, which included but were not exhausted by the capitalist relationships that Marx had analysed so effectively. That Marxist politics was simplistic was and is a reason for complicating it – not for replacing it with another simplistic panacea, such as the one now on offer in Eastern Europe and Latin America.

Somehow the means of delivery from subservience and barbarism must be found in practices that connect with everyday life – in a politics that is here in our localities but radiates effectively into the wider world. This suggests that we must learn to think of our localities in a new way. Statist thinking convinces us that the locality can only be a place within a state, at the bottom of a territorial hierarchy of authority. Local self-government can only mean control over relatively trivial matters, since the character of the locality has already been determined by forces that operate in the wider world. The locality is fixed in a certain way, and the politics within its bounds must conform to the preestablished requirements of the state and the market. When we look at things this way, it becomes clear that the most important political activity has to occur above and beyond the locality, away from people's daily lives. Politics is necessarily alienated. On the other hand, the locality appears as a place of market opportunity, where people can come together to advance their needs as producers and consumers. But, of course, the market has its own logic, and it is one that puts localities under the constraints of economic viability. Economic logic points toward the shedding of labour and the expulsion of the surplus population into the great beyond. Thus, the locality appears as a point from which privileges can be secured, with the world being shut out beyond the locked gates. Statist thinking actually reinforces market logic, in that it points toward an imaginary place where the unseemly problems might be resolved. The locality is preserved as an imaginary place where like can be with like – and forget about the rest of the world. As such, localities are no doubt a comfort to those who can afford the localities they want. For everyone else, they may appear as another dimension of imprisonment.

To think of the local in a different way is to free oneself from the assumptions implicit in the reification of community in liberal/national terms. When we think of people in their actual complexity, we are confronted not with a set of individuals whose wants and needs arise from within, but with people who are involved in complicated social relations within which they develop their sense of identity. Individual self-expression is one thing people seek, but not the only thing. Wants and needs emerge from complex social processes and are generally shared with other people. Who people are, what they want, how they relate to one another – these things are never fixed; they are always being negotiated locally. Thus, the politics in people's lives is always there, as an immediate experience, although not necessarily or even usually as an experience that is embraced. On the contrary, politics in this sense is always frustrating, partly because other people are difficult, and partly because the means for resolving problems are beyond the locality. Local politics is most enervating when it turns in upon itself, and it is most vivifying when it takes people beyond their immediate cares and enables them to deal together with problems that arise in the outside world. The wider world is never simply outside: it is always potentially and most constructively the subject of local politics. People have to find a way to be in the world together – to rid themselves of their own barbarisms and subserviences – and the promise of local politics is that it will enable people to do so. Unfortunately, this is a difficult process under current conditions.

In the 1950s, Hannah Arendt tried to develop a conception of freedom that was consistent with an Aristotelian understanding of politics[36] – that acknowledged the need for a private sphere where people could pursue their economic and social interests, but that also insisted that human freedom could be adequately expressed only in a public realm where people left the cares of private life behind and dealt with one another as citizens. For Arendt it seemed clear that freedom depended on the creation of a public space that was not subject to market relations or state administration. The problem, for her readers more than for her, was to imagine how such a space could be sustained in the modern world. To the extent that this problem has been resolved intellectually, it has been by imagining a third domain of public/social relations: not the state, and not the market, but something else, perhaps to be considered under the rubric of civil society.[37] Conceptions of this other domain are often vague, but it appears to be a place where public-spirited action occurs, apart from the routines of government and the practices of the market. Reminding ourselves of the possibilities for such action is useful insofar as it draws our attention to forms of public activity that have not been organized through the state or the market. However, it is not helpful to reify the social as a domain separate from the economic and the governmental. If politics is confined to one sphere, or separated into three, the possibilities for human action on matters of wider and deeper concern are severely limited.

We should remember that Aristotle himself had not far to go to find barbarism and servitude. There were slaves in his own household, and the women there were confined in ways that foreshadowed the practices now identified with Islamic fundamentalism. Moreover, the free-spirited Greek cities engaged in savage and debilitating warfare, among themselves as well as with their foreign neighbours. Ancient Greece may have been more like contemporary Bosnia than we like to imagine, and the socio-economic and political inequalities at that time were at least as pronounced as they are today. No doubt, to put politics in a place where these things do not have to be dealt with can seem attractive. In fact, the logic of the state is very similar to that of the polis in this respect; both point toward enclosure or privacy as the technique for creating a secure space in which proper politics can occur. The world is wished away, and the noble few are supposed to relate to one another as dignified equals in the places they have made for themselves. However, as Aristotle knew from his experience of Macedonian hegemony, these privileged spaces tend to be fragile or illusory. The world keeps intruding, for the conditions that give rise to barbarism and servitude are not being addressed. While the privileged retreat into their mock parliaments, the real battles for power are fought elsewhere, and these usually are not very pretty. Civilization becomes a mockery of itself.

A politics that repeats the 'solution' of enclosure at a different level or in a different form will simply repeat the problems of the state and the polis. Such are the illusions implicit in the claims of subject peoples to national sovereignty, or in idle speculations about re-creating the city-state. Similar illusions also appear in fundamentalist social movements – not least in the movement that goes under the guise of liberalism and celebrates individual sovereignty. The self-contained individual, the self-contained tribe, the self-contained community of believers, the self-contained state – all are gestures toward an independence that can only be sustained by violence toward others. Thus, servitude and barbarism flow from the reaction they generate, in a seemingly endless cycle of reproduction. A more humane and realistic politics is one that shakes the grip of these illusions and plunges people back into the problems they must deal with. Insofar as the relocalization of politics encourages people to deal with the inequalities, exclusions, oppression, and violence that are there among them, it serves to burst the enclosures that keep us from dealing with reality honestly.

Everyday life and actual local experience tend to make nonsense of the idea that there are separate spheres of human existence that can be neatly distinguished from one another. On the contrary, the divisions that seem so secure in the wider world tend to dissolve into the messy relations between particular human beings. What is private is public, what is personal is political, what is local is global. Nothing is quite what it seems; everything is to be negotiated; nothing is completely fixed. To inquire into local politics in its fullest sense is to explore the flows of activity, to note the stoppages and diversions, to follow the sudden transformations and eruptions – in short, to be confronted with the real complexity of unfixed human existence. Locality itself is always relative, always temporary, always to be defined by human actions. Thus it emerges, dissipates, and is reconstituted by complex political movements. Understanding these movements seems to be the key to comprehending the political as democratic possibility.

**Social Movements and Political Communities**

As usually articulated, the theory of democracy is just an aspect of the theory of the state. It offers an ideal of state organization and specifies the conditions for realizing it. What democracy means as a condition for international relations – rather than as a condition for making foreign policy – is not considered; also not considered are the conditions for democratizing emergent transnational communities, such as those of feminists, or environmentalists, or pacifists. Although localities seem to get more consideration, this is deceptive, for local democracy is usually regarded as an aspect of national democracy. State-centred accounts treat municipalities as ministates and apply to them the democratic prescriptions (e.g., representative institutions) that have been developed for the nation-state. Market-centred theories, such as those about public choice, subordinate democracy to the satisfaction of consumer preferences. In either case, little remains of local democracy as a distinctive political ideal.[38] The venue for everyday life, everyday politics, and everyday democracy fades as an object of political theory, in favour of the state that stands over/against it. In this way, the idea of democracy as an aspect of everyday life also fades, along with the political communities that could sustain or extend it. The latter are unintelligible as aspects of the state and hence are beyond the ken of political theory as normally conceived. That there might be forms of political community that resist enclosure or are stifled by it is barely considered. How these forms might sustain or extend common political ideals is not a serious subject.

Arthur Bentley's famous book, *The Process of Government* (1908), marked a shift toward a 'society-centred' theory of politics.[39] Some political scientists believe that this shift has gone too far and have announced with some pride that they are 'bringing the state back in.'[40] However, it is clear that the state never went away: it was merely renamed. The supposed shift from a state-centred to a society-centred perspective is really just a move from one vantage point to another. The object of study remains the same: 'societies' are constituted by states, and 'politics' is defined by the process of government, the activity internal to states.[41] Groups are deemed to be political insofar as they address themselves to the process of government – that is, insofar as they seek to influence government policy, to secure representation within the state, or, at the extreme, to take over the government itself. If government is the output, politics is the input that connects civil society to the state. It affords space both for parties that seek to control the state and for pressure groups that want to influence it. Thus, in a properly ordered democratic regime, parties and pressure groups monopolize the space for politics.

The theoretical impoverishment that results from a state-centric conception of politics can be seen in the conventional treatment of social movements.[42] On the one hand, everyone knows that social movements are important politically. On the other hand, no one is sure how to fit them into state-centric political categories. Clearly, a movement is neither a pressure group nor a political party. Nevertheless, parties and pressure groups are often spawned by movements, and just as frequently attempt to speak authoritatively for them. For the state, the institutionalization of a movement as a pressure group or party is often essential for containing and dealing with the threat it represents. The enclosure of a movement within an established political space allows for regularization of the relations between the state and the group concerned. This regularization may have the effect of stilling the social movement. For the state, this return to calm is usually welcome. For those involved in the social movement, the party or the group remains as institutional detritus from their efforts. The interests or concerns embodied in the original movement are given a form appropriate to the smooth functioning of the state.

From the vantage point of the state (which is the normal vantage point of political analysis), the institutionalization of social movements is simply a matter of regularizing their political form. In this sense, social movements become political actors only when they are institutionalized. Before that, they appear simply as prepolitical disturbances in civil society.[43] This suggests that the collective activities of ordinary people, in working out new understandings of themselves and bringing those understandings into the world, are themselves prepolitical. Thus, the creative social activity in which ordinary people are most likely to be engaged appears beyond or outside politics. In the political sphere proper (as in the governmental sphere), the important activities demand expertise and afford opportunities for creative action only to the élite. 'The people' are just the chorus and audience – and the beast without. It seems that such prepolitical, merely social creatures are best confined to the harmless dramas of local politics or to the pseudopolitical rituals of television.

Such an account is a distortion of political reality. It seems natural only because of our acceptance of state-centric conceptions of politics. If we begin with popular political activity, rather than from the enclosure imposed upon it, another dimension of reality emerges. Politics might be defined as purposive social action directed at the conditions of social existence. From this perspective, social movements are the politics of the people and government is the politics of the state.[44] Parties and pressure groups are the forms imposed on popular politics, under state hegemony. For the most part, they seem to quell social movements, thereby curbing the politics of the people. The fact that movements can and do burst the enclosures of the state is evidence not of their prepolitical but of their *political* character – of their capacity to *found* or create new forms of political community, political identity, and political action. This alternative conception of politics seems to capture the agonistic character of political action, and to free us from the easy assumption that politics is where the authorities want it to be. On the other hand, it may lead us to reproduce the false dualism that puts government and the people, or the state and social movements, into separate spheres. We need to locate movements in a space that is not simply an exterior to the state.

It is worth considering what democratic theory would be like if it were a theory of social movements rather than just an elaboration of the theory of the state. A more comprehensive theory would have to contend with some complicated facts.[45] The social movements that engage people democratically tend to have these traits:

- They are **pluralistic**, in the sense that there is not just one movement in any place, but many; a person may be part of as many movements as he or she has energy for, and the number of simultaneous movements is in principle unlimited.
- They are **impermanent**. Movements last only as long as the enthusiasm for them, after which they become bureaucratized or they disappear.
- They are **inchoate**, with no definite membership, authority relations, purposes, or programs.
- They are **inclusive**. In principle, anyone can be part of a movement, and there can be no definite means of excluding a person.
- They are **unbounded**. A movement takes in as many people, as much territory, and as many issues as seems appropriate to the people involved.

Not every movement displays each of these features, but in principle movements are the antithesis of enclosures. They lack fixity, boundaries, and determinacy.

It should be stressed that social movements are not organizations in the usual sense. Rather, they are ways of being, thinking, and acting that challenge established routines. In this sense, social movement organizations (SMOs) are reifications of what they represent. They are not the movements themselves, and – as Michels pointed out a long time ago – good organizations can kill good movements.[46] We all have a tendency to forget this. We identify movements with the organizations that purport to embody them, and we suppose that when the organizations are flourishing, so are the movements. The reality is that the death of an SMO may be a result of the success of the movement itself. Once certain ways of acting are embedded in the culture, the organizations that called for them may seem superfluous. Of course, this often is an illusion; even so, it can take time for people to realize how much more change in the culture is required. Once this recognition spreads, a new generation of SMOs is likely to emerge. The labour movement has gone through many periods of organization and re-organization since the early days of capitalism. The 'conservation' movement was born again in the 1970s as the environmental movement. Modern feminism has gone through at least two (and probably more) 'waves' of activism. These are all signs of the fact that the work of great social movements is never done – and that the organizations they create are bound to be temporary.

How then can social movements be conceived in terms of democratic theory? The perplexity with which we approach this question reflects the hold of state-centric political theory. Don't we need definite bounds for the theorization of democracy? (Or liberty, or equality, or justice?) How can we attach democratic conditions to such inchoate phenomena? If we think of environmentalism, we might pose the following criteria:

- The movement ought to address itself to all people, regardless of class, nation, race, gender, or social condition.
- The movement ought to offer all people the opportunity to participate in defining its goals and carrying out its activities.
- It ought not to discriminate in favour of some people at the expense of others.
- It ought not to claim exclusive loyalty, or seal itself off from other movements.

These criteria might be questioned, but they are sufficiently clear to suggest that relating democracy to a social movement is by no means impossible. And what is true of democracy is likely to be true of other political ideals. We are suffering from a lack of political imagination in this respect.

The progressive social movements that have been generating new hopes in the last thirty years all express demands for democratization. More than that, they enact democratization, insofar as they empower oppressed or marginalized people and give effect to practices that facilitate both the criticism of existing institutions and relationships and the exploration of new possibilities. Democracy is thus a movement *within* the movements, where it finds expression in self-education and consciousness raising, communication and direct action, affinity networks, information exchanges, cooperatives, institutions for public service and self-help, and so on. Whether we are talking about feminists, native people, environmentalists, labour activists, or any number of others, we can sense the development of new institutions and practices that embody an ethic of democracy. There is a richness of democratic practice that radiates outward, links the movements with one another, and connects with the popular culture. Although there are many resistances to it, the presence of democracy is fullest in the world of the progressive, critical social movements. This fullness overflows the boundaries established by states, corporations, and families, and in so doing meets up with the flood from within. Indeed, social movements are both inside *and* outside the oppressive relations that have to be changed. Thus, the movement for democracy radiates from centres inside and outside the state, fed everywhere by the movements that embody this demand. No one centre has any obvious privilege in relation to these processes of democratization. Any attempt to privilege a given centre – be it an agency, a party, or an SMO – is likely to be a sign of antidemocratic efforts to inhibit change.

A century ago, Engels talked about the administration of things rather than people.[47] More than he could have imagined, people have since been turned into things to be administered, so that the difference between the two is not always apparent to us. This 'thing-ification' or reification of people as employees, clients, patients, consumers, managers, and residents is implicit in the main practices of public and private administration. In a sense, the point of administration is to turn people into things that can be easily handled. Fortunately, people do resist this, and their resistance finds expression in democratic social movements. With respect to administration, democratization is a process of popular empowerment, whereby people displace the external administration of themselves by processes that enable them to administer together the things that interest them. This necessarily means what Engels forgot – an expansion of the political as a domain in which people work out their purposes in discussion with one another. For this to be productive, the spheres of individual autonomy and collective decision must be expanding simultaneously. People have to find the process empowering for themselves individually; at the same time they must be gaining access to collective decisions. Such individual and collective empowerment can only occur at the expense of the main institutions of social control, most notably the state, the market, and the patriarchal family. In this sense, demands for democratization are inherently revolutionary: they threaten the structures and practices that fix us as subordinates.

If, as suggested, the politics of the people is a politics of movements – not always progressive or democratic, but potentially so – the implications for political theory are profound. It suggests that the key considerations of democratic theory ought not to be the traditional matters of state, but the relations within and between social movements. Indeed, it suggests that, insofar as political theory has become simply the theory of the state, it serves as a legitimating ideology that obscures the very possibility of politics of, by, and for the people. The effects of this are particularly evident in the United States, where the main principles of the conventional liberal-democratic theory of the state are reified as constitutional law. Unfortunately, it is not much of an exaggeration to describe American political theory as a series of footnotes to the U.S. Constitution.[48] Although theorists elsewhere lack such a touchstone, the phenomenon of the state still largely determines their expectations of political theory. Good theory is supposed to offer a critique of the modern state and specifications for changing it. What it says about movements is mere sociology. Thus, the conditions for barbarism and subservience are often treated as externalities in the theory of democracy.

Obviously, to shift from the state to movements, and to ignore the former as an object of theorizing would be wrong. Movements are as much within as outside the state: that is one of the keys to their effectiveness. A woman does not cease to be a woman because she becomes a politician or a civil servant. Nor does she stop being a consumer, property owner, environmentalist, or whatever. This means that social movements are always there within the state, just as they are there within civil society. The operations that secure the state as state (and hence bring about political closure) must suppress this internal presence of other social movements and somehow relocate those movements in a domain external to the state. This means getting state operatives to feel the social movements in their lives as externalities – which is not an easy thing to do. The 'representation' of social movements can be part of an operation to secure externality. Social movements are identified with SMOs; the SMOs are asked to send representatives to meetings or to put them on commissions of inquiry or administrative boards; these representatives are then designated as the legitimate spokespeople for movements that exist legitimately only *outside* the state. This expulsion of the movements is never fully successful, but it serves to encourage public servants to treat movements as objects outside themselves upon which they have the authority to act in the name of the state. The development of progressive, democratic social movements depends on challenging this externalizing process, and on encouraging people within the state to recognize and act on the internal presence of the movements.

As we shall see in Chapter 12, the state itself can be understood as an effect of a particular hegemonic movement, which intersects with other movements such as capitalism. People are not outside the hegemonic movements, and the movements that challenge the dominant ones are not necessarily outward-looking or self-critical. Thus, a politics of movements is not necessarily what we want it to be. Perhaps the most important thing to recognize is that social movements actually create or constitute the political space (or hyperspace) within which the state appears. When we focus on the state exclusively and imagine that it somehow contains everything that is important politically, we avoid the wider political realities, in which both the best and the worst of human life become apparent. From a statist perspective, it is especially difficult to make sense of what ordinary people are thinking and doing, since the political communities that people create are so diverse and amorphous. The word *community* conjures up an image of people in their everyday lives, but the concept of *political* community, as used in political theory, is one of enclosure. Thus, the predominant theories of political community today are just theories of the state disguised.[49] This makes it extraordinarily difficult not only to theorize democracy realistically, but also to deal with other political challenges.

Social movements seem to have localized origins, but typically they spread beyond their original centres. They develop complex systems of communications and invent new authority relations. They convert masses of people, leading them to reconceive their own identities as well as their activities, which include working out goals, strategies, and tactics, and acting on them. They are always in development (or decline). They have no necessary bounds in space or time. Their extent and longevity depend on the enthusiasm of their participants, the nature of their objectives, and the conditions they encounter. They attempt to fix themselves in appropriate forms, but they are in constant tension with the political enclosures they encounter and the social relations that have been fixed by earlier movements. The forms of political community embodied in movements such as socialism, liberalism, feminism, and environmentalism are not easily contained, even when the established containers seem to have arisen from the movements concerned. The Soviet Union was undermined not only by liberalism but also by socialism, and the dominant liberal states are in constant flux because of the activities of people who insist on living out their freedom.

By problematizing standard conceptions of political community, we can begin to examine politics as people actually experience and practise it. In this sense politics is a matter of everyday life, where barbarism and subservience are never far away. This does not mean that everything is political (although it may mean that anything is worth examining politically). It does mean that politics involves people's everyday experience of those practices which define their social identities, social goals, and modes of social action. In part, politics is a matter of participating in or challenging practices of domination, some (but not all) of which are organized through the state. It also involves people's creative social actions: their inventions, not just their resistances. The most powerful expression of this second dimension of politics is encountered in critical social movements. Every critical social movement has its own conception of what is fundamental politically: which human identities are crucial, what forms of social action are necessary, what political communities have to be created. As such, critical movements are the creative edge of politics as an everyday experience. Localities are the venues for such politics, in the sense that they are the places where the various practices of domination meet with the practices of political resistance and invention. Politics as creative popular activity thus occurs at the juncture of localities and movements. To focus on this juncture is to open two analytic dimensions: first, *locality* as the place where movements arise and where they meet; and, second, *movement* as a mode of action that redefines political community and thereby connects localities to one another. Where that takes us in time and space is to be discovered.

# 3

# Critical Social Movements

I picked up the local paper the other day and found a picture of my thirteen-year-old daughter and her friends on the front page.[1] They were demonstrating on the steps of the British Columbia legislature against the logging at Clayoquot Sound. Clayoquot is the latest and most dramatically contested of the environmental hot spots in the B.C. wilderness.[2] Like the Stein, the Carmanah, the Walbran, and others before it, Clayoquot is the focus of protests from those who insist that quite enough of B.C.'s ancient forests have been logged and that most if not all of the untouched valleys should be preserved in their present state. The issue has touched the hearts and minds not only of young people in Victoria, but also of established environmentalists worldwide. Robert F. Kennedy, Jr, came to visit the sound, and Tom Hayden – once famous as Jane Fonda's husband and before that as a leader of the SDS (Students for a Democratic Society) – remarried on the beach nearby. Midnight Oil, the Australian band, entertained at the protesters' camp, with MuchMusic in attendance. And in Europe the dispute over Clayoquot fed into widespread concerns, marked by alarming television documentaries, about the 'scandal' of clear-cut logging in the Pacific rain forests.[3] In many people's minds there is a clear link between forestry practices in B.C. and more disturbing activities elsewhere. The havoc currently being wreaked by the logging companies in Southeast Asia, West Africa, and Brazil seems to mirror what has happened on this continent, first in the East, now in the North and West. That havoc is obviously connected with the progress of industrialism, a progress that now seems to threaten the biosphere.

When B.C.'s New Democratic government had to make a decision about logging around Clayoquot Sound – which is on the west coast of Vancouver Island, near Pacific Rim National Park – it carefully considered the political costs. On the one hand, severe logging restrictions at places like Clayoquot might precipitate mill closures and spell doom for small towns where the unionized work-force had traditionally supported the NDP. On the other hand, the government's failure to address environmental concerns would alienate many of its urban, middle-class supporters. The best political solution seemed to be a careful compromise that would balance job preservation with forest preservation within a framework of 'fiscal responsibility' (i.e., not paying too much money for reclaiming lands from the forest companies). This was the government's theme, and at Clayoquot it resulted in a Solomonic division of the area into loggable, unloggable, and mixed use lands.[4] Whether or not the compromise made sense in terms of the environment or the economy, it was certainly intelligible politically. That is, it was intelligible in terms of a traditional, statist conception of political space. Whether that conception is actually the relevant one is another matter, as the explosion of the issue indicates.

Once upon a time – not too long ago – it seemed as if the most important political issues could be contained quite effectively within the spaces defined by the state system. Provincial politics was provincial politics, and it was about the things that the government could do in relation to a society and economy bound within the province. The political compromises that had to be made (as between loggers and environmentalists, for instance) involved groups that related to one another within the same space – a space that could be governed more or less independently. This space, moreover, had its own distinct history, one that was intelligible in terms of the relations between different segments of the same society. The provincial boundaries defined a time and place at which people could act, knowing that they all shared the same location. However else people might differ, they were relating to one another about the same things within the same bounds, and this gave rulers – and many others – a sense of security. It is this security that is now being lost. For better or worse, the political containers that gave rise to security seem to be disintegrating – at Clayoquot, in the courts at Victoria, in provincial and national politics, and more generally in the world around us. It seems that we are all caught up in a process of dislocation or decentring that is rendering the political spaces of the past less coherent and making it increasingly difficult for people to relate to one another's histories. People in the same place or at the same moment in history are no longer together, and as a result their actions often are mutually unintelligible.

As I write this (late in 1993), the Clayoquot protesters are preparing for a long winter of dissent in an encampment on the sidewalk outside the courthouse in Victoria. Not long ago, Mr. Justice John Bouck of the B.C. Supreme Court was the first to sentence some of the protesters who had been arrested for blocking the logging road into Clayoquot.[5] As he handed down his sentences, he struggled to make himself understood by the people before him. Significantly, he abstracted himself from B.C., instead explaining his decision in the context of the traditions of civil disobedience associated with Mahatma Gandhi and Martin Luther King. Instinctively, he knew that his history of B.C. – a history of civilization – was irrelevant to the people before him. If they had a B.C. history, it was an unedifying tale of corporate greed and exploitation in which the B.C. government and the B.C. courts were obviously complicit. The history that he wanted them to hear was different: a tale of the majesty of the law, the triumph of parliamentary democracy, and the solemn duty of the courts to uphold everyone's rights even when it was unpopular to do so. In that tale – a sort of Whig history of Western civilization as described through the institutions of the state – Gandhi and King functioned as the international symbols of legitimate civil disobedience. Mr Justice Bouck emphasized the civility rather than the heroism of their disobedience, stressing the willingness of the two leaders to accept their lawful punishment. More forcefully still, he stressed that these men had been excluded from political systems that might otherwise have enabled them to achieve their objectives by lawful means. He scolded the Clayoquot protesters for assuming the mantle of right when they had failed, despite all the opportunities available to Canadian citizens, to convince their fellow British Columbians of the need for a complete stop to the logging. That the protesters did not seem contrite, and indeed seemed to think that they ought to be recognized as heroes in the environmentalist cause, was infuriating to the judge. It exasperated him that many of these people did not even bother to read the newspapers.

Little of this meant anything to the protesters, who, although they stood before the judge in his courtroom, were actually in another time and place. They saw themselves as part of the great movement to save the earth from the depredations of the judge and his friends.[6] What the newspapers or the government of British Columbia had to say about logging was of little interest, except as an indication of their obtuseness. The majesty of the law and the state was irrelevant, for it was by these institutions that the rape of the earth was legitimized. No legal or democratic process could really justify what was happening, and the wishes of the people who happened to live in British Columbia at that time were of marginal importance. The story that counted was one of life on earth, of which the human story was just a part. The latest phase of human life was one of industrialism, pollution, and overpopulation, all of these brought on by the 'advances' of Western civilization. That the judge should appeal to one aspect of that civilization to justify its other evils seemed perverse. Moreover, it was deliberately deceptive for him to suggest that the battle for Clayoquot could be won by appealing to the voters of British Columbia. British Columbians, like the ranchers and gold miners of the Amazon, were profiting from the plunder of the rain forests. If the political battle was to be won, it had to be in the court of global opinion, among those who could take a more objective, long-term view. Americans and Europeans had to be shocked out of their complacency, and as necessary led to boycott B.C. as a tourist destination and source of lumber.[7] In the battle for the hearts and minds of the people of the planet, the attitudes of the B.C. government and B.C. electorate were largely irrelevant. Moreover, the only way of winning global attention in face of competition from other issues was to dramatize the struggle by confronting the logging company and the provincial government directly. From this point of view, the 'rights' recognized by the B.C. courts were as irrelevant as the ones bandied about in the Amazon. Who could take them seriously, except someone so obtuse as to be living still in the 'Province of British Columbia' rather than on the surface of an endangered planet?

Of course, the loggers, mill workers, and small-town people whose jobs were threatened by the protests did not have the luxury of living either on the environmentalist's planet or in the judge's lawful state. For them, as for many Canadians, 'global competitiveness' was not just an abstract phrase: it was the force that was taking away their jobs, reducing their wages, removing their economic security, and destroying their communities. In that context, the relevant place was where they lived and worked, and the relevant story was one of human survival. The majesty of the law was not of immediate concern to them, nor was the saving of the biosphere. The place and time for such ordinary people was the day-to-day struggle for survival, focused on the particularities of jobs, homes, families, and communities. To the extent that there was a relevant wider reality, it was the global marketplace being negotiated by the logging companies. The province and its laws and judges and the environmentalists and their distant supporters were interveners from other worlds, where the hard laws of economic competition were kept at one remove. Those spaces of privilege were not available to workers in the forest industry; the histories played out at such a distance were for them scarcely more relevant than the tales from Bosnia and Somalia.

There were yet other worlds involved in this drama, not the least of which were the ones that 'British Columbia' originally was designed to suppress. The Pacific Northwest was the site of an extraordinary flowering of Amerindian cultures. The peoples concerned were among the last to have their lives disrupted by the European invasions that plagued the world from the 1490s onward. As elsewhere, the impact of disease, drugs, and alcohol, commerce, and settlement was disastrous for the indigenous peoples; but, as elsewhere, those same peoples have been reorganizing themselves and reasserting their claims to the lands they had occupied for countless years before the invasions.[8] In this context there has been a reassertion of the indigenous histories of the region, within which the incursions of the new settlers are seen as unfortunate disruptions. The political authorities that are most relevant from this perspective are not the ones imported by the foreign settlers – that is, not the colonial empires and nation-states nurtured in the endless wars of Europe – but the ones that emerge from the peoples who occupied this land from time immemorial.[9] Affirming their authority means setting the alien 'British Columbia' aside and redefining the time and place in terms of the cultural recovery of oppressed peoples. The B.C. courts, the companies in the global market, and the environmentalists in their ecospace fade into insignificance as the practice of cultural renewal expands to include the recovery of the ancient forests by the people who long made their homes there.

In lecturing to the protesters, Mr. Justice Bouck echoed the aspirations toward sovereignty of the B.C. government and the Canadian state in general. To realize sovereignty is to fix everyone in a particular place in the same story, so that they are living their history together in accordance with the same rules.[10] If this fixing is accomplished, then the sentences judges give and the compromises governments make become intelligible to all concerned, even when the decisions seem misguided. Everyone is led to see that politics and the law – the inputs and outputs of public life – come out of a common existence that can only be changed by action within the system. To fix and thus to contain politics in this way – to put it at a certain place on the globe and a certain moment in history – is no small feat and usually requires considerable violence. 'Canada' is no exception in this respect, having been established by force of arms. Once created, as an offshoot of the British Empire, it effaced the histories of indigenous peoples and established a pretended sovereignty in relation to the United States and Europe. From that moment, it had an existence that had to be enforced on the inhabitants of its territory. This was pursued not only through the laws and the courts, but also through a variety of propaganda campaigns in the schools and elsewhere, which were designed to foster a sense that Canadians shared a common country with a common history and a common future. Mr. Justice Bouck demonstrated the continuing seriousness of this project by putting the protesters before him in jail, where he thought they would learn that they were in the same place as he was.

Judges have always been desperate characters, trying to enforce an order that seems just out of reach. The dilemmas of judges and governments seem particularly pressing now, as the securities of the state system come under increasing pressure. It seems very unlikely that my daughter's world will fit into the neat boxes that political scientists – as well as judges and governments – have imagined as the eternal containers for politics. The fixings of statehood, which have underpinned politics and its science in this century, seem to be coming loose, and we will need other guides for understanding and action. How can we negotiate different conceptions of time and place? Can we do so without imprisoning, impeding, suppressing, or killing one another? How can we deal with global processes that are clearly beyond the control of any state, but that affect us locally in quite different ways? How can we achieve identities that are not sovereign, and that admit the commonalties and differences that characterize actual human beings? While there are no easy answers to these questions, the paths of discovery will be easier to find if we unmoor ourselves from a state-centric conception of politics.[11]

## The Illusions of Sovereignty

As we have noted, the early texts of political science – which are only about a hundred years old – typically describe the subject as the *science* of the state or statesmanship. Actual statesmen have been as dubious as natural scientists about these claims, since it is not clear that there can be a science of political leadership or effective government: action rarely can wait on scientific discovery, and political judgment depends heavily on instinct and intuition. Even so, political science does much to orient politicians and give them a sense of self-worth. It is not just that political scientists act as electoral wizards and policy analysts – although this is important enough. Political science also defines the object of political activity. It indicates that serious or 'high' politics relates to the state, which is the sovereign authority with respect to the nation's business. The state is supposed to have control over matters of ultimate importance, and this suggests that politics has a special dignity, or at least that it can rise above its own venality and become 'statesmanship.' If the state is at the centre of politics, in the way that God is at the centre of religion, then political science can be understood as the theology that makes sense of state-worship and that offers its practitioners the guidance they require in their devotions. According to the orthodox religion of the state, political activity that takes place in a different time and space is heretical – perhaps dangerous, perhaps only farcical.

Actually, most people are even more sceptical about politics than they are about religion. Patriotism (idealism?), they say, is the last refuge of scoundrels, and politicians undoubtedly cloak their greed and ambition in high-sounding phrases. However, the scepticism we feel runs deeper than our revulsion toward hypocrisy. The great religions have long taught that politics is not the path to personal or social redemption. Modern economics suggests that prosperity is to be achieved by a mode of production that keeps the state at a distance. The satisfactions of youthful adventure and family security are supposedly found in private, not public life, and the creativity of art and science is at several removes from politics. Thus, the activities that seem most important to our well-being appear apolitical: not properly organized on political principles or to serve political purposes, and not properly governed by political authorities. It certainly seems admirable to keep politics out of the things that matter, and the modern state indeed appears to ensure that politics stays separate from what is most important to our lives. Ostensibly, the state stands apart as a domain where the rules for other, more important activities can be adjusted, and where people can be mobilized to endow or protect what really matters. The government is supposed to facilitate rather than suppress or control people's activities.

In a sense, sovereignty – the organizing principle of the state system – is a contradiction in terms, because it implies a form of totalitarian control that can never be realized. Although the state seems to make civil society and individual freedom possible, it only grounds or completes what we create by our other activities. The separation of the ruler from the ruled, and of the state from civil society, involves relative autonomy for each side.[12] Moreover, the division of the world into separate sovereignties creates spaces above, below, and between states where the writ of governments does not run. In a way that was barely imaginable a few decades ago, the world is integrated by ungovernable systems of electronic communication. Capital moves instantaneously from one part of the world to another; the latest fashions come before us immediately in Djakarta, Bulawayo, and Berlin; diseases circulate almost at the speed of sound; and people push at the barriers that limit their movement from one country to another. Increasingly we have moved toward globally integrated systems of design, marketing, production, and distribution. This global economy sustains, develops, and draws sustenance from a global culture with its own language, music, food, dress, entertainment, and styles of life. Although it evolves in accordance with its own relentless logic, there is no 'centre' from which it is controlled. The states that function within it may claim authority to set the rules, but the activities concerned actually determine what states can be and do.

The processes at work are not new, and indeed it was one of Marx's great insights a century and a half ago that the states of the modern era only *appeared* to be masters of their own destinies.[13] He saw the capitalist economy developing behind the backs of the leaders of his day. He thought that these leaders would inevitably be servants of the system, whether they recognized their role or not. And yet he also thought that the class struggle generated by the antagonistic relationship between capitalists on the one hand and the mass of working people on the other would generate a new politics of hope. In the past, he thought, the struggles of the exploited had been futile, because the existing modes of production condemned the vast majority of people to lifelong toil. However, the immense productivity of capitalism opened the possibility of a free and fulfilling life for all. The point of the new politics was to enable people to understand the new mode of production, to take control of it for their own purposes, and to transform it into something different and better. To Marx it seemed that the new politics would allow people for the first time to become masters of their own destinies, and so to realize the promise implicit in sovereignty – that it would be a system of self-government rather than exploitation and domination. This was the promise of the American and French revolutions, carried forward unsuccessfully in the twentieth century by Marx's own political heirs.

Marx himself thought in terms of dissolving the state in the process of achieving communism. In doing so, he pointed back toward a time when states did not exist. Many students are surprised when they learn that states are a relatively recent innovation in human history. Obviously, there have been ordered societies since time immemorial, and these societies have had some means of enforcing their rules on their own members. If we think of politics as the process for developing and enforcing such rules, it clearly has existed for a very long time and taken many different forms. However, the principles that define the modern state only emerged in early modern Europe. Each state was supposed to have complete autonomy from foreign powers, so that it could determine its own religion, organize its economy as it chose, and have its own language and culture. All of this implied that there would be a supreme authority from which the order of the state emanated. This authority would be impersonal, permanent, and transcendent, yet at the same time internal to the state itself. The establishment of 'sovereignty' involved a radical simplification of the earlier pattern of divided, overlapping, and essentially contested jurisdictions, which had different origins, different histories, and different conceptions of political space.[14] In Europe, sovereign statehood undercut the claims of the universal church and empire, as well as those of many intermediate authorities, from baronies and bishoprics to municipalities and corporations. To most progressive thinkers in the eighteenth and nineteenth centuries – including Marx – the advance of sovereignty seemed essential to clear away the clutter of history. The question was whether the progress should or could continue to the point at which separate sovereignties dissolved into a single, ordered whole.

In its ultimate logic, sovereignty reduces everyone to the status of an individual citizen with equal rights under the laws established and enforced by the state. According to liberal-democratic doctrine, which became increasingly important from the eighteenth century onward, such rights could come to reflect the needs and interests of individuals in general, if the state were properly ordered. At the same time, according to nationalist doctrine, each state could also achieve its own individuality by expressing the culture of a particular people. However, in a community of properly ordered states (so the liberals argued) there would be a common culture that secured basic rights to all individuals and enabled them to participate in a global order that facilitated economic and cultural exchange. By the nineteenth century that global order came to be understood as a marketplace in which autonomous individuals, states, and intermediate organizations could deal with one another on terms of equality. A universal community was to emerge out of the activities of particular states, which produced individuals with similar rights, similar needs, and similar understandings of their duties in relation to one another. Whether this universal community would ultimately need – or be able to produce – a universal government only time could tell, but the efforts in the twentieth century to create a League of Nations and a United Nations seemed to point in that direction.

It has taken hundreds of years for the principles of sovereignty to be worked out, and the process is by no means complete. We have seen in Europe the reduction of extraordinarily complex cultures into increasingly homogeneous nation-states – so homogeneous, in fact, that their integration into a transcendent European Community no longer seems a pipe-dream. In North America, Australia, New Zealand, and to a lesser extent other European settler societies, the indigenous cultures have been overwhelmed by the projection of a homogenized Europeanism, now increasingly understood as 'American.' The Europeans, with their navies and armies, their missionaries, traders, planters, industrialists, and magistrates, carried this activity forward in every corner of the globe, and then the civilizing mission was taken up by the more vigorous Americans. The combined achievement of the West – interrupted in the twentieth century by the civil wars in Europe and the revolutions in Russia and China – has been to replicate its own institutions throughout the world. The effect has been to override what existed previously, to bring everyone into the same history, and to situate everyone in the same system of states and global marketplace. Although this process is still celebrated – most recently in terms of bringing 'democracy' to the benighted peoples of Asia, Africa, Latin America, and Eastern Europe – it can be more accurately understood as a totalitarian project. It is becoming more and more difficult for people to live in a way other than what the West defines as best.

Ostensibly, sovereignty secures differences by enabling each state to go its own way. However, as an internal order, sovereignty tends to reduce people to abstract individuals who have to be related to one another in the same way. Thus, each state is increasingly a clone of the next. This is reflected in the similarities between constitutions in different parts of the world. As Marx recognized, states are autonomous only in the abstract; the division of the world into self-subsistent spaces flies in the face of reality. There are flows of air, water, diseases, animals, ideas, people, drugs, guns, and whatever we might imagine, and these wash over the earth in ways that states can regulate only with enormous difficulty. We have only to look at the experience of the Soviet Bloc in the twentieth century – set up in defiance not only of the global economic system but also of the cultural linkages between Eastern and Western Europe – to understand how fragile the divisions are that set one state apart from the next. The lesson seems to be that sovereignty can only be invoked in conformity with the transcendent global order that reduces the differences between states to variations on the same theme. Much the same might be said of the vaunted individualism of the modern era. With luck, we all can be exactly what we want to be, as long as we conform to the same model of individuality, which precludes anything that does not accord with the principles of modern citizenship and the practices of the global marketplace.

The illusions of sovereignty and the illusions of liberalism are two sides of the same coin. The vaunted differences between states and among individuals conceal the uniformities imposed by the practices that generate these differences. These practices are bound up with a particular conception of what it means to be human – a conception that had its genesis in Europe. As such, they constitute the non-European, non-Christian, nonliberal as an 'other' – as possessing a sort of savage, untamed identity that cannot be reconciled with civilization. Only to the extent that these others adapt their identities to conform to the normative practices at the centre of the system can they be admitted as civilized. As various feminist critics have pointed out, the normative identities of the autonomous individual and the sovereign state seem to be expressive of masculine notions of freedom.[15] As environmentalists have noted, they also seem to entail a kind of detachment from the earth that reflects a peculiarly Western religious sensibility.[16] Finally, as Marxists and other critics of capitalism have explained, the autonomous individual and the sovereign state are the poles between which the 'free market' has been constructed. In that market we have little option but to turn ourselves into commodities that can be exchanged for the goods the economy produces.

From the beginning, the constitutive practices of sovereignty/liberalism faced massive resistance. The non-Western peoples struggled to sustain their own ways of life, and in the West itself older traditions asserted themselves in relation to the new order. These traditions included the particularistic claims of villages, regions, orders of nobility, suppressed nationalities, crafts, guilds, corporations, and much else. They also included the alternative universalisms of transcendent religion and secular rationalism. Out of the latter especially came the most powerful of the twentieth-century alternatives – socialism in its many variants. From the social-democratic movements in the West itself to the communist governments that created a Second World and the revolutionary nationalist regimes that attempted to redeem the Third, the great resistances of the twentieth century were organized around the ideal of socialism. This ideal was premised on the claim that the promise of sovereignty/liberalism was undercut by the operations of the global market. By somehow overcoming that market, it seemed possible to redeem the promises of individual liberty, equality, and democratic self-government, which were contained in the practices of sovereignty/liberalism but never fully realized. The apparent failure of the various socialist projects – symbolized by the collapse of the Soviet Union and its client states in Eastern Europe – has put these aspirations into serious question. In the end, it seems, sovereignty/liberalism can give us only one thing – *what we already have.*

**New Times and New Places**

The protesters at Clayoquot and the First Nations in British Columbia are among the many who resist this conclusion – who insist that genuinely different and better ways of life are possible. However, the history of protests like theirs is scarcely more encouraging than the history of socialism in the twentieth century. Indigenous peoples have been squeezed to the margins and then offered access to modernity through the state, the market, and Western culture. In the face of such overwhelming pressures, few of these peoples have been able to negotiate an autonomous existence on acceptable terms. Meanwhile, environmentalists have been fighting a rearguard action to save some of the remaining wilderness and to keep the pollution of the biosphere within bounds. It would be hard to argue that any of these resistances has done much to slow the relentless progress of capitalism, or to limit the power of the state system, or to secure the possibility for modes of life that do not fit into the dominant order. All of this has long encouraged most socialists to think that the road through the state is the only viable way to an alternative future. To use the power of the state against itself to shatter the conditions of capitalist exploitation has seemed an attractive possibility. But this too has turned out to be a chimera.

Soviet communism was not the only statist project associated with twentieth-century socialism. Nor, perhaps, was it even the most important. In the West the dominant socialist parties identified themselves with a strategy of peaceful democratic reform that relied heavily on the power of the state to regulate the economy, appropriate resources for public purposes, and establish a system of social welfare. In this way socialism or social democracy came to be associated with Keynesian economic management, high taxes, social security, public enterprise, and expanded state bureaucracy. This approach to social reform was premised on the capacity of democratic institutions to ensure sensitive and responsible government. It also depended on the state's capacity to internalize the capitalist economy – that is, to create and maintain a clearly bounded national economy that could be regulated from within. Since the 1970s, this capacity for internal regulation has been steadily eroded, and it has become more and more difficult for governments to diverge from the paths favoured by global capital. The present difficulties of the NDP provincial governments in Canada are indicative of this; in this regard, they reflect a pattern already well established in Western Europe, Australia, and New Zealand. The crisis of statist social democracy also reflects increasing popular concerns about the inadequacies of existing institutions for ensuring government accountability. It seems that the state is neither very effective nor very responsive.[17]

It would be a mistake to suppose, as many people do, that the disempowerment of the social democratic or welfare state has occurred 'naturally,' without any active intervention on the part of those who are hostile to socialism. On the contrary, the project of deconstructing the social democratic state has been at the forefront of conservative politics for decades. The successes of Margaret Thatcher in Britain and Ronald Reagan in the United States were emblematic of a more widespread movement that had a long genesis.[18] The deregulation of financial markets, reduction of taxes, imposition of fiscal restraints, privatization of public enterprises, and reorganization of public services on competitive principles were all intended to reconstitute the state in liberal rather than social-democratic terms. The deregulation of financial markets turned out in the end to be the most significant move, for by freeing up the movement of capital from one state to another the neoconservative governments helped to create truly global capital markets in which global capitalist enterprises could operate. With astonishing rapidity, companies have been reorganizing themselves to operate within globalized systems of resource extraction, manufacturing, marketing, and distribution. This has resulted in relentless pressures for further trade liberalization. At each step it becomes more and more difficult for particular states to resist the trend and establish alternative modes of social and economic organization.

None of this could have happened without conscious political action on the part of capitalist leaders. The key figures were not necessarily the conservative politicians, although people like Thatcher and Reagan clearly played an important part. Central bankers, finance department officials, investment fund managers, securities regulators, insurance executives, money traders, commodity brokers, bond raters, and countless other obscure but important figures in the private and public sector were involved in developing the consensus about what had to be done. Privately funded think-tanks, international conferences, scholarly and popular books, journalistic articles, and learned reports all were important. There has been a massive effort on the part of the capitalist class as a whole to rethink and reorganize the global economy. The reconstitution of states in a mode that precludes social democracy has been a major part of this drive,[19] which has been much more successful in a political sense than even its proponents could have imagined two decades ago. Not only have the social democratic parties had their props cut out from under them, but the external socialisms of the Communists and the Third World also have been driven to collapse. The world now seems free for capitalism in a way that it has not been since the Bolshevik Revolution of 1917.

Marx himself might have predicted that capitalism would ultimately burst the integuments that contained it. The borders of the advanced capitalist world to the east and the south gave it particular stability after 1945, and this worked to the advantage of the working class, women, and socially marked minorities in the prosperous countries. It was in this context that social democracy, the welfare state, and various movements for social justice flourished. In the East and the South, it was possible for at least some of the economically weaker countries to pursue their own social experiments, for good or ill. (This depended in part on the ability of the Soviets and the Chinese to counter Western influence.) The opening of the boundary between the West and the Second and Third worlds has had profound effects. To an extent few in the West realize, the poorer countries have been driven to the wall by Western banks, Western aid agencies, and multinational institutions controlled by the Western governments.[20] These countries have been forced to open up their economies to American, European, and East Asian capital, and in this context hundreds of millions of people have been drawn into a global economy that has little immediate use for them. The teeming slums around the Third World cities are a sign of this 'restructuring.' The governments that supposedly have sovereignty in these countries have little or no capacity to deal with their people's problems, and hence have only a tenuous legitimacy.

In the Soviet Bloc since 1989 there has been a particularly rapid movement in the same direction. The most obvious effect is 'wilding':[21] the social glue that held societies together has been dissolved, and the new glue has yet to take. Yugoslavia is the most obvious example. It should be noted, however, that the disorder in the Balkans and in the Caucasus mirrors conditions in other parts of the world: Sudan, Somalia, Burundi, Haiti, Cambodia, Sri Lanka, East Timor, Afghanistan, Kashmir, Angola, Mozambique, Liberia, Peru, Colombia, Guatemala, Lebanon, Northern Ireland ... the list seems endless. Moreover, wilding can take forms other than civil war. The international drug trade creates its own disorder at the sites of production and consumption, as evidenced by the poles of violence in Colombia, Jamaica, and the American inner cities. As Americans and gradually other Westerners have been discovering, the wilding of the world is the dark side of reorganizing it into a global market. As hundreds of millions of people are made redundant in the new global economy, and their governments are reduced to shadows, desperate solutions become the only ones that are practical. A wild world of armed violence and intimidation develops around the edges of the tame, and penetrates the territorial bastions of capital in the West. Refugees mass at the borders, and an urban underclass lives out the life of the Third World within a stone's throw – or a bullet's glance – of the glitzy office towers where the best and the brightest of capitalism work.

In this context we can see the signs of a recidivist politics of the state, keyed on the idea of creating strong governments that rid the streets of crime and drugs and re-create impenetrable borders. In a sense this is a continuation of the politics of deconstruction that has shattered the hopes of social democracy. However, we can predict with some confidence that the project of social cleaning and containment will not be as successful as the effort to liberate global capital. This is because the progress of capital is itself disruptive to neat boundaries and clean streets. What we can expect instead is a leaner, meaner state that does its own wilding in a desperate effort to establish control. In this respect, Los Angeles is truly an image of the future – a place where the Third World meshes with the first in unstable zones of the tame and the wild, and where the violence of the state is itself a source of disruption.[22] Canada may well be spared the worst effects of such politics, but many Canadians obviously believe that the force of the state ought to be deployed on the American model. That appears to be the conviction of many if not most Reformers. A politics of fear feeds off a politics of deconstruction that cannibalizes civil society as well as the welfare state.

In this desperate situation, many people in the West have been looking to 'the new social movements' as bearers of hope. These movements have gained strength because of the weakening of class-based socialist politics in North America and Western Europe. Environmentalism and feminism are two of the most important movements, but we can also identify ones for peace and human rights, multiculturalism, recognition of the gay and the disabled, and so on. What characterizes a movement in this sense is a break in consciousness that leads to political mobilization, usually outside the framework of the state and the established parties and interest groups. So long as it preserves its vitality, a movement maintains itself in its own time and space. It defines its own origins, articulates its own history, and marks the territory for its actions in a distinctive way. For good example, feminists have been rewriting history as the story of women from women's points of view, and have redefined politics to encompass 'personal' relations between the sexes at home, at work, on the street, and elsewhere. The space for feminist action transects the boundary between state and civil society and between one state and the next. Moreover, the meaning and purpose of feminism is largely unintelligible in terms of the history of states. The same might be said of many other social movements.

It may be well to remember that socialism originally set itself outside the framework of the state in a distinctive time and space. Only gradually did the movement come to be identified with parties that sought and sometimes gained state power. Once these parties came to monopolize the movement, the time and space of the state – defined by elections, legislative sessions, and bureaucratic procedures – became predominant. In this alien environment, the movement atrophied and the parties it generated became vulnerable to displacement. What is more, socialism came to be identified with particular statist projects, such as the nationalization of industry, economic planning, and extended social services. Whatever their socialist origins, these projects were modified in terms of the requirements of specific states, whether those were advanced capitalist countries in the West or revolutionary regimes in the Second or Third World. These requirements had little to do with socialism but much to do with the internal and external security of the states concerned. Thus, aspirations toward socialism – originally understood not only in terms of the transcendence of capitalism, but also in terms of the dissolution of the state system – were increasingly identified with the violence and oppression of state bureaucracies.

The 'new' social movements – some of which can claim longer histories than socialism – have generally avoided the trap of party politics, but often at the expense of framing themselves as pressure groups. The pressure group is the legitimate, statist alternative to the party: a political formation that does not seek state power but instead attempts to influence the state from the outside. The traditional socialist critique has been that mere pressure groups cannot have the same power as parties, since they deny themselves the possibility of taking charge of the state. On the other hand, a pressure group need not compromise itself so much in the search for power. However, this purity is relative, and it can be argued that organized groups that must seek the favour of state bureaucracies are really entrapped on the terrain of the state. Like political parties, they must adapt themselves to the agenda of the state, monitoring day-to-day administration, lobbying policy-makers, and injecting their ideas at every stage of government. As they come to orient themselves to the rhythms of the state, these groups internalize the state's story and begin to operate in a time and space that is alien to their own supporters. At that point the breach between the organized groups and the movement that generated them may become as severe as it has been for socialists. In Canada the various women's and aboriginal peoples' movements have been marked by recurrent concerns about the 'co-option' or 'unrepresentativeness' of their leadership – concerns sparked by the financial dependence of these organizations upon the federal government. It would be hard to say that other social movements have been free from these concerns, even when they have been more self-reliant financially.

Clearly, there is no easy way of keeping the state at a distance, and the market offers no real alternative, since its strictures are at least as severe. In any case, a politics of purity is futile, since it defines itself in terms of what it is not rather than what it is.[23] To find a space and time adequate to people's concerns means originating practices that have their own logic and effectiveness. Whether these practices can become powerful enough to challenge the routines of sovereignty/liberalism is impossible to judge in advance.However, the most promising practices are those which on the one hand are rooted in everyday life and on the other hand are connected with movements that transcend the state.[24] The early practices of socialism had this character. Marx and others stressed the rootedness of socialism in the everyday struggles of working people, especially at the point of production. At the same time, there was a firm sense that these struggles were in principle international and as such required the development of international networks of socialist activists. The density and complexity of these networks was – in the context of travel by rail and steamship and of communication by letter and telegraph – truly remarkable. The socialists were not the only ones who organized in this way: the abolitionists, prohibitionists, conservationists, and women's suffragists were among the other pioneers in the development of international networks for political struggle. In many ways these efforts anticipated important initiatives in the late twentieth century.

Just as we take the state for granted as an eternal feature of politics, we tend to suppose that nineteenth- and early twentieth-century modes of political organization will be with us forever. Thus, we imagine that democratic politics will always culminate at the place where parties and pressure groups meet the state. However, the strategic sites for politics may well be different in an age when states are everywhere imploding, and reopening the old division between the tame and the wild. In the last federal election in Canada, the NDP, the Bloc Québécois, and the National Party all seemed to point back toward the sort of nationalist politics that underpinned postwar social democracy. In different ways, they envisioned a 'national' state that could somehow stave off the effects of globalization and secure a protected space for its inhabitants. This is the politics of nostalgia, which has always been played more effectively by the right than by the left. Those who are seeking a realistic progressive politics for the twenty-first century will have to orient themselves to the flows of globalization and pay particular attention to the margins at which different times and places collide.

**Inventing Politics**

One way of understanding politics is as the mode of activity that emerges when other forms of government fail. Normally, our lives are governed by various routines, some of which we have internalized, others of which are imposed from without.[25] Institutions such as the state and the market develop and enforce such routines. When they fail, overt violence may be used to enforce some sort of order. When that fails, or when people decline to resort to violence, politics is the only answer. Politics has its own routines of bargaining, persuasion, and negotiated agreement, sometimes facilitated by special rules of procedure like majority decision. Nonetheless, the politics appropriate to a particular occasion always has to be invented. What makes a situation political in this sense is that the routines have been disrupted and people no longer agree about who or what should govern. Thus, the appropriate procedure cannot be read off, as from a manual, or dictated by a judge. It must emerge somehow from the interaction of people who are living – or trying to live – in different times and places.

Capitalism tends to reshape resistances to fit the spaces it provides for them. It governs a state system in which the people of each country can engage in a show of self-government without disturbing the processes that determine their future. Increasingly it also provides a kind of Disneyland of politics, in which people can live out their fantasies through media shows, styles of dress, forms of music, rituals of protest, alternative communities, and so on. These projections of difference lend colour to an otherwise drab culture of accumulation and consumption. They also prove the truth of capitalism's claim to offer room for alternatives. In fact, the system positively encourages alternatives – when they can be turned into marketable fantasies. In this sense, the protesters at Clayoquot are shock troops for the outdoor recreation and health food industries. In much the same way, the gay and ethnic communities open up urban neighbourhoods for redevelopment and reshape consumer taste. From a marketing perspective, even indigenous and 'foreign' cultures serve mainly as reserves for fashion designers and interior decorators. Everything seems to have its place and value in this system of differences, and there is ample room for a kind of 'virtual politics' that allows people to imagine that they are changing the world. The young, the alienated, and the marginalized – who are unwilling or unable to participate in the 'realistic' politics of the state – get to live out dreams that the media are happy to treat as dangerously radical.

In this context, politics is liable to be a series of meaningless shows. That is when violence and terrorism become especially appealing to the desperate and the disturbed. The precondition of such violence is dehumanization of the enemy, which in turn requires a denial of common humanity. Thus, the sealed identity – the one that admits of no ambiguity – is the fortress from which violence can most easily be perpetrated. States and markets are designed to provide us with such sealed identities. Other social processes reintroduce ambiguity. If the model of identity is fortresslike, people may seek self-certainty through alternatives that brook no questions. These alternatives can be based on ethnic or national identities,but they may also be derived from apparently biological characteristics like sex or skin colour, or from the communities of faith that develop around religious or quasi-religious commitments. In its more innocent forms, a politics of sealed identities takes the form of elaborate shows of difference that are intended to mark the boundaries between one group and the next. However, these shows are a sign of the inward-turning that makes unconditional violence possible. It is when the boundaries of identity are disrupted, and people are forced to discover their connections, that we find a more creative politics emerging. At present there is a particular need to develop connections on a global scale.

Two of the organizations that have been pioneering in global politics are Greenpeace and Amnesty International.[26] The latter began in England, the former in Canada, but both are now multinational. Like multinational corporations, they take advantage of the fact that they can move operations from one country to another to escape government regulation. Greenpeace especially exploits the high seas, where the authority of particular states is ambiguous.[27] However, both organizations orient themselves to the global media, which establish transnational networks for the formation of public opinion. At the same time, Amnesty and Greenpeace have their own independent communications networks, which link groups of activists in different parts of the world. They also have sophisticated fund-raising organizations that reach out more widely and mobilize the resources necessary to support research, publicity, and more direct interventions in the activities of states and corporations. In a sense, they have constituted themselves as autonomous powers in the ambiguous field of global politics.[28] They are by no means alone in this respect: there are now many multinational organizations, with mandates related to human rights, environmental protection, refugee assistance, and economic development, that create spaces for citizen action on a global scale. Some of these, such as the Red Cross, we can trace to a much earlier era. Their politics vary dramatically, and some of them make a show of being apolitical, but they share a sense of a global community in which connections have to be developed.

Such global reach depends on local rootedness. One of the remarkable features of contemporary politics is the proliferation of groups that constitute themselves in particular communities as nodes within international networks. These organizations inside/outside the locality often interact with one another in complex patterns of support and competition. As such, they help to generate a loosely articulated alternative consciousness that defines itself in terms of a critical relationship to globalized capitalism and the state system. It is in this milieu that protests like the ones at Clayoquot and Oka can gain substance as significant expressions of human possibility. Moreover, a field appears in which ordinary people can live their ideas about alternative ways of doing and being. The Raging Grannies in Victoria are a brilliant example in this respect – acting out their protests in song, dance, and street theatre and making the most of their position as grandmothers to undercut the legitimacy of military violence, corporate greed, and governmental insensitivity.[29] Like other originally local groups, they have spawned imitators and so generated a power beyond themselves. Indeed, all these groups, organizations, and networks tend to make a virtue of necessity and reach out to others who have different but compatible objectives. Such outwardness and mutuality reflect a sense that our local and personal identities are incomplete without the connections that bring us into the world at large.

In that larger world, the refugee – the one who has been displaced from home and now wanders in search of new connections – has come to symbolize everyone's fate. To identify with the refugee is to insert oneself, if only imaginatively, in the actual conditions at the margins of capitalism. The young girl selling her body in a mining-town shanty on the edge of the Brazilian rain forest, the old man fleeing the wreckage of his village in Bosnia, the impoverished mother treading her sewing machine in a dank factory in Bangkok, and the boy on Baffin Island finding oblivion in a bag soaked with gasoline are all refugees. A realistic politics would connect their lives with yours in mutually empowering ways. The search for such a politics depends on disrupting the smooth routines of the state and the market, and this will no doubt put many judges in a spin. But then, judges are usually the last to find out what is happening.

# 4

# Radical Municipalism

Ivan Head tells a wonderful story of his days as an adviser to Prime Minister Pierre Trudeau.[1] He was with Trudeau on a visit to Guyana in the late 1970s. The Guyanese were anxious to show their Canadian guests that they were dealing fairly and sensitively with the tribal peoples of the rain forest, and so they flew the Canadian party far to the south near the Brazilian border, landing in an area where the local people could communicate with North Americans only with the aid of a sequence of interpreters. After exchanging greetings, Trudeau remarked rather inanely, 'I suppose we must be the first Canadians you have ever met.' This message went from the first interpreter to the second, from him to the third, and thus to the Indian spokesman. The reply came back equally slowly: 'No.' Nonplussed, Trudeau asked, 'Who did you meet from Canada, then?' Again he had to wait for the interpreters. Finally, the last one turned to Trudeau and declared: 'The National Indian Brotherhood of Canada.'

This story can be read in a number of ways, not least as a tale of the spreading apparatuses of the Canadian state. After all, the National Indian Brotherhood of Canada was heavily funded by the Canadian government, and Guyanese concerns about demonstrating their sensitivity to aboriginal peoples were no doubt prompted by the Canadian International Development Agency. However, it would be more accurate to suggest that the concerns of the Canadian and Guyanese governments were effects of a global social movement – the movement of aboriginal peoples to reclaim their lands, their autonomy, and their identities. The resurgence of the First Nations in the United States and Canada in the 1970s forced the federal governments to respond (perhaps more liberally in Canada). Funding for Indian, Inuit, and Metis organizations in Canada was one result. The First Nations' presence in the heartland of North America brought the plight of the world's aboriginal peoples 'home' to the West in a way that nothing else might have done. The parallels were clear, and the First Nations in North America had the resources – or could get the resources – to begin establishing the connections necessary for a global movement of aboriginal peoples.

This movement has not been an isolated one; rather, it has been strongly connected with environmentalism. Aboriginal peoples are often understood as unique custodians of the earth. Unlike the rest of us, they seem to live close to the land in its natural state, feel deeply connected to the places where they live, and understand the local ecology. The survival of their lands is so tightly connected to the survival of their culture that neither seems possible without the other. Thus, the movement of the aboriginal peoples and the movement to protect the natural environment are symbiotic.

This has been illustrated by the campaign of the James Bay Cree against the Great Whale hydroelectric project.[2] Throughout the campaign, the Cree have found their natural allies in environmentalist organizations like Greenpeace. Interestingly, their campaign has been no more confined to Canada than the activities of the National Indian Brotherhood. Although the Great Whale project is in Quebec, its essential customers – the ones who could make it economically viable – are in New York and New England. But New York and New England are home to American environmentalists, Indian activists, and their progressive sympathizers, who do not regard the exploitation of foreign rivers as a good response to the escalating costs of electrical power in their own homeland. For them, the limits imposed by current power supplies should be respected, because even as it is the regional economy wastes energy and is environmentally destructive. According to this view, protecting the ancient tribal lands of the Cree from the destructive effects of drainage, flooding, and road-building would have no cost to the American Northeast. Rather, it would be a welcome move toward environmental discipline.

One of the key connections the Cree made was with the Progressives in Burlington, Vermont. Although quite small, with a population of about 37,000, Burlington was the largest city in the state, as well as the centre of a metropolitan area of more than 120,000. As such, it was a key site of struggle, for in the populist constitution of Vermont local people had the right to vote in binding referenda on questions such as whether to purchase foreign electrical power. Vote they did, and on the second occasion the local Progressives – who controlled the mayoralty and a plurality of seats on the council, and whose former leader (Bernie Sanders) had recently been elected to Congress as a socialist independent – delivered the victory the Cree wanted.[3] This was the key, they thought, to statewide success. They also saw it as giving a boost to their campaigns in the larger neighbouring states of Massachusetts and New York. Significantly, Mayor David Dinkins of New York City – that city's first black mayor – gave his support to the campaign that evening at a concert headlined by a Canadian singer and environmental activist, Bruce Cockburn.[4]

A few months later, the Cree won their biggest victories: the New York State Assembly passed a resolution in favour of a separate environmental review of the proposed power purchase, and the New York Power Authority decided to cancel its contract with Hydro-Québec. The power authority claimed that its decision had not been influenced by the Cree, but the responsible minister in Quebec was not persuaded.[5] The Cree had certainly succeeded in turning a straightforward commercial transaction into one with serious political repercussions, even in the huge state of New York. No doubt it had originally been thought that purchasing power from Hydro-Québec would be safer politically than constructing a new plant in New York, since there inevitably would be serious environmental objections to any New York facility. The Canadian border was supposed to provide political protection for the power authority, but the Cree and their environmentalist allies had simply ignored that border and turned a Canadian hydroelectric project into an American political issue.

It is significant that the key actors in this story were not the governments of Canada and the United States – the supposedly sovereign authorities. Far more important were the movements that transected every boundary, the most important of these being the hegemonic movement of global capital (which made the Great Whale a 'natural' resource for American industry) and the critical movements of environmentalists, aboriginal peoples, and others (who were resisting the logic of capital). The struggle between these movements was played out over a territory that extended from the Great Whale to New York, and it involved a series of contests in different political venues. To the frustration of the Quebec government, the critics of the Great Whale project were little interested in claims of sovereignty – and those claims would have been heard no better if Quebec had been an 'independent country.'

The movement for self-government among Canadian First Nations has put 'sovereignty' into a dizzy spin, not because sovereignty has been ignored, but because it has been claimed by peoples who do not fit the model of independence that sovereignty presupposes. Of course, Canada does not fit that model either, nor do most of the states represented at the United Nations. Indeed, sovereignty is almost always unreal, either because the state has too little autonomy to be really self-governing (e.g., Canada), or because it has too much power to be considered a state like the others (e.g., the United States). In any case, the movements that govern our lives most intimately – including the movements of capital or scientific reason – are not effectively controlled by states, but only *mediated* by them.

Even so, 'Canada' or 'Quebec' seems to fit the model of sovereignty better than the little Mohawk band at Kanesatake, near Oka in suburban Montreal, which disturbed the country in the summer of 1990.[6] There are less than 900 Mohawks at Kanesatake, but they regard themselves as part of the larger Mohawk Nation. Their cousins are at Kahnawake (on Montreal's South Shore), Akwesasne (straddling the international border near Cornwall, Ontario), and Ganienke (in upstate New York). Together, the Mohawks are the Keepers of the Eastern Gate of the Iroquois Confederacy, and one of the Six Nations scattered across the traditional Iroquois lands in southern Quebec, northern New York, and southern Ontario. The entire confederacy numbers no more than 50,000 and is divided not only by provincial and national borders but by tribal and clan loyalties, as well as by differences in interpretation of the Great Law of Peace, which is the basis of the confederacy. These differences have been exacerbated by the imposition of standardized institutions of Indian government by the Canadian and American authorities. Unlike the aboriginal peoples of the Amazon, the Mohawks and the other five nations of the confederacy long ago abandoned most of their traditional ways and adapted themselves to their peculiar position in a predominantly capitalist, Euro-American society. Young Mohawk men, both American and Canadian, routinely do stints in the U.S. Marines or U.S. Army, often returning with their experience to become leading Mohawk Warriors. Other Mohawks go off reserve to find civilian employment,[7] and recently some Mohawks on reserve have exploited their claims to sovereignty by selling untaxed cigarettes and by organizing gambling casinos for outsiders. These are hardly traditional, ecologically sensitive activities, but many Mohawks see them as necessary to provide the resources to sustain their sovereignty so that they can protect and nurture their traditional culture.

When the Mohawks asserted their sovereignty in the summer of 1990 at Kanesatake and Kahnawake, they did so against the full force of the governments of Quebec and Canada. The incident was provoked by the municipal council at Oka, which had resolved to extend a golf course onto land the Mohawks traditionally had claimed. The result was a months-long siege that put armed Mohawks behind the barricades, defending their traditional lands at Kanesatake from the Quebec police and, later, Canadian ground troops. Mohawks from Kahnawake also seized the Mercier Bridge, leading from the suburban South Shore into the city of Montreal. Although the Quebec and Canadian governments had overwhelming forces at their disposal, they could not use them ruthlessly, for they were hostages to the global media. Respect for the Mohawks was a condition for international respect, and equally importantly for peaceable relations with aboriginal peoples elsewhere in Canada.

The power of the aboriginal peoples' movement in Canada was demonstrated by the support for the Mohawks that came from native people across Canada, and by the many road and rail blockades erected in sympathy in northern Ontario and British Columbia. In B.C., Indian militancy had long been at a high level, reflecting the uncertainty of Indian land tenure in the province.[8] Faced with a provincial government that had consistently denied aboriginal land claims, B.C.'s Indians had been pressing their demands in a variety of ways, which included linking up with local environmentalists. The list of 'hot spots' in B.C. – South Moresby, Meares Island, the Stein Valley, the Stikine, and so on – lengthened during the 1980s as various bands organized themselves to reassert their ancient claims, both in the courts and through civil dis-obedience. Almost all these claims were backed by environmentalists, who saw the native peoples as a bulwark against the destruction of B.C.'s ancient forests, and as protectors of its river valleys and seacoasts. In every case the claims were advanced by nations of only a few thousand people (sometimes only a few hundred). Like the Mohawks, these were nations that lived among the 'whites' and had adopted many European ways.

The consistent demand of Indians and Inuit throughout Canada has been for a form of self-government or 'sovereignty.'[9] For many Canadians this remains an unintelligible demand, since it seems clear that scattered bands of people cannot aspire to statehood. Something different is at stake – something that puts the very notion of statehood into question. The either/or of statehood – either the Indians are citizens of Canada or they are citizens of their own states – is simply inapplicable. The

First Nations are seeking a form of sovereignty that presupposes a democratic dispersal of power and puts the hierarchical notions derived from European kingship aside.[10] Since the latter notions still inform Canada's Constitution, and more generally our conceptions of sovereignty, we are faced with a challenge to our most basic political assumptions. By comparison, Quebec nationalism seems quite old-fashioned, replaying as it does the themes of nineteenth-century Europe.

That small nations might have the same rights as big ones; that there might be nations within nations within nations within nations within nations (that is, Mohawks within the Iroquois Confederacy within Quebec within Canada within America); that the movements in which we participate – both the hegemonic movements of capital, scientific reason, and Western culture, and the critical social movements of environmentalists, feminists, aboriginals, and so on – might be simultaneously local, national, and global; and that our politics are played out in venues that defy the logic of the state system, is all quite dizzying. Most of the discussion around the Canadian Constitution is underpinned by conscious or unconscious denial of our dizziness. The air of disbelief with which most Canadians approach the constitutional discussions may reflect a general sense that the participants really *don't* know what they are doing and that all of them are wilfully denying their own vertigo. Thinking realistically about constitutions seems to require something utterly different from what we have done to date.

What follows in this chapter is a series of meditations on questions of constitution, movement, and identity that reflect the vertiginous patterns of contemporary politics. If, as I imply, our politics now mainly involves a relationship among global movements, what can we make of the attempt to give ourselves a new constitution? In particular, what is to be made of the fact that localities – like the lands claimed by small Indian bands, and the municipalities that precipitate struggles (Oka, Quebec) or advance them (Burlington, Vermont) – seem to be so crucial to movement politics? Contemporary politics seems to be found at the juncture between localities and movements. How are we to think about this in terms of constitutions? Does it point to the need for reviving the city or the region as the primary political unit? And if it does, can we find in the traditional municipality any clues to the forms of political organization we need?

## Privileged Spaces

A constitution at once enables and forecloses. It enables the actions it authorizes, facilitating and protecting what it renders legitimate. In this respect it works like the rules of a game, literally *constituting* the game and thus enabling a mode of activity that otherwise would have been subject to constant disruptions. At the same time, a constitution forecloses activities by proscribing them or rendering them unthinkable: if this is hockey, we cannot slash or cross-check – and trying for a home run is ridiculous.

That states must be constituted has always been at the heart of anarchist objections to them. Every constitution is a fixing, a reification, a stoppage of the flows of social life. Yet we cannot do anything at all without fixing, objectifying, or 'constituting' our activities at least temporarily. Not only hockey and baseball, but schools and hospitals, families and movements, have to be constituted to make them effective in our lives. The question is whether we can constitute our activities without reifying them; give them form and presence while ensuring that they don't become things that dominate our lives; open possibilities without foreclosing our means to reconstitute our activities in accordance with our changing needs and desires. There is no abstract answer to this question: it is simply a continuing dilemma. That is why anarchists have often been charged with bad faith – offering an end to practices that appear inevitable. Anarchism and statism are two sides of the same coin, in that they offer abstract resolutions to concrete organizational problems. The same can be said of capitalism and socialism.

The truth in anarchist and socialist criticisms is that states and markets are constituted in ways that foreclose the most humane, ecologically sound, pacifist, egalitarian, and emancipatory possibilities. In the ensemble of practices that constitutes this foreclosure, the Canadian Constitution is only a minor element. No change in that one element could have more than a minor impact on this ensemble of practices, which includes the constitution of the global economy on capitalist principles, the constitution of gender relations on terms that privilege the male, the constitution of the natural environment as a human dominion, and the constitution of the state system to provide nominal national sovereignty in the context of the global hegemony of the West. What is, or ought to be, at issue is the constitution of movements which can challenge the practices that form this ensemble, and which can begin establishing alternative practices.

Unfortunately, discussions of the Canadian Constitution are often motivated by a concern for maintaining Canada as a privileged space in the international order. At the moment, the ensemble of practices that constitutes our lives establishes the West (or the OECD bloc) as a privileged space where people can enjoy access to a wide range of commodities, have good housing, food, and health care, get the education and training they need to win privileged positions in the global economy, live near the control and production centres of the economy, have privileged access to the dominant culture of that economy, enjoy pensions and disability benefits – and generally go about their lives under conditions that only the wealthiest Asians, Africans, and Latin Americans can aspire to. These privileges are not just economic, for with them come personal mobility, a choice of lifestyles, freedom of speech and expression, and freedom to organize and act politically. That we do not have as many privileges as we would like politically or economically is clear, but from the vantage point of those who are excluded from the privileged space, most of our complaints in this respect seem like whining.

Of course, exclusion is not just a matter of citizenship. To be more precise, citizenship is no longer a guarantee against exclusion, and perhaps it never was a full guarantee. Even so, the promise of Keynesian welfarism was that every citizen of a country like Canada – indeed, every resident – would be included in this privileged space. Minimum incomes would be guaranteed, along with good health care, education, and transport – indeed, everything necessary to be a full participant in society. That this promise was never fully realized was in a way less significant than the fact that it informed the psychological sense of citizenship. To be a citizen of a country like Canada was not like being a Bangladeshi. Even the lowliest Canadians were privileged in relation to the global economy, and would be secured in their existence if they could not participate in that economy effectively. The protection of the Canadian state would even follow the citizen (and his money) around the world, bursting open jails and markets. To live in a country with a hard currency and a hard passport was – and is – a privilege indeed.

What we have seen as a result of the globalization of the economy and the neoliberal advance (the two are not easy to distinguish) is an erosion of the privileges of citizenship. While the effects have so far been less dramatic in Canada than in some other industrialized countries, the number of homeless and abandoned people has still increased painfully. More subtly, the already marginalized – the full citizens on sufferance – have had their benefits and opportunities reduced, so that the gap between those who are in the economy of the privileged and those who are not has widened. This has exacerbated the insecurities of the included. It is no longer clear that a fall from the privileged economy – because of illness or unemployment, for instance – will be temporary. The ranks of the permanently excluded seem to be growing. At the same time, the pressures from outside the protected space that is Canada have increased. To be included even marginally in the citizenry of an advanced industrial economy is more attractive economically than to be left in the utterly insecure spaces of the Second and Third Worlds. Thus, the refugee camps swell, and Canadians rely on Hong Kong and Thailand, Pakistan and Sudan, Germany and Austria, and, of course, Texas and California to keep the hordes at bay. A trickle of claimants is allowed through – enough to satisfy our self-image as the nicer Americans – even while Canadian passports are put up for sale to the highest bidders.

The aboriginal presence in North America is a continuing sign that one can be 'in' the privileged space and yet remain outside it. As many have remarked, living conditions on Canadian Indian reserves are not much better than in Mexican barrios. In this sense, aboriginal demands for sovereignty – like earlier sovereignty claims in Latin America, Eastern Europe, Asia, and Africa – can be read as demands for *inclusion* on terms that are respectful of traditional cultural identities. As experience since 1948 suggests, however, the granting of sovereignty can be used instead as a means for exclusion, as were the original treaties signed with the Indians throughout North America. If we seek something different now – if we want to offer and exercise sovereignty on inclusive terms – then we have to think about constituting states in ways that redefine the relationship between the inside and the outside.

In a way, movements do this for us, since they sweep through the boundaries of states, putting the inside outside and the outside inside. Movements do not occur in abstract space. They exist, like the states that try to contain them, in the everyday lives of ordinary people. The most fundamental political problem for us is to strengthen the benign movements – or the benign tendencies within movements – and to disperse the malignant ones. Malignant tendencies and movements appeal to suspicion and hatred of aliens and to a narrow and myopic self-interest. They depend particularly on claims to privileged spaces of race, class, nationality, culture, and gender – spaces not to enable inclusion but to enforce exclusion, like the white districts of South Africa (and Southern California). The more benign movements promise to open up the privileged spaces, to put the hegemonic movements of control and containment into question, and to constitute relations of inclusion.

The danger for the aboriginal peoples of Canada is that the recognition of their inherent right of self-government will be used to enforce exclusion – to create either/or sovereignties of the sort that turned the original Canadian Indian reserves into domestic refugee camps. At the same time, the promise of the movement for aboriginal self-government is that it will create nodes of empowerment for people who are inside/outside Canada, and open up new ways of thinking about the way 'national' institutions might mediate the relations between the local and the global. If aboriginal peoples have an inherent right of self-government that should not exclude them from the privileged space of Canada, what are we to say about other peoples who have been displaced from their traditional lands by wars or economic revolutions? Do they not also have a right to be included? If so, how can we include that right in our Constitution?[11]

This raises serious questions not only about the state, but also about municipalities, which are supposed to provide institutions of local self-government for everyone. If they are not be organized, like many American municipalities, as domestic refugee camps – for the urban poor on the one hand and the suburban middle class on the other – their relations with the world around them have to be rethought. This is a matter partly of problematizing their subordination to the state and private capital, but also of making a strength of an apparent weakness. The very inadequacy of the municipality is what can lead immediate, local, popular politics beyond itself, just as the limitations of particular Indian reserves and band councils have led aboriginal groups onto the national and international stage.

## Ambivalent Spaces

Contemporary municipalities are designed to fix localities and hence local politics in forms compatible with the global capitalist economy, the bureaucratic nation-state, patriarchal gender relations, white/Western cultural hegemony, and the human domination of nature. As such, they are supposed to function as part of the apparatus of political containment – in other words, to ensure closure. Yet they are also, by virtue of their manifold connections to everyday life, especially susceptible to the disruptions of social movements that challenge the hierarchies of identity and the relations of exclusion that mark the contemporary world.

A municipality is by definition a *subordinate* political unit – one denied sovereignty. In this sense, it affords a space that is always inadequate politically. There is always a higher authority to overrule it, to deny it resources, to undermine its legitimacy. Its leaders appear as politicians of the second rank, who have not yet ascended to the highest offices and perhaps never will. Its measures are always partial, contingent, insufficient for the problems people face. Meanwhile, the government above it, from which it derives its authority and many of its resources, appears as the source of fully adequate solutions – or, at least, solutions as adequate as any government can provide – precisely *because* it is a sovereign authority with the plenitude of powers and resources that sovereignty implies. Not surprisingly, Indian bands demand not municipal status but sovereignty, even when they have fewer people than a small city neighbourhood. In making this demand, the bands mock the political pretensions of the white cities and put the sovereign identities of the modern state into question.

In the modern era, political identities have been constituted between the two poles of the sovereign state and the sovereign individual. The economy is the domain *par excellence* of the sovereign individual. Within the economy, people are free to sell their own labour or whatever else they have or are able to produce. In turn, everyone is free to buy what he or she wants, including places of abode. These freedoms are granted to or claimed by individuals, as against their families, tribes, communities, religions, ethnicities, professions, corporations, or other intermediary associations. To be free in this sense is to be able to abandon one's family, community, or traditional place in society, to immigrate to a new land, to assimilate with a new group, to take up a new occupation, to renounce one's religion, to become other than what one's ancestors were. At stake are the rights of the individual against all the ties that bind. Economic freedom is fundamental to these rights, for it opens the possibility of breaking all the ties that bind and reestablishing oneself as a stranger in a new place, a new occupation, or a new business. Thus, the sovereignty of the individual points toward globalization of the economy, society, culture, and politics. Only if the world as a whole is open to us all can we be as free as possible individually – or so it is claimed.

The idea that the Great Whale is *naturally* a resource, a *natural* resource, for the people of Boston and New York follows directly from the idea that we are sovereign individuals or sovereign consumers, who can purchase whatever we want, wherever we want, from whomever we want. According to this view, everything belongs to someone and can be bought if the price is right. No land is sacred, no culture sacrosanct. There are no trustees for the past or the future, only individuals whose present interests determine present values and whose rights as such constitute the highest moral claims upon us.

Of course, the world as a whole is not constituted as a single political unit that can secure the rights of individuals. Only *states* have the sovereign authority to secure the rights of sovereign individuals – and, in so doing, to override the objections of aboriginal peoples and environmentalists who point to higher rights. In the absence of a world-state, nation-states seem the most effective protectors of individual sovereignty, for they establish worlds unto themselves for people sharing common cultures. For the most part these boundaries are established linguistically, with uniform national languages, national educational systems, national histories, and national cultures. This, at least, was the original European model. However, it is possible, as the Swiss have shown, to create a national identity despite linguistic differences, provided that the appropriate political institutions have been established. Today, more people than not are forced to have the states they have, because the costs of redrawing boundaries are so horrific. Although some people have nation-states, most people have states that are trying to make nations.

The ideal of the state is of a political unit that is as large as it can be, given people's fundamental identities. If the nation is the largest community with which people can identify – because it is a community of shared language, history, and culture – it seems the suitable unit for statehood. On the other hand, if circumstances fragment the linguistic nation or put more than one nationality in the same territory, statehood can be a means of creating an identity that holds people together. In either case, the ideal of the state is to establish a protected space where people can live out their lives in individual freedom. In particular, this means creating an economic space where people can move about, change occupations, and do business as they like. It also means creating a political space in which people's basic rights are the same and there is common law to protect those rights. The liberal ideal of individual freedom is thus bound up with the existence of the state, whose sovereignty is supposed to be its guarantee.

In contrast to the sovereign state and the sovereign individual, the municipality signifies the claims of a territorial community that does not pretend to be sufficient unto itself. It exists within a state, within a global economy, and within an ensemble of social relations [illegible] can affect locally but cannot by itself transform. The governr[illegible] a municipality depends on its position within the ens[illegible] tions in which it is embedded. Unlike the state, w[illegible] stand over/against the ensemble of social relatio[illegible] relations, to regulate them, and in principle to [illegible] capacity to transform those relations – the muni[illegible] moment within the relations it is supposed to govern. What it requires for its own effectiveness is always beyond itself.

Conventionally, modern politics is understood as a relationship between sovereign individuals and the sovereign state – a relationship mediated by interest groups, political parties, and even social movements. However, the important movements today point beyond the state and the individual. Thus, the identities claimed by aboriginal peoples are antithetical to the claims of the bourgeois individual, with his (her) market freedoms and mobility rights and ostensible capacity to reinvent a personal identity. Similarly, the claims of environmentalism, feminism, and socialism are keyed to identities that transcend the individual and can never be adequately expressed within states that are organized as ensembles of individuals. Such identities cannot even be adequately expressed by movements that are radically distinguished from one another. A politics of movements can mobilize identities that point beyond themselves. Like municipal politics, movement politics occurs in those ambivalent spaces where nothing is ever adequate to itself.

Such movements highlight what has been lost in the process of constituting the modern world between the polarities of the state and the individual. Small Indian bands are poignant reminders of forms of community that once were universal, and that somehow remain present even in their absence. They also point toward forms of community rooted in the postmodern identities expressed by contemporary social movements. It is no accident that so many in the present day have looked to the aboriginal peoples for models of a better way of life. Municipalities are similarly Janus-faced, in that they are reminders of medieval and early modern local autonomy as well as signs of new political possibilities. Those possibilities are to be found in the social movements that dissolve the sovereignties of the state and the individual, and that privilege the local and the global. Whether we are talking of the pacifism of nuclear-free zones, the environmentalism of land trusts, the feminism of affirmative action, or the socialism of workers' cooperatives, the spaces defined by social movements within municipalities – or by municipalities within social movements – disrupt the hierarchies that trivialize local politics. They also create important possibilities for a democratic globalism.

## Sealed Spaces and Unsealed Identities

There is an intellectual if not a political temptation to respond to these possibilities by positing the local and the global as sovereignties of their own. The global can be posed as the world-state in embryo, while the local can be understood in terms of the sovereignties-in-waiting of the civic polis, the ecoregion, and the tribal community (perhaps conflated in the notion of an ecopolis). As critical ideals, these alternatives disrupt the claims of the individual and the state, but they can also take the shape of sealed spaces that reestablish exclusions and hierarchies in forms little more benign than the ones we know. We have only to think of the General Agreement on Tariffs and Trade, the North American Free Trade Agreement, and the European Union to remind ourselves of how wider-than-state sovereignties usually work. Similar scepticism is required in considering the ideals of municipal or local sovereignty.

The common ideal of the *civic polis* derives from a romantic view of the ancient city and the early Renaissance republic. In these 'city-states' – it is no accident that we commonly describe them as such – citizenship involved (or is supposed to have involved) active participation in government. Their comparatively small scale made it possible to overcome the sharp distinction between rulers and subjects, and turned democracy into a system in which citizens took both collective and individual responsibility for the government of the community. What is attractive about this is not only the inclusiveness and egalitarianism of the polis, but its dynamism. A city in the proper sense is open, energetic, expansive, and free in spirit. Thus, it is a place where individuals can be at home. The polis-ideal is of a reformed liberal democracy that encourages the development of individuals but also brings those individuals together in a democratic political community. This is consistent, many would claim, with the requirements of a global market economy. By forming itself into an autonomous political community, the city would be reinforcing itself as a centre for business. The self-governing city would improve itself as a community and foster the enterprises necessary for its economic success. Thus, it would be doing what nation-states pretend to do, but cannot: fostering the dynamism of local economies.[12]

The *ecoregionalist* ideal stands in contrast to this, for it derives from a fundamental suspicion of cities and the economic dynamism they generate. Cities are perceived as signs of the hubris of man – of the effort to create artificial human environments in which people can live free from nature. The ecoregional ideal is of a form of human life that fits into the natural environment, reconnects people with the spirit of the places where they live, and respects the limitations implicit in nature itself. Thus, the emphasis is on discipline – on what we must give up to restore health to our environment and to our lives. In practising the new ecological disciplines, people are expected to discover new sources of freedom. All this is supposed to point toward political organization on as small a scale as the city-state, and probably smaller. However, the territorial bounds of organization are to be given naturally, not determined by the sprawl of man-made cities. Within these natural bounds, communities are to be formed that resist rather than exploit the global market.[13]

*Tribal* communities too are supposed to be communities of resistance, but the enclosures they provide are more psychological than physical. The appeal of a tribal identity is that it is always already there, ready to be taken up at any time. It is in some sense genetic, and thus it is not subject to cultural, economic, political, or even territorial destruction. Such genetic identities are available even to those of us who cannot trace our tribal origins. The categories of race, ethnicity, sex, and sexuality can be invoked to constitute a new community whose claims are overriding. It is possible to deploy such identities critically, as various oppressed groups and social movements have done.[14] On the other hand, such essentialist categories can also be invoked as a way of resealing identities and territories. It is easy enough for us to see this happening when the white tribe of Africa tries to seal itself off from the black tribes around and within it. It is more difficult to see that something similar may happen if we turn the civic polis, the ecoregion, or the tribe of gays or Mohawks into a substitute for the state.

These ideals all express our yearnings for a final resolution to the problem of political identity. Instead of the nation, established by all the forces of the state, we have something more intimate, communal, economically dynamic, democratic, and ecologically sound. However, such a new and better centre for political life cannot be sustained without social engineering. Thus, we are led to talk of draining the powers of the nation-state and infusing the civic polis or ecoregion or tribal community with what is extracted. We also think in terms of establishing clearer physical boundaries, organizing the communal infrastructure within these boundaries, centring public facilities and services, organizing regional markets, developing regional media, fostering regional culture, developing new social and political organizations, and policing the movements of people, wastes, goods, and services across the new boundaries.[15]

Boundary policing is implicit in these ideals because the forces of the present – the ones that re-create national economies and national political identities – have to be resisted in order to give effect to the goals at hand. There is reason to think that such policing would have to be more rather than less intensive than the policing we experience today. This is because the socio-political self-sufficiency of the civic polis, the natural self-sufficiency of the ecoregion, and the cultural self-sufficiency of the tribal community must be secured against the relationships that constitute the individual as sovereign within a global economy. Otherwise, the autonomous locality will develop on the model of Hong Kong or Singapore – not as an ecological/democratic/tribal community, but as a single node in a totalitarian capitalism.[16]

Liberalism and totalitarianism are usually conceived as polar opposites, but liberalism is in fact a totalitarian ideal. To demand that everyone be first and foremost an individual, and to remake the world to this end, is to engage in a form of totalitarianism. At the ideological level, this is precisely the totalitarianism to which we are now subject. Materially, this totalitarianism is capitalism. Capitalist economic and social relations are being extended into every sphere of life and into every corner of the globe, so that it is becoming increasingly difficult to live a life constituted in some other terms. Communities with other bases are constantly threatened with disruption and are delegitimized by the very restrictions they impose on individuals. The only sealed space permitted in liberal capitalism is the autonomous individual.

The communitarian ideal (in its various forms) gives expression to the idea that there are human identities that take precedence over the identity of the individual. Be it the claim that we are members of a tribe, servants of God, children of the earth, sisters in the spirit, or whatever, the suggestion is that we are not fundamentally or essentially individuals. If this is so, then the demands that arise from our individuality do not take precedence over what is required to sustain the communal identity. If antiliberal communitarianism seems totalitarian because it threatens to suppress the individual, anticommunitarian liberalism is also totalitarian insofar as it threatens to extinguish every communal identity that cannot be reconciled with liberalism. Such extinction is no abstract possibility. Tribes of hunter-gatherers, communities of farmers, ethnic communities, and others are being dissolved daily in the global economy and the attendant forms of liberal individualism.

To replace one totalitarian ideal (liberalism) with another (communitarianism) would not be a great gain.[17] This is what makes the municipality so interesting as a model. As a political organization it is at once liberal and communitarian. Its very *lack* of sovereignty may be its greatest gift and its greatest potential. A municipal community is one that admits its own fragility, contingency, limitations, dependence. It is not a political community that demands overriding loyalty, that asks us to sacrifice our lives for it, that demands precedence in relation to all other identities. It is simply there as a place where people can and must come together to realize their aims. As a centre for our politics, it puts sovereignty in a spin.

Municipalities are organizations of localities, and localities are at the juncture of movements, most obviously movements of capital (or sovereign individuals, in another guise) and social movements responding to that capital or to the fixations associated with it. Movements spill out of localities and overflow the fixations of states, nationalities, corporations, and families – and, yes, also the fixations of ecoregions, tribes, and civic polities – mixing with other movements in streams and eddies. At any point or locality, what we can see are the flows and the efforts of people to dam, divert, combine, or unleash the flows to which they attend. Usually people are conscious of only a few of the flows that carry them about.

If the state is a container, the market is a flow. The state fixes, the market unfixes.[18] Speed is the key to success in the contemporary market. To be at the right place at the right time, or (more precisely) to have one's goods at the right place at the right time, has always been crucial. Instantaneous global communication, combined with computer-integrated manufacturing systems, just-in-time deliveries, continuous inventory monitoring, and so on, has made it possible to react to changing market conditions with great rapidity. In part, this is a matter of responding politically to perceived changes in government policy or to popular movements that may affect profitability.

The big political story of the past two decades has not been the advance of neoconservatism in national politics, but the reorganization of the global economy to facilitate international capital flows. This has involved the mobilization of particular national (and provincial) governments to batter down the obstacles to international trade and investment. However, the success of this mobilization has less to do with the ideologies of particular governments than with the vulnerabilities of each state and its national economy. Under the Bretton Woods system, the United States (and the major American banks and corporations) maintained a global economic hegemony. The price of access to American capital, technology, and markets was a certain openness to American economic penetration. However, the terms that opened other countries to American capital also opened the United States to foreign capital. Once the major currencies became fully convertible, banks and corporations throughout the world worked for new political agreements that would enable them to operate freely across borders. Countries that were open to foreign penetration became favoured sites for the deployment of foreign capital. As it became easier to move money and goods and most importantly information about, banks and corporations gained increasing leverage. Individual governments – such as France in the early 1980s – were no match for the combined forces of international capital.[19] The old social-democratic strategy of containing and controlling capital within nation-states could no longer work, and no alternative strategy for controlling capital on a global scale had been devised. Supranational institutions increasingly served to facilitate the globalization and hence the empowerment of capital in relation to the political centres of nation-states.

The market imposes its own disciplines on people, which are reflected in their day-to-day behaviour and political consciousness. Demands that run counter to the logic of the market bump up against the logic of everyday life. Since the market constitutes our identities in certain ways – as consumers, employees, entrepreneurs, investors, pensioners, homeowners, and taxpayers, and ultimately as individuals – critical responses involve positing alternative identities that are rooted in experiences or aspirations which cannot be subsumed under the logic of the market. These relate to ethnicity, religion, culture, and 'community.' 'Community' means ties – familial, neighbourly, religious, ideological, or whatever – that bind individuals to one another in a way that gives their individuality a new meaning. People who are part of a community see the value of their own lives at least partly in terms of the well-being of the community. If the community flourishes, they share in its achievements, and their individual successes have value insofar as they contribute to the community. A person who strongly identifies with a community enjoys his or her individuality in relation to that community.

Market relations tend to disrupt communities formed on other bases, and to form new ones that make sense in terms of market requirements. Hence, the company and the residential neighbourhood nearby appear as focal points for the construction of identities that conform to the logic of the market. Other identities are also possible: churches (especially ones that counsel acceptance of the existing order of things), clubs, teams, even nations. In the end, most identities can be tailored to the requirements of the market. Witness The Body Shop and the trend toward green consumerism. Witness also the practices of Mohawk capitalism. These are forms – indeed, the predominant forms – of identity containment.

In the face of a totalitarian liberalism that dissolves every challenge to capitalism, it is tempting to insist on essential identities that are somehow given in nature or history. In so doing, however, we gloss over the processes of identity construction. Many people would argue that the essential human communities are established by biological sex, tribal culture, language of communication, race, ethnic origin, sexual orientation, religion, social class, political allegiance, or residential territory. However, the multiplicity and incommensurability of these essential communities are themselves indications of the fact that what people take to be their primary identities is highly contingent. All identities are socially – which is to say *politically* – constructed. Since the situations in which people find themselves vary so dramatically from time to time and place to place, we ought to be sceptical about any suggestion that a particular identity has universal priority. In personal life, the sealed identity is the functional equivalent of the state. It may be held against the state, but it is a fixation that can obstruct the practices that are required to secure people's objectives. Creative politics depends on opening up sealed identities and forming new possibilities.

We are especially conscious now of the dangers posed by sealed religious identities. However, such identities have been more fragile historically than the ones associated with the state. Sealed *territorial* identities are particularly dangerous. It actually is quite difficult to seal nonterritorial identities, because they must submit with others in a common territory: thanks to the interactions of everyday life – which cannot easily be policed – the identities we would seal usually begin to open up, and the communities we would create prove fragile. The seductiveness of a tightly bounded territory is that it promises the possibility of sealing an identity that grows out of an everyday life shared in common. Everything within that territory is, or can be, a part of the identity to be sustained. A territorial identity can, in principle, be comprehensive. This is why the state and its surrogates must be problematized.

From a democratic perspective, the attraction of a sealed territory is that it contains and hence centres politics within a community adequate for the purposes of democracy. As Aristotle indicated, adequacy is in large part a matter of scale: the territory should be large enough for self-sufficiency (economically, militarily, socially, culturally), but small enough for effective citizenship (direct participation in government by the citizenry, knowledgeable scrutiny of leaders). Hence, the polis. From an ecological perspective, the attraction of a sealed territory is that it reins in hubris. No longer can we imagine that our environmental problems can be dumped on our neighbours. This is the only land we have: we must deal with our wastes within this land, grow our food and find our water here, make room for wildlife, keep the air and water and soil clean, make space for ourselves and our children, make the things that we need without poisoning ourselves, create a culture that expresses what we are and do. Thus, to contain people within a particular territory is to make them live within the limits of a sound ecology. A common territory also is a place where we have to deal with others, and to relate different problems to one another. People involved in different movements interact on a daily basis, and the forum where their claims have to be considered is immediately present. People cannot say that the claims of others have to be resolved somewhere else: they must be met here or nowhere. This sense of responsibility for and to one another is invaluable. In any case, it is in considering claims in relation to one another that we begin to see the connections between problems, the commonalities in the solutions.

The democratic/ecological/communitarian logic of the sealed territorial identity is clear. Whatever its attractions, however, it is a logic to be resisted. The most obvious point is that it is no longer possible to seal territories without intensive policing – and even then the policing is likely to be ineffective. People are connected electronically to a world beyond their own territories, they want physical access to that world beyond, they want the right both to use the goods and services and to take advantage of the opportunities that wider world offers. If they are to have such freedoms, the territory they inhabit cannot be sealed. If territories are not sealed, then people are connected to one another in relations of interdependency that have to be dealt with politically. Contemporary social movements tend to recognize this; indeed, they are largely dedicated to working out the political strategies necessary to deal with the interconnections of a global community and the proliferation of identities implicit in postmodern life.

As an organization at the juncture of the local and the global, the municipality is crucial, but its liberation is properly conceived in outward- rather than inward-looking terms. Otherwise, the reprivileging of the local can be an obstacle to the creativity that generates new identities and practices. People have to be free to work out identities such as lesbianism, pan-Indianism, pacifism, social ecology, and so on, and this freedom depends on the right to break out of territorial strictures and form connections with like-minded people anywhere. From this perspective, the municipality is defective insofar as it is constituted as a sealed territory or political discipline. Its real promise is as an organizational node in the flow of critical and creative social movements. It is to *their* constitution that it must contribute.

## Municipalities and Movements

In the early days of the Reagan administration, 120 cities flatly refused to cooperate with the 'civil defense' scheme proposed by the Federal Emergency Management Agency (FEMA), which promoted the idea of a survivable nuclear war. 'Cities effectively destroyed the nuclear war civil-defense planning of FEMA by our non-cooperation,' boasts [Larry] Agran [then Mayor of Irvine, California].

By weight of numbers, municipalities changed the concept of divestment from South Africa from pure symbolism to a real tool for dismantling apartheid. More than 70 cities, 13 counties and 20 states have divested more than $20 billion from companies doing business in South Africa, finally forcing Congress to adopt serious, if limited, economic sanctions.

In addition, the 90–100 US cities that have sister cities in Nicaragua have made an important contribution to providing vital economic aid and to derailing the national government's war effort. 'These cities have sent tens of millions of dollars of humanitarian assistance to Nicaragua,' says [Michael] Shuman [President of the Center for Innovative Diplomacy]. 'In fact, one can make an argument that if you put together both citizen and city-based humanitarian contributions going to Nicaragua, it has been roughly the same as the federal government shipped to the contras.'[20]

One of the little-told stories of the 1980s is of the oppositional foreign policies of scores of American municipalities.[21] More than 160 of them participated in the worldwide movement to establish 'nuclear-free zones' at the local level, and a number of them pushed beyond the symbolic gestures that had characterized NFZs elsewhere, to use their powers against the armaments industry. They tried to 'zone out' nuclear weapons producers, prohibit the storage or transport of nuclear wastes, divest in weapons-producing businesses, search out 'nuclear-free' contractors for local services, organize peace education in lieu of civil defence, and facilitate the conversion of industries to peaceful production. These activities were stimulated by nationwide campaigns for local referenda on peace and jobs and on a nuclear freeze. In turn they were connected to the movement for European nuclear disarmament. The city of Manchester, England, had led the way among European local authorities by declaring its nuclear-free status in November 1980. An International Federation of Nuclear Free Zone Authorities was established in 1984; by the end of the decade, more than 4,000 municipalities qualified for membership.[22] In Canada, Project Ploughshares initiated a campaign in 1981 that resulted in almost 180 NFZ declarations.[23]

Although it was the peace movement that really generated the campaign for nuclear-free zones, it soon intersected with the concerns of environmental activists who opposed the production of nuclear power. After the Chernobyl disaster, European local authorities began paying more attention to issues of nuclear safety, and exploring their own regulatory powers in this area. Generally, municipalities on both sides of the Atlantic found that their powers with respect to health and safety, land-use regulation, emergency measures and policing, public education, contracting, and investment gave them significant leverage in the matter of what many of them regarded as noxious industries. This is not to say that they were free to do whatever they pleased: often the courts overruled them, or their regulations were pushed aside by 'the supreme legislature.' On the other hand, the national governments found it difficult to make their supposedly exclusive jurisdiction in matters of national security effective, since in terms of the established organization of the state the municipalities were quite properly involved in the regulation of industries that could quite literally blow up.

The economic powers and interests of the municipalities opened up other matters. A municipality could adopt an ethical investment plan that expressed its abhorrence of South African apartheid, or nuclear weaponry, or the destruction of the rain forests. It could attempt to make contractors comply with requirements for affirmative action or employment equity. It could also use its economic powers to stimulate the formation of new types of businesses, such as workers' cooperatives and minority enterprises. This could complement measures to extract concessions from corporate developers, who could provide the means for developing low-income housing, job-training, and day care at a time when national governments were withdrawing their support. By virtue of its regulatory authority, its responsibility for the urban infrastructure, and its involvement in social services, a municipality could pursue a socialist strategy for economic and social development even in the face of a hostile national government. The left Labour authorities in Britain during the Thatcher years provided the most striking examples of such an oppositional politics.[24]

Recently, under United Nations sponsorship, 200 municipalities in 41 countries came together to form the International Council for Local

Environmental Initiatives.[25] This group is to spread policy innovations by linking activist municipalities with one another. Its presence is a sign of the variety and significance of local environmental innovations – from regulatory controls on CFCs to new schemes for recycling – and of the emerging importance of policy networks that bypass national governments. All of the innovative activity of municipal governments in recent years has depended on formal and informal networks of communication; these have enabled municipalities to copy one another rapidly. Many of these networks – for example, the Planners' Network and Nuclear Free America in the United States, and the Centre for Local Economic Strategies in Britain – are essentially national, but there also are embryonic systems of international communication. These systems often run through nongovernmental organizations, including academic institutions and nonprofit bodies associated with the social movements.

The oppositional foreign policy of the American municipalities would have had no effect had it not been linked to the activities of a myriad of voluntary organizations. Thus, the aid to the Sandinistas was not primarily a municipal effort: the most progressive municipalities simply lent legitimacy and provided organizational support to citizen activities. This role of supporting and nurturing social movement activity is absolutely vital. A particularly brilliant example of it was provided in Britain by the Women's Committee of the Greater London Council, which, after consulting with women in every part of the metropolis, began a grants program that supported a wide array of women's centres, services, and activities.[26] This fostered a symbiotic relationship between grass roots activities and the work of women on the council and in the municipal bureaucracy.

What stands out in the history of progressive municipalities is the way that they enable different movements to come together in a particular venue and support one another's activities. Initiatives for peace or women's equality, for instance, depend on the presence of supportive networks: on the one hand, networks like the National Action Committee on the Status of Women or the Physicians for Social Responsibility, which concert activity on a national or international basis, and on the other hand, local networks that bring together people who have been working on different issues from different perspectives. Out of the local networking, and even more out of the local action that becomes feasible when the resources of a municipal government are available, comes the sort of mutually supportive activity that breaks down the barriers between people and enables them to discover common concerns and joint remedies. A peace education campaign, for instance, can provide the occasion for examining the relationship between war and rape as modes of male violence. An initiative on nontraditional employment for women can open up questions about authority relations in the workplace, the mechanisms of capitalist planning, and the prospects of converting the economy to entirely peaceful production.

Municipal action can contribute much to the development of critical and creative social movements, especially if it serves to challenge sealed identities. Each of the great social movements involves new practices that challenge existing ways of doing things. They embody alternatives that put existing practices into question, disrupt those practices, substitute new practices for them, and ultimately institutionalize those new practices within or outside existing institutions. To generate, develop, and sustain new practices is to build a social movement. That people identify with the movement is crucial, since identification brings commitment, but the movement is what gives meaning to the identity. The movement is an ensemble of practices in which people engage, and from which they may develop identities that come to inform their subsequent activities. In other words, there is a dialectic of practices and identities. However, there is a danger always that people will fix their identities – 'I am a feminist,' 'I am a pacifist,' 'I am a socialist' – in ways that inhibit the creative exploration of connections and commonalities and freeze the practices that generated the critical identities in the first place.

Most people resist sealed identities, which is why they draw back from people who seem too firmly committed to a particular point of view. Such commitment suggests the sort of fanaticism that regulates everything in terms of a single goal or identity. This was long the mark of socialism, and it is a mark borne by some of the participants in all social movements. However, in the present situation no social movement can claim hegemony effectively. It is not that such claims are not made, but that they have little credibility in the absence of a mass movement that gives clear priority to the goals of any particular social movement. This opens up the possibilities for pluralistic radical politics – that is, for the simultaneous development of critical social movements that are genuinely different from one another but not antagonistic. Environmentalism is not feminism, but there is no obvious reason why the two should not coexist, why people should not identify with both movements simultaneously, why those people should be asked to give priority to one movement rather than the other.

If there is common ground between the movements it is in the recognition that the dominant contemporary practices – of capitalism, patriarchy, human ascendancy, bureaucracy, and so on – are not conducive to the aims of any of the great social movements. Thus, there is a basis for joint action on many issues. Some would say that there are underlying commitments to human emancipation, social justice, community, democracy, nonviolence, mutual respect, and respect for the natural environment. This may be so, but the different movements interpret and order these commitments in their own ways, and it is dangerous to suppose that there is an overarching theory that would reduce these movements to particular expressions of something more general. To recognize the specificity of each movement is to accept that there is more than one important thing to be said, more than one great goal to be accomplished, more than one set of practices worth developing.

Contemporary social movements tend to destabilize the relationship between politics and the state, because they politicize matters outside the realm of state regulation. This is partly a matter of making public issues out of private behaviour (for example, the abuse of children, the disposal of wastes, the use of language) and partly a matter of making issues out of activities that cannot be regulated within existing political boundaries (for example, the release of CFCs, the organization of male violence, the exploitation of labour). The practices at issue are generally global, but nonetheless local in their effects. It is simply not clear that alternative practices can be developed within the containers established by states: critical social movements destabilize the containers.

This suggests again the outwardness, expansiveness, and inclusiveness of movements at their best. It also suggests how movements reposition the locality in relation to the state, disrupting the hierarchy that privileges national politics relative to the local. If national politics is no more sufficient unto itself than local politics, and if localities are where movements connect with and arise from everyday life, the municipality appears as a privileged site for political activity. Indeed, we might argue that municipal politics is the most significant indicator of political vitality in any community.

It is, of course, comparatively rare for municipal business *per se* to emerge as the central political concern in a locality. This reflects the fact that everyday life transcends the immediate locality, and that, in any case, the municipality is severely constrained in its ability to deal with local matters. Legal restraints are implicit in the hierarchy of the state, and from these come extraordinarily effective fiscal constraints. It takes considerable political imagination – or an obtuse determination to act –

to overcome these immediate obstacles and widen the field for local politics. When this happens, however, it is remarkable how the municipal council can serve as a centre for connecting different movements with one another, legitimizing their concerns, exploring the possibilities for local initiative, and establishing links between similar movements in different localities. In this process, the municipal council constitutes itself as a site for global politics.

To do this means decentring the concerns that traditionally have been at the heart of municipal politics – concerns about land use, amenities, and territorial development. Such concerns are bound to remain important, but what is vital is the opening of the political field to people who do not understand their gut issues in these terms. Concerns about global disarmament, greenhouse effects, violence against women, mass unemployment, cultural survival, and so on are definitely local, but they cannot easily be squeezed into a rhetoric of neighbourhood protection and waterfront development. Such a rhetoric, even when opened out to encompass the broader concerns of urban planning, tends to seal municipal politics in a form which excludes most people's immediate concerns and which implicitly privileges the social movements that can most easily connect with this rhetoric. Environmentalism, a competitive localism, multiculturalism, and a particular vision of participatory democracy all may find a place, but concerns connected with feminism, socialism, or the global peace movement are liable to be marginalized.

Does this have constitutional implications in the traditional sense? No doubt. We need to broaden the scope of municipal government, not in the sense of conferring exclusive jurisdictions upon it, but rather in the sense of empowering municipalities to act on all the concerns of their own constituents. We need to break down the legal as well as the informal political rules that confine municipalities to their own turfs and that make most important matters off limits to them. This points toward a form of local sovereignty, not in the sense of the city-state but in the traditional/postmodern sense established by the Mohawks, the Haida, and other Indian bands. In this sense, sovereignty is not an 'either/or,' but a 'both/and' – a coempowerment that corresponds to the multiplicity of our identities and of the practices we must pursue to deal with our world. All of us need to have our right of self-government recognized, and this must include a right of *local* self-government. But how that right can operate will only be clear if we attend with more care to the actual history of municipal initiative.

## PART TWO

# Municipal Progressivism

The question of constituting political space at the local level raises a number of hoary issues in the constitutional history of the liberal democracies. Local government reform has always been on the agenda, and the current interest in reinventing government – to use the American phrase – brings administrative issues to the fore. In the first two chapters of this section, I attempt to place these issues in a different context. Chapter 5 is concerned with the metropolitan reality that has long been at odds with the neat schemes of governmental reform. It focuses particularly on the character of the postwar political settlement with regard to the organization of the state, and explores the challenges to that settlement which have arisen from the New Left and the New Right. Canadian experience is again used to focus the discussion, although the analysis has much wider application. In Chapter 6, attention shifts to more recent ideas about the organization of local government in the context of a competitive global economy. The argument is that the municipality is being reinvented as an executive committee for local bourgeoisie – or, to put it otherwise, it is being reconfirmed in a traditional role that it had begun to escape. There is a particular criticism here of liberals and social democrats who have accepted this repositioning on the naïve assumption that local business needs them as much as they need local business. The organizational suggestion that emerges is that progressive politics at the local level must mimic the principles of flexible specialization that have been so successful in terms of the self-organization of the bourgeoisie. Critical, progressive politics necessarily disrupts its own containers.

This leads to a discussion in Chapters 7 and 8 of the two most notable periods of municipal activism: the one ended, symbolically, with the destruction of Red Vienna in 1934, and the other began in the 1960s. In the first of these two chapters, I review the history of municipal socialism in England, France, and Germany, in the hope of understanding what the socialists of that generation were attempting to do. This leads to a revaluation of the effects of 'nationalizing' municipal socialism in the form of postwar social democracy. A challenge to nationalization began to emerge with the development of the New Left, and this had profound effects on local politics in the 1970s and later. A culmination of sorts occurred in the 1980s, when in Britain especially, local socialism was presented as a relatively coherent alternative to a nationalized social democracy. The argument is that the political challenge that emerged in Britain had its counterpart across the Atlantic, where localized movements gained control of particular municipalities and attempted similar reforms. In Part Three, we will look more closely at the sovereignty challenges implicit in some of these practices.

# 5

# Beyond the Metropolis

The metropolis is no respecter of boundaries. However we set boundaries – in our imagination, our maps of urban life, or our political institutions – it soon overcomes them. This is partly a matter of expansion – of the ceaseless spillage of new suburbs, the spin-off of satellite towns, and the transformation of independent communities into appendages of the great city. However, it also involves the constant reorganization of metropolitan life, which disrupts communities, throws up new ones, changes the relationship between city and suburbs, spins off new centres within the built-up area, and almost immediately decentres the nodes it establishes. The very concept of the metropolis is a sign of this, for it was invented to designate an urban reality that could no longer be understood as a self-contained city with a fixed structure.[1] The metropolis may have principles of organization, but it lacks genuine boundaries. This boundlessness is at odds with the political principles of sovereignty, which demand the containment of 'societies' within states, and subsocieties within provinces, districts, cities, or other units with definite geographic limits. The metropolis thus appears to be ungovernable, because it is uncontainable. This has caused great discomfort and has vexed the organizers of states from the very beginning. Unfortunately for statists, this uncontainable urban form is overwhelmingly predominant: what is *not* metropolitan is marginal. Some regions may *seem* to be permanently excluded from the metropolis; in fact they rarely are – logging and mining camps, wilderness reserves, agribusiness centres, and market towns for the tourists and cottagers are outliers of the metropolitan system, no more marginal than industrial sites and shopping strips in 'the city.' The metropolitan system links cities with one another and with the territories they exploit, in ways that make nonsense of political and administrative divisions. The metropolis we would govern is everywhere and nowhere.

This is illustrated by the pattern of metropolitan organization in my own region. I live in Fairfield, one of the older neighbourhoods in Victoria, British Columbia. (To say 'old' in this context is to indicate that many of its houses date from the period before the First World War, when there was a major boom in real estate investment financed by British capital.) The neighbourhood's name comes from one of the Hudson's Bay Company farms that were established near Fort Victoria in 1846, when the company moved its regional headquarters north from the Columbia River in order to escape American jurisdiction. Victoria was not only a trading centre but also an important imperial outpost (for a time the headquarters of the North Pacific Squadron of the Royal Navy was at nearby Esquimalt), and it became the capital of the colony of Vancouver Island and later of the province of British Columbia. Almost from the beginning, it had a large Chinatown and strong connections with the islands of the South Pacific. It was an entrepôt with strong commercial connections to Seattle and San Francisco, and it was an important staging point in the imperial routes connecting London to its North American and East Asian dependencies. It was not until after the completion of the Canadian Pacific Railway in 1886 that Victoria became a Canadian city in the fullest sense, and even then it remained somewhat detached because of its island location and unusually mild climate. Although it never was simply Canadian, Victoria appears now like a suburban node in a multinational Pacific metropolis.[2] It is actually one of a number of cities scattered around the Georgia Basin and Puget Sound. The region is bisected by the international border and has two major centres: Seattle and Vancouver. Victoria is near the midpoint, where the Strait of Juan de Fuca leads out to the Pacific. Although it is the oldest settlement in the region, its island location has turned out to be a commercial disadvantage, and the city long ago lost ground to its mainland counterparts. Nevertheless, Victoria now shares in the economic dynamism of an urban region of more than five million people – a region that is beginning to rival the Los Angeles and San Francisco Bay areas of California and is already much larger and more prosperous than the regions of Montreal or Pittsburgh.

What we might call the Sea-Van metropolis is not yet well integrated politically because of the border that splits it in two. However, most of the people of the state of Washington and the province of British Columbia live in this metropolitan area, and there are strong transportation and communication links between its various cities. A common ecosystem, similar resource industries, a common heritage of aboriginal cultures, and similar isolation from the centres of power to the south and east give the region the elements of a shared consciousness. At the same time, the whole area opens outward in complicated ways into the mountainous interior of the Pacific Northwest and across the ocean to Asia. The transoceanic links that have been forged by the Overseas Chinese community have been particularly important in creating an Asian economic and cultural presence that may ultimately rival the more powerful American and European influences. This is especially obvious in the Vancouver area. At the same time, Seattle is the headquarters of both Microsoft and Boeing, and hence is a major centre for American high-tech industry, with strong links to the American state.[3] Within this wider region, Victoria appears as a tourism and retirement centre and a provincial administrative capital. Its development as a city is largely determined by external forces, and (in the typical North American pattern) there is a ring of suburban municipalities that contain about three-quarters of the 300,000 people in the immediate urban area. Much of the growth pressure is felt far beyond this suburban ring. Thus, even the immediate issues of suburban development are uncontainable. As we have seen, the wilderness/logging areas such as Clayoquot Sound are very much part of Victoria/Vancouver/Seattle in one sense; yet in another sense they are in an amorphous region where local politics opens out into the global. It becomes exceedingly difficult in this context to imagine where political attention ought to be focused or how 'metropolitan' government ought to be organized.

In a sense, the dilemma of the metropolis, which has vexed the architects of local government for a century and a half and stimulated round after round of futile reform efforts, is now the dilemma of government in general.[4] Some, like Jane Jacobs and Murray Bookchin, believe that in the new world order, metropolitan cities will be able to regain their position as autonomous centres for the organization of economic, social, and cultural life, and hence for independent politics and government.[5] Others are not so optimistic. In any case, it seems clear that postwar attempts to 'fix' the metropolis in neat containers, suitable for the Keynesian welfare state, have not succeeded. To many, this has been a grave disappointment, since they believe it is impossible for us to have a better society unless the state gets control of it and regulates it for the public benefit. To others, on both the left and the right, the disruption of the postwar project still appears, in retrospect, to have been essential for human liberation. The facts, of course, are more complex: we have to look at them historically to understand them. For the moment, I will focus on the Canadian example, partly in the hope that it will impress on my American and British readers that the national stories familiar to them are part of a broader pattern.[6]

**The Postwar Orthodoxy**

If the postwar era did not end in 1973, it was certainly over by 1989. The earlier date, associated with the Arab oil embargo, is conventionally taken as the point at which the Keynesian welfare state began to unravel. It is difficult to point to any serious advances in the welfare state in Europe or North America after that year. The fiscal (and, increasingly, ideological) pressures have been in the opposite direction: toward privatizing responsibility, targeting state aid for the most needy, and generally limiting demands on the public treasury. At the same time, the rudimentary systems of national economic management, associated with Keynesianism and French indicative planning, have been under attack as obstacles to economic restructuring and impediments to capitalist efficiency. The political successes of Ronald Reagan and Margaret Thatcher and the failure of the first socialist government under François Mitterrand brought this attack to a head.

In Canada, 1975 is perhaps the most significant marker year.[7] This was the year of the first restraint budget at the federal level, the defeat of the New Democrats in British Columbia, and the collapse of Ontario's program of regional government. The last of these is of considerable interest here, for it marks an important turning point in the drive to rationalize local government on the principles of the Keynesian welfare state. For over twenty years, Ontario had been a leader in the development of modern institutions of local government; its pulling back was symbolic of a change in conditions and a shift in sensibilities.[8] On the surface, the Ontario government was defeated by traditionalist resistance of a sort it had always faced. Traditional municipal government had developed in a pre-Keynesian, prewelfare era. It allowed communities to provide for a few public amenities, but more importantly to promote local business and provide the minimal services and regulations necessary for it to flourish. The market economy itself was expected to provide the framework for community and individual activity; state interventions were supposed to be at the margins. Local authorities were expected to operate within the market economy, responding to its pressures and opportunities. Although they might gain by co-ordinating their actions – as private companies did when merging – this was a matter to be judged from below. To talk of a rational plan of local government organization, with boundaries and functions specified in accordance with some conception of what local authorities ought to be doing, was both utopian and authoritarian. Municipalities, like the private businesses and private individuals they served, had to be free to respond to the changing conditions of a market economy – conditions that certainly were not governed by any central plan.

*Laissez-faire* implied that municipalities could be big or small, active or passive, multipurpose or single purpose. It precluded the sort of strict preconceptions that informed plans of general reorganization. However, such plans were articulated with increasing fervour in Ontario and elsewhere after the Second World War. They presupposed a new relationship between the state and civil society, one in which the state would contain and rationalize the market but not displace it. The unexpressed premise was that, thanks to the new tools of monetary and fiscal policy, it would be possible to manage a national economy to secure steady growth, full employment, and stable prices. The economy would generate a surplus that could be used for public as well as private purposes; indeed, a shift of expenditures in favour of public services was necessary to make up for deficiencies in privately generated demand, and so keep the economy expanding. However, economic efficiency demanded that these funds be spent more rationally than in the past, to improve public welfare and increase economic productivity. As various commentators pointed out, the old rural society, in which cities were isolated centres, seemed to be disappearing; taking its place was an urban or metropolitan society with a rural fringe. This urban society was spreading, and solidifying its internal linkages. As it did so, it was erasing the original communities. Much more intensive, multidimensional planning seemed to be required, in order to regulate urban spread and govern its internal development as well as provide for expensive new public services and facilities. Levels of education and health care and means of transportation that had seemed perfectly adequate for an essentially rural society now seemed woefully deficient. Moreover, a relatively unregulated rural life had to give way to a highly regulated urban life. To meet these demands, more professional governments with wider vision and larger resources were required; the traditionalist municipal authorities had to be displaced.

Up to a point, fiscal equalization solved the problem of inadequately constructed local authorities. Such equalization occurred at both the federal and provincial levels.[9] However, to dump money on authorities that could not use it effectively seemed a waste. To meet the new requirements, authorities had to acquire professional staffs that were capable of planning and administration in accordance with the new standards. To be maximally efficient, they had to be organized on a certain scale, have geographic boundaries that made sense in terms of their functions, and have jurisdiction over complementary activities. This pointed toward the creation of 'metropolitan' or regional authorities to replace the old municipal bodies. Failing that, functions had to be provincialized. The provincialization of public administration was arguably the predominant feature of the reorganization of government after the Second World War. Its effects were most apparent with respect to health, education, and welfare services, transportation, and certain forms of environmental regulation.[10] Although some discretion was left to local authorities, the trend was toward provincial administrative systems that could deliver standard public services and provide uniform regulations for entire provinces. The federal government for its part encouraged more uniformity among the provinces. In this system, traditional municipalities were an expensive nuisance, but they could be more easily tolerated where something like the old rural society retained its vigour. The great pressures for municipal reorganization were in the areas where rural society had been swamped by urbanization, or where it had been transformed so that it now depended on welfare. Municipalities generally were at one remove from the development of the new provincial welfare states. Yet at the same time, they played – or were supposed to play – key roles in developing the physical infrastructure of the new urban society and allocating land use within it. The pressure upon them was to assume responsibility for physical planning, and most of them did this in form but not in substance. Land-use allocation continued to be market-driven, and this allowed for an entrepreneurial politics within and between municipalities that fit better with traditional patterns than with the ambition for a planned economy. Although the trend was toward more effective planning, there were strong resistances to this at every level of government, and Canadian planning never reached European standards of efficiency.[11]

This failure was matched by another: the inability of the modernizers to create a new space for urban and local politics that matched the needs of people in the emergent society. If there was a model of such a space, it was to be found in the provinces themselves. They had emerged by the

1970s as more or less autonomous political units with their own party systems, modern bureaucracies, and responsibilities that extended across the whole range of public concerns. Provincial politics was worth the interest of people who lived in an urban society. It dealt with the governance of significant regions, and there was a sufficient accumulation of power in the provincial capitals to make credible the claim that these were centres from which effective action could be taken on a wide range of problems. Many reformers hoped that metropolitan or regional governments with a similar political significance could be established. But no province was anxious to devolve much authority on such bodies, and nowhere was there strong political pressure to do so. In retrospect, this absence of pressure is hardly surprising, since the provinces themselves afforded more meaningful spaces for regional politics. In a sense, traditional municipal politics had been located in civil society rather than in the state. It was in a domain where people were free to pursue their interests, as individuals or as members of local communities, without much regard for the wider society. Responsibility for regulating this activity rested with a legislature over and above the municipalities. Here, great principles were supposed to be considered; in municipal affairs there was more latitude – more freedom to be self-interested. The effect of the modernizing reforms was to integrate municipal councils into the state – to make them responsible to the wider society for implementing policies and providing services that the legislature had decided upon.

The modernizers thought that regional, metropolitan, or even local authorities could still have considerable latitude as intermediary agencies. This would be especially true if they pressed their powers to the limit and took control of physical, social, and economic development in their own areas. State planning could provide the framework for a principled politics that responded to different conceptions of the future. The trouble with this modernizing vision was that it squeezed local politics between the state and the market. Local councils were to be administrative agencies in a planning system that reserved the most important decisions for higher authorities. The system itself was designed to respect and protect the market. The crucial politics of the day related to the boundaries of state action, and the defenders of *laissez-faire* were largely successful in confining state planning to the public sector itself. This meant that economic development, and hence land allocation, continued to be market-driven, and public planning was largely adaptive. Local authorities thus found that their freedom of action was severely constrained, by the autonomous logic of the market on the one hand and by the requirements of government policy on the other. Really serious differences could hardly be expressed in local politics, because the range of choice for the local authorities was so narrow.[12]

The Canadian situation is somewhat unusual, in that the major political parties have not bothered to contest local elections in this century. In most of Europe and the United States, political parties take an interest in municipal contests. In Europe especially this puts additional pressure on local politics, with the parties treating local elections as preparations for the real thing at the national level.[13] This is less the case in the United States, where the tendency after the Second World War was to focus programmatic responsibility on Washington and to put municipalities in the position of competing with one another for federal aid.[14] The politics of grantsmanship in the public sector was the natural counterpart to municipal competition for private business, and fit well with the American spirit of entrepreneurialism. Compared with their Canadian counterparts, the American state governments were extraordinarily weak and ineffective, and this reinforced the tendency to seek private solutions to public problems. The traditional pattern of competition between ethnic minorities was racialized in the context of the delayed enfranchisement of the nonwhite population, and this gave a new edge to the conflicts in urban politics.[15] By the early 1970s there was an edge of violence and an emotional intensity to American urban politics that was particularly startling to foreign observers, who often concluded that a civilized resolution to the obvious problems was unlikely. This reinforced the common view in Canada, Australia, and Western Europe that a strong welfare state was a necessary bulwark against the savagery emerging in American cities. That the Americans had been unable to develop such a civilized regime, despite their promising start in that direction under Franklin Roosevelt, was taken to be a sign of their political inferiority. In contrast, Canadians could take their own success in maintaining civilized cities as proof of a kind of political superiority, as reflecting a successful adaptation of European statism to North American conditions.[16]

There was, of course, another view, which was that the statist solutions of the postwar years could not be sustained, and that the conditions that had arisen in the United States would soon be quite general. The unrest that spread throughout the Western world in the late 1960s seemed to foreshadow a necessary change.

## New Left Insurgency

The New Left that emerged in the 1960s was not an organization but a movement – a change in sensibilities by no means confined to the left itself.[17] It was marked not only by a suspicion of capitalism, but also by a profound antistatism that found expression in demands for participatory democracy, community control, and the empowerment of the disadvantaged. The disadvantaged were variously defined to include students and young people, racial minorities, countercultural communities, women, gays, and others. Old notions of the left, including those which privileged the working class as the agent of social change, were put into question. So too were the statist assumptions of communism in the East, social democracy in Western Europe, and liberal reformism in North America. The New Left pointed toward a cultural revolution from below that would transform civil society. A new society, one without constrictive boundaries, would take back the powers given over to the state, the corporations, the universities, and all the other bureaucratic institutions that dominated people's lives.

The rise of the New Left was bound up with the emergence of a globalized urban society – an unbounded metropolis – in the capitalist West. This was a society linked by the new media of instantaneous communication and by rapid interurban and intercontinental transportation. It was a society of relative affluence, with a large, mobile population of students and young people who shared increasingly in a distinctive transnational culture. It was also a society in which the urban environment was changing dramatically. Concentrated cities were beginning to sprawl; downtowns were being redeveloped as financial control centres and cultural meccas; and in the shadows between the glittering office towers and the plush suburbs, new immigrants were appearing: black Americans, Caribbeans, Asians, Africans, and Latinos. In the 1960s these processes were more advanced in the United States than anywhere else, but they were also apparent in Canada, Australia, and Western Europe and helped to generate similar unrest. Among the issues identified with this profound change were housing and transportation, both of which fell within the ambit of municipal government.

The New Left sensibility found its most significant expression in a series of critiques of the conditions of life in a globalized urban society: a critique of racism that pointed toward the manifold exclusion of people of colour from a white society; a complementary critique of imperialism that raised issues about Western exploitation and manipulation of the rest of the world; a critique of militarism, as it manifested itself in the Cold War, imperialist domination, and the organization of a military-industrial complex; a critique of capitalism, not only as a system for the exploitation of labour but as a materialist ideology that was blind to spiritual values; a critique of mindless consumption, which wasted people's lives and devoured and despoiled the environment; a critique of patriarchy, as a system that condemned half the species to subordination; and a critique of the various exclusions – of the homosexual, the disabled, and others who could not live up to the models of middle-class suburbanism. These critiques pointed toward forms of politics that challenged existing political, social, and cultural boundaries, including the ones that constituted the Keynesian welfare state and put the municipalities in their peculiar position at the juncture between the state, the market, and everyday life.

It is tempting to distinguish between the *urban* social movements that were identified with the New Left, and the ones (feminism, for example) that focused on something other than the city.[18] However, this would be to impose an academic boundary that is alien to the politics of the New Left. In an important sense, New Left politics reflected the realities of the unbounded metropolis, or global village. For the insurgents, the refusal to acknowledge established boundaries – cultural, social, and political – was fundamental to effective politics. This was true both in the early ferment of the 1960s and in the subsequent movements and organizations of the 1970s and 1980s. Characteristic of the 'new social movements' was the recognition of some global phenomenon as problematic, and the claim that this problem had to be met by immediate *local* action. The supposition was that the existing institutions of the state, and the political organizations that focused on it, were not to be trusted. New communities for change had to be created, and new forms of action had to be developed, in autonomous political spaces. Movements or 'communities' that developed within these spaces could then intervene in the state or in other social institutions. In the process, they could break through the established boundaries and open the space for global change.

Insofar as the municipality was seen simply as a 'local apparatus of the state,' it seemed an unlikely locus for effective politics. On the other hand, it represented, if only in a distorted way, the possibility of an authentically democratic politics that was rooted in the communities of daily life and marked by intense popular participation. Many of the New Left critiques were marked by a radical consciousness of the value of locality – by a sense that economically or culturally disadvantaged communities were being threatened, that democratization entailed 'community control' over the territories concerned, that people had to come together in their own neighbourhoods to resist the interventions that were disrupting their lives, and that people had to create for themselves the institutions, services, and facilities they needed to live better as individuals, families, and communities. The desire to nurture local communities, and even form new ones, was expressed by movements of hippies and students, 'back-to-the land' and later 'urban gardening' movements, gays, feminists, and environmentalists of all stripes. Ethnic minorities and even occupational groups (such as artists and theatre people) also made claims to community. These claims and aspirations did not neatly coincide, and they involved a variety of territories that were 'in and against' existing metropolitan forms and the 'local apparatuses' of the state.

It was in the context of a more general insurgency of the New Left that a new progressivism, focused on municipal politics, began to take shape in the early 1970s.[19] The movement was strongest in large metropolitan centres, where the disruptive effects of urban development were most apparent and the countercultural communities of the New Left tended to collect. Many of the original issues raised were matters of democratic process. It was claimed that the municipal councils had really become the servants of the developers and their allies, that the procedures for decision-making in the municipalities were so secretive that ordinary people could not know what was happening until it was too late, and that little serious effort was made to enable people to work out what they wanted for their own neighbourhoods. These procedural complaints were connected to more substantive issues. It was said that a *sub*-urban form of urban life was being imposed – one that destroyed the diversity of the inner cities, disrupted viable low-income and middle-class neighbourhoods, forced people into automobiles and out of public transit, polluted the air, congested the streets, and made life in the central area more dangerous and less 'liveable.' The new progressives believed that a more authentic urbanism, one that was sensitive to the quality of life in the central cities, would emerge from a more democratic politics at the municipal level. This involved the mobilization of the silent majority, who had heretofore been little interested in municipal politics. In almost every major Canadian city, new progressive political organizations emerged in the 1970s. Some, like the Montreal Citizens' Movement (MCM), and the Committee of Progressive Electors (COPE) in Vancouver, were organized as disciplined political parties. Others, like The Electors' Action Movement (TEAM) in Vancouver, were much looser and practically undisciplined coalitions. In some places, including Toronto, city-wide organizations were weak and ephemeral, and the residents' associations in particular neighbourhoods provided the strongest basis for electoral organization. People from all parties became involved; and despite sporadic efforts by the NDP to alter this situation, the traditional forms of civic nonpartisanship remained strong.

It would be wrong, however, to equate the impact of the new progressivism with the fortunes of the organizations associated with it. Much more significant have been the changes in sensibility, and in practices, within municipal governments, especially in the central cities. Almost everywhere, municipalities have opened themselves up to greater citizen participation and become more sensitive to neighbourhood concerns about the disruptive effects of development. There is greater concern about the quality of the urban environment and the necessity of maintaining liveable city centres. The preservation of historical buildings and old neighbourhoods, the recycling of old industrial sites, the transformation of waterfronts into parklike settings for various uses, and the development of new systems of public transportation all get wide support. The change in sensibilities is reflected not only in public policy but also in the styles of development favoured by promoters. The idea that old cities should be recycled rather than levelled in the process of redevelopment is widely accepted.[20]

It is also the case that the wider concerns of the social movements associated with the New Left have entered public policy. Environmentalism in municipal politics today is not simply a matter of protecting neighbourhoods and urban amenities. It is also a matter of controlling air and water pollution, regulating the production and disposal of toxic chemicals, recycling garbage, controlling smoking, eliminating CFCs, and so on. Many of these measures, such as the control of CFCs, are understood as contributions to the solution of global rather than purely local problems.[21] They command support from conservative as well as progressive politicians. In the same way we can trace the impact of demands from women and minorities: equal-opportunity programs in public employment; pay equity measures; human rights codes and anti-discrimination ordinances; access programs for the disabled; the redesign of public spaces to make them safer for women and more accessible to the disabled and to people with children.[22] We can even find effects of the peace and international solidarity movements: declarations of nuclear-free zones, civic peace marches, 'sister-city' and foreign aid programs.[23] Although measures of this sort by no means commanded universal support, they had become surprisingly common by the mid-1980s.

In its formative years, the new progressivism was rooted in concerns about consumption rather than production. Not jobs and business opportunities, but homes, neighbourhoods, amenities, and services were at issue. The fact that both working-class and middle-class neighbourhoods were often threatened by urban development facilitated some unusual political alliances. However, these alliances were fragile, for reasons implicit in the process of urban development. Middle-class neighbourhoods only needed to be protected against adverse change in order to thrive. From their perspective, half-way houses and public housing projects were often seen as threatening – as were tax increases to support public services. On the other hand, most working-class neighbourhoods needed considerable investment to upgrade housing, add to the stock, and improve neighbourhood amenities and services. In the absence of controls, neighbourhood improvement often took the form of rehabilitation and infill construction by speculators oriented toward the profitable middle-class market. Thus, neighbourhoods were gentrified, and the poor were displaced onto an inflated housing market. Ironically, the more success the new progressives had in preserving the quality of life in the inner cities, the more difficult it was for the poor, the ethnic minorities, the single parents, and the cultural and countercultural communities to remain where they were. These experiences helped to sharpen the divisions between middle-class preservationists and the new progressives in municipal politics, and tended to close the gap between the Old and New Left.[24] The consolidation of the MCM in Montreal, the rise of COPE and collapse of TEAM in Vancouver, and the emergence in many cities of a strong municipal NDP (or surrogate) were signs of this political realignment. The recomposed progressive organizations, which brought people from the new social movements together with labour activists, ethnic and minority leaders, neighbourhood workers, social service professionals, academics, and others, created a political milieu similar to the one offered by the federal and provincial New Democrats. Out of this milieu came strong demands for new programs of public housing, employment, and social services, all of these attuned to the needs of a socially diverse urban constituency. This put the new progressives 'in and against' the agenda of the New Right.

## The New Right Reaction

Throughout the Western world we can see what looks to be the final stages in the reconstruction of old industrial cities as the nuclei of the post-industrial economy. This process involves the conversion of industrial zones and harbour and railway lands to other uses – offices and boutiques, upscale housing, galleries and museums, waterside parks, convention centres, and sports stadiums. American urbanists talk of Rouse-ification, after the firm that redeveloped Faneuil Hall in Boston and replicated its success in city after American city.[25] Canadians might prefer to give more credit to the federal Liberals, who poured so much money into these lands in search of votes. Perhaps we should call the process Axworthing, after the federal minister most responsible; in any case, it is clear that the recycling of inner cities, in which many Canadians took particular pride in the 1970s, was part of a general process that was as evident in New Orleans or Baltimore (or indeed Liverpool or Glasgow) as in Vancouver or Toronto. In its characteristic forms, this process seems to represent the triumph of neoconservatism over the Keynesian welfare state and the insurgency of the New Left.

The New Right represented a change in sensibility: a reassertion of both the values and the legitimizing claims of the old civil society.[26] Although the New Left had been critical of the emergent regime of Keynesian welfarism, it tended to take the triumph over *laissez-faire* for granted, and hence to assume a trend toward ever tighter regulation of the economy, more extensive public services, and at least a modest redistribution of resources in favour of the poor. Demands for more radical action presupposed this social base. Thus, the resurgence of conservatism caught the New Left as well as the Old off guard. Indeed, the New Left was implicated in the rise of neoconservatism, insofar as its own critiques of welfare statism had prepared the ground for a reassertion of the virtues of existing society. For conservatives, these virtues were embodied in the nexus of family, religion, and private property, and were protected above all by the self-organizing relations of the market, which enabled individuals and families to secure themselves by their own efforts. From this perspective, the power of the state was to be invoked only to secure this nexus or to extend the values implicit in it: that power was not to be used for social reconstruction.

The resurgence of conservatism in the 1970s occurred in the context of the fiscal crisis of the welfare state.[27] It seemed that existing welfare services could not be extended or even preserved without unacceptable levels of taxation or public borrowing. Capitalist resistance to these levels became increasingly effective as the development of capital markets enabled international investors to play states off against each other. The crisis was such that capital had to be either appeased, or confronted with a major extension of state control over investment. The apparent failure of the French socialists to make the latter strategy work seemed to confirm the wisdom of the appeasement strategy adopted by all the other capitalist states. However, this strategy had already been legitimized by a massive propaganda campaign that convinced most people that Keynesian welfarism would no longer work.

The Canadian federal government adopted its restraint program in 1975, and the provinces eventually followed suit, forcing welfare agencies, hospitals, school boards, and municipalities to constrain their activities. One obvious effect was to destroy the promise of new inner-city housing for the poor. That promise had been contained not only in the new progressivism of municipal politics, but also in the provisions of the National Housing Act of 1973, which had been influenced by the progressive critiques of the preceding years.[28] The supposition was that federally and provincially supported nonprofit housing, developed by a variety of municipal, charitable, and co-operative agencies, would provide working-class housing on a significant scale. This would make up for the demise of the old public-housing programs, which had been insufficiently sensitive to the urban fabric and to the social requirements of the people being housed. Despite some promising initiatives, however, the new forms of housing had little impact on conditions of life for the poor of the inner cities. There was simply not enough of it, because the federal and provincial governments refused anything more than token funding.[29]

In a similar way, fiscal restraint took the initiative away from a variety of other agencies at the local level. Ironically, this was especially true in the voluntary sector, which the conservatives have touted as the proper locus for most social services. In the context of Keynesian welfarism, the voluntary sector had come to depend on public funding and on the provision of certain core services by government agencies. In a sense, the voluntary sector was supplemental to the state sector. It had more freedom of action, not only to develop innovative services, but to engage in a politics of social welfare – mobilizing constituents, agitating among the public at large, and pressuring governments. As such, it was a site for New Left insurgency. Fiscal restraint forced voluntary agencies to pick up services abandoned by governments and to find alternative funding for their own activities. As a result, much of the energy that had gone into innovative programming and politicking had to be diverted into fund-raising and bureaucratic management.[30]

One way of understanding the neoconservative thrust is as an effort as much to foreclose political spaces as to restrain public spending. (The truth of this will become more apparent when we look more closely at what happened in Britain in the 1980s.) Keynesian welfarism had opened up new political spaces, partly within the administrative apparatuses of the state, but more importantly on their periphery. It enlarged the class of social service professionals and legitimized claims for public action to remedy social ills. Directly or indirectly, it supported an array of groups and organizations that developed new demands, organized new constituencies, and created new political spaces for themselves. Without confronting these groups directly, neoconservative governments were able to constrain them by reducing financial support, off-loading activities, and attacking expectations for new public programs. Thus, political spaces for the New Left, which had emerged in the penumbra of the Keynesian welfare state, were disrupted or constricted.

In Canada, unlike the United States, the conservative revival has not found much expression in 'tax-revolts' or other grassroots movements at the local level.[31] There are no provisions for popular legislative initiatives, and few opportunities for referenda. Conservative populism has been much more apparent in federal and provincial politics, especially in the guise of the Reform Party of Canada. At the municipal level there has instead been a drift back to traditional municipal politics, legitimized by the rhetoric of neoconservatism. Traditional boosterism is thus represented as entrepreneurialism. Deals with developers become 'public-private partnerships,' and civic trade junkets become responses to globalization. For the most part, this is a repackaging of old activities; even so, there is no doubt that the competition for business has forced municipalities to become more innovative. Whether this justifies grand claims about economic development strategies is questionable. The most obvious effect has been to intensify the pressures for downtown redevelopment, as exemplified in the postmodern monuments arising on old railway and harbour lands.

Grass roots conservatism is expressed in resistance to developments that, while they might have wider social benefits, do have adverse local effects. These developments include incinerators, dump sites, half-way houses, and public housing. Such NIMBYism, which can be partly explained in terms of market rationality – who wants a project that will reduce property values? – is fairly easily expressed within the conventional forms of municipal politics, which 'centre' questions of land use. However, the people involved often say that they are trying to protect the environment and preserve the quality of human life. In this way their rhetoric points to values that transcend the market – values which are much more boldly advanced by the New Left. An even more dramatic break from market rationality and the codes of conventional politics is apparent in the anti-abortion movement. To defend traditional religious and social ideas, the movement invokes a language of universal human rights ('the right to life') and uses political tactics developed by the New Left. Anti-abortionists have defied the police and the courts, attacked private and public property, and disrupted the 'normal' political process. Thus, they have pointed, like New Left insurgents before them, to a form of 'local politics' that bursts the bounds of established political spaces. Whether this new politics will be barbaric or civilized remains at issue.

**Toward a New Politics?**

In the nineteenth century, theorists like Mill and de Tocqueville hoped that the municipalities would be the main sources of vitality in the emergent liberal democracies. This hope has never been realized. Instead, municipalities have been trapped between the state and the market – at times expected to serve the purposes of the state (be they for economic planning, welfare administration, or whatever), at times simply to function in the market (promoting the economic interests of their communities), and often to do both simultaneously. These activities always have attracted some people's attention, and have aroused the passions of the majority from time to time, but they have not engaged the popular imagination in the way Mill and de Tocqueville hoped. Such engagement depends on the spaces of municipal politics coinciding with the spaces of popular mobilization. Needless to say, such a coincidence has been the exception rather than the rule.

The new progressivism has produced local parties that are detached from federal and provincial organizations and has provided a means for focusing a variety of new concerns on the municipal councils. However, the neoconservative reaction has made it increasingly difficult for these concerns to be addressed within a municipal framework. One can see the effect of this on ostensibly social-democratic politicians – for example, Jean Doré and Michael Harcourt, who, as mayors of Montreal (1986–94) and Vancouver (1980–6) respectively, adapted themselves to the new entrepreneurialism.[32] Similar patterns are seen in other countries. To the extent that municipal councils succeed in breaking through the boundaries imposed by the state and the market, it is as a result of their relationship to social movements. This creates serious contradictions, for movement politics involves a restless questioning of identities and communities that is inconsistent with fixed political spaces.

The disruption of established political spaces is a fearful matter for anyone who assumes that the familiar boundaries are essential for order. For many, the confrontation at Oka in the summer of 1990 (which we noted in Chapter 4) showed what happens when political practices are followed that defy the norms and limits of the liberal democratic nation-state. It also illustrated the realities concealed by our usual conceptions of 'urban and local politics.' It was, arguably, the most dramatic incident in municipal politics in recent years in Canada, provoked as it was by the municipal council's decision to extend a golf course onto land claimed by the Mohawks. Yet what ultimately happened could not be dealt with or comprehended in terms of municipal politics: an armed band, claiming to represent the Mohawk nation, confronted the armed forces of Canada, Quebec, and Oka; sovereignty was claimed and denied; different nations and communities were defended; a variety of modern and premodern political traditions were invoked. Despite the overwhelming military superiority of the Canadian state, there was no simple way of crushing this challenge to Canadian sovereignty, for the Mohawk Warriors had claimed a space not only in a Montreal suburb, but in the global media. Clothed in a rhetoric of aboriginal rights, asserting a difference legitimized by the norms of the global village, the warriors achieved their victory in the media even as they were dispersed by Canadian troops.

Whatever one thinks of the Mohawk Warriors or the right-to-life campaigners – or the Greenpeace activists who challenged the French government in the South Pacific and disrupted Premier David Peterson's reelection campaign in Ontario in 1990 – they represent forms of politics that will not go away. Current social movements reflect conditions of life in a globalized urban society, in which problems of personal security, economic opportunity, human rights, and environmental health cannot be contained within national, let alone municipal borders. Neoconservatives have thought that the market would provide the discipline to contain popular insurgency; but in every country they have had to rely on the powers of the state to keep people within bounds. The explosions of popular discontent have not only been 'critical' and progressive – as in the movements associated with the New Left – but reactionary and conservative – as in the present attacks on biculturalism, multiculturalism, gay rights, and feminism. Modes of social and political organization that 'fix' people, either as buyers and sellers or as subjects of administration, cannot be very stable in a global village that promises everyone freedom and self-fulfilment.

Neoconservative attempts to reinscribe the old limits of politics, and prevent people from taking effective action on the matters of most concern to them, are liable to add to popular frustrations and to encourage the nastier forms of fundamentalism. To avoid this, we need to keep open the spaces created by the social movements that came out of the New Left insurgency. We should not expect these movements to respect the neat boundaries of the Keynesian welfare state (or the new entrepreneurial state that seems to have succeeded it). Instead, we should expect them to keep disrupting the forms and practices of politics as usual, refusing the existing political agendas, inventing new repertoires of action, and identifying communities for change that we had never anticipated. What we should expect, in sum, is a politics of 'flexible specialization' that mimics the pattern of organization that businesses have adopted in the context of a globalized economy. This type of politics will involve ongoing resistance to the demand that states and municipalities reposition themselves as entrepreneurial bodies.

6

# Flexible Specialization

In the course of working on this book, I was invited to a conference in Brisbane, the Australian city that is most comparable to Vancouver.[1] I had never been to Australia before and knew little about its municipal politics, so I was somewhat startled to find myself listening to a speech from the Lord Mayor that could have been given in almost any Canadian or American city with a supposedly forward-looking municipal government. We even heard a little about the mayor's days as a graduate student in Chicago, when no doubt he was reading some of the same books I was reading at the time as a Canadian at Oxford. The ideas, as refracted through a couple of decades of experience, had a very familiar ring, and so did the situation described by the other participants in the discussion of Brisbane's constraints and opportunities. It seemed as if we were anywhere and everywhere in a metropolis that left everyone slightly confused, and that drove middle-class intellectuals back to their faith in the virtues of individual and local enterprise. Why was it so difficult to imagine something different?

Brisbane is one of a number of cities around the Pacific Rim that are trying to establish themselves as leading centres for global capital. Obviously, it is not in the same league as Los Angeles, Tokyo, or Hong Kong; it is a rung down even from Sydney and San Francisco. However, it is competing with Albuquerque and Phoenix, Portland and Seattle, Vancouver and Calgary – and a host of other cities elsewhere – for a favoured position within the new global order. In this context it can trade on its distance from the old industrial centres, with their decaying infrastructure, obsolescent labour, and endemic social conflicts. It can also trade on its distance from those new industrial centres – especially in Asia and Latin America – where the quality of life seems as low as it was in Engels's Manchester. Practically all the English-speaking towns like Brisbane (that is, the ones that developed into large cities in the postwar era) have become attractive havens for capital and capitalists: places where life can be worked out afresh at a distance from the old and new proletarians. On offer is not only a middle-class style of living but also a configuration of community power that assures consensual support for business leadership. In a city like Brisbane, which has a strong labour tradition, the implicit promise is that working-class insurgency and other social movements will be contained within a new social democracy that promotes the accumulation of capital and checks the redistribution of wealth. The bias, clearly, is toward leadership from the cosmopolitan middle-class.

To a distressing degree, contemporary cities have been exposed to a global competition for capital that encourages the economic boosterism and conservative politics that have long been identified with American municipalities. Paul Peterson in 1980[2] could contrast the American situation with the European, and point to the protective power of national states that regulated capital and redistributed resources, and thus opened the opportunities for more progressive local government. This contrast no longer seems so significant. Even in the guise of social democracy, higher-level governments have been drawing back from their redistributive activities and reconfiguring themselves as organizations in support of capital accumulation. This has intensified the pressure on local authorities to disavow any redistributive capacity and to focus instead on infrastructural development and community marketing. In this context, progressive or social-democratic politics is seen increasingly in terms of its capacity to mediate the requirements of private business with demands for environmental protection, equal rights for women and minorities, minimum labour standards, and public health. This is a role that must be sold to business, which might otherwise flee to safer havens. For marketing purposes, social democrats (or 'liberals' in the American sense) have turned to the idea that strong governments are required to organize business effectively for global competition. They have promised, in effect, to turn 'the executive of the modern state' into a truly efficient 'committee for managing the common affairs of the whole bourgeoisie.'[3]

Much of the commentary in recent years on the stagnating economies of the English-speaking world has focused on the relative disorganization of the anglophone bourgeoisie. Either 'our' capitalists have let us down, or we have let *them* down by not organizing them effectively to compete with Japan, Germany, and the Little Dragons of East Asia. 'Their' capitalists have been engaged in strategic planning, while 'ours' have been left behind squabbling over the rents from their old investments. Whether this is a matter of irredeemable cultural differences or one that can be corrected by appropriate political leadership is the subject of some dispute.[4] There is a noticeable longing in 'our' part of the world for some new leader – Bill Clinton? – who can organize business into a more effective, forward-looking bloc. As many have recognized, for twenty-five years after the Second World War there was a reasonably effective system for global economic management; however, it depended on eliding the distinction between the United States and the 'free world' and allowing the internal management of the American economy to set the parameters for global economic activity.[5] In the long run, this was not a viable arrangement. In the new world order the United States is being forced, like Britain before it, into the role of an ordinary competitor. The spatial logic of the state system seems to give the advantage to countries that can forge a unity that gives them a capacity for strategic action.

A similar logic applies at the local level, and in fact the absence of sovereignty points toward a redoubled effort. Analysts once worried about the domination of communities by power élites, but the aim now seems to be to create such élites where they do not exist. The common complaint is that 'communities' are unable to take charge of their own destinies. In this respect they are like the feckless states of the anglophone world, only worse. What is required from this point of view is to establish a hegemonic bloc within each community.[6] Given the character of the economy and the nature of the state system, the only effective blocs seem to be ones that are organized around local business. Ultimately, it is said, only business can generate capital, establish external markets, and exploit local labour effectively. To tie capital into the local community – to create a genuinely *local* bourgeoisie – appears to be the necessary object of political leadership in the city. Only insofar as the captains of business regard themselves as burghers of the city will they commit the energy necessary to discover their common interests, and begin planning as one for the development of 'the community.' Around this core other interests can constellate; if there is no core, local efforts to boost the community within the global economy may be futile.

There is a widespread perception that the new global economy – the informational economy of flexible specialization, global markets, and global production systems – widens the scope for developmental action at the local or regional level. Thus, there has been a convergence of thinking since the early 1980s around the idea of strategic planning in the entrepreneurial mode. On the left, admiring eyes have been cast toward Emilia Romagna in Italy, where the local bourgeoisie apparently came together with a little help from the Communists, and secured for the region a privileged spot in the new global economy.[7] On the right, American cities like Pittsburgh, Baltimore, and Atlanta have been more widely admired, since their 'public-partnerships' barely involve the unions, let alone socialists, and keep government in its place.[8] In either case, the model is of a politics that puts redistributive or class politics to one side and focuses everyone's attention on the developmental objectives of capital accumulation. Peterson suggested that such a practice was inevitable for a government with scant control over an open economy; for him, *the City, Ltd.* was a necessary consequence of *City Limits.*

Unfortunately, this latest version of the 'end of ideology' analysis asks more questions than it answers. It slides too easily into the assumption that a politics of the disadvantaged is no longer possible, and that the appeasement of capital is necessarily the order of the day. It fails to take seriously enough the possibility that the lines of popular resistance and political exploration have been redefined in the global city, and that the opportunities for a creative politics are quite different from what they were even a decade ago. Moreover, it mystifies our understanding of the organization of political authority in modern capitalist society.

**Bourgeois Self-Government**

From the point of view of capital, the state system divides the world inconveniently. It breaks it up into sovereign units that are often too big or too small for the immediate purposes of capital accumulation. Thus, there is strong business support for the development of global political institutions. At the same time, nation-states are inconveniently large, in that they impose rules that constrain free action within the global system. Thus, there is an apparent need for political organization on different scales and dimensions, to overcome such constraints. It is a particular problem for business to find modes of organization that allow for flexible response to the changing conditions of capital accumulation. The state, in this respect, is very inconvenient, because its operations are inevitably slow (legitimation depends on broad consultation) and its edicts are supposed to have permanence. In contrast, the conditions for capital accumulation are in constant flux and success depends on rapid response. To be caught within a state, in competition with state-free capital, can be disastrous.[9]

This ambivalent relationship between the state and capital is illustrated by the history of local authorities. Political scientists are now so obsessed with the state and its relations with capital that they often neglect the fact that the original political organizations of an emergent bourgeoisie were not states, but guilds, communes, and corporations.[10] Perhaps the most ancient of these political organizations is the Corporation of the City of London, which retains much of its medieval form. The Corporation is still an important organization for managing business in the financial centre of Europe. It is conveniently constituted to keep other interests at bay – including the interests of the state as such. Thatcher's government, which made great efforts to constrain other local authorities, enhanced the position of the City, and began the work of creating a new and larger financial district to the east, under the aegis of another 'public' corporation firmly under business control.[11] This reflects the long-standing pressure on the state to sustain institutions that enable capital to pursue its various projects, clothed as necessary in public authority.

The political institutions for modern business were slowly formed within the ensemble of authorities in medieval Europe. Their character varied enormously, but in the most successful cities – for example, those of northern Italy – the burghers organized themselves into republics as autonomous as royal courts. More commonly, municipalities took the form of chartered corporations, which enjoyed a wide array of rights and privileges. In Britain and the former British colonies (including the United States), the lineal descent of contemporary city governments from these medieval corporations is clear. Moreover, other local authorities, which descend from the baronial courts and parish meetings, have been assimilated into the corporate form of the municipalities. This reflects the universalization of the bourgeois model of local government in the nineteenth century. Gradually, all local authorities were given corporate status, with their powers vested in a board or council chosen by and responsible to the shareholders or propertied inhabitants of the communities for which they were responsible. Corporations were highly congenial to the bourgeoisie, in comparison with the courts and meetings that entrenched the rights of the old nobility and the agrarian landholders.

The history of local government in the English-speaking countries is extraordinarily complex, but since the seventeenth century it has mostly been a tale of the proliferation, consolidation, and reproliferation of authorities for bourgeois self-government. When the old municipal corporations proved too rigid and unadventurous for an expansive capitalism, businessmen in different communities formed a variety of trusts, commissions, and boards to provide services and facilities and to enforce the regulations they wanted.[12] The 'sovereignty' of the Crown, Parliament, or the state legislatures was acknowledged, in the sense that these authorities were clothed with legal rights and privileges. However, this was largely a cover for the self-organization of the bourgeoisie. The whole process was complementary to the self-organization of capitalists in the 'private' sector. One of the great events of the nineteenth century was, indeed, the creation of a 'private' sector in which businessmen could organize and reorganize themselves with minimal interference from the outside. The great multinational corporations that emerged from this sector are now clearly the most important *political* organizations for business.

In the Anglo-Saxon countries at least, the distinction between municipal corporations and business corporations was not established until the first half of the nineteenth century.[13] Creating a right of incorporation for private business and giving such corporations the same rights against the state as natural persons were essential moves in establishing the legal foundations for corporate capitalism. Complementary to this was the recognition that certain corporations – municipalities and local authorities modeled on them – had to be regarded as agencies of the state. This meant that they were supposed to use their powers for public purposes that went beyond the interests of business itself. As public authorities rather than private businesses, they enjoyed special prerogatives, such as the right of eminent domain. At the same time, they were confronted with newly defined limits on the state, intended to secure 'private' property. From this time on there was a distinction – heretofore barely made – between the organizations of the bourgeoisie in the private and public sectors.

If we trace the development of cities since the nineteenth century, we find an array of bourgeois initiatives both 'private' and 'public.' Schools, for instance, were variously organized, some as commercial ventures, others as charities, religious institutions, or nonprofit foundations, still others as institutions of local school boards funded by taxation, and more yet under the aegis of municipal corporations or the state itself. Although the school system has come to be organized increasingly through the state, other modes of organization have persisted and transect the state organization. The right to educate one's children outside the state system is firmly entrenched; non-state schools are publicly subsidized; the state schools are controlled by local school boards or education committees; textbooks, information systems, equipment, and similar, are sold to the schools by commercial enterprises. Thus, the school system straddles the boundary between the private and public sectors and is subject to constant reorganization as a result of bourgeois initiatives, some of which are commercial (the sale of computer systems) and others of which are not (the organization of alternative schools).

What happens in education occurs throughout the field of 'local government.' Whether we look at health care, policing, land use planning, or whatever, we find not an activity assigned clearly to the public sector, but a domain of initiative in which a wide variety of agencies are active. By no means all of these agencies are bourgeois, but most of the important ones are. We find companies planning and developing office complexes, shopping centres, suburbs, and even towns, acquiring whatever public authority they need along the way. We find huge private police forces offering 'security' on a fee-for-service basis. We find ostensibly 'public' corporations acquiring land and selling it below cost for commercial ventures, or operating transit services, or providing water or power at subsidized rates. We find theatres, galleries, museums, and broadcasting stations subsidized by public subscription. We find an array of social services organized by privately funded charitable agencies, alongside services provided by the state and the local public authorities. Although all of this is indicative of the self-organization of the bourgeoisie, none of it is reducible to the presence (or absence) of the state.

In terms of political organization, 'flexible specialization' has always been the rule for the bourgeoisie. There are the business corporations, large and small, that as agencies for capital accumulation are as much political and governmental as economic. There are the trade and professional associations, lobbies, and front organizations. There are the charities and nonprofit foundations for education and culture. There are the regulatory agencies that are clothed with state authority but organized for the self-government of the industries concerned. There are broadcasting outlets, publishing houses, sports teams, and entertainment complexes. And there are municipalities, school boards, hospital societies, planning commissions, and public utilities commissions, and an endless array of other agencies that exercise some measure of public authority. To think of all this in terms of the organizational force of the state – which, no doubt, is there in some degree – is to miss its complexity and diversity. That complexity and diversity is a sign that the bourgeoisie cannot satisfy its needs within a single mode of organization.

**Do the Capitalists Need an Executive Committee?**

The idea that the bourgeoisie needs an executive committee, with the authority to act in the interests of the class as a whole, is a reflection of the statist traditions of continental Europe. It enters into Anglo-Saxon thinking in deference to the tighter logic of the French and the Germans, and in anxious recognition that the more tightly organized states of continental Europe and East Asia might someday push the Anglo-Saxons to the margins. This has not happened yet; indeed, one is struck by the fact that the global bourgeoisie has done very well with a loose political organization that plays states off against each other. One also notices that many of the emergent centres of capital in East Asia – Singapore and Hong Kong most notably – are independent cities rather than nation-states, and are loosely linked to one another by the cultural networks of Chinese civilization. In Europe, of course, the state system is being modified by a complex of European Community institutions, and in North America the latest free trade agreement points in a similar direction. In the most advanced parts of the capitalist world, the trend seems to be toward greater complexity in political organization – a complexity that defies the tightness and unity of the state form.

What applies at the national or global level also applies locally. If we are searching for the pattern that exemplifies purely bourgeois organization at the local level – business at work where it faces least resistance – then we should look to the United States, particularly the southwestern United States. In Southern California, for instance, we find an ensemble of authorities in a complex 'public economy' that replicates most of the principles of 'private sector' organization and is almost completely dominated by bourgeois producers' and consumers' organizations.[14] This public economy is constitutionally entrenched. Once constituted, public authorities (not just municipalities but water districts, school districts, and so on) can rarely be eliminated without the consent of their shareholders. Private property rights are carefully protected; there are constitutional limits on taxation and spending; intermunicipal competition keeps taxes low and directs funds toward services for businesses and middle-class residents; land-use regulation keeps a balance between middle-class amenities and the requirements for capital accumulation.

There is virtually no strategic planning for the region as a whole, which contains over 20 million people; even so, Southern California remains one of the most dynamic centres of global capital.[15]

A different but equally interesting example is provided by the city of Houston, Texas. Houston has emerged in the past thirty or forty years as one of the major control centres for global capital: as a headquarters city for oil, gas, and related petrochemical industries. The political ascendancy of business there is, if anything, more marked than in Southern California. The labour movement is weak and disorganized, as are the displaced Latino peasantry and the descendants of the black slaves. The ideology of capitalism is so deeply instilled that opposition can be crushed by accusing it of socialist tendencies. Success in business is taken as a prime indicator of political capacity. So, how does the bourgeoisie organize itself politically when it has this sort of freedom? Does it create a strong, local executive committee? Or does it contain and disorganize 'the state' in order to secure the power of its own political organizations?

Houston is noted throughout North America as a city where no zoning occurs – that is, where the municipal authorities have not applied the standard system of land-use control. Instead, land use is regulated by 'restrictive covenants' imposed as conditions of sale or rental. These covenants are devised by land developers, who can thereby secure future land use on the estates they are developing. This is a great advantage for marketing, since future householders, retailers, or office tenants want to be assured of conforming uses around them. Provided that they can assemble enough land, developers can create 'planned communities' of any sort the market demands. The municipality is redundant in this process, since the covenants are invented by the developers – or by groups of adjoining land-owners – and enforced as a matter of right by the courts. This system of non-zoning is widely praised by American conservatives, because it provides for a market-driven system of land-use control that seems to illustrate the redundancy of government regulation.[16] If the dominant class can do things within the 'private sector,' why bother to invoke state authority except for enforcing contracts?

Unlike many American metropolises (for example, greater Los Angeles), Houston is not divided into many distinct municipalities that compete with one another for the favour of capital. Such a division is redundant, because the non-zoning, low-taxing, business-controlled Houston council secures uniformly favourable conditions for capital across the entire city-region. The council concentrates on providing roads and sewers, contracts out as much work as it can, and keeps services to the working class as limited as possible. It has a negligible program of public housing, scant welfare services, weak schools, and limited health services – in other words, it provides a welfare state so impoverished that people are strongly encouraged to seek the services they need on the market. This the middle class tends to do. Thus, the local state is constituted in a form that strongly reinforces perceptions that the free market is superior.

Houston's council is involved in economic development activities, but not as an executive committee for the local bourgeoisie. It is there to hold down taxes, act as a lobby for state and federal funding, and promote the city as a site for investment. It does not engage in strategic planning. When the recession of the early 1980s hit the city hard, it was not the municipal council but the Houston Chamber of Commerce – a 'private sector' organization – that set up a strategic planning operation. And even that operation was weak and ineffective.[17] Evidently, for major businesses in Houston, strategic planning on a regional basis was largely redundant. The important planning was being done in the corporate headquarters of the oil and gas industry and related to global operations, not regional ones.

Houston provides an interesting contrast with Pittsburgh, the city most admired by American proponents of 'public-private partnership.' In Houston, local business has seen little point in strategic planning; in Pittsburgh, such planning began with the Allegheny Conference in 1943.[18] Significantly, the conference was a private organization of local businessmen; only later was the city of Pittsburgh brought onside as a participant in strategic planning. The idea was that local business should work out collectively a strategy for civic reconstruction and then bring in governmental agencies to help carry the plan into effect. The 'executive committee of the local bourgeoisie' was outside the state, and organized the state to carry out its projects. Houston's chamber of commerce followed this model forty years later, but the consensus necessary to make it really effective did not exist in that city.

Pittsburgh and other American cities, such as Baltimore, that have gained a reputation for strategic planning have not been on the crest of an investment boom. On the contrary, what stimulated action in Pittsburgh and Baltimore was the recognition that the growth industries of the day were locating elsewhere, and that their own major industries were entering a phase of gradual decline. The local bourgeoisie had to choose between disinvestment and recapitalization. In most cities, mobile capital – big capital – chose disinvestment, and a weakened local business community was left to manage as best it could.[19] What makes Pittsburgh stand out is that a major capitalist – Richard Mellon – used his influence to organize local capitalists for strategic planning. Pittsburgh was rebuilt as a corporate headquarters city, major investments were made in the universities and teaching hospitals, and there was a drive to transform the city into a scientific research centre with spin-off, high-tech industries. These efforts have been remarkably successful, so that the city stands out among the former industrial centres of the Great Lakes Basin as one that is making the transition to a post-industrial economy quite successfully.

Several things should be noted about this Pittsburgh model. In the first place, the political mobilization of the local business élites depended on a unique combination of economic decline and 'place-commitment' on the part of big capital. Mellon, in particular, was unwilling to disinvest, and his commitment to the city was sufficient to secure widespread support from other businessmen. No such leader emerged in Houston, where, in any case, the urgency of the situation was never as great. Second, the organization in Pittsburgh – like the one in Houston that never quite succeeded – kept the state (in the guise of both municipal and other authorities) at a distance. Like the United Way or the Regional Planning Association of New York, the Allegheny Conference acted as a private sector agency and deliberately kept government from imposing its own schemes. Third and finally, the organization deliberately excluded the working class. Union involvement was negligible, and blacks and other minorities were practically unrepresented. The Allegheny Conference was clearly an organization of the bourgeoisie.

The good burghers of Pittsburgh certainly have been successful on their own terms, but it should not be supposed that they turned the regional economy around. Most of the steel mills that had generated profits for a century, and been at the core of the Pittsburgh economy, were in fact located outside the city, in the nearby river valleys. As these mills and their associated industries closed, the mill towns were thrown into crisis. There was an effort on the part of labour (in alliance with churches and community groups) to organize against the closures and for a regional effort at industrial regeneration. This the capitalists opposed: they wanted to concentrate their investments in the new growth sectors of the economy, and hence in the city of Pittsburgh (or outside the region altogether). Only when the process of deindustrialization had become irreversible – and when the labour and community leaders who had resisted it had come to terms with the situation – did the Pittsburgh capitalists become involved in an effort at regional planning. This has involved a sort of 'clean-up' operation around the fringes of the new Pittsburgh economy.

Los Angeles, Houston, and Pittsburgh represent different forms of capitalist self-organization. In each case, the state – or more accurately, the ensemble of 'public' authorities – is kept at arm's length in the processes of economic decision-making. The bourgeoisie organizes itself within the private sector. Local circumstances – including traditions of organization and patterns of leadership – largely determine the particular form of organization that emerges. This may involve a deliberate disorganization of public authority, as in Los Angeles or (in a different way) Houston, or it may preserve the illusion of strong municipal government, as in Pittsburgh. It may inhibit any strategic planning, other than what occurs in the corporate headquarters; or it may provide for transcorporate co-operation within the framework of civic or regional institutions for strategic planning. Both modes of organization involve the appropriation of public authority and public resources in accordance with the plans that are generated. Co-operative politicians are necessary in this regard. However, it is clear in both cases that the politicians are the handmaidens of local business and lack the capacity to impose any different economic direction. From a bourgeois perspective, one can hardly imagine better forms of organization.

It is significant that the major thrust of Margaret Thatcher's policy toward local government in Britain was to disorganize and disempower the existing local authorities.[20] These authorities embodied a social democratic conception of the local state that involved the mediation of urban development and collective consumption by bodies representing a variety of interests, including labour.[21] As some of the Left Labour authorities tried to press forward with an explicitly socialist vision in the 1980s – thereby posing a direct political challenge to the central government in this context – the need to curb them became more pressing. The Thatcherite strategy, which emerged only gradually, was to Americanize the local state in Britain. This meant removing powers from existing local authorities and transferring them to special-purpose agencies under the direct control of business or (in a few cases) middle-class consumers. It also meant trying to stimulate the political organization of business in local communities, so that public-private partnerships on the Pittsburgh model could be established. However, in Britain as in

Houston, bourgeois enthusiasm for such organizations was limited. More fundamental to the requirements of British capital were the Thatcherite projects of deploying the state against itself to free capital from regulation, and smashing the institutions that supported a socialist counterculture.

## So, Do *We* Need to Reorganize the Bourgeoisie?

It is a curious presumption of social democracy that the bourgeoisie needs to be reorganized for its own sake – and that this will somehow benefit labour, or women and minorities, or 'the people.' It seems to have come as a big surprise to social democrats that business did not care very much for the Keynesian welfare state, and was quite happy to get rid of it (or at least many features of it) when a better form of organization seemed feasible. (Just as Marxists discovered the state, the bourgeoisie set about deconstructing it!) Since then, social democrats have been casting about for a new role, and it seems to have brought them some comfort to think that local or regional bourgeoisies could now do with reorganizing, to make them more competitive in the new global economy. The Houston model has of course little appeal to social democrats, since it involves an extreme form of *laissez-faire*. On the other hand, the Pittsburgh model is quite appealing, provided that the strategic planning agencies can somehow be opened up, to allow for more widespread participation.

In the English-speaking countries at least, the social democratic ideal is located somewhere between Sweden, Japan, and the 'Third' Italy – that is, in a mode of organization that permits public officials, as well as representatives of labour and other groups, to participate in capitalist investment planning, in exchange for their co-operation in securing social control, developing the economic infrastructure, training the work-force, regulating unwelcome competition, promoting communication, and opening up markets. There is an emergent recognition that local or regional authorities may have a comparative advantage in doing these things, because they are closer to those small entrepreneurs who are spinning off from the big corporations and seeking to expand their operations. The presumption is that the big multinationals have little need for such authorities – or, rather, that their relationship to such authorities is bound to be instrumental and exploitative – whereas the smaller, weaker companies need an infrastructure of public support and assistance in order to form organizational links and strategic planning systems that will act as a substitute for the hierarchical organizations of the multinationals. The hope is to exploit the perceived needs and vulnerabilities of these smaller firms, to get them to co-operate with the public authorities in strategic planning.

This social-democratic strategy depends on softening the resistance of local business. This means convincing the élites that they need to be organized in a different way, that they cannot do it entirely themselves, and that the public authorities will respect business interests when developing new organizations for planning. It is significant that those social democratic politicians who had some success in organizing local business élites – for example, Jean Doré in Montreal and Mike Harcourt in Vancouver – built on institutions developed by leaders with close connections to the business community. In both Vancouver and Montreal, the idea of developing an economic strategy for the city, in co-operation between the business community and the municipal authorities, had already been adumbrated when the social democrats took office. Basic institutions had already been established, and it was necessary only to fill in the content. This meant organizing the technical staff, working out consultative procedures, and moving toward the definition of strategic objectives. One of the strengths of the social democrats was that they really believed that public-private co-operation in strategic planning could make a major contribution to economic development; their conservative predecessors were much less sure about this.

The interesting thing about strategic planning in Montreal and Vancouver is that it differs so little from such planning in Pittsburgh and Baltimore. When Mike Harcourt was mayor of Vancouver, he devoted great attention to his relations with key leaders in the business community, trying to convince them that it was in everyone's interests to agree on strategic objectives for the Vancouver economy. This led to widespread discussions intended to generate a consensus about the likely character of the city's economy at its best, and the sort of milieu required to attract new private investment.[22] This resulted in recommendations for new institutions and programs in both the private and the public sector: some things would be done by organizations funded and directly controlled by business representatives, and others by ostensibly public agencies. Underpinning the division of responsibilities was the recognition that the autonomy of the private sector – the right to make investment and other business decisions on a purely commercial basis – had to be respected, and that business had to be free to organize its own services as appropriate. The strategic interventions of the public authorities were furthermore intended to encourage and support anticipated private investment. The city's role was to be facilitative, not directive.

Business promotion – 'boosterism' – has always been central to municipal activity, and so efforts at strategic planning are a logical extension of what has been done before. As such, it has a certain legitimacy. From a bourgeois perspective, the fundamental principle of legitimacy is that the bourgeoisie itself should make the major economic decisions, and that arrangements for planning should not interfere with this. In many places, such as Houston, the political institutions of the municipality are largely extensions of business organizations. Whether or not these institutions are used for strategic planning depends partly on economic requirements, partly on the internal politics of the business community, and partly on the perceived dangers of 'going public' with planning, and hence inviting other interests to intervene. If there is to be planning, the preference is clearly for a tame city council like Pittsburgh's, which – to the extent that it is not simply an organization of the bourgeoisie – plays a carefully circumscribed role in organizing collective consumption. The intervention of the social democrats, or any strong organization of subordinate groups, requires local business to set stiff terms for co-operation. It may profit considerably from playing the role of the reluctant bride.

When the Left Labour authorities in Britain began developing radical economic strategies after 1980, they soon encountered the effects of capital's reluctance to participate. Although the intent was to 'plan for labour' – that is, to mobilize the skills of the work-force in established industries to develop alternative economic strategies – relatively little was accomplished, because capital's own strategies involved disinvestment in the industries concerned.[23] Blocked by the central state, the local authorities found that they had few means of raising their own capital. More significantly, perhaps, they lacked the managerial expertise and the access to markets that the private capitalists had supplied. Partly because of the class antagonism they encountered among those who could supply business services, but more especially because they could not adapt to the space/time of global markets, the local authorities were unable to sustain a wider presence for the industries they were trying to support. Local interventions had instead highly localized effects, which made little difference to economic prospects in the communities concerned. As capitalist restructuring continued unabated, and the notion of planning for labour became more obviously illusory, support for alternative economic strategies faded.

In the last few years, the Labour authorities in Britain have been drifting back toward a strategy of 'planning for capital.'[24] This does not mean a return to Keynesianism so much as a shift toward organizing private business for strategic planning. Much has been made of the fact that the local authorities have been beaten into submission by the state itself, which under Conservative leadership has insisted on American-style co-operation with capital. However, the nonco-operation of capital has been at least as important in forcing the shift. Labour authorities have found themselves fussing at the fringes of economic decision-making, and have responded by trying to entrap business organizations in new, co-operative institutions for strategic planning. So far, they have had limited success at this: capitalists are not terribly interested in having local executive committees, and are even less interested in letting socialists organize them. The main effect of bourgeois resistance has been to discipline the Labour authorities, so that they are prepared to play a role acceptable to capital.

All this has occurred in a context in which national governments – including those controlled by social democrats – have increasingly disavowed their capacity to redistribute wealth. This means not only that particular social groups are being thrown back onto their own resources, but also that disadvantaged regions and localities are now expected to fend for themselves. Earlier socialist discourse challenged these limiting assumptions by putting the claims of capital at issue; notions of exploitation and unearned increment were used to undercut both the legitimacy of profits and the claims of the economically advantaged to differential returns. The distribution of wealth and income was posed as a matter for conscious social regulation. From such a perspective, it was the state rather than the market that had the primary distributive responsibility, and it was the redistributive effects of the market that had to be checked. However, this socialist counter-rhetoric has been pushed to the margins, so that there is little challenge, even from social democrats, to market regulation of the distribution of resources. As a consequence, progressive local authorities are caught in a vise that is as much ideological as fiscal.[25]

## Are There Any Alternatives?

The present interest in involving the bourgeoisie in new institutions for strategic planning at the local or regional level reflects the widespread recognition that states are incapable of controlling capital within a global economy. Cities or metropolitan regions have been identified as crucial organizational nodes – as spots from which strategic interventions can be made. The supposition is that capitalists have to make use of such nodes, and that particular spots can be rendered strategic by appropriate public action. Once companies have been enticed into these spaces, and involved in organizational networks that enmesh them with the public authorities, they will supposedly become subject to regulation. In this way the object of creating 'executive committees' for the bourgeoisie at the local level, and establishing a strong public presence on these committees, becomes quite enticing. The industrial region becomes a surrogate for the nation-state in the organizational thinking of social democracy.

Unfortunately, this reasoning reproduces the fallacies of state-centric politics, and simply shifts the centre of action from the nation to the region. What the present analysis reveals is that centricity is not a feature of capitalist organization, and that any hope of centring capital in order to control it must be in vain. An effective politics of resistance must mimic the principles of flexible specialization that give capitalist organization its strength and adaptability. A sense of this is apparent in Marx's focus on the labour movement, rather than the state, as the *other* that must organize itself against the bourgeoisie. Whatever the difficulties in his conception, it at least points to an understanding that sites the state within the field of struggle, rather than putting the field of struggle within the state. It also suggests that effective movements of resistance must be mounted within the space/time of capital, and not be trapped in the reified spaces that *appear* to contain capital but do not. If we have learned anything at all since Marx's time, it should be that neither states nor factories nor 'communities' can contain capital, but that these reified spaces are often effective in containing political resistances.

Marx insisted that it was impossible to draw blueprints for political organization. He looked instead at the concrete resistances of the working class, to get a sense of what had to be done and what could be done. If we were to do the same, our attention would be focused on the flexible specialization of contemporary social movements – movements that are global and local, universal and specific, fluid and solid. These movements involve networks of communication, modes of identity, and forms of action that defy established political containers and open up the prospects for more progressive politics. At their best, they defy fixation and act anywhere and everywhere in the global city. This creativity is perhaps best exemplified by contemporary environmentalism and feminism, but it is also apparent in the global movement of indigenous peoples, the international movement for human rights, north–south organizations for economic development, peace coalitions, and the transnational campaigns of organized labour. Significantly, many great cities and smaller urban communities have served as nodes of interaction among the movements, and this has meant that from time to time, it has been possible to use the instruments of municipal government to promote progressive causes. In turn, this has served to create continuing pressure from below for the democratization of the local state.

Since the nineteenth century, socialist politics has returned again and again to the ideal of the autonomous local community as a venue for action. From the Paris Commune to Red Vienna and the socialist municipalities of postwar Europe, this ideal has found halting expression in the activities of local governments. Postwar social democracy offered a chance to achieve socialism on a much wider scale. Although some of that promise has been realized, it seems clear that the present phase of capital accumulation on a global scale will make regulation and redistribution on a national basis more difficult. On the other hand, globalization is changing the meaning of local community, especially in the more prosperous parts of the world, such as Queensland. A politically significant *locality* at present is both a zone of intervention within a global process and a moment of meaning within a larger movement. It is a spot/moment at which people come together – as at Tienanmen Square or Sproule Hall – for action that may resonate far beyond. In the affairs of a global city like Brisbane, these significant sites/times appear and reappear as people recompose their political location. The spots/moments/locales at which people can act effectively are constantly changing.

In this context, the municipality is a particularly interesting venue for political action, precisely because it is inadequate for its ostensible purposes. On the one hand, it appears in the public consciousness as an organ of democratic self-government, one that enables people to take control of the conditions of their own lives. On the other hand, municipalities were obviously constituted to suit the purposes of a particular class, and they must fit into a global capitalist economy, a state with negative if not positive sovereignty, and a set of cultural practices that disadvantage women and minorities and that orient us toward exploitation of the natural environment. If a municipality is to be a site of political challenge, people have to treat these limits as something other than immovable fixtures. The recent trend in social-democratic or liberal politics has been in the opposite direction, toward the organization of hegemonic blocs around the fixtures of local capital. This is the logic of the 'gateway city.' The alternative is to pose the 'gates' as limits to be overcome or subverted. This is the logic of a progressive politics that flows from critical social movements.

Old ideas of the free city or the socialist state are of little value insofar as they vest our hopes in enclosure. Yet they also remind us that progressive politics has always depended on a certain separation – from capitalism certainly, but also from the practices we associate with statist bureaucracy, patriarchal domination, environmental degradation, and so on. Establishing that distance is a matter of creating fields for autonomous action on different principles, and of inserting ourselves in a time that is not governed by the clocks of modernity. Since a local action group must produce its own time and place, it can never be exactly when or where the authorities/analysts expect it to be. While this evanescence appears to be a weakness, it also reflects the strength that comes from the mobility of popular organization. The people who pose the most significant challenges to the existing order are not the ones who are locked into existing repertoires of action, and fix themselves to particular organizations. Rather, they are the ones who reach beyond the obvious possibilities.

In this century, there has been so much insistence on the powerlessness of the municipality that it is bold indeed for anyone to suggest that the limits upon it are there to be overcome. The resurgence of fascist politics in Europe and religious fundamentalisms elsewhere ought to be a reminder that hopelessness creates a dangerous political vacuum. The contemporary politics of social democracy is a politics of hopelessness, insofar as it is tied to the vain delusion that capitalists need socialists to organize their affairs for them. What should be obvious is that the bourgeoisie can look after themselves. The real task of a progressive politics is to tap into the needs of the marginalized, the excluded, and the oppressed, and to focus organizational efforts not on those who are already well organized but on those who are not. In this context, political maturity is measured not by the size of the gateway for capital, but by the creativity and fertility of local social movements.

# 7

# Municipal Socialism and Social Democracy

Marx may have anticipated the day when the state would be the focus of bourgeois politics, but he himself lived in an era of municipal activism. When we look back at the history of local government in the nineteenth century, we discover an extraordinary record of positive government.[1] National and imperial authorities may have been opening up world markets, developing and protecting new financial institutions, creating the legal forms for modern capitalist enterprise, and overseeing the development of national and international systems of transport and communications, but most of the rest of the work crucial to the development of modern capitalist societies was being done at the local level. Municipal authorities drained the new town sites, pumped in clean water from distant sources, laid out the streets, paved and lighted them, organized fire services, regulated local markets, organized public transit, brought in new public utilities such as gas supply, electricity, and telecommunications, controlled 'vice,' protected employees, guarded public and private property, controlled the spread of disease, fed and disciplined the poor, herded children into schools – indeed, developed in rudimentary form virtually all of the public services we associate with the twentieth-century welfare state. It was this practical and unadmitted 'socialism' that caught the eye of Sidney Webb and other Fabians.[2] It seemed to suggest that a wide range of public services and considerable public ownership were rational necessities in a modern industrial society. Notwithstanding the supposed separation between the state and civil society, local institutions – children's aid societies, street railway companies, and so on – straddled the boundary between the two. Often, they spilled over geographic boundaries as well. The proliferation of organizational forms reflected both the diversity of the new needs and the variety of leaderships that emerged to meet these needs. Although the state intervened periodically to standardize administrative arrangements or to require minimum standards of service, this intervention generally followed upon local initiatives. Most of the innovation occurred beyond the bounds of state regulation.

As Foucault and others have pointed out, this was the period in which modern disciplinary regimes took hold.[3] Public health, education, policing, accounting, traffic control, personnel management – one can name any number of disciplines that emerged, many of them within the broad framework of local government. Each discipline was characterized by its own discourse, standards of conduct and judgment, experts, and physical forms. Well-engineered streets, for instance, had to take a particular shape. So did schools, hospitals, mental asylums, and so on. These forms were both physical and social. To be effective, each discipline had to be internalized by the people involved in it: drivers and pedestrians had to use the streets in a certain way, children had to sit quietly and obey their teachers, patients had to accept the rules of the hospital.[4] Not only were ordinary people required to conform to these disciplines, but political leaders had to adapt to them as well. At the local level, much of the political struggle was between those who accepted the new disciplines and those who resisted them. As time went by, the new disciplines were widely internalized – partly because their efficacy became more apparent, but also because people came to understand them as normal. There was a gradual change of consciousness that led to a new sense of what it meant to be a civilized human being. This fit ill with the older notions of the peasantry and the aristocracy, but it seemed to suit bourgeois conceptions of propriety.

Municipal activity was disciplined by these conceptions, and increasingly constrained by the requirements of the state, which was in the process of asserting its sovereignty over the local authorities. Confronted with much evidence to the contrary – which suggested that local governments derived their authority from the customs of particular communities[5] – states generally claimed to be the founders of municipal government and the source of municipal authority. Throughout the British Empire and the United States, where the principle of local autonomy was supposed to be well respected, the courts struck down municipal initiatives that exceeded what the judges regarded as the proper bounds of municipal activity.[6] These bounds were defined by the statutes and regulations of the central government, and by the doctrines of private property and market freedom. The market economy imposed direct limits, insofar as it determined both the supply of resources to the municipality and the economic opportunities available to its inhabitants. A municipality could only afford to go so far against the logic of the market, before scaring away business or running up against frightening expenses. In any case, it had to respond to the demands of its own inhabitants to do what it could to promote their interests in the market. As the municipalities became enmeshed in the new social disciplines – partly as a result of the demands of the state and the market – they were required to conform to the practices of those disciplines. These practices privileged the knowledge of professionals and determined priorities not already given in the requirements of the state and the market.

The effect of this triple constraint – of the state, the market, and the new disciplinary regimes – was to put municipal politics in a space where the majority of people were bound to be frustrated if they attempted to act directly on their fundamental concerns. This was by no means accidental. Public officials, businessmen, and professionals generally could agree that ordinary people were a nuisance, and that decision-making had to be left to people who understood what was needed. Thus, the model of local democracy that came to be accepted in the late nineteenth century was similar to the one Mill adumbrated in his *Considerations on Representative Government*.[7] If there was to be universal suffrage, it was to be connected to a system of representative institutions that separated the government from the people, insulated a public service appointed on merit, and protected private property and civil liberties from undue government interference. All of this was at odds with the notions of mass democracy that had been expressed during the English and French revolutions, that were alive on the American frontier, and that appealed to the socialist movement emerging within the bosom of capitalism. Despite or because of the constraints implicit in the developing system of local administration, municipal politics became a venue for significant political insurgency in the late nineteenth century. Although the socialist movement ultimately came to be focused on the state, this orientation was strongly contested until the 1930s.[8] Marx's insistence that the state must be overcome, and replaced by a new form of political organization, reflected a more general conviction among nineteenth-century socialists. The anarchists were not alone in thinking that the working masses would have to develop a new form of self-government that broke down the old hierarchies, decentralized authority, and gave people effective control over their own lives in their own communities. Nor were the anarchists alone in believing that the mode of organization of the revolutionary working class should prefigure the organization of the new society, and that the revolution should thus begin with the people taking direct control of what most concerned them. The local community was necessarily a focus for democratic socialist action.[9]

The brief-lived Paris Commune of 1870 was for many a symbol – of the spirit of the working class, of the capacity of the workers to govern themselves democratically, and of the unfortunate vulnerability of any isolated revolutionary community to outside attack.[10] The commune posed the issue of socialist politics in a particular way, so that some could read the events of 1870 as proof that an insurrection could not succeed, others as an indication that such an insurrection had to be mounted on a wider scale. Some saw the potential of democratic communalism in the Parisian experience, others a demonstration of the limits of purely local action. Some were reoriented toward practical reforms, others toward building a mass movement. In any case, issues about the appropriate form and character of socialist politics were there to be resolved, and the question of municipal socialism had to be addressed. Could one, should one, focus one's politics on municipal action, and hope thereby to challenge the strictures of capitalism, the capitalist state, and the capitalist disciplines? Or was such a focus inappropriate, given the centralizing tendencies of the capitalist system? What kind of a political space did democratic socialists have to create?

In working out answers to these questions, turn-of-the-century socialists could not assume (as their successors did) that the world would be naturally divided into nation-states or that the states themselves would be convertible to socialist purposes. They had to take the question of political space seriously, and this meant, among other things, that they had to orient themselves to established traditions of municipal activism.

## The Rise of Municipal Socialism

Nineteenth-century municipal politics generally was characterized by civic boosterism of the kind so well described by Asa Briggs.[11] However, this boosterism was transected by various movements prompted by the appalling conditions of life in the industrial cities: the public health movement, the movement for public schools, the housing, settlement, and charity organization movements, the movements for professional policing and fire protection, the movement for the professionalization of the public service, and so on.[12] For the most part, these were bourgeois movements, but they were given impetus by fears of proletarian insurrection. There were, in any case, a variety of proletarian 'self-help' movements, including benefit societies, co-operatives, dame schools, unions, and political parties.[13] By the end of the nineteenth century, socialist or labour parties had become the dominant working-class political organizations in most of the advanced industrial countries. Many of these organizations began to put candidates forward in municipal elections. Although there were a few notable successes before the First World War, it was not until the 1920s and 1930s that major European cities came under socialist control. It was then, especially in Vienna, that the practical model of a socialist city began to appear.[14]

What was manifest in places like Vienna and Sheffield – the latter being the first major English city to come under socialist control, in 1926[15] – was a drive to create a society on different principles, within the bosom of capitalism. This involved a shift from private, market-mediated consumption, to various forms of collective consumption, mediated by a local authority that was ostensibly under workers' control. Workers in a socialist city could live in public housing, ride public transit, rely on public utilities for water, power, lighting, and telecommunications, send their children to public schools, get health care at public hospitals and clinics, go to the public swimming baths, recreation centres, parks, and theatres, eat at public restaurants, and depend on public pensions and other benefits for people with inadequate incomes. At the same time, workers could look to the local authority for employment in these various works and services. The local authority, moreover, could provide a framework within which workers could participate in planning and developing their own community. The unions and the workers' party would cement the connections between ordinary working people and the authority itself. Where socialist local administrations managed to stay in power for more than a few years, a different way of life was established for hundreds of thousands of working people. It was a way of life largely insulated from the capitalist economy.[16] Working people did not have to go out onto the market to satisfy their basic needs: they looked to the local authority for education, employment, housing, transportation, utilities, health care, and recreation – and for the means for buying the few things they needed that were available only on the market. It was precisely the isolation of a large section of the British working class from the market that provoked Margaret Thatcher's rage in the 1980s. Reintegrating these people into capitalist society meant smashing the power of the local authorities that had been providing for an alternative way of life.

One of the earliest formulations of municipal socialism was Paul Brousse's Municipal Program of November 1880.[17] Brousse, who had been active in both the First International and subsequent anarchist organizations, was the most influential figure in the nascent French socialist party. The Municipal Program was intended not only as a platform for the upcoming municipal elections in Paris, but as an example of a 'possibilist' approach to socialist action. Despite the factional conflicts that led to a vigorous repudiation of possibilism by the Marxists, many of the ideas and practices articulated by Brousse anticipated the reformist socialism of the Second International. As David Stafford observes: 'The emphasis in anarchist doctrine on the need for action outside the framework of the State and within the framework of the local Commune provided the essential groundwork for Brousse's later reformist and municipal socialism.'[18] The Paris Commune exemplified, for Brousse and others in the First International, the revolutionary organization of the proletariat. As Marx himself emphasized, this form was profoundly democratic, egalitarian, and federalist: the commune, not the nation-state, was the primary political unit.[19] In the dark days following the suppression of the commune, Brousse identified himself with the anarchist faction in the International, which resisted Marxist efforts to impose a single program and a centralized organization on the workers' movement. Like Malatesta and Bakunin, Brousse insisted on the need for action, which in the circumstances involved 'propaganda by the deed.' In the 1870s, he, like they, understood this in terms of individual blows against the state. But as the inefficacy of such gestures became clear, and the conditions for peaceful organization of the workers in France improved, Brousse drifted toward a more programmatic or reformist interpretation of propaganda by the deed.

In the anarchist view, the workers' movement had to prefigure socialist society in its practices and mode of organization. This meant that it had to follow the federative principles Proudhon had earlier articulated.

The corner-stone of this desirable future socialist society was to be *contract*, as Proudhon meant it – the source of obligation. The society was to be federal, structured around the autonomy of the individual, the autonomy of the Commune and the autonomy of the trade or industrial grouping ('la corporation'). These three units – the individual, the Commune, the corporation, represented *economic* realities; the worker, the unit of consumption, the unit of production, respectively. Thus, a *practical* socialism, a socialism 'conforme aux principes de la sociologie,' rejecting the abstract bourgeois concepts of the individual and majority will, would emerge.[20]

Within the International, and later within the reorganized French socialist party, Brousse and his allies pressed for a mode of organization and a corresponding doctrinal formulation that would give scope for localized action. Increasingly, they saw such action in electoralist terms. Localism made sense, not only because it prefigured the socialist society, but also because it took advantage of the geographically uneven development of capitalist society. Working-class majorities in the more industrially and politically advanced cities could carry parts of the socialist program into effect and this would provide examples to be imitated by workers elsewhere. If the reactionaries forced a violent struggle upon the workers, the latter would be prepared for the struggle as a result of their municipal experience.

The actual program Brousse formulated for Paris in 1880 involved demands for the following:

- *Communal self-government.* This was to include control of the police, the administration of justice, and the local armed forces, as well as the right to enter into joint arrangements with other communes.
- *Democratization of the commune.* This was to include extension of the franchise to women, payment of councillors, open meetings, rights of recall for nominating committees, provisions for referenda on important questions such as the local budget, election of key administrative officials, replacement of the magisterial courts by popular juries and bodies for arbitration, and replacement of the police by a popular guard.
- *Public enterprise.* Big private companies would be transformed into public utilities that provided services (including gas, coal, and public transit) for free or at cost. New municipal industries would be formed to provide work and enlarge the public sector. Municipal facilities, including bakeries and slaughterhouses, would be established to compete with the speculators and profiteers.
- *Services to workers.* There would be free public education until the age of twenty-one; legislation on employment conditions; aid to co-operatives; and support for workers on strike.
- *Redistributive taxation.* A highly progressive income tax and a confiscatory inheritance tax would be enacted.

Although this was put forward as a program for immediate action, it clearly involved a major shift of authority from the state to the communes.

In the event, socialists elected to municipal councils – Brousse among them – focused on the reforms that could be achieved within the existing framework of the state. It was not in France but in Britain, Germany, and the United States that 'municipal socialism' within capitalist states became most advanced. In Britain, such activity was associated with the Birmingham Radicals of the 1870s and the London Progressives of the 1890s. In his famous contribution to *The Fabian Essays*, Sidney Webb suggested that the continuing expansion of government activity, under the aegis of staunch capitalists like Joseph Chamberlain, was a sign of an inexorable modern drift toward socialism.

> Socialists are only advocating the conscious adoption of a principle of social organization which the world has already found to be the inevitable outcome of Democracy and the Industrial Revolution. For Socialism is by this time a wave surging throughout all Europe . . .
>
> The general failure to realize the extent to which our unconscious Socialism has already proceeded – a failure which causes much time and labor to be wasted in uttering and elaborating on paper the most ludicrously unpractical anti-socialist demonstrations of the impossibility of matters of daily occurrence – is due to the fact that few know anything of local administration outside their own town. It is the municipalities which have done most to 'socialize' our industrial life; and the municipal history of the century is yet unwritten.[21]

Webb identified socialism with the extension of the public sector, and saw the advance of socialism in terms of the permeation of capitalist government with socialist ideas. He and other Fabian socialists associated themselves with the Liberal-dominated Progressives, who won control of the London County Council when it was established in 1889 and stayed in power until 1907.

The first socialist program for London actually was formulated in 1887, by the Marxist H.S. Hyndman of the Social Democratic Federation, in the pamphlet *A Commune for London*.

> In addition to the municipalisation of essential services, gas, water, lighting, trams, parks, poor relief, markets 'and (within limits) education', which had been advocated by James Firth in his *Municipal London* of 1876, Hyndman suggested housing rented at cost rates, free education and the feeding of schoolchildren, municipal supply at cost price of bread, meat and vegetables, the useful

organisation of unemployed labour and a policy of fair wages and reduced hours for council employees.[22]

Eleven years later, an SDF-led Labour Party won control of the West Ham Borough Council in East London. Its program was inevitably more modest, but it pointed in the direction Hyndman had indicated.

The first priority was taken to be the slum housing. More sanitary inspectors were appointed, and a house to house inspection carried out for the first time; although opponents claimed 'in their zeal to exterminate the insanitary landlord, the socialists persist in ignoring the insanitary tenant'. Two new baths and wash-houses were built. Plans were made for 500 council houses, houses for widows and widowers, and municipal lodging houses, known as workmen's hotels. The Council applied for a loan to build 300 further houses when these were finished. A works department was created and given a large initial contract to build a hospital. The local libraries were opened on Sundays, and more branches proposed. More music was provided in the parks, and free winter concerts started. An unemployed register was opened, and the men put to work planting trees. Council employees were given an eight hour day, a 30/- minimum wage, Mayday and a fortnight's holiday. Scholarships to the Technical Institute were founded. Negotiations were opened for the purchase of the local gas and water supply, and tramways. Municipal laundries, dispensaries and insurance were proposed.[23]

In 1903, Labour won power in Woolwich, and followed a similar program until its defeat in 1906.

Among those who were impressed by municipal socialism in Britain was Eduard Bernstein, the German Marxist who became the chief spokesman for 'revisionism' after his book *Evolutionary Socialism* was published in 1899. Bernstein spoke admiringly of the Fabians and their gradualist strategy. He tried to show that Marxist suspicion of municipal socialism – rooted in a hostility to Proudhon's federalism and to all schemes of *petit bourgeois* reform – was at odds with Marx's own praise for the Paris Commune and with the complex requirements of a socialist society. As he said, 'There is not the least doubt (and it has been proved many times practically) that the general development of modern society is along the line of a constant increase of the duties of the municipalities and the extension of municipal freedom, that the municipality will be an ever more important lever of social emancipation.'[24]

Bernstein noted that the Germans had been behind in developing municipal socialist programs, because of the absence of universal suffrage at the local level in Germany. Achieving such a suffrage was, for Bernstein, a paramount objective. Upon its achievement, he thought there should then be (a) an extension of the municipal power of expropriation (not to involve confiscation), (b) an expansion of municipal enterprise, to include all natural monopolies of a local character, (c) an expansion of municipal services (in ways he left undefined), and (d) a pro-labour policy, which would involve union recognition and payment of union rates, the creation of labour bureaux, and the involvement of the municipalities with the trade unions in creating suitable systems of social insurance.

Among Britons and Americans, Germany gradually acquired a reputation for a type of municipal socialism that was derived not from the activities of the Social Democratic Party (SPD), but rather from the ventures of bourgeois authorities that were even bolder than those of their Liberal counterparts in Britain. As the American reformer, Frederic C. Howe, noted of Düsseldorf in 1913:

> The city owns more things and does more things for its people than any city I know. Municipal socialism has been carried far beyond the suggestions of the most radical in this country [the U.S.A.], and it has been done with the approval of all classes. Yet the city is not governed by socialists; it is governed by business men who elect the council, choose the burgomaster and the magistrat, and make the public opinion which approves of these things.[25]

The activist German cities not only took over the 'natural monopolies,' including gas, water, electric supply, and public transportation (street railways), but they also ventured into some unusual commercial activities. Düsseldorf, for instance, operated restaurants, a wine business, and an industrial undertaking – without much worry, apparently, about intruding in activities reserved for private business. The German municipalities had vast landholdings, and generally attempted to buy up land on their outskirts, in anticipation of future expansion. With these landholdings, they were able to secure control over the pattern of urban development – to locate public facilities in advance in accordance with their own plans, to control subdivision, to regulate private development, to tax unearned increments of land values, and so on. They also provided a variety of social services, which were familiar enough elsewhere: hospitals, sanatoria, convalescent and maternity homes, and orphanages; poor relief; and public health services and regulations. They intervened in the labour market by establishing model employment practices and forming labour exchanges. They encouraged working-class savings through municipal banks. They supplemented the mortgage market by establishing their own mortgage-lending institutions, and a few of them began their own public housing programs. Finally, they provided an array of cultural facilities – public gardens, museums, theatres, baths, galleries, concerts, and so on – that were the envy of visiting Americans. What impressed Howe and others was the German willingness to do whatever seemed needful to improve the life of the community, without fear that this would undermine private enterprise.[26]

As noted, the German SPD took little part in these municipal socialist initiatives. An 1888 resolution of the party had declared that municipal politics involved efforts'quite disproportionate to the advantages.' Orthodox Marxists were leery of a strategy that seemed to offer false hopes of a gradual transition to socialism. As Engels wrote to Sorge in 1893:

> The Fabians here in London are a band of careerists who have understanding enough to realise the inevitability of the social revolution, but who could not possibly entrust this gigantic task to the raw proletariat alone and are therefore kind enough to set themselves at its head. Fear of the revolution is their fundamental principle. They are 'eddicated' *par excellence*. Their socialism is municipal socialism; not the nation but the *community* is to become the owner of the means of production, at any rate for the time being. This socialism of theirs is then represented as an extreme but inevitable consequence of bourgeois liberalism; hence their tactics of not decisively opposing the Liberals.[27]

In the orthodox Marxist view, British Fabianism, French possibilism, and German revisionism all pointed toward reformism: that is, toward a political strategy that either postponed the socialist revolution indefinitely or denied its necessity altogether.

It seemed clear to Marx and Engels that a national revolution would be required to break capitalist power, and that the focus on merely local activity could be diversionary. Lenin advanced this argument strongly in 1907, when he criticized proposals to substitute municipalization for nationalization as a goal of the Russian social democrats: 'Municipalisation is a reactionary slogan, which idealises the medieval isolation of the regions, and dulls the peasantry's consciousness of the need for a centralised agrarian revolution.'[28] The idea of the municipalizers had been to make the peasants proprietors of their own plots, and to turn the remainder of the land – the great estates – over to the municipalities or communes, which would be controlled more directly than the state by the peasants themselves. Advocates suggested that this decentralization of land ownership would provide a bulwark against reaction. Lenin ridiculed this claim.

It is not a question of protecting the local regional self-governing bodies from the encroachments of the central government by means of paper resolutions; that cannot be done either with paper, or even with guns; for the trend of capitalist development is towards centralisation, towards the concentration of such a force in the hands of the central bourgeois government as the 'regions' *will never be able* to stand up against. The point is that *one and the same class* should have political power both centrally and locally, that democracy should be quite consistently applied in both cases to an absolutely equal *degree*, a degree sufficient to ensure the *complete supremacy* of, let us say, the majority of the population, i.e., the peasantry. That alone can serve as a *real guarantee* against 'excessive' encroachments of the centre, against infringements of the 'lawful rights' of the regions.[29]

Thus, for Lenin, it was clear that the land had to be nationalized – the power of the landlords broken completely – before it could be redistributed among the peasants and the communes. The municipalizers, like Proudhon before them, ignored the dynamics of capitalism and the power of the central state, and romanticized the capacity of the peasantry and the *petit bourgeois* generally to sustain their way of life in the face of the pressures upon them. The power of capitalism/the state had to be broken at its centre.

'Municipalisation' from this angle, regarded as a means of 'securing' something for the regions against the central authority, is sheer philistine nonsense. If that can be called a 'fight' against the centralised bourgeois authority, it is the sort of 'fight' that the *anti-Semites* are waging against capitalism, that is, the same extravagant promises, which attract the dull and ignorant masses and *the same economic and political impossibility of fulfilling* these promises.[30]

The proponents of municipalization looked to the West for examples of socialist action at the local level. Lenin pointed out that the possibilities for such action were extremely limited, and he condemned as opportunist the shift of attention among some Western socialists from the centre to the municipalities.

The bourgeois intelligentsia of the West, like the English Fabians, elevate municipal socialism to a special 'trend' precisely because it dreams of social peace, of class conciliation, and seeks to divert public attention away from the fundamental question of the economic system as a whole, to minor questions of *local self-government*. In the sphere of question in the first category, the class antagonisms stand out most sharply; that is in the sphere which, as we have shown, affects the very foundations of the class rule of the bourgeoisie. Hence it is in that sphere that the philistine, reactionary utopia of bringing about socialism piecemeal is particularly hopeless. Attention is diverted to the sphere of minor local question, being directed not to the question of the class rule of the bourgeoisie, nor to the question of the chief instruments of that rule, but to the question of distributing the *crumbs* thrown by the rich bourgeoisie for the '*needs of the population*.'[31]

Since the bourgeoisie already recognized the need for public health measures, working-class education, and so on, class struggle hardly arose – as was evident in the gradual spread of public utilities.

The philistine opportunism of that 'trend' lies in the fact that people forget the narrow limits of so-called 'municipal socialism' (in reality, municipal capitalism, as the English Social-Democrats properly point out in their controversies with the Fabians) ... It does not need more than a slight acquaintance with 'municipal socialism' in the West to know that any attempt on the part of *socialist* municipalities to go a little beyond the boundaries of their normal, i.e., minor, petty activities, which give no substantial relief to the workers, any attempt to meddle with *capital*, is invariably vetoed in the most emphatic manner by the central authorities of the bourgeois state.[32]

For Lenin, the great danger of 'municipal socialism' was that it would blunt the class struggle by diverting attention from the foundations of class rule and fostering the illusion that capitalism could be transformed by gradual measures.

However, Lenin implied that there was a form of socialist practice in municipal affairs that could transcend municipal socialism.

'Municipal socialism' means socialism in matters of *local government*. Anything that goes beyond the limits of *local* interests, beyond the limits of state *administration*, i.e., anything that affects the main sources of revenue of the ruling classes and the principal means of securing their rule, anything that affects not the administration of the state, but the *structure* of the state, *thereby* goes beyond the sphere of 'municipal socialism.'[33]

Thus, the main issue was whether one could make of the municipality a venue for the broader class struggle. Could one mobilize the workers in this context, in ways that enhanced their revolutionary consciousness? Could one actually use the municipalities against the state? These became issues of more practical consequence after the Bolshevik Revolution in Russia, as socialists searched for modes of action that would bring about fundamental changes in other countries. In the 1920s, London and Vienna proved to be especially important venues for a municipal socialism that pointed beyond itself in the ways that Lenin demanded. What was at stake, among other things, was the possibility of a revolutionary socialism that did not take its models from the Bolsheviks.

**From London to Vienna and Back**

As John Foster has pointed out, local authorities in certain areas of nineteenth-century Britain came under working-class control, and their powers were used in struggles against the capitalists, the land-owners, and the state itself.[34] In a sense, these struggles were ineffectual, since the workers were ultimately overwhelmed by the powers they faced. Even so, they were important in the development of working-class organization and consciousness. In twentieth-century Britain, especially after the First World War, local authorities were used in a similar way. Until 1919, franchise limitations had greatly limited the political advances of working-class organizations, so that experiences in places like Woolwich and West Ham were highly exceptional. But after the First World War, the reorganized and newly unified Labour Party made extraordinary advances, in municipal as well as national politics. Labour won control of 12 of the 28 London boroughs in that year, and became the largest party in two others. This created opportunities, not only for reformist activity but also for working-class mobilization 'in and against the state.' The London Borough of Poplar, under George Lansbury's leadership, came to symbolize the latter form of struggle.[35]

Poplar, an East End London borough in what is now called the Docklands, had an overwhelmingly working-class population of about 165,000. Within a year after the franchise was broadened in 1918, Labour won solid majorities on both the Board of Guardians (which dispensed poor relief) and the Borough Council. Under Lansbury's leadership, the Poplar Labourites pursued a tough working-class policy. First, they established relief rates on the basis of 'need' rather than on the Victorian principles of 'less eligibility.' Especially after 1920, when money wages began to decline, Poplar's relief rates for men with big families were well above the average wage rates for workmen. The guardians also ignored the Victorian idea that relief should normally be provided 'indoors' – that is, in a workhouse – and offered 'outdoor' relief as a matter of principle. Second, Poplar established a high minimum wage for its own workers, and offered it to men and women alike. When the wage was first set in 1920, it was near the prevailing rate for men, but well above the prevailing rate for women. As money wages declined in the next few years, Poplar kept deliberately to the old rate, in the hope of stiffening working-class resistance to capitalist pressure. Third, Poplar, like some other Labour authorities, provided relief to strikers during trade disputes. This policy was followed, for instance, during the unofficial dock strike of 1923. Fourth, and perhaps most significantly, Poplar pursued all these policies by evasion and outright defiance of the law. It routinely labelled as 'exceptional' the circumstances of anyone applying for relief, so that relief could be offered 'outdoors.' When it found it could not sustain its policies without imposing an inordinate burden on the ratepayers, it began appropriating for its own purposes money that was owing to the metropolitan authorities. When ordered to reverse this policy, the Poplar councillors refused, and went to prison instead. When released from prison, they continued their policies with little modification. In the succeeding years, they pursued a kind of guerrilla war against the government and the courts, as they ignored or evaded ministerial directives and policies.

The Labour leaders in Poplar were not following any well-developed plan. Nevertheless, their actions involved a class strategy that transcended the limits of reformist municipal socialism. The Poplarites treated both the Borough Council and the Board of Guardians as institutions belonging to the working class, whose powers could be used quite rightfully in the class struggle. Other institutions of the state – including Parliament and Cabinet, the courts and the district auditor, the London County Council and the Metropolitan Police – were regarded as agencies of the ruling, capitalist class, whose directives lacked moral authority. Representatives of the working class in institutions under working-class control – including the Board of Guardians and the Borough Council in Poplar – had, it was thought, a duty to use their positions to advance the interests of the working class, and to resist the pressures of both the capitalists and the state the capitalists controlled. Thus, the Poplarites saw their policies on relief and wages as means to resist downward pressure on wages and to establish alternative principles for distribution in society (for example, equal pay for work of equal value, and relief for the unemployed at levels determined by need rather by than market conditions). The hope was that other authorities under working-class control would follow Poplar's lead – as, indeed, a few did: Bethnal Green on wages; Bethnal Green, Stepney, Bermondsey, West Ham, Chester-le-Street, and Bedwellty on different aspects of poor relief – and that this would strengthen the working class (which was also struggling on the industrial front) in its efforts to resist the capitalist offensive of the 1920s. In this context, evasion or defiance of the law was regarded as morally legitimate, especially when it was sanctioned by popular vote. In Poplar during this period, the electors returned their defiant councillors and guardians without fail, and so strengthened their resolve to resist.

Successive governments found it extraordinarily difficult to bring Poplar to heal. The threat of 'surcharges' on individual councillors or guardians was ineffectual, because the people concerned had virtually no assets anyway. On the one occasion when Poplar's leaders were imprisoned – in 1921, for defying a court order to pay Poplar's precept to the London County Council – the government suffered considerable embarrassment. The people of Poplar rallied round their leaders as heroes and martyrs. Local government in the borough was threatened with collapse because its leaders were in prison. Without new legislation, the government could not disqualify the imprisoned councillors. In any case, new elections would probably have led to their replacement by an equally defiant group. Direct rule would also have required new legislation, and in any case would have threatened the government with direct resistance to its rule. In the circumstances, it proved easier throughout the 1920s for successive governments to temporize with Poplarism.

Poplar was in some ways an embarrassment, yet it was also a political asset for successive Conservative governments. The spectre of tough working-class resistance might be appealing in Poplar and other working-class communities, but it was frightening to the middle class. It involved fundamental threats to law and order, the rights of property, and existing class relations. It evoked the spectre of Bolshevism. Thus, it was an embarrassment to a Labour Party that was intent on reassuring the middle classes. The Conservatives exploited this and made considerable propaganda out of the dangers of Poplarite lawlessness. This seems to have helped them reverse Labour's local election successes of 1919 three years later. Labour lost all but four of the metropolitan boroughs that it had controlled, and this electoral defeat – although worst in areas that had not followed Poplar's lead – reinforced the determination of the national Labour Party leadership to distance itself from Poplarism. In turn, that determination – reflected in the views of most local Labour Parties in London – found expression in anti-Poplarite policies on the part of most of the other boroughs under Labour influence. In the end, the Conservatives introduced legislative changes that enabled them to deal more effectively with the Poplarite resistance. Responsibility for poor relief was transferred from the local boards to the County Councils, the majority of which were under reliable Conservative or Liberal control. Another act provided for local councillors to be disqualified from office for five years if they were found to be responsible for making illegal expenditures – which the courts had defined to include unreasonably high wages. Thus, 'unreasonable' socialist councillors could be removed and penalized by a judicial process that would not implicate the government of the day directly. Further legislation allowed the minister to suspend a recalcitrant council and rule directly through commissioners: this power was invoked against several Boards of Guardians before their functions were transferred to the more reliable County Councils.

The great opponent of Poplarism within the Labour Party was Herbert Morrison, then Secretary of the London Labour Party (est. 1915) and Mayor of the borough of Hackney. He denounced the 'spendthrift illegality' of the Poplar leaders, because he feared the effects of government reprisals and thought that Poplar was setting an unfortunate example for Tory authorities who might want to resist a future Labour government. He saw the value of action at the local level mainly in terms of the extension of public services and enterprises – both for their own sake, and for their demonstration effects. Morrison wanted to show potential Labour supporters – especially among the middle class – that the party had the capacity to govern, and that its policies made sense. He was mainly responsible for the Party's 1922 London manifesto, which set forth a bold plan of positive government.

> Under Labour the LCC [London County Council] would undertake a large program of house building at low rents, and seek to create a regional plan for building new towns on garden city lines in the home counties. All London passenger transport facilities would be owned and operated by the LCC which would also take over gas, electricity and water supplies, and coal, bread, fish, meat and milk supplies, slaughter houses and markets, and set up a bank. There would be no

poverty bar on an able child receiving a good education, for higher grants would be paid. The LCC would be a model employer, adopting trade union conditions for its employees and for those of its contractors, who in any case were to be eliminated wherever practicable. Finally the health services of London were to be improved; municipal management and control of a wide range of medical and welfare services were to replace provisions through the Poor Law.[36]

Although Labour was soundly rejected in 1922, Morrison led them to victory in the 1934 county elections, introducing thirty years of unbroken rule at that level. Under his leadership in the late 1930s, the LCC made vigorous efforts to improve and extend public services – clearing slums and building houses, improving and liberalizing public assistance to the poor, extending school health services, building more parks and offering fuller recreational services, constructing new schools and facilitating working-class entrance to them, increasing funding for the hospitals and other health and welfare services, improving the roads and drains, establishing a 'green belt,' intensifying town planning, and – as war approached – upgrading civil defence provisions. However, the distinctively 'socialist' measures of the 1922 program – setting up a bank, taking over food supplies, and so on – were quietly forgotten.

To a significant extent, Labour's program for London was inspired by the activities of the socialists in Vienna. Morrison, like other socialists who were looking for a practical alternative to Bolshevism, turned to Vienna for an example of what could be done even without control of a national government. The Austrian Social Democratic Party (SPAD) had emerged from the First World War as the strongest single force in the German remnant of the Austro-Hungarian Empire.[37] Liberals and conservatives rallied to its side, in the hope that SPAD leaders could impose order on the workers' and soldiers' councils springing up across the country. Elsewhere, as in neighbouring Hungary and Bavaria, such councils had provided the basis for short-lived revolutionary dictatorships. The Austrian socialists refused to follow this Bolshevik direction, but unlike their German counterparts, they also refused to mobilize the forces of the Right against the workers' councils. Instead, they won the councils' support for the establishment of a new Austrian Republic. At first it appeared that the socialists might well win a majority in the country as a whole, but the elections of February 1919 made it clear that the conservatives were firmly entrenched outside the Vienna region. Although the SPAD dominated the first Republican government and made some moves toward socialism, support for its agenda rapidly evaporated as the threat of revolution diminished. A reorganized conservative coalition took power in June 1920 and forced the SPAD back into its Viennese bastion.

That bastion was formidable. The SPAD had won a majority of seats on Vienna's council in May 1919; in so doing it became the first socialist party in a liberal democratic state to govern a city of more than one million people. It went from success to success in subsequent years, raising its share of the popular vote to two-thirds in 1923. But the extent of the popular mobilization went much further.

By 1924 the city of Vienna, which had 1.8 million residents, had 266,415 Socialist party members, one of every five adults ...

The Socialists created their own 'public sphere,' maintaining active organizations in each of Vienna's twenty-one districts, which were broken down into sections for electoral work, and into house and street associations. Party publications, including the daily *Arbeiter-Zeitung*, the hundreds of *Vereine* encompassing all possible free-time activities, party clubs and taverns provided a constant level of activity and support for party members.[38]

The socialists even had their own army – the *Schutzbund* – which had been formed in 1923 as a bulwark against the new right-wing militias. Until 1927 at least, the *Schutzbund* was probably the strongest military force in the country, and gave the socialists confidence that they could defend themselves against rightist aggression. Fears of such aggression increased as proto-fascist movements gained strength in the countryside, where the conservative national government found most of its support. Thus, the Viennese socialists appeared to be ready to defend their revolutionary gains as necessary.

Vienna was both a province and a municipality. As such, and in consequence of Germanic legal traditions that allowed municipalities to do whatever was not specifically forbidden, the city government was able to move with considerable freedom, especially before 1930.

The most significant and symbolic achievement of the party was the construction of Socialist housing for workers, sorely needed as a result of the housing shortage that had existed since before the war. The ambitious new housing program was financed by a 'housing construction tax' levied against luxury rents, imposed in 1923 as part of the radical redistributive fiscal program created by the city's Socialist finance minister, Hugo Breitner ... By the end of 1933 the city had built more than 61,175 new apartments, mostly in the form of large housing blocks, the *Wiener Hofe*, with parks, swimming areas, schools, kindergartens, gymnasia, health facilities, and community centers.[39]

The great housing blocks looked like military bastions for the *Schutzbund* – as indeed they were. More importantly for the party, they were supposed to be milieux for the development of a new socialist culture, in which workers would share equally in the means of consumption and engage in cultural and educational activities that would contribute to the social environment of their *Bildung*.

The SPAD – like the prewar German SPD – was distinguished by its vigorous and innovative pursuit of cultural politics.[40] For the party's Marxist leadership, this was an extension of class struggle by other means, and it reflected the fact that the Austrian party had maintained its unity despite splits that in other countries had made moderate leaders suspicious of communist agitation. The aim of the SPAD was to form a working class that was capable of taking power and creating a socialist society. This meant that the workers had to learn to live as socialists – as in the *Wiener Höfe*. It also meant that they had to appropriate the best of bourgeois culture, and re-frame it in democratic terms.

> The designers of the new Vienna ... completely renovated the educational system, abolishing the old hierarchical class divisions (*Einheitsschule*), eliminating corporal punishment, democratizing the administration, and introducing widespread changes in educational structure and pedagogy to stress the formation of democratic values, experimentation, and the promotion of social mobility without regard for class or sex. Moreover, the municipality introduced an extensive program of adult education that supplemented the party libraries, bookstores, and 'Bildungs-commissions' that were set up in all Vienna districts.[41]

All these changes – and the new forms of living in the *Wiener Höfe* – were in aid of a cultural revolution that would be a prelude to socialism. The SPAD took heart from its growing support in the Vienna region, which could be attributed partly to these cultural policies. Although the party made little electoral progress outside the Vienna region, its growing strength in the capital boosted its share of the national vote from 34 percent in 1919 to more than 41 percent in 1930.

Much of what happened in Vienna actually flowed from the traditions of municipal interventionism that made even conservative German cities seemed 'socialistic' to foreigners. Tight planning controls, vigorous development of public utilities, and the provision of many health, educational, and welfare services were common enough. The Viennese socialists really distinguished themselves by imposing strongly redistributive taxation, and by taking almost complete control over the housing industry. This strong intervention in the sphere of consumption was not matched by comparable initiatives in the sphere of production. The SPAD shared the Bolshevik assumption that action in the latter sphere required national power. On the other hand, revolutionary cultural policies could be pursued locally. Unfortunately, the SPAD had a rather paternalistic, almost repressive approach to working-class culture.[42] There was an exaltation of classical bourgeois forms as a model of being, and the communitarian life of the *Wiener Höfe* was organized around patriarchal nuclear families. The bourgeois proprieties were carefully policed in this communal setting, and those who failed to abide by them could lose their homes or their children, or both. Not surprisingly, 'municipal socialism was often viewed as regimentation from the top.'[43] As one critic observes:

> In both political and cultural work, [SPAD] party leaders assumed a tutelary attitude toward the workers. They assumed the mission of bringing about socialism through political means (electoral politics) and when these lines were blocked, they turned to the cultural realm. But in neither case were they concerned with fostering the kind of self-consciousness that would have led to self-direction and creativity from below. That would have required a kind of familiarity with and sensitivity to the actual lives of workers which the leaders, despite their sympathies for 'the proletarian condition,' were incapable of. In both cases, the rank and file was relegated to the role of consumers of party programs and shut out from their creation or management.[44]

This suspicion of the rank and file seems to have contributed to the ultimate demise of the Viennese socialists. Party leaders were firm in their commitment to the republic and its legalities – so firm, in fact, that they refused to mobilize the *Schutzbund* against the fascists until it was too late. The turning point came in 1927, when the conservative national government turned its guns on Viennese workers demonstrating against an abuse of legal process. Out of respect for the law, the SPAD kept its own, superior forces in check. The right-wing militias and the government itself interpreted this as a sign of socialist weakness. By 1932, when Engelbert Dollfuss staged a *coup d'état*, the balance of forces had shifted decisively against the socialists. Thus, when the *Schutzbund* was finally provoked into action in February 1934, it was easily destroyed. The three-day civil war ended with the surrender of the Karl-Marx Hof, the most famous of the socialist housing complexes. The Dollfuss regime moved quickly to take over the government of Vienna and disband the SPAD. Four years later, when Hitler's soldiers arrived, 'Red Vienna' was already just a memory and the world was presented with chilling pictures of people lining the streets to cheer their Nazi 'liberators.'

This was the context in which Morrison and the other Labourites had to consider the options for a more lasting municipal socialism. Perhaps it is not surprising that they chose to tuck themselves safely into the bosom of the liberal-democratic state.

**Welfare States**

For the Bolsheviks, the collapse of the socialists' bastion in Vienna was the final proof that the 'third way' of the Austro-Marxists could lead only to defeat.[45] The Austrian socialists had refused the opportunity for revolution in 1919 and showed the same timidity in the face of fascism. They had tried to create a socialist city in a capitalist state, in the vain hope that their opponents would allow them to continue their 'experiment' until the whole country had been won over to the socialist idea. Instead, the conservatives had isolated the socialists in their vaunted municipality, gathering their strength in the rest of the country. When they were ready, the conservatives threw off the mantle of bourgeois legality and destroyed Red Vienna. Surely, claimed the communists, this was proof that a purely municipal socialism could not work – that socialists had to be prepared to smash the bourgeois state and constitute their own national regime. Ironically, on the latter point, the social democrats of the West could agree. Stalin, despite or because of his brutality, seemed to have succeeded in establishing a sort of socialism in one country, with state ownership of the means of production and a planned economy. At the same time, the Swedish social democrats – in power nationally from 1932 – were having obvious success with 'state regulated economic planning' along the lines later identified with Keynesianism. Austrian cultural politics might or might not have had promise. What was clear was the popularity and practicality of public action to provide housing, education, health care, social services, and an array of public utilities such as water and power supply and local transit. From a social democratic perspective, the failure of Red Vienna was not a failure of reformist socialism but of its purely municipal variant. For the Labour Party in Britain – and for Herbert Morrison, now a senior minister in

Britain's first majority Labour government – municipal experience seemed only a preparation for the real thing. A national government could make a reality of the welfare state and the planned economy.

The political orthodoxy that emerged in the West after 1945 was profoundly statist, not only in the sense that it posited a role for government that seemed to put the supremacy of the market at risk, but also in the sense that it focused political attention on the possibilities for national or parliamentary action. There was a consensus across the political spectrum that the important decisions had to be made at the centre, and that this centre was constituted by the nation-state. On the left, this meant that interest in localized action tended to fade in favour of a politics of national legislation. The American New Deal, Sweden's Third Way, and Britain's experiment with Labour all seemed to suggest that significant social change could be achieved by a determined national government that had strong popular support and that kept to the forms of legality. Economic crisis, totalitarian repression, world war, and the threat of nuclear annihilation contributed to a sense that strong states were a bulwark against disorder, and helped to persuade leading capitalists that they should accommodate themselves to a regime of public management that offered them greater security in return for some restrictions on their freedom of action. Thus, the liberals and social democrats in Western Europe, North America, and other industrialized countries conceived of their political mission in terms of the completion of the welfare state and the effective management of what came to be called the 'mixed economy.' Criticism of this mission from the socialist left was framed as a critique of timidity. It was said that the capitalists could be pushed much harder and that an irreversible movement toward socialism could be set in train. However, the socialism at issue was essentially a democratized and liberalized version of the Soviet state, and put the centre of decision firmly in the national capital.[46]

It is well to remember now that the prevailing view in the early 1960s was that the Soviet Union actually worked – if only in the sense that Mussolini's trains or Hitler's war machine worked.[47] Especially among progressive thinkers, the presumption was that the Stalinist system of economic planning had succeeded in transforming a backward country into a great industrial power. Soviet science and technology were impressive, and so were Soviet athletes and dancers. There might not be much freedom in the Soviet Union, and the secret police were still terrifying, but there seemed to be full employment, a wide array of health and educational services, and a kind of economic security for the average person that the unemployed in the West might envy. Obviously, the might of the Red Army was a sign that the Soviet state had been able to mobilize resources in an impressive way. For social democrats in the West, the Soviet Union was a warning of what happened when socialism ceased to be liberal and democratic; yet it was also a proof that, despite the deformations of Bolshevism, socialist practices were capable of delivering a better future for ordinary people. Western social democracy could be even better, it was thought, because it would preserve the advantages of liberalism and parliamentary democracy, while making the state into an effective instrument for social and economic improvement. From this perspective, the requirement of the day was to fill in the content of the New Deal – to make real the claims of the welfare state and the planned economy. For these purposes, the models were to be found in British labourism and Swedish social democracy.

Significantly, the influential models for democratic socialism were provided by European national governments. These were the models that captured the imagination of the left in North America – a left that was increasingly sensitive to its own inability to carry forward the New Deal promise. There was more progress in the latter respect in Canada than in the United States, but even here it became clear by the early 1960s that there would probably never be a Swedish-style social democratic government for the country as a whole. Such an ambition could hardly even be entertained in the United States once the Red Scare had taken hold.[48] Social democrats were faced with the embarrassing realization that the most attractive model of socialism – the apparent harbinger of the future – was confined to a relatively small part of the industrialized world, and that it could not easily be extended beyond its current redoubts. One might be comforted by the recognition that even conservative governments, like the one in West Germany, had adopted policies that could be identified with the welfare state and economic planning. Indeed, one could look – as Frederic Howe did in an earlier generation – at the socialist practices of right-wing governments as a sign that socialism in some sense was inevitable, and that it was only a matter of time before the welfare state would be completed in the United States as well as elsewhere. However, the continuing power and increasing self-confidence of the antisocialist governments did not bode well.

The advance of the welfare state and of the new systems of national economic management lulled the left into a false sense of security. It seemed that the space for progressive politics had been fixed forever and that the only movement possible was forward. The neoconservative revival, which began in the United States in the early 1960s, foreshadowed changes that would put the certainties of the postwar left in crisis. But even before the left had to deal with this challenge seriously, it was faced with a kind of internal revolt. This was associated with the rise of the New Left, which not only put the statism of the postwar orthodoxy at issue but also raised the question of cultural politics in a form more challenging to bourgeois sensibilities than the sober paternalism of Red Vienna. Suddenly, socialists had to think again about the kind of politics they were practising, and its relation to the everyday life of ordinary people. The New Left implied that the problem of postwar social democracy was not that it had been too timid in the use of state power, but that it had relied on the state rather than on the people in pursuing change. The renewed search for political space led back to the local community, and thus to the issues that had been raised by the Paris Commune.

# 8

# Radical Municipalism and Local Socialism

By the early seventies, thousands of former student activists were engaged in a myriad of collective experiments and projects in institution building, cultural expression and political organization, in deliberate efforts to find 'roots' and 'base' in local communities and institutions and to develop a left in the academic disciplines and professions. These efforts ought not to be interpreted as the meager remnants of the New Left; they were understood as ways to carry the projects forward into new terrain, to create workable personal integrations between politics and livelihood, to institutionalize the New Left and try to practice radical democratic principles in the real world. These experiments and borrowings soon fed into and helped develop what came to be called the 'new' social movements – both feminism and environmentalism had roots in the sixties movements, and were efforts to transform and extend the ideological content and practical relevance of radicalism.[1]

It is common enough now to suppose that the New Left was just a passing phenomenon, no longer of much relevance in the age of Newt Gingrich and Preston Manning. However, as Flacks indicates and as Gingrich himself has emphasized, the political presence of the New Left in the 1970s and 1980s was far more pervasive than a superficial analysis would reveal.[2] This is not just a matter of middle-aged people romanticizing their youthful radicalism. The political practices that have become familiar in the last thirty years owe much to the innovations of the New Left, and the New Left sensibility – experimental, anarchistic, antibureaucratic, populist, movement-oriented – has been reproduced in other oppositional movements. Moreover, the graduates of the New Left have moved into settings where there are opportunities for lifetime activity. The moment of student rebellion has thus been transmuted into a way of life that sustains at least some of the earlier creative energy. While it is impossible to explore all the effects of this here, it is worth thinking more carefully about the kind of progressive *municipal* politics that emerged in the wake of the New Left. The New Left paid particular attention to the possibilities for immediate, local action, and it was relatively undogmatic about the form such action should take and the issues it should address. Implicitly, it posited a political space that was at once local and global, and as such displaced the state (and the parties focused on the state) as the natural and inevitable focus of political activity. The New Left oriented itself toward the cultural domain, but dismissed the barriers that protected the state and the market from cultural revolution. It claimed a space for action that was anywhere and everywhere, and refused authorities the right to disclaim responsibility for the effects of their actions. Thus, the relationship between the local community and the governments, corporations, and other authorities that acted upon that community was an obvious subject for the New Left's attention.

The American New Left first encountered local government on the streets, in its guise as the apparatus for enforcing racial segregation and repressing protest against the Vietnam War. Local government was also encountered as the apparatus for repressing and controlling minority communities – not only communities of colour and language, but also those of style and culture, such as the ones created by distinctive patterns of sexual activity or drug use. Thus, municipal authorities (for example, Mayor Richard Daley and his Chicago police) were seen as particularly obnoxious apparatuses of the state: as responsible for suppressing minorities, controlling dissent, and containing the counterculture. It seemed to many observers that municipal government, which was supposed to be closest to the people, actually was remote, insensitive, and often authoritarian. It certainly did not provide a framework for democratic self-government in the communities with which the New Left could identify. On the other hand, the fact that municipal government was formally democratic was an indication that cultural revolution and not just institutional tinkering was required to make democracy effective. In the American context, there were strong traditions of local autonomy and democratic accountability, which could be asserted in more challenging ways. In the black ghettos and Hispanic neighbourhoods of big cities like New York, this might take the form of demands for community control.[3] In smaller municipalities such as Ann Arbor, Madison, and Berkeley, which had previously been dominated by middle-aged, middle-class, business-oriented élites, the call for political transformation could be oriented toward the young. In either case, the implication was that communities at odds with the American mainstream could have a wider than local impact if they asserted their own right to democratic autonomy.

In Berkeley, California – site of the original student rebellion in 1964 – the New Left was drawn into municipal politics as a result of its encounters with the local police, and not because of any preexisting theory about the importance of the municipality as a political venue.[4] The attempt there to articulate a program for community control of the police led to the formation in 1971 of the April Coalition – the predecessor of Berkeley Citizens' Action, the left grouping that eventually won control of the city council in 1984. It was in the context of the initial controversy over policing that the New Left in Berkeley discovered the possibilities of municipal politics: chances to link the concerns of student activists with those of poor blacks and other minorities; to open up issues about the control of public lands, public facilities, and public services; to challenge the power of capital and of the propertied classes, not only in the disposition of public resources but also in the use and development of 'private' property; to invest the apparatuses of the local state with the principles of participatory democracy, community control, environmental sensitivity, and equality for women and minorities; and to legitimize the New Left's critique of American foreign policy by clothing it with the authority of an elected government.[5] Significantly, a grouping that had originally focused on questions of policing (which were of great concern to students before the Vietnam War ended in 1975) eventually shifted focus to the issue of rent control, which became the mobilizing issue for its later political successes. Moreover, the same coalition took on board the growing environmental consciousness of the 1980s, and attempted to make Berkeley into a lead municipality in the development of local environmental initiatives. There were efforts to translate concerns about cultural insensitivity and systemic discrimination into programs for affirmative action and school reform, and there were also attempts to foster an alternative business sector that was not dominated exclusively by whites or by outside capital or by entrepreneurs who refused to engage with their employees as equals. Domestic policies of this sort were complemented by a relatively aggressive and critical foreign policy that put Berkeley at odds with the State Department and the U.S. Immigration and Naturalization Service. Thus, the powers of municipal government were pushed to their limits, the aim being to turn a radical ghetto into an exemplary outward-looking community that could help to empower the critical social movements with which many if not most of its inhabitants identified.

Such a conception of the potential for progressive local politics could be seen in other American communities. Burlington, Vermont,[6] and Santa Monica, California,[7] were perhaps the most notable in this respect; but there were others, such as Davis and Irvine, California, and Cambridge and Amherst, Massachusetts, where local progressives pushed at least some of the elements of this same agenda, with varying success.[8] Moreover, in larger cities like San Francisco,[9] Boston,[10] Chicago,[11] and New York,[12] one could discern the effects of a similar progressive politics, especially in the 1980s. Clearly, local progressivism in the years following the New Left upheavals was by no means confined to a few university towns. In fact, the radicalism of communities like Burlington and Santa Monica had little to do with a university presence; it was much more obviously connected to the more general development of a post-industrial economy. These towns owed their prosperity to the new information businesses, and hence were caught up in the contradictions of capitalist dynamism. These contradictions resulted in escalating land values that threatened renters, encouraged speculation, and ultimately disrupted established communities. The effects of the dual economy – increased poverty, homelessness, drug addiction, and street violence – were felt strongly in communities that were otherwise filled with promise.[13] And, of course, the contradictions of prosperity in terms of traffic congestion and environmental degradation were certainly apparent. Although the same phenomena fed into a neoconservative reaction in many parts of the country, it should not be surprising that more progressive responses emerged in some communities. For the most part, these communities had a strong 'liberal' tradition in the American sense, and thus felt a connection with less-favoured communities. Thus, the activists in Berkeley yearned to connect their own predominantly white radicalism with the black radicalism in neighbouring Oakland. A similar outwardness and commitment to a politics of solidarity with the poor and the oppressed is visible in the politics of other 'radical ghettos.'

The great disappointment of progressive activists in American municipal politics has been this: it is very difficult to forge effective alliances across the barriers of class and race. Within all classes, racial divisions have become deeply entrenched; and a progressive intelligentsia that is predominantly white has great difficulty connecting with an inner-city proletariat that is predominantly nonwhite. The alienation of the progressive intelligentsia from the white working class and the labour movement has exacerbated these difficulties. Nevertheless, there have been strenuous efforts in many large cities to create progressive coalitions, which are often organized around mayoralty candidates – for example, Harold Washington in Chicago, Ray Flynn in Boston, John Agnos in San Francisco, and David Dinkins in New York. The victories have often been Pyrrhic, but these efforts are another sign that localist progressivism tends to produce outward-oriented, coalition-seeking activity. Although there is continuing tension between parochialists focused on a particular neighbourhood or community and leaders who are movement-oriented, the impact of people in the latter category is greater than they themselves realize. There is a continuing impulse to relate localized action to wider social concerns; this finds expression not only in electoral activity but also in propaganda campaigns, lobbying, political demonstrations, and practical projects. The 'project focus' of American local activism – establishing a shelter for the homeless, creating bicycle paths, setting up an alternative school, offering health care to unregistered immigrants, testing the soil for toxic wastes, training women for construction jobs, and so on – reflects both the absence of a tightly organized welfare state and the presence of a relatively vibrant network of activists with a strong sense of self-sufficiency. The alternative to an insensitive market and an uncaring state emerges from a pattern of activity that, though localized, is meant to have wider social effects.

In this context, relatively progressive municipal councils or other local authorities – or even councils that have a substantial progressive minority – can and do play an important part in sustaining an American left. This is not a left that is under the hegemony of a particular party, although many of its activists take part in Democratic politics from time to time. It is a diffuse, open, ideologically diverse, multinucleated, movement-oriented, locally based, outward-oriented network of networks that defies control from any centre and often seems (especially to foreign observers) not to exist because its presence cannot easily be marked. A council like Berkeley's or Burlington's is actually an outcrop of a left that has a much wider and deeper social presence. Local electoral success helps to crystallize important aspirations. More concretely, a progressive municipal council offers a venue for debate, a focus for popular mobilization, a source of political, administrative, and financial assistance, a means of legitimation, and a centre from which to develop demonstration projects of wider practical consequence. Burlington, for instance, pioneered in the development of land trusts and established a Women's Economic Opportunity Program; [14] Berkeley advanced a more effective system of rent control and created new guidelines for waste reduction and recycling; and Santa Monica developed new schemes for linking development approvals to social benefits for the poor, and began at a remarkably early date to explore the democratic potential of new information technologies. Many other examples could be cited. Fed into interlocal networks of communication between activists and professionals, these activities helped to establish the legitimacy of progressive alternatives in other communities. [15]

The analytic question we face is not whether this sort of activity has transformed the United States – obviously it has not – but whether it foreshadows the pattern of progressive politics in the twenty-first century. As Marx said in *The Eighteenth Brumaire*, people make their own history, but not under circumstances of their own choosing.[16] There is reason to think that the circumstances that allowed for the fusion of socialism and nationalism and hence for the practice of a statist socialism have already passed. If so, the condition of the left outside the United States will increasingly resemble that of the American left, and activists will have to adjust themselves to a politics that is much more American in style than they would like. To some extent, this has already happened; indeed, the European interest in the new social movements in the 1970s and 1980s reflects a coming to terms with a form of politics that no longer fits the old spaces defined by state-centric political parties and that has a looseness, openness, particularism, and globalism that seems almost American. In this context, it is worth looking more closely at the recent pattern of municipal progressivism in Britain and Canada, where the supposed empiricism of English-speaking politics has met with the strictures of statist social democracy.

## Local Socialism[17]

The most sustained and innovative challenge from local authorities on the left to a conservative central government occurred in Britain in the early 1980s. This was in the context of a crisis within the Labour Party, during which insurgents from the right and the left were attempting to redefine the character of progressive politics. The emergence of the New Left in Western Europe and North America had coincided with the first period of Labour government nationally since 1951.[18] The Wilson government of 1966–70 was only the second Labour government ever to have a decisive majority in the House of Commons, and for that reason there were great expectations associated with it. Unfortunately, Wilson and his ministers proved to be timid in their socialist initiatives, ineffectual in their economic policies, and obsequious in their relations with the United States. Thus, the New Left critique came to be focused on a government that was supposed to carry forward the struggles for peace and socialism, but seemed to be doing nothing of the kind. This gave the critique a focus comparable to the one in West Germany, where the SPD had been participating in the government since 1966. It was less a matter of rethinking communism (as in France and Italy) or of coming to terms with the absence of a socialist party (as it was in the United States), and more a matter of dealing with the perceived failure of a socialist party that was as open and undogmatic as critics of communism could want, but that seemed incapable of acting effectively on the socialist vision it was supposed to embody.

In Britain in the 1960s, most of the political and intellectual energy of the new generation of the left was directed outside the Labour Party. Radical activists in Britain were disappointed in the Wilson government's domestic performance, and appalled by its support for the American war in Vietnam and by its failure of nerve in Rhodesia. Also, they were much influenced by Miliband's critique of parliamentary socialism, by German and American analyses of the totalitarian culture of capitalism, and by the revival of critical Marxist theory in France; and they were drawn to the modes of action in civil society pioneered by the Americans and developed by the Germans, the French, and the Dutch. For all these reasons, they generally declined to join the Labour Party and sought other milieux for their activity. An upsurge of militancy among the organized working class helped to save middle-class radicals from the illusion that the working class was dead politically. The working-class militants were sufficiently influenced by communism and Trotskyism that their activity had a patina of Marxist orthodoxy; among the middle-class radicals, this stimulated interest in the Trotskyist sects. Thus, although many of the radicals drifted into unorthodox activities such as community organizing, they tended to see what they were doing as connected to the traditional project of mobilizing the working class and building a socialist party.

In its social policy, the Wilson government was much influenced by the American War on Poverty. The techniques of area-based positive discrimination, community organization and client participation, and locally differentiated systems of service delivery were largely modelled on American initiatives. They were seen as ways of making up for the deficiencies of Fabian welfarism, with its uniform programs and bureaucratic administration. They were also seen as ways of reaching out to neglected constituencies – especially to the growing immigrant population and to marginalized elements of the urban working class. The Labour government's programs in this respect were hardly more successful than their American counterparts, but like their American counterparts they provided employment and political experience for a generation of middle-class radicals. The main criticism from the left with respect to these programs was that they were much too timid, and in any case that they were unrealistic in the absence of a socialist economic policy. This line of thinking found its classic expression in the final report of the Community Development Project, which was the last of Labour's urban initiatives before the government fell to Margaret Thatcher in 1979.[19]

By the time James Callaghan was defeated, many of the left's criticisms of the Labour government had become conventional wisdom. Unfortunately, it was the New Right that made most decisive use of these criticisms in delegitimating Fabian welfarism and Keynesian economic planning. The Thatcherite project of subjecting the British state and civil society to the discipline of the market emerged as the alternative to the drift of Butskellism.[20] Few at first believed that this project could succeed, but its pursuit by Thatcher convinced many on the left that the time had come to wrest control of the Labour Party from the right-wingers who had been responsible for the drift that she had so effectively attacked. It was in this context that the Campaign for Labour Party Democracy was mounted, and that Tony Benn made his dramatic bid for the deputy leadership of the party. It was also in this context that many of the middle-class radicals began to drift back into the Labour Party, and to discover the possibilities of local politics.[21]

In Britain perhaps even more than in North America, the perception had been that municipal politics was a black hole: it was where parochial people dealt with parochial issues, and where moribund local Labour parties dealt with the routine administration of the Fabian welfare state. The middle-class radicals and working-class militants had run up against these local bureaucracies in various contexts, and tended to regard them as alien. However, it became clear during the Campaign for Labour Party Democracy, and during other nationally oriented left initiatives within the party, that many constituencies and District Labour Parties were ripe for the picking *because* they had become so moribund.

In different ways and in different contexts, the 1960s generation of left activists began moving back into the local Labour parties, and positioned themselves to take control in a number of cities by 1980 or 1981. Unlike their North American counterparts, these left activists did not have to build popular political organizations from scratch. In many places, once they had won control of the local party, they could take over the local council almost automatically, since Labour electoral majorities were virtually guaranteed. This facilitated the pursuit of more ambitious and ideologically coherent objectives.

The crown jewel of Labour government in the 1980s was the Greater London Council, much the largest local authority in the country and, more important, the ostensible government of Britain's metropolis. Ordinarily, local government in Britain tends to be invisible, because of the extraordinary centralization of the news and cultural media. Under Ken Livingstone, however, the GLC became news.[22] He and his colleagues seemed to embody the new Labour left, which was then contending for supremacy within the national Labour Party. When they became the governors of the nation's metropolis in 1981, and began to pursue the policies the left was advocating as the real alternative to Thatcherism, their activities gained national significance. The leaders of the GLC saw their own mission in terms of national politics; although they were exploring the space for action at the local level, they understood their project as one that could only be accomplished at the national level. They were involved in a sort of demonstration of what the left alternative would be like, and as such they were engaged in continuing propaganda by the deed. They also became engaged in more overt propaganda against the Thatcher government. As the media gave them increasing attention, Thatcher herself responded with a series of measures to choke off this propaganda for socialism in all its forms. The struggle culminated in the abolition of the GLC by Parliament in 1986.[23]

Although Livingstone's GLC of 1981–6 was the most prominent of the new left Labour authorities, it was by no means the only one. In the 1982 local elections, a number of the London boroughs – indeed, all but the ritziest parts of inner London – fell to Labour and hence to Labour's left. Sheffield, a traditional Labour bastion in the north, swung to the left under its own charismatic leader, David Blunkett.[24] A Labour Group dominated by the Trotskyist 'Militant Tendency' won control of Liverpool, which had been a Liberal bastion in the 1970s.[25] All six of the Metropolitan Counties, around the six biggest English cities other than London (Birmingham, Manchester, Liverpool, Leeds, Sheffield, and Newcastle), were under Labour control and varying degrees of left influence. In urban Scotland, especially Glasgow, there was a similar left presence. Thus, Thatcher was confronted from 1982 onward with a left that had a powerful influence, if not tight control, over local government in most of the largest cities in the country. It was a left with strong ties to the trade unions, to social movements, and to community organizations. Moreover, it was a left that, in the provinces as much as in the metropolis, saw its political mission in national terms. As such, it posed a threat that Thatcher could hardly ignore.

From a North American perspective, the most distinctive feature of the Labour left authorities was their commitment to 'socialism.'[26] This commitment was embodied in efforts to pursue a radical version of the Alternative Economic Strategy at the local level. This strategy had been articulated originally as a national policy, and had been conceived essentially as an industrial strategy. As such, it was little concerned with land-use planning, and much directed toward the manufacturing sector. It was informed by the hope of planning with and for labour rather than capital. The idea was to involve workers on the shop floor in an effort to develop alternative plans for declining industries – plans that would protect and enhance employment rather than shed labour. Governments would use their regulatory authority and their financial resources to push and pull capital into line. On its own, a government might have difficulty doing this; however (so it was thought), organized labour could use its own power to hold capital to account. This power would be positive, insofar as workers would be able to use their expertise to develop alternatives for capital as well as for labour. The vision was socialist in the sense that it anticipated an economy in which the organized working-class would ultimately become the main agent of economic planning, and the role of government would be to facilitate this autonomous activity. This conception clearly was closer to nineteenth- and early-twentieth-century ideals of socialism than to the models of state enterprise and economic planning that had become associated with socialism after 1929. It was informed, moreover, by the New Left critiques of bureaucracy that had gained currency in the 1960s.

Pursuing an alternative economic strategy at the local level proved extraordinarily difficult, because local authorities lacked both the financial resources and the regulatory authority to push and pull capital into line. Problems were compounded by the recession of the early 1980s, which was exacerbated by Thatcher's own economic policies. The manufacturing industries, where labour was best organized and most sophisticated, were hit particularly hard, so that local authorities like Sheffield's found themselves planning with and for an industrial labour force that was in the midst of massive layoffs. Although job-saving alternatives were desperately mooted, few of them made sense without massive investments. These investments were not forthcoming from the private sector, and were beyond the financial capacity of the local authorities. Thus, the left Labour councils could only gesture in the direction they *would* move if they had the support of the national government. Inevitably, much of their energy was diverted toward the third sector of the economy: small business. They could and did develop innovative programs for this sector – networks to provide access for small business to technological innovations; management assistance for workers' co-operatives and minority businesses; regulations to ensure equal opportunities for women and minorities, as well as union rights; access to capital for high-risk applicants – but the impact of these programs was limited: this sector of the economy simply could not generate enough employment to replace what was being lost.[27]

The economic initiatives of the left Labour authorities were of less practical than ideological significance. Ideologically, they were important both as an illustration of what a national Labour government might attempt – presumably with greater effect – and as an exploration of the space for socialist intervention in a capitalist economy at the local level. The GLC in particular focused on modes of intervention not normally associated with local authorities, and tended to neglect the possibilities inherent in the traditional instruments of land-use planning.[28] This reflected the influence of economists who had come to the GLC from backgrounds dissociated from local government, and the ambitions of the left to engage in the sort of activity they thought should be pursued by the next Labour government. Ironically, the activities of the left Labour authorities alerted the Conservatives to the possibilities of using local authorities as agencies of economic development. The Thatcher government used its parliamentary majority to choke off the possibility of socialist initiatives at the local level, while enhancing the capacity of local authorities to pursue initiatives supportive of local capitalist development. This meant turning to the United States for models, and attempting (rather unsuccessfully) to reproduce the public/private partnerships that were heralded there.

It is difficult to find, among progressive municipal politicians in Canada and the United States, anything like the keen British appreciation of the differences between a capitalist and a socialist strategy of local economic development.[29] Whatever the failures of the British efforts – and there were many – they at least posed the question of whether a socialist local authority in a capitalist country could use its powers to foster alternatives to capitalism. Partly because this question was often posed in abstraction from the traditions of British local government, the left discovered more opportunities than anyone had previously recognized for significant economic intervention at the local level. Thus, the left authorities had policies for technological development, foreign trade, labour relations, the finance of investments, and so on – policies that might have been unremarkable at the national level but were of a scope never before contemplated in British local government. Significantly, these policies were informed not simply by a commitment to socialism, but also by a sense that socialism had to be achieved by a transformation of social relations within the state and civil society, and not by an enhancement of the power of the state as against civil society.

This relational understanding of the struggle for socialism clearly reflected the influence of New Left ideas. The emphasis was on the following: facilitating workers' control of capitalist industry, by encouraging union recognition and pressuring capitalist enterprises to involve workers in the processes of industrial planning; assisting in the creation of new worker-controlled enterprises on a human scale, and helping these enterprises to survive capitalist competition; providing for greater worker control and greater client control over public services; and facilitating the provision of services to communities by the communities themselves. In contrast, Labour had, since the 1930s, put its faith in centralized, bureaucratic state organizations that could manage the economy with Keynesian techniques and provide the required public services without involving the community in a serious way. The new emphasis led the left Labour authorities to explore means for democratization and decentralization within the public sector, to open up relations with the third sector of noncorporate private business, and to address the concerns of groups that did not identify themselves in class terms.[30] This tampering with orthodoxy created tensions within the left itself, since some elements of the left – especially the Militant Tendency, which dominated Liverpool's council – insisted on an orthodox workerist approach to socialism (which Michael Parkinson has called municipal Stalinism). However, the predominant tendency was away from orthodoxy and toward the modes of practice that have come to characterize municipal radicalism in Canada and the United States.

Ironically, Thatcher's counter-attack against local socialism forced the left authorities into a defensive posture with respect to the Fabian welfarism they were attempting to change. The reforms the left contemplated cost money, and money was precisely the thing Thatcher wanted to deny to the local state. The result was an extraordinary battle between the central government and the local authorities.[31] Not until Thatcher was well into her third term did she finally succeed in forcing the left authorities into line, and for her to do so she had to apply the sovereign authority of Parliament, the full weight of the civil service, three decisive electoral victories, and her own iron determination. Despite difficult internal divisions, the left authorities were stubborn, artful, and daring in their resistance, successfully evading and frustrating wave after wave of legislation designed to curb their activities. In the end, they succeeded in burdening Thatcher with an unpopular measure – the 'poll tax' – that contributed much to her own political downfall. If Labour returns to national government in the 1990s, it will owe much to this defensive struggle, which highlighted the statist centralism and ideological extremism of the Thatcherite Conservatives.

The local socialist program always was conceived in terms of extending and improving the socialist initiatives of the past – initiatives which, whatever their deficiencies, had produced an extensive sphere of collective consumption with respect to housing, transport, education, health care, and social services, and which had subjected land development to tight public regulation. From this perspective, to democratize the provision of public services and facilities, to democratize the process of planning, and to extend democratic planning into the workplace required an extension, not a contraction, of the public sector. Contraction was, of course, Thatcher's objective. To protect their base, in both a political and an administrative sense, the left authorities had to become the chief defenders of the public sector which they had so vigorously criticized in the past. This enabled Thatcher to turn their own critiques against them. What is more, the resources of the left authorities were so much absorbed by the defensive struggle to protect the 'old' public sector that there was little remaining for the new initiatives. As the fiscal and regulatory squeeze on local government continued, the 'soft left' were able to assert the need for a 'new realism' that pointed toward accommodation with the market-oriented principles that Thatcher had imposed.

Restricted as they were, the left authorities were able to make symbolic gestures toward the new constituencies that they hoped to integrate into the left coalition. Thus, women's committees[32] and race equality committees[33] were established in most of the left authorities. These new bodies undertook various measures to improve service and employment opportunities for the target communities, as well to publicize issues related to racism and sexism. Also, there were a variety of foreign policy initiatives from the left with respect to disarmament, Third World liberation movements, and the guerrilla war in Northern Ireland.[34] Significantly, the efforts of the left authorities to articulate an alternative foreign policy, break free from the workerist traditions of British labour, and develop a socialist alternative to Thatcherism were condemned as 'loony,' not only by the Tory press but also by the national Labour leadership. It was clear that everyone at the centre was unnerved by the pretensions of those local politicians who were attempting to intervene in the space reserved for serious politics. What was actually a widespread and innovative movement that promised to create new possibilities for political action was widely condemned as a form of lunacy – mocked in the terms that the American media had developed for the 'People's Republic of Santa Monica' and the 'Sande１istas' of Burlington.[35] An aggressively radical local politics was evidently too dangerous to be tolerated.

**Urban Progressivism**

Local socialists in Britain and the Greens in Germany echoed many of the themes of the American New Left, and practised a politics that in many ways imitated urban progressivism in North America.[36] Because municipally focused progressive activity had little impact on the national political parties in Canada and the United States, it gained less national and international publicity. However, this does not mean that it was any less significant. If one were to summarize the progressive initiatives advanced by Canadian and American activists in the 1970s and 1980s, they would fall into several categories:

- **Development Control**. Efforts to protect established neighbourhoods from intrusive development by means of restrictive zoning, height and density limits, and design regulations. Ordinances to protect designated buildings from demolition or alteration. Measures to encourage medium-density, lowrise, mixed-use development of obsolescent industrial districts.
- **Housing**. Support for nonprofit housing alternatives. Rent controls. Restrictions on conversion of low-cost rental accommodation into

high-cost condominiums or hotel spaces. Shelters and support services for the homeless. Agreements requiring developers to provide low- or moderate-income housing and/or public services as part of any major project.

- **Transportation**. Opposition to urban expressways and road widenings. Limits on downtown parking spaces. Encouragement of car pooling. Improvements to public transportation, and limits on fare increases.
- **Affirmative action**. Codes prohibiting discrimination in employment or services, on grounds relating not only to race and gender but also to sexual orientation and mental or physical disability. Efforts to encourage or require hiring of women and minorities in the public sector and to require contractors in the private sector to comply with similar standards. Job training for people entering nontraditional occupations. Special support for female and minority entrepreneurs. Sensitization training for police and other public officials.
- **Environmental protection**. Programs for recycling and waste reduction. Stricter controls on toxic waste disposal. Prohibitions or restrictions on the use of dangerous materials. Encouragement of or requirements for energy-efficient construction or retrofitting. Preservation of forests, parks, farms, and wetlands. Opposition to nuclear energy, dam construction, and thermal plants.
- **Democratic participation**. Requirements for timely dissemination of information about public decisions. Measures to increase the opportunity for public input. Storefront information and service centres in poorer neighbourhoods. Support for community associations and community organizers. Decentralization of service delivery and decision-making.
- **External affairs**. Disinvestment and/or refusal of contracts with businesses supporting oppressive regimes abroad, dealing in armaments, or participating in the nuclear industry. Support for refugees and/or illegal immigrants. Twinning with 'red' communities in the then Soviet bloc or the Third World. Support for foreign aid and foreign witness programs. Declaration of a nuclear-free zone.

One could add to this list. In doing so, it would become apparent that progressive initiatives were not confined to progressive municipalities, and that few supposedly progressive councils would be able to demonstrate action on all fronts. The real point is that we can relate this pattern of activity to the presence throughout North America of an urban progressivism that is in some respects comparable to the movement in the early years of the twentieth century.

The Canadian experience of this movement is interesting because Canadian cities were not as vexed by racial conflict as their American counterparts; also, although there was a strong social-democratic tradition in Canada, the New Democratic Party and the Parti Québécois showed only passing interest in municipal affairs. Thus, urban progressivism developed outside the framework of traditional party politics, and was not confronted so directly with the racialization of class divisions that was so apparent in the United States. At the same time, however, the provincialization of responsibility for health, education, and welfare tended to narrow the focus of Canadian municipal government.

It is not surprising, therefore, that civic progressivism in Canada had its origins in the reaction to rapid urban development in the 1960s.[37] There were two dimensions to this: complaints about the disruptive effects of urban development on the quality of life generally and on the particular quality of life in front-line communities; and objections to the neglect of the poor in creating new housing and urban facilities. The latter objections gave a class character to urban issues. However, the tendency in most cities was to mute the class character of the conflict, on the grounds that an effective alliance for reform depended on cross-class solidarity. Part of the common ground within each alliance was a demand that urban development proceed in accordance with the expressed interests of those affected. This translated easily into a series of concerns about democratic process – openness in government, careful scrutiny of development proposals, widespread public consultations, and so on – concerns that sometimes obscured the substantive issues involved.

To the extent that there was a socialist tinge to the new progressivism in Canadian city politics, this colouring derived from ties to New Left radicals, labour organizations, and community organizations in working class neighbourhoods. The New Left radicals provided a bridge between the other two. Socialist political culture in Canada was greatly weakened in the 1950s, but it did not die out, partly because of the continuing presence of the Co-operative Commonwealth Federation, the immediate predecessor of the NDP. After the NDP strengthened itself in the 1960s, the possibility of social democratic government – and hence, the political possibility of some sort of socialism – seemed to increase rather than diminish. There were particular hopes for the newly empowered provincial governments, and the NDP had a series of electoral successes at that level in 1969–72, gaining power in Manitoba, Saskatchewan, and British Columbia. The Canadian labour movement went through a period of growth in the 1960s and 1970s, thanks especially to legislation that opened up the public sector to unionization. Old conflicts faded between social democrats and communists; the Catholic trade unions in Quebec became radicalized in the context of a modernizing French-Canadian nationalism; Canadian nationalist feeling began to develop in the 'international' (i.e., American-dominated) unions; intellectuals influenced by the political culture of the New Left began to appear on union staffs. All of this contributed to increased militancy and socialist consciousness among organized labour. In turn, this meant that the labour movement, and the socialist ideals associated with it, remained central to the Canadian left at a time when the American left was becoming increasingly alienated from organized labour. At the municipal level, this meant that civic progressives sought to make organized labour a pillar of their political coalitions. Indeed, in the three largest Canadian cities, labour councils helped to create the progressive organizations that structured leftist politics municipally from the mid-1970s onward. In Vancouver, the Committee of Progressive Electors (COPE ) began as a Labour Council initiative; in Toronto, the Labour Council worked through the NDP; and in Montreal, its equivalents stimulated the formation of the popular committees that were the basis of the Rassemblement des Citoyens et Citoyennes de Montréal (RCM) in francophone neighbourhoods.

Labour's vital role in progressive city politics should not obscure the fact that the immediate protests generative of the new progressive coalitions arose mainly from development issues. This created certain tensions, because working-class jobs were often threatened by middle-class protests against development. To overcome these tensions, crucial links had to be forged between the labour movement and community organizations in working-class neighbourhoods. Middle-class radicals imbued with socialist notions were often important in this respect, but indigenous working-class leadership was just as apparent. The Downtown Eastside Residents' Association in Vancouver – which had strong links to the Vancouver Labour Council and to COPE – was a good example of this.[38] The various popular committees in Montreal – stimulated by the Conféderation des Syndicats Nationaux, the once-Catholic trade union central – performed a similar political function, in that they organized concerns about public services and regulations in forms that were consistent with labour's imperatives. For instance, the tenants' slogan in

Montreal – *On reste ici!* ('We're staying!') – embodied the notion that development should not be at the expense of working-class housing and amenities: the opposition would not be to development as such, but to a form of development that was an invidious exercise of class power. Resistance on these grounds made perfect sense from the vantage point of a radicalized labour movement.

Urban progressives in Canada had some success in dealing with class relations but were much less successful in breaking out of their downtown ghettos. In practically every metropolitan area, progressive politics was concentrated in the central city, where the pressures of urban development on existing neighbourhoods are strongest and the social problems arising from the gap between the rich and the poor are most evident. The central city is where the liberal middle-class tends to congregate, and where youthful movements of environmentalists, feminists, gay-rights activists, and campaigners for peace and Third World development flourish. Working-class organizations also tend to be relatively strong. In the suburbs, the pressures and problems of development are diffused; the working-class is disorganized; and conservative elements of the middle class predominate. The strong trend toward suburbanization in Canada means that most Canadians – even in the largest metropolitan areas – live in municipalities where no significant challenge has been posed to the traditional discourse of nonpartisan politics and value-free development. Obviously, this has limited the impact of urban progressivism, as it has in the United States and Britain.

Although Montreal's metropolitan area is no longer Canada's largest, the city of Montreal is by far the biggest lower-tier municipality, with a population of nearly one million. Before 1978, the Montreal Citizens' Movement (MCM, as the RCM is called in English) was probably the most radical political organization of any consequence at the civic level in North America.[39] It was influenced both by French Marxism and by American 'libertarian socialism.' Although it never developed a coherent program, it envisaged both a radical decentralization of political authority within the city, as well as serious efforts to check capitalist development and open up the possibility for economic alternatives. However, the party split, and suffered a serious electoral defeat in 1978. A centrist leadership took firm control and brought in cohorts of reformists from the Parti Québécois. (The latter is an uneasy alliance of left and right under a nationalist banner. After 1980, it began to drift further to the right, and many of the militants on the left began to desert it. The MCM provided a home for many of them.) The MCM regained lost ground in the 1982 elections and won a decisive victory in 1986, with its leader, Jean Doré, becoming mayor.[40] Doré and the party remained in power until the fall of 1994, when both were badly defeated at the hands of a right-wing populist. Its program in office was only moderately progressive. Rather than radical democratization and decentralization, it offered more openness in government; even then, by the standards of English Canada or most parts of the United States, Montreal's administration remained aloof and bureaucratic, and this contributed to the MCM's ultimate defeat. For the most part, its program of reform was to bring the civic administration up to the standards of 'good government' as practised in Toronto and Vancouver, and to be more sensible and innovative than its predecessors in its support for private capital. Not surprisingly, the party's left wing broke off in 1989–90, and an independent left began running its own candidates, although with indifferent success.

In Vancouver, both the Communist Party and the Labour Council were influential in creating of the Committee of Progressive Electors in 1968. This connection was always controversial, and COPE never succeeded in winning control of the city council. However, a loose alliance between it and Mayor Harcourt – a New Democrat from the centre-right of the party who went on to become provincial premier in 1991 – dominated the council in 1982–6. Vancouver had been governed by a liberal-reformist regime in the early 1970s, which had opened up city hall, tightened planning procedures, and introduced various measures to enhance citizen participation. The COPE-Harcourt council tended to continue in this same direction, but COPE's influence also was used to secure a 'fair wages' policy for the city (that is, to require civic contractors to match union wages and fringe benefits), to direct more attention to the impoverished Downtown Eastside, and to make some symbolic gestures on matters of foreign policy. Among the latter, steps to make Vancouver a nuclear-free zone (which involved protests against the visits of American warships to Vancouver's harbour) and support for the annual Peace Walk (an enormous event that has involved 60,000 or more marchers annually) were particularly significant. By the late 1980s the Peace Walk had become so popular that it could command the support of the city's new, conservative mayor. When Harcourt departed for provincial politics, COPE lost its key ally and was reduced to an embattled minority on council.

In Toronto, the left-reformers were in a position of influence but not control on the city council in 1972–6, 1978–80, and 1988–91. They had the most success when they aligned themselves with the liberals under a banner of 'reform' to secure greater openness in government, tighter planning controls, and more citizen participation. As a policy committee of the Metro Toronto NDP noted in a 1988 position paper:

The Reform Movement, which began some twenty years ago, had two basic principles: to protect and strengthen neighbourhoods and to open up and democratize City Hall and the city as a whole. These principles were a timely response to a vision of a city of expressways and development run rampant. While still relevant, these principles had some great weaknesses. Reform's neighbourhood protection theme did not capture the essential egalitarianism of a socialist vision. It spoke to the democratic process, but did not accomplish a redistribution of power or wealth. Instead, Reform largely consolidated the power of the wealthy in their neighbourhoods. Neighbourhood preservation has focused on land use to the exclusion of other issues; for example, the workplace was largely untouched by the reform vision. A new vision must go beyond a geographic definition of community.'[41]

In trying to develop this new vision, the Toronto NDP tried to address a much wider range of issues, and to develop a political coalition that included feminists, labour activists, ethnic and racial minorities, gays and lesbians, tenants, seniors and the disabled, children and youth, and so on. In doing so it opened itself out in a way that would have been familiar to American activists. Whatever the merits of this strategy, it proved insufficient in 1991, when the party made its most determined attempt to win a majority on council. Although a moderate New Democrat was elected as mayor in 1994, she came in without a majority on council and on the basis of a nonpartisan campaign that marked a strong contrast with the ambitiously leftist initiative of 1991.

The quandary of urban progressivism in the major cities in Canada reflects a wider dilemma. The federal NDP has been in crisis since losing its major-party status in the 1993 federal election. In Ontario, the New Democrats were crushed in the May 1995 election by a Conservative Party that had moved far to the right. In British Columbia, the NDP narrowly averted the same fate, winning re-election in 1996 with only 39 percent of the vote. The social democratic hope of achieving at the provincial level what has been denied federally seems to be fading. Such hope was associated with the first Parti Québécois government in Quebec (1976–85), and it inspired a generation of New Democrats in English-speaking Canada as NDP governments came and went in four of the provinces. However, the NDP governments of the 1990s have been caught in such a tight fiscal squeeze and have been so uninspired generally that they have failed to satisfy the longings of their own supporters. It is now becoming apparent that the federal Liberal government is hardly more capable of challenging the bond raters and money traders, and is certainly more reluctant, and so the prospects of a progressivism centred at either the federal or the provincial level of government seem dim. Municipal activism is generally dismissed as a third-rate alternative to the real politics in Ottawa and the provincial capitals. And yet, the idea remains that there must be a centring for effective action. It is difficult for Canadian progressives to give up on the idea that some variant of European social democracy can hold the dike against the Americanization of Canadian politics.

**In the Shadow of the Empire**

We have become so used to the idea of an antisocialist United States that we forget that American socialism was not as weak before the First World War as it became later. The United States, like Western Europe, had an early history of municipal socialism, in both the senses to which we referred in Chapter 7.[42] In the late nineteenth century, American cities, like German ones, were noted for their progressive approach to the development of public services. Despite their reputation for corruption, American municipal councils actually pioneered in the development of public transport (especially tramways and subways, and later also motorized buses), water supply, public health services, general education, and even planning controls. Although in the early twentieth century Germany may have seemed ahead to American visitors like Frederic Howe, this perception was itself related to the sense that, in light of past experience, it was the United States that *ought* to be ahead, since it had always been ahead in the past. Among progressives like Howe, there was a sense of frustration that the great potential for public-sector development in the United States was being squandered because of corruption, inefficiency, and a growing ideological antipathy to public enterprise. This antipathy was connected both to the emergence of a strong socialist movement in the United States and to the presence in the large industrial cities of a huge, alien working-class. The appeal of the socialist movement was well demonstrated during the 1912 presidential election, when Debs made a major impact. In the preceding few years the socialist party had had some significant successes in municipal politics; these mirrored the advances of its sister parties in Europe. It was in this context that nonsocialist progressives could look to Germany for examples of vigorous, efficient, non-ideological government of the sort that would meet the needs the socialists had identified, and yet would not threaten the United States with a revolution against private property.

The story has often been told of the destruction of American socialism following the declaration of war on Germany, the Bolshevik Revolution, and the subsequent Red Scare campaign.[43] The combination of anti-German, anti-Russian, anti-Semitic, and anti-Communist feeling proved overwhelming; the United States, alone among the major industrialized countries, emerged from the postwar crisis without a socialist party that was strong enough to define the underlying issues in electoral politics. In Europe (and in Australia and New Zealand), the question of socialism was central to electoral politics for decades afterwards, even in places where it was clear that the socialists were not strong enough to win an election; in the United States, the Democratic and Republican parties were able to maintain their virtual monopoly on electoral politics and thus to write socialism off as an un-American alternative. The Cold War and the second Red Scare that developed after 1948 helped to cement this pattern; as a result, for the generation that came of age in the 1960s, the possibility of an explicitly socialist politics in the United States seemed so remote that hardly anyone could credit it. People who regarded themselves as radical or progressive had to invent a politics that was distinctively American and that did not simply copy the alien forms that had been successful in Western Europe. Even a Canadian example like the CCF government (1944–64) in Saskatchewan – a government that understood itself as socialist, was rooted in the agrarian populism of the American West, and took inspiration from the British labour movement and Swedish social democracy – could hardly be a model, since its presence was an anomaly even in Canada, and Canada was at one remove from the vigorous antisocialism of the United States. In North America, clearly, progressive politics could not draw its models from Europe.

Crucial to European socialist thinking was the idea of a rigorously centralized state. This was the Bolshevik model, and it was also the model in Britain and Sweden, which had traditions of centralized government that were at odds with the federalism of Canada and the United States. British-style parliamentarism, in which legislatures were typically dominated by a single, disciplined party, and in which the premier and his cabinet had virtually complete control over law-making, budgeting, and administrative policy, had been reproduced in Canada but not in the United States. Thus, in most of North America, the power to make political decisions was divided and redivided in bewilderingly complicated ways. There was a territorial division of power between the federal, state, and local governments; and at each level, legislatures were weakly disciplined, executive authority was divided among officials who enjoyed considerable independence from the legislature and from one another, the courts played an increasingly active role in overruling political decisions (on constitutional or other grounds), and the electorate had many more opportunities for direct intervention than was common in Canada or Western Europe. In the western United States especially, the turn-of-the-century progressive reformers – some of whom had strong connections with the nascent socialist movement – had succeeded in introducing a range of populist measures that allowed for direct voting on matters of law or public policy. They had also reformed political practices in a way that had further weakened the political parties and made it difficult for leaders to discipline their followers effectively. The political and governmental reality of the United States was – at least in appearance – one of decentralization and dispersal of authority.

Of course, from another perspective the United States was not at all decentralized. After the Second World War, Washington became the imperial court of the Western world, and the President of the United States was less the head of a particular government than the Leader of the Free World (to use the favoured American phrase). As Leader of the Free World, the American president had responsibilities that had little to do with the domestic politics of the United States, except in the sense that they were connected to the country's own sense of itself as the natural and inevitable centre of freedom and justice in the world. To maintain America's preeminence – and Washington's stature as the imperial centre – the president, the congress, and much of the federal bureaucracy had to devote themselves to tasks that were related only obliquely to America's needs as a particular country. To put it another way, the requirements associated with America's imperial position overdetermined domestic politics and made it difficult to pursue certain issues that anywhere else would have been at the centre of national politics. With respect to America's imperial role, there were demands for absolute loyalty, discretion, and solidarity. A politician could not question these demands without appearing to be un-American. Thus, the emperor's freedom of manoeuvre was less than it had been in Franklin Roosevelt's time, when the New Deal had given inspiration to European social democrats.

The state-centricity of the study of comparative politics has been such that a crucial difference between American and European politics in the postwar era has been obscured. The European countries and even Canada enjoyed an autonomy from the imperial centre that was not granted to the American states. Whereas the latter were profoundly constrained, the former were free to follow policies that were at odds with the orthodoxy established in Washington. Moreover, as non-American governments they were at one remove from imperialist fervour and imperial responsibilities. Most important, they were spared the requirement to put military duties at the top of public priorities. The consequence was that Western countries outside the American union could still adhere to an illusion of national independence, and of an independent national politics. Politicians and voters in these countries were encouraged in the belief that American tolerance could be secured at the price of anticommunism, and that matters of social and economic policy could normally be resolved without reference to the American ambassador. Although conditions were different on the frontiers of the empire – where imperial security concerns were paramount – this situation encouraged progressives everywhere outside the United States to associate national independence with the possibility of progressive action. To be progressive politically was to work for autonomy in relation to the United States, and to insist on the prerogatives of the national government and the national parliament. This reinforced the statist tendencies of European social democracy and of Asian, African, and Latin American anticolonialism. Even in Canada, where the sense of being different from America was least pronounced, there was a strong sense that national independence was necessary if creative responses to local problems were to be found.

The simple solutions of regional nationalism were not available to the fifty states that were part of the American union, even though some of them (California, New York, Texas, and Illinois) could have rivalled the major European states as powers in their own right. Instead, these states were implicated in an American nationalism that inevitably took an imperialist guise. The two main critical responses to American imperialism – isolationism and internationalism – tended to wish the world away. In the one case, the United States was imagined as a country just like the others, which could focus on its own problems and pretend that what it did had limited external effects. In the other, the world was reimagined as the United States on a larger scale, governed by the same principles of political and social organization. By comparison, American imperialism was more sensitive to actual differences in the world. In the heartland of the empire, it was difficult to imagine that fundamental change could occur on any scale other than a global one. This meant that those who addressed themselves to the question of a progressive politics had to orient themselves toward a political space that opened outward to the furthest reaches of the American empire, and yet was constrained by the wants and needs of the heartland. The politics they wanted to practise was made doubly difficult by the fact that imperial authority was relegitimated every two years by popular vote in the heartland. It is difficult enough to criticize imperial policy from within the imperial court; when that policy appears to command massive popular support, the danger of dissent is greatly enhanced.

This helps to explain the apparent ideological uniformity of American politics. However, it is easy for foreigners to be deceived about American conformism, since the forms and practices of critical politics in the United States are necessarily different from what they are elsewhere. In the United States, the imperial presence is felt day by day in the minutest details of life, and to pose alternatives to the regime is to threaten not just the government of a particular province such as France or Sweden, but the whole imperial order. In this context, American progressive politics has been marked by a series of strategic shifts that have given it a quite distinctive character. Most obviously, it stopped being socialist after socialism came to be identified with anti-Americanism. Instead, it situated itself in the distinctively liberal, populist, and democratic traditions of the United States, proclaiming thereby the possibility of realizing the American dream and fulfilling the American Revolution. That there was an indigenous revolutionary tradition to which Americans could appeal was of major importance, since it gave the American left a means of presenting itself as hyperpatriotic in a context in which the charge of un-Americanism was bound to be advanced. The suspicion of socialism was that it would be illiberal, undemocratic, and centralist; American progressives had to counter this by appearing more liberal, more democratic, and more decentralist than their political opponents. These tendencies were especially marked in the New Left.

A postsocialist progressivism was also encouraged by the relatively advanced state of the American economy. It was already clear by the early 1960s that the future economy would not be dominated by the old heavy industries with their masses of organized workers. The moment of social democracy, with a left based in the labour movement, had already passed, as the moment of agrarian democracy had passed before. American progressives had to deal with a reality in which the majority of people had come to understand themselves as middle class, and resisted the strong distinctions between manual and nonmanual workers that had informed an earlier class consciousness. In this new reality, the natural constituency of the left was difficult to identify, and the tendency was to respond opportunistically to whatever discontents emerged. Thus, the struggle for the civil rights of black Americans, the protest against an unpopular war in Indochina, the concern about poverty in the cities, and the resistance to a conformist national culture came together in the movements associated with the New Left; these in turn spawned new forms of protest associated with feminism and environmentalism. The lack of a hegemonic socialist party encouraged experimentation, allowed people to make unlikely political alliances, focused attention on particular local issues, and transformed ideological militancy into a kind of tactical daring. American progressivism came to be characterized by extraordinarily heated conflicts with the authorities over relatively small issues. Moreover, the movement as a whole developed as a cultural presence rather than as an organization, and as such spread far beyond the boundaries of the United States.

Socialists have long stressed the fact that revolutionary change depends on cultural transformation, but many of them have had trouble with the idea that the change could come in such a disorganized fashion. The efforts of the SPD in Germany before the First World War, the SPAD in Vienna before 1934, and the Communists in the U.S.S.R., China, Cuba, and elsewhere have provided various models for an organized cultural revolution. Usually the experience has seemed more appealing at a distance than up close. In any case, the notable fact is that these cultural revolutions seem to have been quite transitory compared with the fundamental changes that have come with the advance of capitalism. In contrast, the New Left presented itself as the effect of a cultural revolution that it did not pretend to control: it was the political expression of something that came up from below and that could not be harnessed or disciplined for anyone's purposes. Although there is reason to doubt the permanency of some of the cultural changes associated with the New Left, the form of politics it practised does seem to have been prefigurative. By de-emphasizing class, focusing on issues of race and gender, representing the national as global, and defining the issues in terms of a variety of different but compatible social movements, the New Left articulated a more complex space for progressive politics; in this sense it anticipated political conditions that have become more obvious since 1989. The political space in which the New Left operated did not have the same slope everywhere, give everyone the same political schedule, or centre activity in the same spot. As the conditions that allowed for the linkage of nationalism and socialism have deteriorated in the 1980s and 1990s, even the European left has had to come to terms with a political space that lacks the simple form to which it had become accustomed.

The collapse of the Soviet Bloc and the reorganization of global capital have weakened American hegemony, and the effect of this has been to reduce the political differences between the American heartland and the other advanced industrial countries. International capital – especially in the form of the bond-rating agencies – is an obvious presence in the domestic politics of every country. One need only turn on the television or pick up the paper when the government's budget is being discussed to learn what the 'sovereign' authorities will and will not be permitted to do. National autonomy with respect to fiscal, monetary, and commercial policy is becoming increasingly illusory; the regulative presence of global capital in people's daily lives is becoming more apparent. As I write this in 1995, popular resistance to the disciplinary measures of global capital is weak and confused, and there is little immediate prospect of an effective challenge to policies that transfer more resources to the wealthy and enhance capitalist freedom. Nevertheless, it seems clear that the modalities for a future socialist politics – for a politics that mobilizes those people who cannot depend on their capital for a living in a struggle with the capitalist system – will be quite different from what they were in postwar Sweden, interwar Vienna, or revolutionary Russia. This new socialist politics is likely to be articulated in a political space more like the one that the American New Left encountered. If so, the socialist organizations that once hegemonized the politics of the left will be replaced by a panoply of institutions with more modest aims and with a more complex relationship with other critical social movements.

In this context, the frustrations of local socialism in Britain and urban progressivism in North America do not prove that municipal politics is futile; rather, they prove that municipal politics must be taken more seriously. Implicit in the dismissal of municipal activism is the belief in a sovereign who could sweep the obstacles away if he were so inclined. Implicit in this belief is that the answer to one's political frustrations is to win the next election, if not nationally then provincially. Only when people are blocked out altogether do they retreat to their radical ghetto, to nurse their political wounds and plot revenge. In this conception, the local is *always* a poor alternative, and local objectives are *always* subordinate to the struggle at the centre. What seems clear, however, is that the centres established since 1932 in the belt around America cannot hold. It is a comforting illusion to think that power comes with the accoutrements of sovereignty, but it is an illusion we must overcome.

# PART THREE

# Beyond Sovereignty

The challenges posed by local socialism, progressive cities, and radical municipalism obviously have not been able to halt the trend toward neoliberalism and neoconservatism. Progressive politics seems more confused now than it has ever been, and the apparent failure of socialism as a political movement hangs heavily upon us. It seems that in trying to be too much – the source of spiritual and cultural renewal, the centre of humanism, the alpha and omega of politics – socialism has become too little: a shadow of itself, unable to mount any serious opposition to capitalism. In this context, it is worth considering more carefully the initiatives associated with radical municipalism. Three are given particular attention here: the unsuccessful attempt by local authorities in Britain and British Columbia to defy the fiscal restraints imposed upon them in the mid-1980s (Chapter 9); the efforts by women's organizations to create and sustain their own institutions inside/outside the local state (Chapter 10); and the foreign policy initiatives on the part of local authorities on both sides of the Atlantic in the context of an escalating Cold War (Chapter 11). These stories are of particular interest because they expose the problem of sovereignty in different ways. What we see in these examples are the efforts of local people to create for themselves their own political spaces, in opposition to the practices of sovereignty. None of these efforts were entirely successful, but they shed light on the need and the opportunity for creating expansive political spaces at the local level.

In Chapter 12, I draw back and pose some of these issues in a different way. The state system appears as an overwhelming reality, and students of international relations tend to take as a ground for theorizing that which is external to domestic politics. In a rather speculative vein, I attempt to draw out the idea that the current world order is best understood as a global city or as a movement toward urbanism as a way of life. This leads to the suggestion that world politics must now be conceived as urban politics, and that states should be understood as glorified municipalities. While such an analysis can only be sketched here, its full implications would obviously take us beyond sovereignty as the organizing principle of political understanding.

# 9

# Fiscal Struggles and Municipal Autonomy

It is a major historical irony that a left that had denigrated local government for forty years had to defend it so vigorously in the 1980s. As we have noted, one of the premises of postwar social-democracy was centralization. To deal with capital effectively, to provide uniform social security, and to ensure the same high standards of public services everywhere, it was deemed necessary to move the power of decision upward from the locality to the region, from the region to the nation, and (if possible) from the nation to the world as a whole. Thus, to be socialist or social democratic in the 1940s and 1950s was to be centralist. The rhetoric of local choice was essentially conservative and antisocialist. Two developments reversed this ideological division: first, the rebellion within the Left against bureaucratic socialism and the rediscovery in that context of the virtues of communal self-government; and, second, the rediscovery by conservatives of the double power of the sovereign state and the sovereign individual in the struggle against socialism. There was a major theoretical effort on the right in the 1940s, 1950s, and 1960s to refurbish the nineteenth-century theories that glorified the strong state and the strong individual as bulwarks of the good society. However, it was not until the fiscal crisis of the state developed in the mid-1970s that these theories gained wider currency.[1] It was in that context that local government was redefined on the right as a problem to be resolved by stripping it of most of its powers.

There were really two neoconservative strategies for the destruction of local socialism and radical municipalism, one populist and one statist. In most respects these strategies were complementary. The populist emphasis was most apparent in the United States, where conservatives have long invoked fears of big government, and where the constitutional entrenchment of local government is such that direct attacks are difficult to mount. The simple solution for conservatives was to push the demand for local autonomy to its logical extreme and interpret it as the right of every individual to do what he pleased with his own money.[2] It followed that every individual should be able to get the public services he wanted and was willing to pay for. It also followed that charity toward others should not be compulsory: people should be allowed to decide for themselves what their duties ought to be. In the context of the developing fiscal crisis of the state, it was relatively easy for conservatives to say that people were being taxed for services they did not want and were also being forced to extend charity to the ungrateful and the undeserving.

It was in this context that the California tax revolt developed in the late 1970s.[3] Local governments were faced with popular initiatives – that is, laws adopted by statewide ballot – that imposed limits on their capacity to tax and spend. Municipal councils like those in Berkeley and Santa Monica soon found that, despite local majorities in favour of taxing and spending for certain purposes, they were prevented by state law from moving in desired directions. In effect, local socialism (if that is what was wanted) was legally prohibited. Californian activists found that their only recourse was to fight fire with fire – that is, to launch their own statewide initiatives and to pursue their options locally by means of ballot initiatives that could override state restrictions. Thus, the rent controls that were introduced in Berkeley and Santa Monica came by means of local ballot initiatives, and so did Berkeley's mandatory recycling program.

In Britain and Canada, there was little scope for ballot initiatives, and so the struggle over fiscal limits took a different shape. The conservatives were obliged to use the power of the central state more directly, and the left had to claim for local authorities a kind of sovereignty in relation to the centre. There were remarkably similar struggles along these lines in British Columbia and in much of Britain in the early to mid 1980s. These struggles came to a head almost simultaneously. On 15 March 1985, thirty-five of British Columbia's locally elected school boards defied a neoconservative provincial government by submitting for approval 'needs' budgets that clearly exceeded provincial budgetary guidelines.[4] A week and a day before this, fifteen local councils in England had taken similar action, by declaring that they were unable to finance their services with the 'rates' they were allowed to levy.[5] On 6 May 1985, the most militant of the B.C. authorities, the Vancouver School Board, was dismissed from office, and the Vancouver school system was placed under trusteeship. On 26 June 1985, legal action began in Britain, which led ultimately to the surcharge and disqualification of the defiant Labour majorities on the Lambeth and Liverpool councils. These measures delivered the councils concerned into the hands of the local opposition. When new elections were held in Lambeth, Liverpool, and Vancouver, a defiant left was returned to power locally, in a scenario reminiscent of Poplar in the 1920s. Some elements of the left took heart from these shows of resistance, but others were disappointed by the fact that most of the initially resistant local authorities quickly capitulated when faced with the choice between 'going illegal' and accepting what they regarded as illiberal and undemocratic restrictions on local autonomy.

Although these struggles took place more than a decade ago, they remain of interest, and not only because the effort to put fiscal restraints on local authorities has continued to the present. What was at issue in these struggles was the nature of sovereignty. Did the principle really imply that a central government could deprive a democratically elected local authority of the right to tax and spend as it chose within its own territory?[6] Or was there in fact a democratic right of self-government that entitled such a local authority to defy a supposedly sovereign legislature so long as the people in the community concerned were prepared to support it? Did local authorities, their leaders, and their work-forces have a right of civil disobedience when they were confronted with a central government that was abusing its own authority and preventing municipalities from exercising their own autonomy? What, in a practical sense, could the aggrieved local authorities hope to accomplish by resisting a determined central government? How effective were tactics of evasion and delay, and in what circumstances could authorities hope to be successful in outright resistance? These cases offer no simple answers to these questions. However, it is worth looking again at what happened, if only because most local authorities – and indeed most national governments – seem to have given up on their efforts to resist the fiscal restraints that are being demanded by the bond and money traders. Whatever else these stories show, they indicate that local resistance can put the higher authorities in a difficult dilemma, and open a public debate about where major decisions on taxation and public spending should be made.

### The Rate-Capping Campaign in England

One of the remarkable features of the Thatcher government in Britain was the close and continuing attention it paid to the organization of local government. Whatever Thatcher's original plans may have been, her government had to devote as much time and attention to restraining the local authorities as it did to restraining the unions. Few people would have predicted this when she came to office. However, in retrospect, one can see that the suppression of local socialism and the reorganization of local government on American lines – with smaller-scale authorities offering assistance to capital and mediating the provision of public services by the private sector – was as important for her program as weakening the unions. Thus, her government introduced a series of measures to privatize public housing and public transport, enforce competitive tendering for public services, abolish the metropolitan planning authorities, limit local controls over private business, and so on.[7] These measures were broad and extensive enough that they generated wide opposition among groups with vested interests in the previous arrangements. The government intended to 'make Britain safe from socialism,' at a time when socialists were making political gains at the local level. This put the left in a position where it had to mount as stiff a resistance as it could to Thatcherite initiatives.

Thatcher's government certainly was not the first to be concerned about local spending and taxation.[8] The rates – the taxes levied on the rental value of property – had long been the most important source of income for local authorities. However, in the nineteenth century, grants from the central government began to grow in importance as an element of local finance. Since the 1920s, what Canadians would call the unconditional portion of these grants had been increasing. Legislation in 1929 (and 1948) introduced (and strengthened) the equalization formula used by the central government. The Conservatives especially were concerned about relieving the 'burden on the rates' resulting from the expansion of local services. Labour was more concerned about providing fiscal incentives to authorities who might otherwise neglect what was required. Generally, however, in the thirty years following the end of the Second World War, national governments of both stripes tended to take a positive view of local spending. In 1974, there was a major reorganization of local government, under Conservative aegis. The new arrangements were premised on a continued expansion of public services and interventionist economic management, not necessarily informed by the logic of the market. These structural reforms coincided with a shift in opinion in both major parties about the value of local spending. Local expenditure came to be regarded – after the oil shock of 1973, the consequent inflation, and the subsequent stagnation of the economy – as a problem rather than as a solution to problems. It was said that the public sector could not continue to expand more rapidly than the economy as a whole without inducing inflation and impairing productivity in the private sector. Since spending by local authorities was such a large component of total public expenditures, the widespread assumption was that the local councils would have to be induced or required to restrain themselves.

In October 1976, Anthony Crosland, environment secretary in the Labour government of James Callaghan made a famous speech to the local authorities in which he announced, 'The party is over' (that is, the era of rapid increases in local spending had come to an end).[9] This followed Britain's resort to the International Monetary Fund to rescue the pound, and the IMF's insistence on a series of austerity measures. The previous year, Chancellor Denis Healey had established a Consultative Council on Local Government Finance, which was intended to involve the local authorities in formulating plans for expenditure restraint. Although in the preceding decades Labour had been more interventionist than the Conservatives with respect to local government having nationalized a number of local government services, set standards of provision for others, required land-use planning, and generally stimulated local spending with relatively generous grants – it moved cautiously to impose restraint. At first it relied strictly on persuasion; only later did it move to freeze and then reduce grants to the local authorities. In the Conservative view, these cautious measures were insufficient. After their victory in the 1979 elections, the Conservatives pursued more vigorous policies. Labour's subsequent criticisms of the Thatcher government tended to obscure two important facts: that the new policies of fiscal restraint were initiated by Labour, and that Labour itself had accepted the principle that the national government could intervene to influence if not regulate local budgets. In the period of expansion, there was little question of regulation, since fiscal incentives could do the job. In the new conditions of the mid-1970s, the Layfield Committee on Local Government Finance had speculated about the need for direct central control over local budgets.[10] Although the Callaghan government was uneasy about going so far, it clearly believed that it had the right, and indeed the duty, to intervene in local financial affairs in whatever way was necessary to ensure proper balance in the national economy. This was the rationale offered by the Thatcher government for moving toward direct budgetary control.

The preceding Labour governments had altered the grants system to take account of the high spending requirements of urban authorities – most of which, as the Conservatives noted, were normally under the control of local Labour parties. Although the formula for determining grants to particular authorities had become exceedingly complex by the late 1970s, a major factor was the authority's level of spending in previous years. The more an authority needed to spend – as indicated by its spending in the past – the more grant it could attract. To the Conservatives, this seemed like an incentive to profligacy. When they came to power in 1979, they were determined to revise the system of grants so as to provide incentives to economy and disincentives to high spending. During Thatcher's first term, granting arrangements were revised constantly with these objectives in mind. Each authority was subjected to a 'grant related expenditure assessment' (GREA) that was intended to show what the authority ought to be spending in light of its needs. On these assessments, most of the urban authorities – and especially the Labour ones – were spending far too much, and some of the rural Conservative authorities too little. An authority spending at or near its GREA could expect to have a given proportion of its expenditures funded by central grants. Additional money would be provided to make up for resource or rate deficiencies. However, authorities that went past a certain threshold in spending would be penalized by having their resource estimates raised and their percentage grants reduced. Most urban authorities faced thresholds so low that they were bound to be in this penalty range. The government recognized that it could not expect the dramatic cuts it wanted immediately, so it set more realistic targets for expenditure reduction. Authorities that exceeded their targets by more than a certain percentage were subjected to a further penalty in the form of grant hold-backs. These hold-backs became progressive claw-backs in 1981. Their effect was to take as many as four pounds of grant money away for each pound of excess expenditure.

At the beginning, the Conservatives (like Labour before them) had assumed that local authorities would be unable or unwilling to resort to the rates to make up for lost grants. After all, the rates – like property taxes in the United States – were highly unpopular. However, the high-spending authorities soon found that they could raise the rates dramatically at small political cost. Most of the authorities concerned were solidly held by Labour and could tolerate a big swing against them. In any case, many of their poorer constituents were protected against rate increases because they were 'on benefit' (that is, getting welfare); or they were entitled to rate rebates because of their low incomes. In the case of 'council' (that is, public housing) tenants, authorities could partly conceal the size of the rate increase by holding the line on rent increases. Moreover, the government's restraint measures could easily be characterized as *so* unjust and *so* arbitrary that people ought to be prepared to defy them, even at the cost of huge rate increases.

As the objecting authorities pointed out, the new grant system was introduced without consultation, by a government that was unwilling to change it in face of criticism. In both respects, this was a break from past practice.[11] It was also clear that the whole system was biased in favour of the (Tory) shires and against the (Labour) urban authorities. Estimates of required spending in the urban areas were unrealistically low, and there seemed to have been many fiddles in the grant calculations that saved Tory authorities who might have been caught by the rules. As the Labour authorities began to incur penalties and the Tory authorities got the rewards of good behaviour, the disparity in grants increased. Thatcherite authorities such as Wandsworth and Westminster emerged with sweetheart deals that enabled them to set rates artificially low, while neighbouring Labour authorities had to raise their rates to extraordinary levels to make up for lost grants.[12] This certainly convinced many electors and local politicians that the price of resistance to Thatcherism was too high; but it also stiffened the resistance of those who believed that the government's measures were arbitrary and unjust.

Some of the local authorities – including the Greater London Council and the Inner London Education Authority, the two biggest in England – were so much above the government's targets in their spending that they no longer got the unconditional grants. This made them immune to further grant penalties. Other authorities that were still getting grants wre prepared to ignore the government's wishes, because they could evade many controls by 'creative accounting' and make up for grant deficiencies by raising their rates. Creative accounting became increasingly important after 1983. Authorities found that they could minimize the effects of government controls by shifting money in and out of reserve accounts, changing definitions of current and capital expenditures, and mortgaging fixed assets under lease-back arrangements – in short, by adopting every possible accounting trick. Since the government had to lay down the rules before the authorities made their budgets, local treasurers always had the benefit of the last move in a complex game. One of the reasons the rules kept changing from year to year – a source of much complaint from the local authorities – is that the local treasurers kept discovering new loopholes.

Some of the creative accounting was necessary to enable authorities to go on making capital investments, especially in new public-housing stock. Borrowing by local authorities for capital expenditures had long been subject to central approval, and both Labour and Conservative governments had used this power over local investment as a tool of national economic management. After 1973, there had been a dramatic decline in investment by local authorities, partly as a result of national policy. Also, authorities responded to higher borrowing costs by finding other means of financing capital expenditures. When the Conservative government obliged local authorities to begin selling council houses to sitting tenants, this raised the prospect that the capital receipts could be used to build new public housing. That was the last thing the government wanted. In 1981 it assumed the power to limit the total capital spending, from any funding source, of any local authority. In subsequent years it put increasingly stringent limits on the use of money from house sales.[13]

While these various measures made life difficult for the local authorities, the total effect on spending was more limited than the government had hoped. This ultimately led to the Rates Act of 1984, which – though it still left the local authorities free to determine their levels of current spending – gave the government the power to cap the rates of authorities that were, in its view, guilty of overspending. The effect of capping rates was (or so it seemed) to force a reduction in expenditures, since the rates were the only significant source of tax revenue available to the local authorities. Local authorities were required by law to balance their budgets. Moreover, local councillors were subject to surcharge and disqualification from office if they caused financial loss to their authorities by neglecting to make a legal budget on time. An authority without a legal budget could not collect rates and so would have to either suspend operations or sustain itself with expensive bridging loans. Either course of action would involve huge costs, for which the councillors responsible would be legally liable.

The Rates Act was foreshadowed by the 1983 White Paper on the Rates and by an item in the Conservative Party election platform that year.[14] It followed on from what the Conservatives regarded as a series of highly successful measures in Scotland. The Scottish authorities were then as now under a different fiscal and legislative regime from their English counterparts. In 1981 the Secretary of State for Scotland had assumed the power to reduce central grants to authorities that were (in his view) overspending. This gave him more powers than his English counterpart, because the grant cutbacks were applied after the rates were set for the year in question. Since supplementary rates were already illegal in Scotland and any borrowing required the secretary's approval, the Scottish authorities had little room for manoeuvre. Several authorities – including Lothian Regional Council, which covers the Edinburgh region – were caught by these measures in 1981. In 1982, the secretary of state was given the additional power to limit rate increases. Lothian and other councils were victims of this as well in 1983. Not only were local taxes and expenditures reduced by these means, but the local socialists in Lothian were so battered by the experience that they lost the local elections.[15]

The government evidently was heartened by the Scottish experience, but its opponents were equally heartened by the experience in Liverpool. Liverpool's council had been controlled since 1983 by the Militant Tendency, a Trotskyist grouping within the Labour Party. When the time came to set the budget for 1984–5, Militant declared that it could not do so without breaking its electoral pledge to maintain jobs and services while keeping (public housing) rents and rates stable. Liverpool was thus without a rate until July 1984, when it finally reached a settlement with the government that raised its share of central grants. The government understood this as a special case – Liverpool was desperately poor and yet was not getting as much in the way of central grants as richer authorities such as Manchester. However, Militant claimed a great victory when the settlement was announced. It took it as proof that militancy worked – that the Thatcher government could be intimidated by the threat of chaos or revolutionary resistance in its major cities.[16]

The left looked back to two other instances in which rebel Labour councillors had defied a Conservative government: Poplar in the 1920s, when the issues were relief rates and public sector wages; and Clay Cross in the 1970s, when the issue was council house rents.[17] The Clay Cross case was still fresh in people's minds. The national leadership of the Labour Party was criticized on the left for its reluctance to give any substantial support to the Clay Cross councillors. The situation in 1984 was not much different, in the sense that the Labour leadership wanted to distance itself from any hint of illegal activity – especially since the miners' strike, which the Labour leaders regarded as an embarrassment, was becoming violent. The Militant Tendency was a grave embarrassment to Labour leaders trying to win back the centre vote; its apparent success in Liverpool was probably as much of a disappointment to the Labour Leader, Neil Kinnock, as it was to Thatcher.[18] At the same time, the Militant success gave 'small m' militants within the Labour Party good reason to stiffen their own resistance to Thatcher. It seemed that between them, the miners and the local socialist authorities might actually force Thatcher to back down. In any case, it was dangerous for the rest of the left, which was generally anti-Militant, to let Militant claim that only it was prepared to fight.

At the Labour Party's Local Government Conference on 6 and 7 July 1984, the left authorities, which governed most of the country's bigger cities, agreed on a strategy of noncompliance. The Local Government Campaign Unit was to co-ordinate their activities and press their case publicly. A number of trade unions – especially the ones involved in local government – joined the unit as well, and contributed resources to supplement the ones made available by the local authorities. The unit also attempted to involve the voluntary sector in its campaign, arguing that voluntary organizations were bound to have their grants from local government cut if the authorities lost their power to levy adequate rates. There was much lobbying of Parliament, along with various rallies and marches and a media campaign that was supposed to culminate in the Trade Union Congress's Democracy Week – itself coinciding with the crucial budget meetings of the rate-capped councils.

Even though Liverpool escaped rate-capping in the July determination, the councillors there decided to join with the rate-capped authorities in resisting the government's measures. This reflected Militant's determination to be seen as the leader of what it saw as a class struggle.[19] Militant's leaders understood their activity in terms of a struggle that was ultimately revolutionary. The same was true of many of the leaders in Lambeth, who were connected to a different Trotskyist grouping that was quite hostile to Militant. In the other Labour authorities, Trotskyist elements had much less influence, even among the 'hard' left. Generally, the noncompliant authorities were dominated by loose coalitions of the Labour left, with 'softer' leaders than the ones in Lambeth and Liverpool. These softer leaders were more hesitant about 'going illegal,' if only because they were more sceptical about their capacity to maintain the necessary political support, and more leery of what the government could do destroy their fragile bases of power.[20]

The Labour groups on local councils normally tried to act in a disciplined way. Party policy was worked out in group meetings, and dissenters were expected to abide by group decisions. This meant that a left minority could actually control the council, by virtue of controlling the group. In some places, including Liverpool, the group actually was controlled by the executive of the District Labour Party, whose policies Labour members were pledged to execute. Thus, an authority could be controlled by a minority of its council members, acting in accordance with instructions from an external body. In most cases, however, group discipline was rather fragile, since the means of enforcing it were not very effective and the groups were divided into hostile factions. In the arguments over rate-capping, councillors disposed toward compliance could take comfort in the fact that the national leadership of the Labour Party disapproved of any illegal action and generally regarded the party's left wing with great suspicion. As the threat of surcharge and disqualification became clearer, and the rumblings of disapproval from the National Executive Committee of the Labour Party grew louder, it became increasingly difficult for the left leaders to maintain control over their own groups.

The hard-left leaders fully expected betrayal. In some ways they even welcomed it, since it would show who really could be trusted to fight for working-class interests. The soft left had the greatest interest in maintaining unity but the least capacity for enforcing it. It could not move toward compromise without losing the support of the hard left, and it could not hold the loyalty of the waverers in the centre unless it could show that there was no alternative but compliance. As the time for budget-making grew closer, the leading councillors began to realize that creative accounting actually could enable most of the authorities concerned to maintain or even expand services without levying an illegal rate. As events proved, the Greater London Council – the flagship authority of the Labour left – was able to expand services while levying a rate well below the figure the government had set. None of the other councils were quite so flush with cash, but the plasticity of creative accounting was such that all the councils could avoid the drastic cuts in jobs and services that they had earlier declared would be inevitable because of government rate-capping. Thus, the waverers had somehow to be convinced that, even though there was a way out, they should incur disqualification from public office and personal bankruptcy in order to make a political point. Needless to say, many of the waverers were not convinced.

Most of the left leaders probably knew that all but one or two of the Labour groups would break under the pressure. Labour had a slim majority on many of the councils, and the left in turn had a slim majority in many of the groups. Thus, only a handful of councillors had to defect to make a policy of noncompliance impossible. This was especially true in the flagship authority, the Greater London Council. However, once committed to a strategy of noncompliance, the left was virtually obliged to see it through, hoping against hope that it could maintain a facade of unity long enough to scare the government into some concessions. The implicit threat to the government was that it would be faced with a simultaneous breakdown in local government services in a number of Britain's major cities, including London. Ultimately, it would be forced to 'send in the commissioners' – that is, put its own agents in to run the town halls and enforce the cutbacks it wanted. However, the commissioners would be faced with a hostile labour force that was loyal to the disqualified local councillors. The workers might go out on a general strike, or occupy all the administrative offices, or simply engage in an extended campaign of nonco-operation. In any case, it would be impossible for the commissioners to accomplish their mission, and the government would be revealed as incapable of governing. This is what the revolutionaries in the Labour Party hoped for; the soft-left leaders hoped the government would see it as a realistic enough prospect that compromise would be worthwhile.

In the event, the government decided to wait things out, in the expectation that the opposition would eventually crumble. And crumble it did.

On 18 December 1984, the noncompliant councils had agreed on a common resolution that they would all adopt the following spring. After an unfruitful meeting with the government on 4 February, the exact terms were set, and the resolution was duly adopted by fifteen councils on 7 March 1985. Among these fifteen were Liverpool, Manchester, Sheffield, and nine of the London boroughs. The form of the resolution was soft, in that it simply declared that the councils concerned were unable to set a rate at that time. Since they were under no clear legal obligation to do so then, their resolutions did no more than hold out the possibility of illegal action in the future. However, the upper-tier authorities were under a legal duty to set their rates (technically their precepts on the rates levied by the lower-tier authorities) by 10 March, and so had a much more pressing decision to make about illegality. None of the upper-tier authorities were controlled by the hard left, and in many the leaders had made it clear from the beginning that they could not carry their groups into illegality. Continuation of the campaign of defiance really depended on the Greater London Council, the crown jewel of the Labour left, which was led by the most famous of the local socialists, the bête noire of the Tory press, Ken Livingstone.

Unfortunately for the campaign, the left in the GLC Labour group had already split by the time of the meeting of 10 March. The boroughs' decision to go with soft resolutions on 7 March had helped secure unity then, but at the price of increasing the GLC's exposure. The miners' strike had collapsed shortly before, so Thatcher was no longer fighting on two fronts. The national Labour leadership was anxious that the GLC comply with the law. The left majority in the Labour group was razor-thin at best. Then, Livingstone and his hard-left deputy, John McDonnell, had a bitter falling out over the implications of the budget figures. Livingstone claimed that McDonnell had concealed the fact that the GLC could actually increase spending within the rate limits. McDonnell said Livingstone had known this all along and was simply seeking an excuse to 'bottle out.' The left split between them, the right and centre of the party aligned with the Tories, and a compliance budget was set at a rate well below the legal limits. The media were treated to explosive recriminations between the leading figures on the left, and it became clear that the national rate-capping campaign was bound to fail.[21]

One by one, the other defiant authorities fell into line and set rates.[22] Only where the competing Trotskyist factions were strongest, in Lambeth and Liverpool, did the councils hold out until the summer. The district auditors set in motion the legal proceedings that ultimately led to surcharge and disqualification for the councillors involved. Liverpool tried to proceed with what was in fact, if not in form, a deficit budget. As in 1984, it tried to threaten the national government with a breakdown of services in Liverpool. But Thatcher had been embarrassed by her minister's weakness the preceding summer and was quite prepared to call Liverpool's bluff. The council in Liverpool tried to convince its workers of the need for an all-out strike to back its demands. By this time, however, the workers' confidence in the ultimate success of the campaign had been shaken, and the necessary majority for a strike was not secured. In September, the council infuriated its employees by issuing three-month redundancy notices in anticipation of a possible shutdown of the civic government in December. In October, at the Labour Conference, Neil Kinnock launched a fierce attack on Militant, and began moves to break its control of the party in Liverpool.[23] As their support dwindled, the Militant leaders finally backed down and reworked the budget to avoid the predicted collapse.

Many of the same councils faced rate-capping in 1986, and responded to it with creative accounting rather than with outright resistance. The GLC and the metropolitan counties, which had given the Labour left such a strong national presence, were abolished that year. The remaining left authorities had neither the will nor the capacity to continue the fight on their own. Especially in London, many of them were wracked by internal divisions, as the soft left accused the hard left of adventurism and the hard left accused the soft of selling out. Although many of the initiatives associated with local socialism in the early 1980s continued in one form or another, the left authorities generally retreated into a defensive posture and tried to deal with continuing Thatcherite measures in the spirit of the 'new realism.'[24] That new realism was to keep the left authorities on the sidelines during the campaign against the 'poll tax,' the new flat-rate per capita tax that replaced the rates in the spring of 1990. Militants in the streets led the campaign – in some cases attempting physically to prevent left councils from setting their poll tax charges – but no local council tried again to go illegal. Despite or because of this, the unpopularity of the poll tax contributed substantially to the turn of opinion against Margaret Thatcher and the Conservative Party.[25]

**Restraining the School Boards**

In British Columbia, the conflict between the Social Credit government and the municipalities never got as fierce as in Britain, because the municipalities were little involved in social spending. Health, education, and welfare expenditures were beyond municipal control; municipal public housing programs were insignificant; and public transit was under provincial control. Municipal spending was largely confined to infrastructural investments and housekeeping services of the types that even conservatives regarded as necessary. At the same time, however, the school boards were in charge of what conservatives regarded as a lavish and inefficient school system that (together with equally lavish and inefficient health and welfare systems) was threatening to bankrupt the province.[26] Since the school boards were the only elected local authorities the province had to contend with in the process of imposing fiscal restraint on social spending, it was perhaps to be expected that those boards would emerge as important centres of opposition. For this to happen, however, extraordinary pressures had to be placed on them, since they traditionally had been apolitical.

The postwar political landscape in British Columbia was in some ways very similar to the one in Britain, in that provincial politics was ideologically polarized.[27] However, the social democratic left in B.C.

never enjoyed the successes of the Labour Party in Britain. By 1985 the NDP had formed the provincial government only once (1972–5), and at the local level the left generally was poorly organized. However, the left made significant gains in Vancouver municipal politics during the 1970s, and emerged very strong in 1980, when New Democrat Mike Harcourt captured the mayoralty and the Committee of Progressive Electors won a majority on the school board.[28] Harcourt remained in office until 1986; in the last four years of his term there was a centre-left majority on the council, with COPE controlling four of the eleven seats. COPE lost its majority on the school board in November 1982 but regained it two years later. Thus, in 1984–5, the Social Credit provincial government was confronted with what it regarded as hostile local authorities in the city of Vancouver. Given that about half the people in B.C. live in metropolitan Vancouver, the emergence there of potential centres of resistance was of great political significance.

As Michael Howlett and Keith Brownsey have reminded us, the conservative coalition that governed B.C. with just one break between 1941 and 1991 was always concerned about fiscal restraint with respect to social spending.[29] When Social Credit returned to office in December 1975 – just after the federal government began its own restraint program – it began immediately to develop plans and proposals for limiting the growth of public spending and employment. In the late 1970s the restraints applied were comparatively moderate; in the early 1980s they intensified as the province entered a severe recession and provincial revenues declined. In a formal sense, the restraint program began in February 1982, and was – in the government's view – ratified by the electorate in May 1983. The July budget of that year intensified restraint and introduced a variety of measures that were widely viewed as an attack on established social rights.[30] This resulted in mass protests under the banner of the Solidarity Coalition, and escalating strike action spearheaded by the B.C. Government Employees' Union and co-ordinated by Operation Solidarity. The strikes and protests reached a peak in November 1983, when a settlement was reached that involved some minor government concessions. The B.C. Teachers' Federation had been among the organizations that pulled its members out on a strike of doubtful legality.[31]

In terms of its emotional impact on the left in B.C., the Solidarity campaign was comparable to the miners' strike and rate-capping campaign in Britain. The Kelowna Accord, which brought the Solidarity protests to an end, was regarded by some as a victory but by others as an outrageous sell-out.[32] In any case, it brought many to the brink of 'illegal' action or beyond: the BCTF, for instance, would have had to defy court injunctions to continue its strike. The withdrawal from the brink had left many so emotionally drained – and so doubtful that an illegal protest could be sustained – that it was difficult to contemplate any repetition. The government obviously relied on this emotional and political exhaustion in pressing its advantage over the next three years. By avoiding issues that would unite the opposition and by moving in fits and starts in many different venues, the Socreds were able to maintain the pressure without creating the explosion they had faced in 1983.[33]

In attacking the labour unions, the government could count on considerable public support. However, the schools and the teachers were more difficult to deal with politically, because of the depth of concern about education among the conservative middle-class. The teachers could be labelled fairly effectively as a privileged group in need of restraint, but children and school boards were another matter. At the beginning of the formal restraint program in 1982, budget cutbacks in education were not really unpopular; but as one restraint measure followed another over the next few years, middle-class opposition on the school boards and in the electorate intensified. This allowed the left to begin organizing more militant opposition. COPE's success in the Vancouver School Board elections of November 1984, during which it pledged to resist further restraint, is perhaps indicative of the shift that had occurred. Only two years earlier, in November 1982, the conservative Non-Partisan Association – then led by the future prime minister, Kim Campbell – had argued successfully that a more moderate approach in dealing with the government would bring better results for the city's schools.

The key restraint measure with regard to education was the Education (Interim Finance) Act of April 1982.[34] This act gave the education minister the power to control school board budgets. School boards were stripped of their access to nonresidential property taxes – something Margaret Thatcher did not do to the local authorities in England until 1990. The budgetary controls also placed limits on what could be raised from residential property taxes; this ultimately involved limits not only on total spending but also on expenditures in various categories. The fiscal framework was changed frequently and retrospectively – four times during 1982 – so that school board budgeting was extraordinarily difficult. Gradually, the financial controls became tighter and more effective. By November 1984, many relatively conservative school boards were claiming that fiscal restraint had already gone as far as it reasonably should. In that context, demands that fiscal autonomy be restored to the school boards became more pressing.

The government claimed that the loss of autonomy was temporary – hence, the 'interim' designation of its key measure. There was also a precedent, in that fiscal limits had been imposed on the school boards by an earlier Social Credit government in 1969. As the education minister reminded everyone, he had the power under the School Act to place a recalcitrant board under trusteeship, and thus enforce the restraint the board itself was not prepared to implement. This threat remained abstract until the spring of 1985, when thirty-five school boards across the province submitted 'needs' budgets that exceeded provincial guidelines. Opposition among the school boards had by then become much stronger, especially in metropolitan Vancouver. In January 1985 the Metropolitan Education Association was established to co-ordinate the struggle. The Vancouver School Board, with its COPE majority and strong connections to the BCTF and to the unions, was clearly the leading centre of opposition, but the suburban Burnaby and Coquitlam boards were also promising to hold out against further cuts, whatever the government might do.[35]

On 6 May the province took preemptive action and dismissed the Vancouver School Board. Allan Stables was installed as sole trustee of the system. A week later, the Cowichan board on Vancouver Island was also placed under trusteeship. The Burnaby and Coquitlam boards avoided dismissal by submitting compliance budgets. As in England, creative accounting tended to blur the political issues involved. The province claimed that the boards could make economies without reducing services or letting more teachers go. The boards claimed that this would be impossible without using capital reserves that the province said could not be allocated for such purposes. When Stables took over the Vancouver board he made precisely such a use of the reserves. Burnaby and Coquitlam were encouraged to take similar action to avoid trusteeship. COPE's critics alleged that it had persisted in an illegal budget when it could have used creative accounting to maintain services without going illegal. COPE suggested that the government had been looking for an excuse to override the decision the Vancouver electors had made in November 1984.

The teachers in Vancouver refused to co-operate with Stables on a number of administrative committees. COPE organized various protest meetings and demonstrations, and led a petition campaign for new elections to the school board. It also brought an unsuccessful suit under the

Charter of Rights, alleging that the dismissal of the school board had violated the rights of the school trustees.[36] Until December, the education minister steadfastly refused to contemplate special elections, saying that a new board would be selected in November 1986. Unexpectedly, he then ordered special elections for January 1986, announcing simultaneously that the restraint program would come to an end that year. COPE organized effectively and won all of the school board seats in the special election. COPE's leaders hailed this as a complete vindication. However, by November, the political situation had changed: Bill Bennett had been succeeded by Bill Vander Zalm as Social Credit leader and premier, and Vander Zalm won a smashing victory in the October election, promising to end the conflict of the past few years. A revived and reorganized NPA capitalized on this spirit to regain control of the Vancouver council and defeat COPE in the school board elections. It has remained in power since.

Social Credit promised a permanent solution to overspending at the local level that was more American than British in inspiration. In 1984 the government introduced and then dropped a scheme that would have forced school boards to secure referendum approval for spending (and hence property taxation) above the levels recommended by the government. This use of the local electorate as fiscal disciplinarian was no doubt inspired by the American experience; in the United States, electors have been fairly consistent in turning down proposals for increased taxes to finance schools. In Britain the idea of requiring local authorities to hold referenda in similar circumstances had been introduced in Parliament in 1981, and then withdrawn in face of backbench Conservative opposition. In British Columbia the idea was revived in 1989: school boards seeking extra funding were obliged to seek referendum approval.[37] Significantly, the Vancouver School Board did so successfully in the spring of 1990; however, other boards without such a history of militancy refused to test the electoral waters. Generally, a new realism took hold in British Columbia as well as in Britain, and sapped the political will to resist.

**The Conditions of Effective Resistance**

In the fall of 1991, an NDP government again took power in British Columbia, having promised a balanced budget and respect for the market. It has adhered to centrist policies of the sort that the leaders of the Labour Party in Britain have been promising since the mid-1980s. (Early in 1996, the NDP education minister dismissed the school board in suburban North Vancouver because it refused to balance its budget.) This has not brought electoral rewards; on the contrary, the NDP premier is at the moment about as unpopular as Margaret Thatcher's successor, John Major. This suggests that policies of fiscal restraint offer little long-term electoral advantage to parties of the left, which must necessarily appeal to those who expect positive action in the face of market constraints. If that is the case, the resistance developed by left local authorities in the mid-1980s may be more instructive than the capitulation offered by provincial and national governments in the 1990s. Is the failure of this local resistance really a sign that there is 'no alternative'? Or can subsequent timidity be attributed to a failure of political imagination?

Local authorities are obviously at a disadvantage in relation to the state in terms of their legitimacy. The deficit in this regard is both formal (in both Britain and Canada, local authorities are constituted by ordinary statutes and as such are subject to restriction or even abolition by ordinary legislation) and political (although the right of local self-government is widely acknowledged, the locality is generally regarded as an inferior political community). Nonetheless, there are limits on a central government's capacity to endow its own acts with legitimacy, and these limits can be exploited by the local authorities. The radical local councils in Britain and British Columbia gave a good illustration of how these limits can be tested.

To retain its legitimacy, the central government must always act within the rule of law. This means following the required procedures scrupulously. Since these procedures are often complex, action may be so delayed that it becomes ineffective. Moreover, where the rule of law is followed, independent courts get to decide whether the procedures have been properly observed. This gives local authorities the opportunity to harry the central government with legal challenges, and in some cases to frustrate central action by securing an appropriate court order. One of the significant developments associated with the struggles in Britain was the exploration by local authorities of their means for challenging central government in the courts.[38] These means proved to be more extensive than many had imagined possible in a country that affords no special status to local government. Other limits on the central government are posed by constitutional understandings that are widely accepted, though unenforceable in the courts. It seems clear that the Thatcher and Bennett governments undermined the legitimacy of their own activities by acting outside the accepted norms. It is one thing to change the boundaries or functions of local government; it is another thing to abolish it altogether. It is one thing to limit central assistance to local governments; it is another to prevent a local authority from raising taxes for its own purposes. It is one thing to demand compliance with central policies; it is another thing to remove elected officials from office. Thus, the rate-capped authorities in Britain and the school boards in British Columbia could act under cover of legitimacy, in the face of the law itself, when they insisted on their right to tax and spend as they pleased. One might also cite related constitutional understandings about rights of consultation, procedural due process, and acceptance of difference that were violated by the central governments concerned. The Thatcher and Bennett governments both were accused of acting dictatorially, in the sense of refusing to canvass opinion before acting, ignoring all forms of criticism, conceding nothing to opposition views, and insisting on a uniform mode of local government even in areas of the country where that mode was wildly unpopular.

At the time they mounted their resistance, the local authorities could also rely on certain understandings about people's entitlements with regard to day-to-day life. These entitlements related to such matters as the right to health care or an education, the right to decent housing, the right to a job or to an income, and so on. The left authorities were able to enhance their own legitimacy by presenting themselves as the defenders of the welfare state. Since the central governments concerned had been elected without a clear mandate to dismantle the welfare state, and since the regime of Keynesian welfarism seemed to command majority popular support, it was possible for the resisters to present themselves as the defenders not only of local autonomy but of the democratic rights of the population as a whole. Of course, in this regard they were up against the statist assumption that elections for the sovereign authority provide a final resolution to such disputes.

It should be noted that in British Columbia, the Canadian Charter of Rights and Freedoms proved to be utterly ineffective in securing the right of local self-government (or any of the associated democratic rights). The legal suit by the dismissed school trustees in Vancouver was summarily dismissed by the B.C. Supreme Court, and those trustees lacked the resources (both financial and legal) to appeal this decision to the higher courts. The essential problem was and is that, though a right of local self-government may be widely asserted, it has never been accepted by the courts in any of the Anglo-American jurisdictions. The American view – and American jurisprudence is probably more sympathetic on this point than British or Canadian – is that any such right is inchoate and hence unenforceable. It must, in any case, be derived from other constitutional principles.[39] The Canadian Charter of Rights and Freedoms has been of little use in this regard, since it is designed essentially to protect individual rather than collective rights.

Note, however, that in Britain, the local authorities discovered that they had a far greater capacity to evade, delay, and obstruct than anyone had imagined. This reflects the fact that earlier relations between central and local authorities in Britain had been based on a set of understandings that promoted mutual accommodation. When the left Labour authorities launched an attack on Thatcherism, and Thatcher launched an attack on them, these earlier understandings evaporated, and those on each side of the barricades were forced to use whatever means they had available. In the case of the local authorities, these were essentially means of resistance. All orders from the centre are subject to evasion because there are such limited means of surveillance; the centre must rely on the fear of repercussions from illegality – a fear that is particularly strong among professional officers, without whom policies cannot be implemented. This fear is effective enough, but imaginative officers can usually find omissions or ambiguities in the orders they receive. With appropriate political support at the local level, they can act on these omissions or ambiguities to evade or frustrate the evident intent of the orders from the centre. Moreover, once given, an order is subject to judicial interpretation, and as such can be contested in the courts. It may be advantageous for a local authority to act on quite a bizarre interpretation of the law, if it can thereby hold out longer in the course of action it prefers. The British experience is a reminder of the cumbersomeness of the law: it took Thatcher nearly a decade to bring the local authorities to heel, despite all the parliamentary powers at her disposal. One is reminded of the difficulties governments have in taxing the wealthy effectively: every tax law is subject to avoidance and evasion, and every measure to close a loophole seems to create new loopholes. Fiscal controls over local authorities are not much different: a major local authority, like a big corporation, can hire good accountants and lawyers to advise it on ways of avoiding fiscal controls. The magic of creative accounting makes monies appear and disappear in ways that baffle the ordinary administrator as well as the ordinary citizen.

However, a struggle between central and local authorities imposes great economic, social, and political costs, which are not evenly distributed. Local authorities can wage a kind of guerrilla war that imposes considerable costs on the central government in terms of political attention, administrative resources, parliamentary time, and credit with the general public. Like any guerrilla army, however, the fighting authorities must be prepared to sustain disproportionate losses if they are going to inflict serious damage on the centre. In Britain, for instance, the resisting local authorities were able to sustain current operating expenditures only by running down their capital assets. Moreover, their political leaders – all amateurs – pushed themselves to the brink of exhaustion in trying to sustain campaigns over a long period. Their officials were equally overworked. Unless the issues are absolutely clear – and in fiscal matters they rarely are – it is difficult to sustain resistance over long period, especially when the people in a particular locality are isolated.

By their nature, local authorities are parochial, and their leaders are unlikely to have strong political links outside their own areas. In these two cases of local resistance, the left authorities were hampered by lack of support from the relevant local-authority associations, professional associations, and political parties, although they could count on some assistance from the unions. For career reasons, professionals generally were unwilling to contemplate actions that would have taken them outside the law. For similar reasons, provincial and national politicians wanted to avoid the taint of illegality. Generally, any strategy of resistance will involve an unequal distribution of costs among the resisters, and this is bound to create problems. For instance, in any resort to illegality, the councillors or trustees are on the front line: their supporters may be urging them on, but they are not the ones risking disqualification from office, fines, and imprisonment. For lawyers, penalties can include professional disqualification. In the English case, the threat of 'surcharge' was particularly significant, since the sums at issue were large enough to bankrupt the ordinary person. One must have considerable confidence in one's own supporters to incur such risks. A council that is attempting to maintain services in the face of centrally imposed cutbacks may find natural allies in its own work-force. On the other hand, the tactics the council uses in resistance may put people's jobs at risk, and when the local authority gives in, and begins making cutbacks – either as a stopgap measure or as a full-scale capitulation – this may make the work-force especially bitter. Also, client groups may be reluctant to support tactics that deprive them of essential services; similarly, ratepayers may balk at strategies (such as creative accounting) that ultimately cost them substantial sums. Thus, the politics of resistance is ultimately divisive.

If these cases have illustrative value, it seems that some form of party discipline is essential for effective unity. (However, see the discussion in Chapter 10: discipline may arise from other sources.) In the case of B.C., there was effective resistance to the end only in Vancouver, where there was a disciplined party in control of the school board. In Britain, the most disciplined Labour groups held out longest. Parties can be important in supplying back-up candidates (for those disqualified or imprisoned), maintaining coherent policies over time and space, and providing an organization of trust for people unfamiliar with one another. Disciplined unions can of course back up disciplined parties, as socialists always have believed. On the other hand, local resisters who depend on established parties and unions become vulnerable to pressures from those organizations, which may have reasons of their own for timidity. Thus, the Solidarity Movement in B.C. was ultimately broken by the labour organizations that were its main support, and the local Labour parties in Britain had to fight for their own legitimacy against a more timid national leadership.

As long as local authorities remain within the law, they may be able to resist the central government without intense and widespread popular support. Local councils are often elected on small turn-outs, so that to stay in power, one need only avoid stimulating strong new opposition. Guerrilla tactics of administrative resistance, court challenges, creative accounting, and so on may be tolerated or even mildly supported by the electorate; it is a different matter when resistance involves people putting their bodies, their jobs, or their entitlements to income and services on the line. Generally, the resisting authorities in Britain and B.C. found that they lacked the intense support necessary to stand the central governments down. As these crises developed, there were some important demonstrations, and tough words from union leaders, but nowhere was there mass action in support of the dissenting authorities. In Vancouver, for instance, little happened when the school board was turned over to a trustee, and he was able to do his job with little difficulty. It seems that in these instances, the protesters were hampered by their internal differences and by the widespread fear that successful resistance would lead to an utter breakdown of public authority. Although the Trotskyist militants would have welcomed such a breakdown, the vast majority of the people involved were attempting to contain their protest within their own conceptions of law and order. The central governments were able to exploit the popular belief that law and order depended on central rather than local authority, and so push people to the point where their own resistance became self-limiting. Such self-limitation may be a sign of civilization, but it also points out the difficulties involved in resisting governments that show no similar restraint.

The implication seems to be that local authorities can protect themselves from a determined central government only when a political culture has been created that legitimates the locality as a political unit with a dignity that is equal to the nation's. In Britain and Canada, the claims of the locality have been denigrated for so long that it is difficult for politicians to advance them effectively. Historically, the left played an important part in undermining local autonomy; more recently, it has been paying the price. Central to the left's failure of political imagination is that it has never adequately grasped the analogy between national and local governments. The whole story that has been told here could be repeated in a 1990s context, but with national governments in the role of dissident local councils. If anything, 1990s national governments have been weaker and less effective in resisting the demands for fiscal restraint than 1980s local authorities. Sovereignty confers no political courage. In fact, the effort to maintain the illusion of sovereignty in face of the globalized economy usually results in the repression of democratic resistance.

# 10

# Women in Transition

(with Leslie Kenny)

Many of those who have been activated by contemporary social movements have little use for elected governments. They tend to conceive of their activity as occurring in a political space 'outside' the state, and they are not inclined toward municipal politics. In Chapter 3, we noted some of the effects of this in relation to the environmental movement, and in Chapter 11 we will be discussing the municipal impact of pacifism, antinuclear activism, and other outwardly oriented social movements. Before we do so, we need to think about the movement that has revolutionized our conceptions of the outward and the inward, the public and the private, the political and the personal: namely, feminism. This may be the most powerful of the contemporary social movements, and the new political spaces it develops cut across the old spaces afforded by the local state. If women become organized around their own issues (such as personal safety, childcare, and employment equity), can they advance those issues effectively when faced with a state that is disposed against them? Can women be more effective in their autonomous action than elective local authorities? Are the modalities of women's resistance, self-affirmation, and self-development the same as for other social movements? Is autonomous action likely to turn inward and become self-destructive?

These are large questions, for which we have no complete answers. However, we may be able to shed some light on the issues by looking at one interesting example: the Women's House Saving Action of 1985–6 in Vancouver. This action was contemporaneous with the school board struggles we have just discussed. For the local feminist movement, the action involved issues of deepest concern, and dramatically posed the question of whether organized women could sustain institutions of their own despite a hostile government. The activists who came forward were by no means parochial. Many of their leaders were prominent in the national women's movement, a movement that had been remarkably successful in developing and sustaining its own organizations despite all the obstacles to action in a large, thinly populated, culturally divided country. Moreover, these leaders were highly attuned to the triumphs and defeats of the American women's movement and aware of the efforts of the GLC Women's Committee and other innovative feminist organizations in Britain. The Vancouver activists regarded themselves as participants in an international struggle, one that took a particular local form. From their own perspective, what they were doing was of world-historical significance.

The action to which we are referring brought scores of women together in an eight-month occupation of Transition House, which was the city's only facility exclusively for battered women as well as a major feminist institution and advocacy centre. The Social Credit government of British Columbia had slated the house for closure; the occupation was intended to preserve it, not only as a feminist institution but also as a unionized public facility. Despite a remarkable effort, the occupiers ultimately had to abandon the house and shift their focus to City Hall, where they found more support for their demands. A long lobbying campaign ensued, in which feminist activists on Vancouver City Council, in the municipal bureaucracy, and in the wider community worked to get federal and provincial support for a new Transition House. They were again disappointed: the province funded other facilities but refused support for what was bound to be a centre of feminist practice. Ten years later, the city still lacks the kind of open, secular, unionized public facility that the occupiers were trying to defend; even so, the action itself remains a symbol of what women can (and cannot) accomplish.

For most of those involved, memories of the Women's House Saving Action are at once deeply painful and profoundly exhilarating. It was a time when women came together quickly and effectively and sustained a vital service against extraordinary odds. No local event did more to express the power of women's liberation. Yet by the same token, it was also a time of deep division, when many of the conflicts within feminism were sharply expressed. It was a struggle without obvious victories, and it left the putative feminist leadership at one remove from the city's remaining facilities for battered women. For many, the results were proof of the power of patriarchy, which divides, marginalizes, and oppresses women. For some, the lesson was that women should establish their independence from the patriarchal state, and not be seduced by offers of friendly support. For others, the lessons were more complex – fraught with a confused sense of failure and triumph. For many of those now involved in transition house services in Vancouver – and certainly for most battered women – the Women's House Saving Action hardly figures at all: it is there, but not *there* in what they do.

In many ways, the action encapsulates the experiences of the women's movement, which gets stronger with every defeat and more pervasive with every act of containment yet still disappoints many activists. In trying to tell the story of the action, we encounter many of the things that make social movements so hard to analyse: the elusiveness and contestedness of movement identities, the fluidity of movement structures and organizations, the absence of definite frontiers between one movement and the next, the implication of movements in the relations of ruling, and the apparent irrelevance of ordinary standards for judging organizational success. We also encounter the elusiveness of the state, whose apparent fixity conceals a shifting ideological boundary. The conflicting interpretations of the action that we find among movement activists mirror the analytical confusions of traditional and critical sociology. Our own view is that the activities the action was intended to save – the practices of the transition houses – themselves generate understandings that we can use to model wider social movements. As battered women have discovered, transition is not a simple movement from 'here' to 'there,' in which the 'inside' and the 'outside' can be kept distinct. Nor is it a process marked by sudden enlightenment or triumphant victories. It involves a deeper recognition of complexity, an enhanced sense of one's power and responsibility, and a feeling of community that opens a person toward the wider world. These are paradigmatic experiences of critical social movements in relation to the state and to one another.

**A House for Women: 1973–83**

For those removed from the women's movement, it is difficult to understand how central shelters and refuges are to the practices of feminism. Recognition of the male violence and misogyny at the core of patriarchy was crucial for the development of feminist thought in the 1970s. It helped constitute a distinctively radical feminism that was different from earlier liberal, maternal, and socialist variants. It also put the issue of women's safety – on the street and in the home – at the forefront of feminist practice.[1] The failure of the police, the courts, and the social service agencies to recognize the character of male violence against women, let alone to deal with it effectively, illustrated with particular clarity the need for an autonomous women's movement to provide the services and facilities needed. It was in the context of such a movement, which spread rapidly from city to city and country to country in the 1970s, that the particular problems of battered wives were first clearly identified. Women's centres, which had originally been places for women to meet and discuss their ideas and problems, soon spawned informal refuges where women could escape from abusive partners. These refuges in turn became sites for developing distinctively feminist work practices that challenged the hierarchies of professional service and administrative organization, and politicized activities that had been considered private.

Transition House, established in December 1973, was among the pioneer facilities for battered women in Canada. It was formed by a network of feminist organizations in Vancouver, including Status of Women, Women's Place, Rape Relief, the Women's Health Collective, and the women's caucuses at the University of British Columbia and Simon Fraser University. The purpose was to provide battered women with a protected alternative community – an environment for transition. As Megan Ellis explained:[2]

> The battered woman, whatever her class or background, is rendered powerless and degraded by the man who violates her. Her transition thus necessitates finding a way to regain a sense of control over her life, to re-learn independence and find her strength. The experience of living cooperatively with other women allows her to recognize herself in the lives of these other women and to both give and receive assistance and support. Sharing in the day to day tasks of maintaining the house, trading off childcare with other residents, taking on the struggles with the welfare office and family courts, and finding a place to live, all contribute to a woman's regaining a sense of being able.

Such empowerment depended on egalitarian relations between staff and residents, which were uncommon in traditional social services. Sponsors and staff believed that women in transition had to be protected, not only from their former partners but also from the courts, police, and social service agencies, which tended to blame women for their own victimization. The house as an institution had to be a strong advocate for battered women, and this meant that it had to be politically engaged.

The initiative to establish Transition House coincided with three key events: the launching of the federal Women's Program,[3] a provincial effort to create community resources boards,[4] and the organizational campaign of the Service, Office, and Retail Workers' Union of Canada (SORWUC), an independent feminist union.[5] The Women's Program of the secretary of state's office was created in 1973, following the 1970 report from the Royal Commission on the Status of Women in Canada. It soon became a source of core funding for women's organizations – many of which focused on issues of male violence – and it stimulated similar initiatives at the provincial level. In British Columbia, Vancouver Status of Women (1971) was joined by the Women's Research Centre (1973), the B.C./Yukon Society of Transition Houses (1978), Battered Women's Support Services (1979), Women Against Violence Against Women (1982), and other organizations; these gave the women's movement in general – and the transition house movement in particular – greater institutional density and created a network of mutual support. Practically all these organizations depended on federal or provincial grants, not only for core funding but also for specific projects, including the provision of transition house services. This reflected a more general pattern in which the Trudeau government, picking up on the themes of 'participatory democracy' articulated in the 1960s, institutionalized support for groups of people at a disadvantage in Canadian society: native people, ethnic and linguistic minorities, people of colour, the handicapped and the disabled, and women generally.

Participatory democracy was also one of the themes of the Barrett government's efforts to create community resources boards in B.C. These new elective agencies were to do for the social services what the school boards had done for education since the early nineteenth century – provide decentralized, democratic control. The operative legislation was not proclaimed until November 1974, but it had been foreshadowed in February by the establishment of the Vancouver Resources Board, which became the central agency for a network of fourteen locally elected community resources boards in the city. The board took over the functions of the municipal welfare department and the children's aid societies, and had a mandate to integrate and co-ordinate statutory and nonstatutory social services throughout the city. It thus became the granting agency for Transition House. This was a fortunate circumstance, because the claims for autonomy and democratic control advanced by the house's supporters accorded well with the proclaimed objectives of the VRB and the provincial government.

The government and the VRB were also sympathetic to unionization. They worked out a multiparty agreement with the four main unions affected by social services reorganization, and struck a separate deal with SORWUC, which insisted on a distinctive approach. SORWUC was a small, feminist union at odds with the labour establishment. It naturally appealed to the transition house staff, because of its orientation toward women workers neglected by the mainstream unions and its insistence on grass roots organization, bargaining unit autonomy, and bottom-up control. Under the agreement between SORWUC and the VRB, International Women's Day was recognized as a statutory holiday at Transition House, and the staff were given the right to bring their children to work in emergencies. More crucially, the staff gained some protection for their distinctive work practices, which were those of a feminist collective. As far as possible, the Transition House workers operated by consensus, sharing work between themselves and the residents and resisting demands for an administrative hierarchy.

This sympathetic environment did not last for long. Social Credit won the provincial election of 11 December 1975, having promised to dissolve the community resources boards and the VRB. For practical reasons, the VRB got a reprieve, but its activities – including those of Transition House – were taken over by the province's Ministry of Human Resources in October 1977. In this context, the Transition House staff opted to switch their allegiance from SORWUC to the B.C. Government Employees Union (BCGEU), which could offer better protection against an unsympathetic provincial government. The staff soon found themselves subject to the combined pressures of the ministry and the BCGEU, both of which required conformity to conventional administrative controls. After the appointment of a supervisor for the house in 1978, the collective decision-making process was compromised and political activism curtailed, partly because of BCGEU's fears of government reprisals. Some of the more militant staff became uncomfortable and quit, and less militant people were hired in accordance with bureaucratic recruitment and selection procedures. Without losing entirely its commitment to feminist principles of organization and advocacy, Transition House began to resemble a more traditional social service agency.

In society at large, the issue of violence against women was gaining prominence. However, the government, courts, police, charities, and allied professions tended to present matters in terms that obscured the gendered character of violence and marginalized the activities of the women's groups that had put the issue on the public agenda. This was particularly evident at the United Way's 1977 Symposium on Family Violence.[6] The feminist activists who had developed Transition House found themselves struggling to prevent the absorption of a movement by and for battered women into a normalized, professionalized, depoliticized social service under the control of governments and traditional charities.[7] As the transition house movement spread from the cities to the suburbs and the outlying towns, its radicalism was muted. As one result, the house in Vancouver became increasingly important as a symbol and centre of innovative feminist practice. Its links with other feminist organizations were unusually strong, and it was a focus of practical initiatives and ongoing experience for a network of prominent advocacy groups. In a politically hostile environment, the staff within the house could still work privately with battered women, social workers, police officers, and ministry officials, to raise consciousness and change administrative practices; more public activity could be left to the supportive feminist organizations. Personal and organizational linkages ensured a symbiosis of practical experience, theoretical reflection, and political action.

Unfortunately, these relations were soon threatened by a major split in the Vancouver women's movement. From one point of view, the underlying issue was the movement's relationship with the state: Could it sustain its autonomy while submitting to state regulation? From the other point of view, this was a false issue that obscured differences about appropriate standards of conduct toward women and children who were assaulted by men. The debate was joined between two of the city's major feminist institutions: Transition House and the Vancouver Rape Relief and Women's Shelter.

Up till this time, things had been different. Like Transition House, Rape Relief was started in 1973 with funding from the NDP government, and for several years the two organizations were the closest of allies. Rape Relief's mandate was different: it was not a shelter per se, but a crisis and resource centre that provided advocacy, court accompaniment, and referrals to women who were sexually assaulted. During the late 1970s, under the Social Credit government, Rape Relief came under increasing pressure to give a bureaucratic accounting of itself. One of the key issues concerned the collective's defiance of guidelines for reporting child sexual abuse. Rape Relief was critical of the way cases were handled by ministry child-abuse teams and had at times counselled the teenage women who came to them not to seek help from police and social workers. Also, government was demanding access to the personal files of women who used the service, and Rape Relief was refusing to co-operate. The collective's concerns about the government's access to records at Transition House – where it was not lawful to harbour minors without reporting them to the ministry – led to the decision to open an alternative facility. Using money raised by a variety of creative means – including a men's fund-raising committee – Rape Relief was able to buy its own house in 1981 and open a women's shelter with no links to the ministry.

This decision did not sit well with other feminist groups, who were concerned about the kind of service the shelter would deliver. There was a pervasive feeling in the women's movement that pressure should be maintained on the state to 'pay up' – to assume its proper share of responsibility for violence against women, and to provide adequate resources and appropriate compensation for women dealing with the consequences of that violence. Rape Relief defended its use of unsalaried volunteers in terms of the more egalitarian, sisterly relations that could be maintained between staff and clients in the shelter. From this perspective, Transition House was becoming too professional. Rape Relief was also criticized for its irreverence towards the system of criminal justice, which it regarded as abusive of women, biased in terms of class and race, and wholly ineffectual in dealing with male violence against women. The nonjudicial alternatives Rape Relief offered often involved direct confrontation with an attacker at his workplace or in his home community. Aside from the obvious risks to the women involved, this policy – according to Rape Relief's critics – was being imposed on vulnerable women in a dogmatic and moralistic way.[8]

Rape Relief's final breach with the provincial government came in February 1982, when it refused to participate in a government evaluation of its non-shelter services; the consequence of this was a complete termination of public funding for the organization itself and for the four other centres under its umbrella. Feminist critics accused Rape Relief of jeopardizing the financial resources and public credibility of the women's movement as a whole. By the time the dust settled, Rape Relief had been officially denounced by important sectors of the feminist community,[9] and its rape-crisis advocacy functions had been replaced by a new agency, Women Against Violence Against Women (WAVAW). From then on there was a definite polarization between Transition House, backed by WAVAW, which claimed to represent the mainstream of the women's movement and was ready to use all the legal channels to help women, and Rape Relief, which regarded itself as independent of the state. While lacking the radical edge that made (and continues to make) Rape Relief an important element in the national campaign to end violence against women, Transition House still provided the most convincing model of high-quality feminist services connected with advocacy work within and outside the state. Because the house accepted provincial funding – and indeed, after 1977 was actually an arm's-length agency of the Ministry of Human Resources – the staff could provide shelter and services for free. There was no need to charge women for room and board, as happened at the Rape Relief shelter. Moreover, the staff were not just volunteers, but paid, professional, unionized shelter workers who had the training and experience to deal effectively with the difficult problems that battered women faced. This not only ensured higher-quality service but also gave shelter workers the recognition they deserved. As far as its supporters were concerned, Transition House had staked out a new territory for women's self-organization and feminist practice within the state, the social services sector, the professions, and the unions. This was not a territory to be surrendered in a quixotic quest for autonomy.

**Privatization and Resistance: 1983–6**

As it happened, Transition House never had the opportunity to withdraw from the state: it was expelled. The context was the provincial government's campaign to privatize public services. This had been signalled as early as 1979, but it had gained momentum with the 'restraint' budgets of 1982 and 1983. The latter had prompted massive social resistance, in which women's groups played a prominent part along with organized labour. A general strike was averted when the government reached an understanding with the main labour organizations, including the BCGEU.[10] Women's groups and other organizations felt that they had been betrayed by the unions, but the succeeding struggles often forced them together again. The BCGEU in particular had to fight a long rearguard action against job loss and privatization, which brought it onto a terrain shared by women's groups threatened by a loss of funding and deterioration of services.

Along with many other public services, Transition House was scheduled for privatization early in 1984. The BCGEU tried to block this by prohibiting unionized staff from bidding on the new contracts and threatening the charities it supported with loss of funding if they entered the bidding themselves. If this slowed the momentum of privatization, it certainly did not prevent it. Again, the feminist supporters of Transition House were not about to have the facility closed for reasons of ideological purity, and they encouraged the YWCA to bid for the contract, which it did, successfully. When the YWCA assumed responsibility for the house in March 1984, this brought a 'first wave' feminist organization – one with traditional administrative practices, non-unionized staff, and a low political profile – into a direct relationship with a militant, unionized, participatory 'second wave' institution. The mixture proved to be explosive. The Transition House staff found the YWCA more difficult to work with than either the ministry or the VRB. The feelings were reciprocated. Faced with administrative difficulties and a renewed threat to its funding from the BCGEU, the YWCA decided in April 1985 not to renew its contract to operate the house. To the shock and dismay of everyone involved, Grace McCarthy, the human resources minister, took the opportunity to let the contract for services expire; this forced the YWCA to send dismissal notices to the eighteen staffers and schedule the house for closure on 28 June 1985.

This is when the Women's House Saving Action began. At first, the action took the form of a political campaign: a group of prominent feminists quickly formed a Vancouver Transition House Society and made public their bid to take over the contract from the YWCA. They were ignored by the provincial government, but found more sympathy at the civic level, where an informal centre-left coalition dominated the municipal council. On 23 May, the council unanimously declared:[11]

(1) Vancouver must have an emergency facility, specifically for women and children who are victims of domestic violence;
(2) the facility must be staffed on a 24–hour basis by women experienced in working with battered women; and
(3) the sponsor must not represent any particular religious or philosophical viewpoint. That is, the facility must operate and be perceived to operate in a manner that is open to all women regardless of race, economic status, religious preference, etc.

The idea that there should be a secular, multiethnic facility near the centre of the city had a particular appeal to politicians representing a diverse inner-city constituency. The provincial government claimed that there were adequate alternative facilities for women in crisis, but critics pointed out that these other shelters were located in the suburbs, or were run by religious groups to which many women would not turn, or were open to such a variety of women in crisis – including alcoholics and drug abusers – that they could not provide healing communities for battered women in transition. In any case, available beds of any sort were few. Supporters of Transition House relayed these messages through the media, and also through bureaucratic channels, where feminist staffers in the city's Social Planning Department were particularly effective.

It soon became evident, however, that the house would probably be closed despite pressure from the city and other sources. Its supporters held a public meeting ostensibly to consider alternatives, but direct action had already been planned at a secret gathering organized by leading feminists associated with WAVAW. This 'emergency tea party' had been called without the knowledge of the Transition House staff, who could not be implicated in any illegal action if they were to be re-employed at the house. The Rape Relief collective was also kept in the dark, for political reasons. Thus, ony a few people had any prior knowledge that the house was to be occupied beginning on the day of its official closure, 28 June. Staffers were surprised by the women who entered on that day and declared to the press:[12] 'We're here, and we'll remain here, providing what level of service we can, until the government reinstates Vancouver Transition House. This service, even if the government doesn't realize it, is a life and death matter for Vancouver women who face violence in their homes.'

As it became clear that the occupiers represented a much larger group that included many prominent feminist leaders, most of the staff gave them their implicit support. A well-planned media campaign, which took advantage of women's networks that extended into the editorial rooms, helped to generate surprisingly favourable publicity. This reinforced the work that was being done through feminist organizations and networks of victims of violence. In the months that followed, over a hundred women took turns working in the shelter; others provided food and supplies or engaged in lobbying and organizational work. Eleven functional committees organized the work, and linked volunteers to the 'core' that took responsibility for tactics and strategy.

As the action proceeded, it became clear that neither the police nor the provincial government would intervene. Indeed, both were complicit in sustaining the occupation. The house still belonged to the Ministry of Lands and Parks; it continued to receive electricity from B.C. Hydro (a provincial Crown corporation), telephone services from B.C. Telephones (a private, federally regulated monopoly), water and sewerage from the Greater Vancouver Regional District, and garbage collection from the city of Vancouver. Although telephones and electricity had been cut off before the occupiers entered the house, these were quickly restored. The ministry never sought an order to have the occupiers evicted, and the police never interfered with the occupation. In fact, the Vancouver police and the local social-service agencies continued to refer battered women to the shelter for assistance. At least sixty women and children were given refuge and provided with help during the occupation. In short, this now 'illegal' operation continued to function as a public service, with implicit support from the police, the courts, and other agencies of the state.

The occupiers clearly benefited from the skills and social class of their leadership, the solid presence of the women's movement within the state and the media, and the past success of Transition House as an agency within the social service sector. After twelve years of operation, the house enjoyed wide acceptance within the network of institutions dealing with the consequences of violence against women. Unlike Rape Relief, it had not spurned connections with more conventional organizations. The occupiers thus could count on sympathizers within the key provincial ministries, the police force, and the public utilities. They had advance warning of adverse government actions, and they could quietly arrange for the restoration of vital services. At the same time, they could act within a framework of favourable publicity, generated by friendly women reporters. The fact that the leaders of the occupation were prominent and credible within the city's women's movement gave the occupation a legitimacy it otherwise would have lacked.

It became increasingly apparent that the government's decision to close Transition House was not motivated by a desire to eliminate the service; the real point was to eliminate its feminist content. This was evident in the government's rejection of a take-over proposal from the feminist-sponsored Vancouver Transition House Society, as well as in the wording of the ministry's advertisements for the new contract. As one critic noted, the tender called only for the provision of an 'emergency family shelter' and a program 'supportive to the integrity of the family unit'; it made no mention of battering, or male violence, or the specific protection needs of women and children escaping life-threatening situations.[13] In response, a 'women's summit' was called under the sponsorship of the city of Vancouver, at which a coalition of thirteen women's organizations called upon the government to award a contract that would ensure the following: a 'woman only' environment for the victims of battering; unionized staff; a confidential address; a self-help and co-operative approach; referrals to community services; and an ability to serve disabled women and women from ethnic minorities – in other words, a facility that would be as much like the old Transition House as possible. The ministry ignored the groups' proposal, however, and two weeks later, on 6 August, awarded the contract to the Salvation Army, a fundamentalist Christian organization that had opposed the establishment of Transition House in 1973. This seemed like a deliberate rebuff to the women's organizations, as well as an obvious ideological ploy: the minister, Grace McCarthy, even served on the army's board. When Kate Booth House, the army's new facility, opened on 9 October 1985, it was clear that the government regarded the issue as closed and would be prepared to let the occupiers sit in the old house as long as they liked. Implicitly, feminist women were being offered the freedom to operate an alternative service on public property if they so chose.

This put the leaders of the occupation in a nearly impossible position. Their purpose was not to show that voluntary women's groups could provide good services to women: that had been demonstrated many times over. The point, rather, was to claim as women's own a public service that was provided by unionized professionals who were motivated by feminism and loyal to the women's movement. The idea that Transition House belonged to the women's movement even though it was located in the extended apparatuses of the state was absolutely crucial. So too was the idea that a women's organization of this sort had a right to its share of public resources. In turn, this implied that women working with women should enjoy the same pay, professional respect, and conditions of employment as other highly qualified public servants. If women were to be properly recognized within the state, the kind of activity symbolized by Transition House had to be recognized as an institutional necessity and integrated with the activities of the women's movement as a whole. But how could this claim to a stake in the state be pursued when the government was so determined to expel the offending organization?

As the occupation wore on, divisions within the group began to emerge.[14] There were complaints that class divisions were being replicated in the division of labour, with middle-class women doing the planning and organizing and working-class women providing the frontline service. There was also a growing concern that a temporary occupation was turning into a permanent service of quite a different kind from the one the women were trying to defend. Some of the socialists argued that the occupiers were really playing into the government's hands by privatizing the service themselves, and substituting volunteers for laid-off unionized workers. These issues came to a head in November, when a number of socialist-feminist/NDP women decided to abandon the occupation. The split was played down in public, and the core leadership intensified its efforts to find a face-saving way out of the occupation. To be declared a success, the occupation had to generate some sort of positive response from 'the state' that would give symbolic recognition to women's claims. The city of Vancouver eventually obliged.

If the province would not acknowledge its responsibility to provide suitable transition services, the city was the obvious alternative. Like most Canadian feminists, the leaders of the action had generally been little involved with municipal politics, focusing instead on grass roots activity and federal and provincial lobbying. Thus, they were somewhat surprised to discover that they had relatively easy access to the municipal bureaucracy and the civic leadership. Working with planners, social workers, and representatives from ethnic and minority communities, they developed a strong proposal for a multiethnic, multicultural Transition House and Advocacy Centre, to be run by the city with financial support from the federal and provincial governments. Vancouver's council gave its commitment to the plan on 28 January 1986 – no doubt encouraged by the fact that it was not being expected to fund the facility – and this promise was enough to enable the occupiers to bring their action to an end.

**Transitions: 1986–93**

Obviously, the occupation had not achieved its original objectives: the house was closed, leaving the Salvation Army's facility as the city's only refuge exclusively for battered women. On the other hand, to sustain the occupation and continue the service 'illegally' for eight long months was no mean feat. Although the Social Credit government was not moved, the occupiers had had repeated propaganda successes, and had managed to raise consciousness about male violence and the need for transition house services in the city among a wider and wider constituency. Moreover, they had been effective in distinguishing the kind of service generated by the women's movement – grounded in women's shared experience, informed by feminist analysis, and inspired by the openness and egalitarianism of women's collectives – from the depoliticized charity favoured by the government. At least a majority of the city council had been won over to the idea that effective facilities for battered women in transition had to be based on the principles that had emerged from the women's movement. Thus, the ideal of a restored Transition House and Advocacy Centre, open to all women and operated as a feminist agency within the state, remained on the political agenda. This gave focus to lobbying efforts for a number of years.

In 1990, feminist activists had another disappointment, when the provincial government again rebuffed a request from the city of Vancouver for funding for a municipally operated transition house. By this time the city council had a conservative majority, but its support for the feminist proposal held. However, the province did offer funds to Helping Spirit Lodge, a new facility exclusively for native women and their children. Helping Spirit interpreted violence against native women in terms of the ongoing effects of European colonization, and insisted on the importance of traditional healing practices in the context of native self-government.[15] This emphasis on the particularities of women's culture was echoed in another service that gained provincial funding: Vancouver and Lower Mainland Multi-Cultural Family Support Services, sponsored by B.C. Immigrant and Visible Minority Women. The idea was to provide liaison and support services in six minority languages to the twelve transition houses in the greater Vancouver region; this would enable immigrant women to function in predominantly English-speaking settings. The hope in this case was to mediate the transition from isolating cultural contexts, while reinforcing the legitimacy of cultural differences.[16] By responding to these demands from immigrant and native women while continuing its support for the Salvation Army, the province was able to undercut feminist claims that it was unresponsive to the diversity of women's needs. It seemed rather that the feminists were insisting on uniform, all-in public facilities, and not responding adequately to the problems of cultural diversity.

To characterize the situation in this way is highly unfair to the feminist activists who worked hard to deal with the issues of racial and cultural diversity, but it highlights the fact that the transition house movement – and indeed both the first and second waves of Canadian feminism – originated within the white Anglo community. In 1985, the issue of diversity was not even addressed in a major statement from the feminist leaders associated with the Women's House Saving Action.[17] Thus, it is not unreasonable to suggest that there were assumptions of cultural uniformity at work in the original practices of Transition House. As the years passed, assumptions of uniformity were increasingly difficult to sustain, but they were still implicit in the demand for a 'one house fits all' model of transition house practice. This exposed the feminist leadership to the divisive action of the provincial government, which could claim the high ground of respect for women's diversity.

Read more positively, the emergence of Helping Spirit Lodge and Multi-Cultural Family Support Services – indeed, even the development of Kate Booth House as a Salvation Army facility – can be understood in terms of the spreading effects of feminism. None of these initiatives would have been conceivable without the pioneering feminist efforts to clarify the issues and develop the most appropriate responses to male violence against women in the home. These new organizations may relocate their efforts in the context of cultural difference and lend more support than feminists would like to 'traditional family values,' yet they still bring feminist practices to bear in contexts that would otherwise be immune. Under suspicion of proselytization, the Salvation Army had to put itself at one remove from Kate Booth House. That group hired a feminist to run the service and allowed her to develop a set of healing practices that approached (without entirely duplicating) the forms pioneered at Transition House. Thus, the Salvation Army facility – which is still not completely endorsed by many feminist organizations around the province – is extending the practices it was designed to contain. The same might be said of other transition houses that were developed by women less radical than their Vancouver counterparts.

This illustrates how a social movement overlaps itself and thereby generates effects beyond its ostensible boundaries. The women's movement is unusually powerful in this respect, since it speaks to an identity and a set of life conditions that involve half the people in the world. It is significant that almost all the major actors in the story of the Women's House Saving Action were women – from Grace McCarthy and the Salvation Army captains to the social workers in the welfare agencies and the radical feminists in the occupation. Superficially at least, this was a tale of struggles among women to define an issue and organize practices that necessarily put women at the centre. The primacy of women was a given in most of the debate – a remarkable fact in itself. At the same time, it is clear that women's networks, especially the ones generated by feminist activity, were essential for generating and sustaining the occupation and the subsequent lobbying activity. Without those networks, the closure of Transition House would have been a non-event for the state, the media, and even for the unions, which were preoccupied with what they regarded as wider struggles.

Clearly, feminism has established a terrain of political action that overlaps the state, civil society, and other social movements. It is inside and yet outside them all, co-present with each, autonomous, but deeply implicated in all the relations of ruling and resistance. As such, it directly challenges the spatialization of the state – and indeed other social movements and institutions – as an autonomous domain. The Women's House Saving Action made this challenge explicit by claiming a state institution for the women's movement. It also mobilized women (and some men) within the state in activity directed against the government of the day. We may think of this as a mobilization of the state against itself – as a challenge to the univocularity of the state and hence to sovereignty. If the state does not belong to the sovereign authorities in any simple way, its unity can only be understood as an ideological fiction enforced by various social practices. These practices are contested by social movements. Thus, there was the strange dance in which the B.C. government tried to cleanse the state of an unwanted feminist institution, while the women's movement tried to occupy the state and establish its own presence there. Although at first sight it seems that the cleansing was successful, feminist institutions and practices have reappeared like stubborn spots on the garment of the state.

The unions, the 'helping' professions, and the traditional charities have been similarly vulnerable to feminist practice.[18] Although SORWUC is gone, and transition houses have increasingly been normalized as agencies within a network of social services, these are not signs of defeat, but of a double movement of disruption and absorption. No more than the state have the other social institutions been able to set the women's movement outside, and maintain the purity of their traditional practices. Certainly, unionism and social work have both become more feminist. Ironically, this shift is often seen in terms of a loss of purity that can only be prevented by turning the movement back onto itself. Thus, the government's effort to constitute itself as sovereign was echoed in Rape Relief's quest for autonomy. That quest, which radiates throughout contemporary social movements, is the state-mimicking drive to establish a source of sovereign identity that will render the movement secure. The illusion is that a movement can become a self-constituted fixture, independent of the rest of the world. This is the illusion of statehood replicated on a smaller scale, where the pretense is even less credible.

A more realistic model for social movements can be derived from the process of transition – that is, from the original feminist practices that informed and inspired the Women's House Saving Action. Transition, as it relates to women who have survived a battering relationship, is a process of moving out of isolation, of walls coming down, of opening up one's own sense of identity. Typically, the conditions for surviving a relationship with a violent man require a complete shutting down of life energy on the part of the woman. She finds that she cannot speak her mind, trust her feelings, or reach out to people without punitive consequences. All contact with friends and family is compromised, or severed completely. Any prospect of change, growth, or movement appears increasingly remote. The complexity of identity is subsumed by a rigid, static, and predominantly negative sense of self. Unfortunately, such is the invisibility or namelessness of this condition that women often exist within such a closed system for years without any conscious awareness of what has been lost. Transition enables a recovery of the self, but it depends as much on a woman's capacity to choose and create the kind of person she wants to be, as on her discovery of aspects of herself that have been hidden or repressed. In this context, recovery comes from the strength that is gained by letting go of the assumptions, the denials, and the inflexible truths that dominated one's existence, and by learning to make oneself open to the complexities and undetermined opportunities that life offers. As the early proponents of feminist consciousness-raising discovered long ago, the most powerful moments of transformation, or recovery, occur in collective settings where the experiences and pain of individual women can be received by a supportive group of peers without judgment or interference. Hence the emphasis within the movement on establishing safe and comfortable residences for transition.

In the imagery of women's transition – tentative, vulnerable, without definitive guarantees or conclusions, ever subject to external conditions of violence, but enormously powerful in its personal and social dimensions – lies an important clue to understanding the complex character of social movements. As recent scholarship on the relationship between 'self-help' and social change has indicated, the recognition of boundaries internal to one's identity or movement, and the development of new strategies for breaking through such boundaries, is rapidly posing a new kind of challenge to the state-centric politics of sovereign identities. It is a challenge marked by the contrast between the regressive retreat of fundamentalism – akin to the battered woman's defensive enclosure – and the real promise of self-examination, exploration, and development that is manifest in the process of transition. In this context, the fragmentation of the Vancouver women's movement amidst the struggle to ensure services to battered women ought not to be regarded negatively, for it reflects the radical diversity of women's choices for resisting abuse. The women's movement is inherently transitional and cannot be pinned down. It is this quality that enabled some positive institutional results to emerge from the Women's House Saving Action: new feminist institutions that defy the principles but express the practices of the original Transition House. On such an understanding, Rape Relief, Transition House, Kate Booth House, and Helping Spirit Lodge all appear as necessary moments in a wider movement promoting the ongoing transition of all women.

# 11

# Municipal Foreign Policy

As we have noted, municipalities occupy ambivalent spaces between the state, the market, and everyday life. They are constituted as expressions of local community, and as such are designed for local self-government; yet they also operate as police agencies of the state and as businesses seeking profits for their shareholders. This ambivalence is expressed in the legal status of the municipality as a corporation – at once a political *association* of the inhabitants of a place, a *public agency* that derives its powers from the central authorities, and a *business* whose shareholders are the owners and occupiers of land in the community. In the rhetoric of statism, each of these is a mark of subordination: the state itself is the supreme political association; it claims authority over every business within its territory; and it governs public agencies under its constitution. Nevertheless, the subordination of municipalities is never complete. The people who enter these ambivalent spaces can tap into demands for local autonomy, wring concessions as agents for the centre, and connect with processes beyond the control of any state. As such, they can, by artful practices, begin to disrupt the oppressive enclosures and the relations of domination that characterize the contemporary world.

There is no guarantee that the political spaces afforded by municipal government will be used in innovative ways, and indeed there is strong pressure to fix municipalities as executive committees for the local bourgeoisie. In this respect, Singapore and Hong Kong are postmodern exemplars of the civic republics of an earlier era, prospering in the gaps between states and empires and organizing themselves as nodes in the global economy. In an era of diminishing nation-states, the free marketeers imply that aggressive municipalities, by putting business first, can aspire to 'world city' status. (There is even a social-democratic variant of this theory that points to the possibility of binding labour to capital by appropriate 'social contracts.') It is thus that we see cities opening offices of international affairs, developing 'sister city' linkages, sending trade missions abroad, fostering cultural exchanges, competing for international games and expositions, and generally promoting themselves independently of their national governments.[1] For the most part, the states concerned have treated such municipal activities with benign neglect if not active encouragement, since there is nothing at stake that threatens the existing order. Yet at the same time, a surprising number of dissident or insurgent municipalities have begun, since about 1980, to challenge the policies of their national governments and to open up international relations focused on matters like global peace and security, universal human rights, environmental protection, and conditions of life for the poor. These activities have been facilitated by the globalization of international communications, but they have not been geared to the market purposes implicit in the drive toward world-city status.

In the United States and Britain, the development of dissident foreign policies at the local level can be attributed in part to the triumph of neoconservatism in national politics. Whatever the ideological inclinations of the left, dissidents in the 1980s were forced to operate within the political spaces that remained to them. On the one hand, there were social movements such as environmentalism and peace activism, which increasingly defied the boundaries between states; on the other hand, there were enclaves of provincial or municipal authority that the left could take by electoral means. Without much sense of an overarching strategy, 'left' municipal councils began to use their own authority to challenge national policies on nuclear armaments, civil defence, relations with revolutionary regimes, the reception and treatment of refugees, the control of pollutants, and the character of assistance to the poor. By connecting with one another in national and international unions of local authorities, tapping into the programs of the United Nations and its agencies, and coordinating their activities with those of wider social movements, progressive municipalities were able to articulate alternatives on a global scale. This activity has not received much attention from political scientists, and it is often discounted as purely gestural,[2] even by participants. Nonetheless, in a world of weakening states and strengthening cultural and economic connections, the political possibilities foreshadowed by these practices deserve closer attention.

### Free Zones, Sanctuaries, and State Sovereignty

Many of the dissident municipalities have declared themselves 'free zones' or 'sanctuaries,' the former in relation to nuclear weaponry and the latter in relation to refugees or military deserters. The language of the declarations is redolent of the medieval German idea that 'city air makes free' – that a serf could win his freedom by living peaceably in a city for a year and a day. Civic authority originally was rooted in popular freedoms and had to be won from both the nobility and the clergy. The postmodern notion of the free zone or sanctuary is an expression of similar claims that people in particular communities have the right to opt out of practices that, while they may have the sanction of regal or national authorities, are at odds with more fundamental principles. The question is whether such 'opting out' can be made effective despite the apparently overwhelming power of the nation-state. The history of the free zones and sanctuaries is surprisingly positive in this respect.

The sanctuary movement in the United States began within religious congregations, which invoked the ancient principle that churches and temples are spiritual sanctuaries that should be respected by the secular authorities.[3] Since the ministers and priests within these sanctuaries were to provide help and succour to any who sought it, they could not be expected to reject or expel anyone who looked to them for protection. By extension, this principle could apply to the whole of a congregation and their property. Moreover, people who wanted to live out their religious convictions could well claim the right to extend help to those who were seeking refuge but who had not yet arrived in places of sanctuary. In the case of Central Americans fleeing oppressive regimes, this pointed toward helping refugees across the border with Mexico, transporting them to more northerly cities, getting them food, shelter, and medical care, finding them work, and shielding them from the U.S. Immigration and Naturalization Service.

Municipal 'sanctuary' declarations originally were intended to provide local political support for sanctuaries established independently by religious congregations and similarly minded secular groups. In 1971, in the context of protests against the Vietnam War, Berkeley had actually declared itself a 'sanctuary' for draft resisters and deserters from the U.S. Armed Forces. At a conference in Tucson in January 1985, the old Berkeley resolution was brought forward as a model response to recent arrests of activists accused of aiding illegal immigrants. Delegates went home and quickly secured council resolutions in a number of cities, beginning with Berkeley and Madison. As the municipal sanctuary movement spread, the religious and secular activists intensified their efforts. A version of the Underground Railroad was established to get people from the Mexican border areas to sanctuaries farther north, and it was in this context that a number of sanctuary workers were arrested for transporting illegal aliens. A National Sanctuary Defense Fund was established, partly with money raised by sympathetic European churches, which were involved in their own refugee work. The sanctuary workers were connected informally with various other organizations doing Central American support work. Thus, they became involved not only in providing refuge, but in accompanying people back to the areas from which they had fled and to which the U.S. government thought they should return.

When municipalities got involved, they appealed not only to principles of morality but also to their rights and duties under international law. For instance, the city of Madison, Wisconsin, adopted the following resolution on 5 March 1985.[4]

WHEREAS, the United Nations Convention relating to the Status of Refugees has defined the conditions of political refugee as 'any person who owing to a well-grounded fear of being persecuted for reasons of race, religion, nationality, membership in a particular social group or of a political opinion, is outside the country of his(her) nationality and is unable, or, owing to such fear, is unwilling to avail himself of the protection of that country'; and
WHEREAS, the United States Congress has adopted this convention in the Refugee Act of 1980; and
WHEREAS, the United Nations High Commission on Refugees has recognized that persons fleeing El Salvador and Guatemala are bona fide political refugees, yet fewer than two percent are being granted that status by the U.S. Immigration Service; and
WHEREAS, deportation of those seeking asylum has often meant disappearance or death upon their return home; and
WHEREAS, members of those religious communities offering sanctuary to the refugees believe themselves to be acting not in civil disobedience but under the law of the land; and
WHEREAS, both refugees and sanctuary workers in Texas, Arizona, Washington, New York, California and Pennsylvania have been detained or indicted in recent days; and
WHEREAS, within the City of Madison, we have both refugees and sanctuary providers for whom fear of deportation and the threat of arrest have an increasing immediacy; and
WHEREAS, the Common Council passed a resolution on June 3, 1983 in support of those sanctuaries when first refugees came to our City;

NOW THEREFORE, BE IT RESOLVED, that the Common Council of the City of Madison reaffirms that resolution, declares Madison a City of refuge and supports the religious communities of the City of Madison in their efforts to provide sanctuary; and
BE IT FURTHER RESOLVED, that the people of Madison will not condone for its own citizens who are providing sanctuary the harassment, indictments or arrests which have been experienced by sanctuary workers in other cities at the instigation of the U.S. Immigration Service; and
BE IT FURTHER RESOLVED, that no employee of the City of Madison will violate the established sanctuaries by assisting in investigations, public or clandestine, by engaging in or assisting with arrests for alleged violation of immigration laws by the refugees in the sanctuaries or by those offering sanctuary, or by refusing established public services to the established sanctuaries; and
BE IT FURTHER RESOLVED, that the Madison Common Council urges the Immigration Service to provide the refugees with the status of 'extended voluntary departure,' so that they may live among us free of the threat of deportation until conditions allow their return home.

The Madison City Council was by no means isolated. By mid-1989 there were twenty-nine declared sanctuary cities in the United States,[5] including Detroit, Los Angeles,[6] and San Francisco.[7] In some but not all of these cities, the police and other local officials were ordered – as in Madison – not to co-operate with the INS in its investigations. Where there were large numbers of 'undocumented' migrants, as in California, local authorities could invoke legitimate concerns about public health and welfare to resist demands that they should police immigration. Since illegal immigrants would be afraid to present themselves for medical treatment, send their children to school, or complain about unsafe working conditions if they thought they would be deported as a result, there were credible local policy reasons for not inquiring about people's citizenship status.

This resistance activity of the sanctuary movement in many ways paralleled the activities of the antinuclear and disarmament movements, not only in the moral fervour it generated but also in the use it made of municipal powers. In December 1979, NATO decided to modernize its nuclear weaponry and prepare itself to fight a 'limited' nuclear war with the Soviet Union.[8] In response, in Britain the Campaign for Nuclear Disarmament (CND) began to mobilize its supporters in a major struggle for European nuclear disarmament. This effort was soon matched throughout Western Europe, and was echoed in a 'call to halt the arms race' issued by American peace groups in April 1980.[9] In Santa Cruz, California, local activists picked up on the idea of a municipal 'nuclear-free zone' – an idea pioneered in Japan in the late 1950s and imitated in Australia and New Zealand in the 1970s, but never before attempted on the home territory of one of the nuclear powers – and tried unsuccessfully to get local ballot approval to zone out a proposed weapons factory.[10] There was a much deeper well of support for disarmament initiatives among the Labour-controlled local authorities in Britain. The Manchester City Council took the lead on 5 November 1980 by declaring the city a nuclear-free zone. The council appealed to the British government 'to refrain from the manufacture or positioning of nuclear weapons of any kind in the boundaries of our city' and called upon other local authorities 'to make similar statements on behalf of the citizens they represent.'[11] Within a year, 119 councils in Britain had followed suit. The movement spread to other European countries, especially Italy, Holland, and West Germany; by 1984 there was enough interest to hold the First International NFZ Local Authority Conference. Two years later, an international secretariat was created in Perugia, Italy. By that time there were 3,000 nuclear-free-zone authorities in seventeen countries worldwide.

The movement spread slowly in the United States, partly because of the need for grass roots initiatives to get popular support for ballot measures or town meeting resolutions. The 'nuclear freeze' campaign, in which resolutions were presented to 'initiate an immediate, verifiable, mutual halt to the production, testing, and deployment of new nuclear weapons and their delivery systems,' dominated peace politics at the local level in 1980–2.[12] The first American antinuclear ordinance, which banned the transport or storage of nuclear materials, was adopted in Hawaii County in February 1981. By the end of 1982 there were still only half a dozen American NFZs, but this number had climbed to fifty by the spring of 1984 and to one hundred by the fall of 1986. The communities concerned were often very small, but they included cities as large as Chicago and New York.[13]

The exact wording of an NFZ declaration varied from one community to another, but it generally takes this form.

(1) The territory is declared off-limits to the design, testing, manufacture, and deployment of nuclear weapons. The declaration (ordinance) may also ban the transportation of such weapons through a community; or ban radioactive materials, whether related to weapons or nuclear waste from power plants. Signs may be erected on property declaring its nuclear free status.

(2) Any activity which, in a local government's view, promotes nuclear weapons or nuclear war can be condemned or prohibited. Often this means that a community decides not to invest in or do business with industries that make nuclear weapons components.
(3) The community – or school, church, office, or other organization – renounces its right to be defended with nuclear weapons held by any government, including its own.
(4) The NFZ community or entity asks the nuclear powers to take it off their target lists. Letters are sent to the proper authorities in Paris, London, and Peking as well as to Washington and Moscow; and possibly to officials in India and Israel, whose nations may also be producing nuclear weapons.[14]

Thus, particular American municipalities tried to zone out nuclear industries,[15] divest from companies involved in nuclear weapons production,[16] redirect contracts to nuclear-free businesses,[17] block (or at least regulate) the transport of nuclear materials,[18] turn civil defence into peace education,[19] facilitate the conversion of industries to peaceful production,[20] and encourage the development of non-nuclear energy sources.[21]

Particularly on matters of contracting and investment, the NFZ municipalities in the United States followed practices pioneered by the anti-Apartheid movement, which had begun in the 1970s to pressure local authorities to break their economic links with South Africa.[22] Measures of this sort involved a more indirect challenge to the national government than attempts to zone out armaments factories, block convoys, or ban nuclear research. To protect themselves, local authorities usually tried to claim that they were acting within the limits of their traditional responsibilities for health, safety, and economic well-being. Thus, the city attorney in Portland, Oregon, advised the council there to avoid reference to matters of national defence or foreign affairs in developing its NFZ policy.

The present revised ordinance should be redrafted to restrict its purposes to (a) enhancing economic stability in the City; (b) improving the psychological health of City residents; (c) protecting the civil liberties of City residents; and (d) accomplishing other traditional local police power purposes. There also should be a full record made before City Council containing evidence that the ordinance in fact will contribute to the achievement of these purposes.[23]

This was the strategy followed in Chicago in 1986.[24]

The Ordinance seeks to ban the manufacture of nuclear weapons and nuclear

weapons components by private parties in the City of Chicago for the following reasons:
Economic instability: the nuclear weapons industry is unstable 'because the demand for nuclear weapons may decline drastically in the event of an arms control agreement or a freeze or reduction in the United States Government nuclear weapons arsenal.'
Depletion of the community's limited resources: nuclear weapon-related activities divert the City's limited public and private resources to non-productive uses.
Excessive security: 'security requirements accompanying the nuclear weapons industry unduly restrict the dissemination of information' and require 'the reallocation of scarce police and fire department resources.'
Public health: the presence in the City 'of an industry which could make the City a target of terrorism or nuclear attack' threatens the public health.
Morality: 'the public morality is affronted by the presence of an industry profiting from activities which may ultimately lead to unprecedented death and destruction.'

As the lawyers for the NFZ proponents noted, all of these reasons related to 'the traditional police powers of the state to regulate the community's public health, safety, morals, economic well-being, and general welfare.'

A case can also be made, as with respect to refugee sanctuaries, that international law *requires* a municipality to act on these matters, even in defiance of the federal authorities.

All of these affirmative actions are supported by the body of law that has come to be designated peace law. The fundamental source of law supporting such action is the UN Charter, a treaty ratified by the United States in 1945 (89–2) and signed by the President as one of the treaties of the United States and therefore part of the supreme law of the land under the U.S. Constitution, Article 6, Sec. 2. The UN Charter provisions most frequently used are Articles 2.3, 2.4, 55 and 56. These establish standards of conduct for the United States, individually and collectively as a member of the United Nations. Another basic source of peace law is the Nuremberg Principles, which are also part of U.S. law as an executive agreement between the United States, England, France, and the Soviet Union, signed on August 8, 1945, and made part of international law at the request of President Harry Truman in 1946, in order to make permanent these rules originally used to try Nazi war criminals. They are now found in the U.S. Army Field Manual (FM 27–10, 18 July 1956) and 59 Stats. at Large 1544, et seq. (1945), and clearly govern the conduct of all U.S. military personnel and all U.S. civilians.[25]

The key claims that arise from this analysis are as follows: Americans (including American officials at all levels) have a legal obligation to assist refugees, abstain from the use of nuclear, biological, and chemical weapons, and abide by the decisions of the International Court of Justice. According to this view, then, Americans (and indeed, citizens of all the countries in the United Nations) have a legal obligation to create refugee sanctuaries and nuclear-free zones. This is one of the grounds offered for the NFZ ordinance in Berkeley, California.[26]

Such claims about the positive duties of municipalities complement the arguments advanced by Michael Shuman and Larry Agran of the Center for Innovative Diplomacy, to the effect that the paramountcy of the American federal government with respect to foreign affairs does not preclude local action. Shuman notes:

Legal scholars have pointed out that the Constitution forbids local governments from assembling their own army or navy, declaring wars, entering treaties, violating national treaty commitments, and levying duties on imports or exports. Since they could not imagine how else local governments might influence foreign affairs, the legal case against municipal foreign policies has always seemed obvious. But almost all of the municipal activism now underway does not fall into any of these forbidden categories. And as attorneys and courts have examined specific municipal foreign policies, they have found that countervailing constitutional principles render the general legal wisdom practically meaningless.[27]

A generous reading of local powers under the U.S. Constitution is certainly possible.

Indeed, the Constitution grants to states and localities numerous foreign policy making powers. The First Amendment guarantees the right of all citizens, even mayors and city council members, to speak out on foreign policy. The Fifth Amendment grants them the right to travel abroad. The Compact Clause allows states and cities to negotiate agreements with jurisdictions abroad, providing Congress does not object. Article III, Section 2, gives federal courts jurisdiction over 'controversies between a State ... and foreign States' precisely because it envisions communications and deal-making between U.S. local governments and foreign nations. Similarly, when the Framers gave Congress the power 'to regulate commerce with foreign nations' (Art. I, Sec. 8), they assumed that vigorous economic intercourse between local and foreign jurisdictions would continue. The Tenth Amendment further underscores that 'powers not delegated to the United States, nor prohibited by it to the States, are reserved to the States respectively, or to the people.'[28]

Be that as it may, conservative courts and state officials still take the view that matters of foreign and defence policy are properly within the jurisdiction of the national government. In Massachusetts the attorney general consistently refused, between 1983 and 1987, to register NFZ by-laws adopted by town meetings, on the grounds that they involved unconstitutional incursions on the federal powers to provide for the common defence and to determine the foreign policies of the United States. Concerns were also raised by the attorney general and other commentators about possible interference with interstate commerce, vested property rights, and rights of free inquiry.[29] It was on such grounds that the tough NFZ resolution in Oakland, California, was overturned by the courts in 1990, as a result of a private suit by a military researcher supported both by a conservative 'public interest' group and by the federal justice department.[30] Some of the space left to municipalities exists only because of inaction by the senior governments, and could be closed off by adverse legislation or even executive decrees.

However, the British experience suggests that even a tightly centralized and strongly led government like Margaret Thatcher's can run into serious difficulties in trying to impose its policies on determined local authorities. There are striking parallels, for instance, in the fate of 'civil defence' in Britain and the United States in the early 1980s. The U.S. Federal Emergency Management Agency ultimately had to abandon a new civil defence scheme, because it could not generate enough support at the state and local levels, and could not get Congress to force the junior governments into line – something that Congress could in theory have done.[31] Thatcher's ministers had the support of a tame Parliament, and theoretically had the means to impose whatever duties they liked upon 'nuclear-free' authorities. Nonetheless, civil defence planning was an exercise in frustration for the Conservative government throughout the 1980s.

Problems began for it in 1980, when the British Home Office issued a pamphlet, *Protect and Survive*,[32] that told people what to do in case of a nuclear attack. E.P. Thompson's brilliant riposte, *Protest and Survive*,[33] was a propaganda triumph for the resurgent nuclear disarmament movement, not least because the government's advice about hiding under a table in the parlour was so silly. Two years later, the NFZ authorities had their turn, when they responded to the government's civil defence exercise, 'Hard Rock,' with a peace campaign under the slogan 'Hard Luck.'[34] So many local authorities refused to participate in the exercise that the government was forced to cancel it. Embarrassed, the Conservatives responded with their own propaganda campaign, which emphasized the need for 'all hazards' planning for disasters ranging from major fires to nuclear wars. They stressed the prospect of conventional attack on Britain[35] – which evoked memories of the Blitz – and criticized the dissident Labour authorities for politicizing what ought to have been an uncontroversial process of emergency planning. More forcefully, they required the local authorities to prepare plans under the new civil defence emergency regulations of 1983.

This might have ended the matter, but the NFZ authorities complained that they lacked the information necessary to prepare for nuclear war. They needed to know where and how they could expect to be hit in a nuclear attack, the extent of the likely damage, and so on. When the government responded with planning assumptions that offered only sketchy information, the dissident authorities began their own planning assumptions studies, and insisted that they could not comply with the government's requirements until these were complete.[36] The best publicized of these studies, the GLAWARS Report on Greater London,[37] was another propaganda success for the NFZs, because it detailed the horrific effects of an attack on London, suggested that civil defence was largely useless, and pointed to the need for action to prevent nuclear war. The government again was embarrassed, and it brought in new legislation – the Civil Protection in Peacetime Act, 1986 – to bury civil defence in an 'all hazards' approach to emergency planning.[38] By separate legislation, it abolished the Greater London Council and other metropolitan authorities, which had had responsibility for civil defence in the major cities, and replaced them with new, special-purpose bodies, including fire and civil defence authorities. The powers of the latter were carefully circumscribed, so that it was clear that they could plan only for the consequences of nuclear war, and were not allowed to explore the possibilities for preventing it.[39] That same year, all the local authorities responsible for 'civil protection' were given deadlines for completion of their nuclear plans.

The NFZ authorities – whose representatives dominated many of the new fire and civil defence authorities, as well as most of the key urban local councils – responded with a strategy of 'critical compliance.'[40] They proceeded with planning, but at every stage made it clear that they were being asked to work with unrealistic assumptions and without sufficient resources. They managed to get deadlines extended, and meanwhile pressed their case publicly, trying to show that the government was actually sacrificing the opportunity to develop an effective national system for responding to civil disasters by diverting scarce resources into a futile war-planning scheme that had more to do with keeping people out of the military's way than with protecting civilian lives. Again, propaganda by local authorities on this and other matters proved to be quite effective. The government tried to control it by legislating new limits on local authority 'publicity.'[41] This was supposed to make it impossible for local councils to engage in 'propaganda on the rates.' However, as an NFZ legal opinion indicated,[42] the legislation still left scope for carefully constructed information campaigns, since the government did not dare silence the local authorities altogether. They were entitled, as ever, to advance their own policies with respect to their own activities, which included civil defence.

At each stage in this battle, it became more difficult for the local authorities to pursue their dissident policies; however, it never became impossible for them to act critically. The government's 1988 legislation removed the right of local authorities to impose 'contract compliance' conditions that were extraneous to the business at hand; this made it impossible for those authorities to follow the American lead in boycotting nuclear weapons contractors. However, this only highlighted the fact that the NFZ authorities had been laggard in using their powers in this respect. As an NFZ working party reported in 1987:[43]

> NFZ Authorities have, over the last 5 years, contributed positively to public debate about nuclear issues, and have given significant support to the wider movement for peace. However, when NFZ Authorities are publicly visible it's often because of symbolic initiatives such as NFZ roadsigns, stickers, or peace gardens. Where those initiatives have been pursued without a complementary development of policy in respect of those responsibilities of the local authority which are affected by the actual activities of the nuclear state, NFZ Authorities have become vulnerable to attack and ridicule. An over-emphasis on the symbolic to the detriment of policy development may also have limited the number of authorities who are willing to spend money on NFZ initiatives. If it is accepted that this is the case, then it is recommended that the NSC [National Steering Committee] should give emphasis to substantive policy development on nuclear issues in its work programme. This policy should be developed in respect of those responsibilities of the local authority which are affected by the

nuclear state, in particular an authority's responsibilities for its citizen's safety, general education and future livelihood and well-being.

In response to the Chernobyl disaster a year earlier, the NFZ authorities had agreed to campaign against nuclear power as well as nuclear weapons. This facilitated a 'shift to the mainstream' in the development of NFZ policies.[44] For local authorities responsible for public health and safety, there clearly were many practical issues related to nuclear accidents and radiation levels, which they had an obligation to deal with. These issues arose in relation to nuclear power plants and weapons facilities, disposal sites for nuclear materials, and shipments of nuclear fuels, reactors, weapons, and wastes. Although the national government might claim to have all of these matters under control, it was obviously sensible for local authorities to take an interest as well.

Thus, NFZ authorities took it upon themselves to monitor radiation levels,[45] track nuclear convoys,[46] publicize nuclear hazards,[47] educate people about the dangers of nuclear materials,[48] develop plans for nuclear accidents,[49] and lobby the central government continuously for more information. The complaint that the government was denying the public what they needed to know for their own safety was crucial to the continuing campaign against the nuclear state. Demands for information about the transport of nuclear materials might still seem like posturing if the local authorities had no power to regulate shipments, but it was posturing related to an issue close to the centre of local government responsibilities, and as such had greater legitimacy. Similar was the campaign around 'conversion' of nuclear plants,[50] weapons installations, and armaments factories. Clearly, the closure of such facilities would have serious effects on the local economy, so it was logical enough for a local authority to explore the possibilities for conversion or diversification before the event happened. This suggested that long-term discussions were required with local defence contractors and their employees. The logic of this was recognized even by local councils that had little sympathy with the NFZ movement.[51]

The 'shift to the mainstream' in British NFZ policy involved a retreat to the redoubts of local authority, where dissident activity could not easily be controlled by the national government. Within these redoubts, practical work could be done that related to a wide range of popular concerns. This helped to legitimize peace action that might otherwise have appeared quixotic. It also made an essential connection between the foreign policy initiatives of the dissident authorities and the traditional concerns of local government.

**Healthy Cities**

Issues of war and peace are not the only ones that engage municipalities in activities that transcend the limits of national policy. Municipalities are the primary environmental authorities, and thus have a legitimate interest in many issues of global concern, including ozone depletion, acid rain, and toxic waste disposal. One response for a local council dissatisfied with the national government is to make common cause with its counterparts elsewhere. This logic is implicit in the activities of the recently formed International Council for Local Environmental Initiatives. As Jeb Brugmann, acting secretary general, indicated in 1990:

> Right now, there are a handful of municipalities in the position to test new and risky strategies for environmental protection. Without a vehicle for the transfer of successful innovations, many years pass before other municipalities, which cannot assume the political or financial risk, begin to adopt proven policies and techniques. We'll be trying to speed this transfer process by supporting the innovation process, identifying and sharing successes and working directly with communities to implement them.[52]

Thus expressed, the role of the council seems apolitical; however, the networks it embodies are the children of political insurgency. Brugmann, for instance, was first director of the Peace Commission in Cambridge, Massachusetts, a body established in the wake of the 1981 nuclear freeze initiative in that city. As such, he was involved in campaigns around nuclear disarmament and the conversion of factories to peaceful production, as well as in the development of sister-city relationships and new peace curricula for the local schools.[53] Later he became field programs director for the Center for Innovative Diplomacy, which was perhaps the most important agency for promoting radical foreign-policy initiatives among American municipalities in the 1980s. It was at a CID-sponsored conference in Irvine, California, that an intermunicipal Stratospheric Protection Accord was first promoted.[54] Also, the CID was one of the sponsors of the 1990 World Congress of Local Governments for a Sustainable Future, a New York gathering facilitated by both the International Union of Local Authorities and the United Nations Environment Program. Out of this conference and the activities associated with the Rio Conference on Environment and Development came the new international council.

This intersection of local and global initiatives had been anticipated within the field of public health. At the 1978 International Conference of Primary Health Care in Alma-Ata, U.S.S.R., the World Health Organization had adopted a new global strategy, that 'stressed the close and complex links between health and socio-economic development, and proposed the primary health care approach as the key to attaining health for all.'[55] This had two immediate implications: an explicit recognition that poverty and the 'inequity'[56] that generated it were at the root of the most serious health problems; and a commitment to 'health promotion' as a strategy for dealing with these problems. The latter idea arose largely from the experience of development programs in Asia, Africa, and Latin America. Efforts at immunization and disease control were often defeated by the desperate poverty that led to poor nutrition and inadequate sanitation. Although economic development was clearly the key to better health, it could not be secured by big projects that bypassed ordinary people and required massive injections of foreign capital and technical assistance. It depended instead on community organization, appropriate technology, and social and ecological sensitivity – all of which were also required for health promotion. Outsiders – be they engineers, accountants, or public health nurses – had to support the local people as they identified their priorities, serve as advocates for them in the outside world, and learn to make their expertise, resources, and external connections relevant to the situation at hand. This implied a far more egalitarian relationship than the ones typical of traditional aid programs.

European municipalities were among the first to reconsider their relationship to Third World development in this context. At a 1983 conference in Florence on Towns and Co-operation for Development, delegates from a number of local authorities and nongovernmental organizations agreed to co-ordinate their efforts. Two years later they issued the Cologne Appeal, 'From Justice to Charity,' for joint action by NGOs and local communities in North-South development. The delegates looked toward activities that would combine the expertise, experience, and external connections of the NGOs with the organizational resources, legitimacy, and local presence of municipal governments. They foresaw major educational and informational efforts to raise consciousness about North-South issues, a joint planning process involving all sectors of the community to develop links with the South, and projects for 'establishing friendship, solidarity and partnership with towns and rural areas in the South on a community-to-community basis.' Linking projects would be guided by the principles developed by the NGOs and their partners in the South; these principles included 'equality, reciprocity, absence of paternalism,' 'focus on the poorest,' 'recognition of the significance of women,' 'environmental impact [assessment],' and '[respect for] cultural diversity.'[57]

These principles echoed the practices of community development that had been evolving in the rich countries themselves, from Saul Alinsky's time onward. In Toronto, these practices fed into the 'health promotion' ideas coming out of WHO and helped to transform the local board of health. In 1978 a radicalized board adopted a new program that involved 'community development and advocacy directed toward the social and political determinants of health.'[58] Led by a one-time African aid worker and NDP official, the health advocacy unit established an impressive international reputation. In 1984 the board celebrated its centenary with a major international conference, 'Healthy Toronto 2000.' This proved to be of major significance, because it was here that delegates worked out an agenda for 'healthy public policies,' aimed at creating 'healthy cities' by the year 2000. The European region of WHO picked up these concepts and began to promote them under the rubric of its Health For All by the Year 2000 campaign. Thus, a local initiative became much more general.

In Britain, the 'healthy cities' campaign was a godsend to Labour authorities looking to break out of the strictures imposed on them by the Thatcher government.[59] The Black Report of 1980,[60] commissioned by the previous Labour government, had documented the connection between ill health and economic and social deprivation in the northern cities. As such, it offered strong evidence that the Third World concerns that informed WHO's new Health For All (HFA) global strategy were equally relevant in a First World context. These concerns pointed toward a broader approach to public health, one that would emphasize environmental improvements, increased social and economic opportunities for the deprived, and both individual and collective participation in health improvement. Under such an approach, the elected local authorities, which had been pushed to one side by the National Health Service and the district health authorities, would again have a key role to play in public health. Moreover, they would have reason – validated not only by the Black Report but also by WHO – for pursuing a socialist health strategy with strong environmentalist, feminist, and collectivist elements.[61] As Barbara Lane notes:

> By June 1987, approximately 50 cities in the U.K. were participating [in the Healthy Cities project], some of them communicating with the Regional Co-ordinating Centre at the WHO Europe Office, or with each other informally through the newly formed, loosely-knit U.K. Healthy Cities Network, or a bi-monthly Healthy Cities newsletter published out of Liverpool, or in April 1988, at the first United Kingdom Health Cities Conference, held in Liverpool. WHO had designated Liverpool and Bloomsbury/Camden as 'Project Cities,' to be joined in 1988 by Glasgow and Belfast. However, relatively few cities in the U.K. have aligned themselves with WHO, preferring to declare their own projects without waiting for the results from demonstrations projects.[62]

This burst of activity outside the WHO framework reflected the fact that the activist Labour councils had already identified health as an issue that would enable them to reopen the socialist agenda in Britain. As a leading Sheffield activist noted:

> In the years to 1985 claimed for municipal socialism we used local experience and experiment to create a vision of primary care challenging the dominance of hospitals and medical professionals, democratically accountable to neighbourhood communities, planned to prevent illness and eradicate inequalities in health across the city and building on the skills of grass roots workers like home helps, health visitors, general practitioners and district nurses.[63]

Similarly, the board of health in Toronto continued to pursue a more radical version of 'healthy cities' after the Conservative federal government gave its blessing to a Canadian Healthy Communities Project in 1986.[64] While other Canadian cities contemplated modest efforts,[65] the Healthy Toronto Subcommittee of the city's board of health advanced a series of bold proposals that would have reoriented local government.[66] These included the creation of a Healthy City Office, a Healthy Public Policy Committee, a Food Policy Council,[67] and a 'safe city' task force,[68] as well as measures for 'community empowerment,'[69] a Healthy Housing Policy, an environmental bill of rights, and economic 'sustainability.'[70]

Such initiatives illustrate how dissident authorities have linked their activities to the broader concerns of progressive social movements. The connective presence of these movements, the stimulative effect of international organizations of all sorts, and the shared experience of social, economic, and environmental problems have all contributed to the development of common fields of action that disrupt the hierarchies of the state system. It is by no means clear that the initiatives of the Toronto Board of Health, the mayor of Irvine, California, or the Manchester City Council are 'local' in the sense of 'confined to a particular place.' Rather, they open up to and are informed by complex international networks that cut across the boundaries between states and create empowering interlocal and global/local relations.

**The Scope for Municipal Foreign Policy**

The collapse of the Cold War security system, which kept the East 'out' and the South 'down,' has added immeasurably to the uncertainties of international relations. Some of the initiatives of the dissident authorities in the 1980s seem to belong to a world that has passed. Still, it is clear that borders are less stable and more difficult to police, that individual states have less control of economic matters, that disease and decay spread relentlessly over the globe, and that national governments are everywhere struggling to maintain their authority. In this context, both the need and the scope for vigorous municipal action are great. What is apparent from the activities of the 1980s is not that municipalities can easily overcome their own subordination, but that determined action at the local level is difficult to crush. In 1987 the Institute for European Defence and Strategic Studies warned of the 'potential of the municipal anti-nuclear movement to cause havoc throughout the Western world,'[71] and one of its academic supporters suggested that it might be necessary to suppress democratic local government to protect the state from the 'incipient challenge' to its own integrity.[72] Such alarmist reaction is the sincerest form of flattery, and indicates that the most effective limits on municipal action may not be the ones established by states, but rather the ones that exist in the imagination of those who have convinced themselves that local actions cannot have global effects.

Whatever their limitations, municipalities are still vehicles for *public* action at a time when privatization remains the watchword. The apparent privatization of world governance, which is symbolized by the growing power of the currency exchanges, has not been effectively challenged by national governments. In the circumstances, the need for direct municipal action is likely to become more acute. If this action is not to be confined to what enhances economic competitiveness, it has to be framed in terms of a wider right of local initiative. Thus, the idea that a municipality may act on any matter of immediate concern to its citizens is of extraordinary importance. This is the idea implicit in the activities we have considered in this chapter, and it has profound implications for the way we orient ourselves toward the hyperspace of the global city.

# 12

# Social Movements and the Global City

The organizing assumption of international relations theory is that the political universe is to be conceived primarily in terms of relations within and between states. The belief seems to be that the state is so powerful that, in the end, everything of consequence in world politics is forced through the system of states and inter-state relations. This belief is an old one, and it reflects the organizing assumptions of 'political science,' a discipline that emerged in Germany and the United States about a hundred years ago. That discipline was originally conceived as the science of the state. It aspired to be the Aristotelian master science – a way of understanding human action on the grand scale. However, it was challenged from the beginning by its sister disciplines in the humanities and social sciences, all of which pretended to have discovered a more fundamental human reality, of which the state was a mere reflection. In the past few decades, political scientists have been more and more beleaguered by sociologists, economists, geographers, anthropologists, cultural theorists, and historians who claim to have better ways of explaining politics – ones that point beyond the state to something else. These claims have naturally been treated with some scepticism by political scientists, who suspect that they are being victimized by a reverse disciplinary imperialism. It has not escaped everyone's notice that analysts from the sister disciplines tend to reintroduce the state without explaining it, or to substitute terms like 'the nation' or 'society' for what we might otherwise call states. Political scientists in general and IR theorists in particular may be forgiven for supposing that their own approach is at least more honest, because it names the state as the ultimate regulator of social, economic, and cultural life and focuses attention on the politics of state policy-making and inter-state relations.

The unfortunate effect of this defensive response is that 'world politics' has come to be conceived within a single analytical frame. It is not just political scientists who have adopted this frame: sociologists, economists, anthropologists, geographers, and other analysts of the modern world have imported the same basic assumptions into their work.[1] Although people may talk about civilizations, world economies, and other transcendent formations, statelike entities keep popping up as the governing authorities in even the most innovative accounts of world order. Worse, the political analyses that have been drawn from these accounts tend to follow the familiar demarcations between domestic government and international relations. It seems that we are doomed to have more and more of the same until the 'specialists' in political analysis seize the initiative and show others how the old categories can be rethought.

Fortunately, there are some signs of rethinking, even within the theoretically backward discipline of international relations. Most of us have sensed, since the collapse of the bipolar world order and the emergence of a global economy and culture, that the old ways of conceptualizing world politics are not really adequate. As well, political scientists have grown generally uneasy about their ability to account for changing conditions. The neat patterns of politics in the postwar liberal democracies have been disrupted, and the textbook accounts no longer make much sense. Our analytical tools for understanding politics outside the West seem even less adequate. And, of course, the ontological and epistemological assumptions of the social sciences have been seriously challenged. More and more, political scientists are putting the state at issue – that is, they are coming to see it as a historically, culturally, and geographically specific form of political order; beginning to inquire into its conditions of possibility; and recognizing a wider field of 'politics' within which state formation, state policy-making, and inter-state relations are seen as particular activities that do not encompass the whole. Some believe that the 'new' social movements have changed the conditions for political action and generated 'spaces' for politics that are incommensurate with the ones defined by the state system.[2] For instance, to think of Amnesty International, and Greenpeace International (let alone the global environmental movement, and the international movements for human rights and women's emancipation) as domestic 'pressure groups' or as 'non-state actors' in the international system misses much of what is significant about these new formations. To grasp what is not contained within the old categories, we have to loosen the hold that those categories have upon us, and experiment with different paradigms for political analysis.

It is in that spirit that I will be presenting a different approach to understanding world politics. This approach focuses on the global city[3] and its social movements rather than on the state system and the actors within it. Two conceptual shifts are involved: from the state system to the global city as the form of world order; and from the political actors defined by the state system to the social movements that constitute or challenge that system (as well as the other modes of governance or social regulation present in the world). Although this approach decentres the state as the object of political analysis, it does not ignore the state or pretend that it is about to wither away. On the contrary, the state system is analysed as the effect of a particular social movement interacting with other social movements in the domain of world politics. This new approach concretizes a mode of analysis to which others have pointed, by suggesting that world order takes the form of a global city. If that suggestion is correct, world politics has to be understood as a type of urban politics, in which inter-state relations occur as a particular form of activity. Not many will take kindly to this idea, because it disrupts conventional notions about the hierarchy of disciplines in political science. Nonetheless, I ask readers to pause, and follow me in exploring the implications of this paradigmatic shift. We need to open up the study of world politics, and the approach suggested offers one way of doing that.

If we were to historicize the analysis that follows, we might relate it to contemporary accounts of postmodernity. It has been suggested that the contemporary world can no longer be understood as 'modern,' and that it has to be reanalysed as a 'postmodern' phenomenon.[4] It is not clear exactly what this means, but if we identify modernity with the state system, we might conceive of the postmodern order in terms of the global city. The processes of decentring, proliferation of identities, pluralization of histories, destabilization of authority, and so on are all recognizably 'urban' phenomena, which to date have been analysed mainly in terms of the advanced urbanism of Western Europe and North America. There is a dim sense that these processes have their analogues in the massive new cities in other parts of the world, and that what happens in one place is intimately connected with developments elsewhere. California and Mexico, France and Algeria, Germany and Turkey, Canada and China resonate with each other in ways that could hardly have been imagined a few decades ago. If there is some truth to the notion that we have entered – or are about to enter – a new era, the transition may be amenable to analysis in terms of the displacement of the state system by a new political order that we can best understand as a 'global city.'

The account that follows does not adhere to such a simple periodization. On the contrary, its implication is that the global city was 'always there' from the beginning of modernity, but that its presence has been only dimly recognized. In the first section of this article, we explore the Weberian/Wirthian idea that 'urbanism' is a distinctive way of life, and argue that this insight needs to be developed as a *political* theory of world order. In the second section, we look in more detail at that order. The focus is on the city (and thus the global city) as a self-organizing (or 'anarchic') system that defies the principles of state sovereignty (and with them the familiar analytic principles of international relations). In the third section, we re-pose the question of world order in terms of the constitutive politics of social movements, whose venue or 'space' is the international urban system or global city. We argue that this venue can be conceived as a political hyperspace. In the final section, we consider rather tentatively the analytical and political implications of thinking of this hyperspace in urban rather than state-centric terms.

**Urbanism as a Way of Life**

Once again, as a beginning, we can invoke the figure of Max Weber, but this time not the Weber who is celebrated or maligned by theorists of international relations. At issue, rather, is the Weber who theorized the city as a sphere of 'non-legitimate domination.'[5] His idea of the city – or at least the European city – as a site of domination unlegitimated by the state or the church ought to have been extremely suggestive for students of world politics, but it seems to have been generally neglected. When Weber wrote, it was already a commonplace notion that the distinctive politics of the West had been shaped by the struggle between church and state – a struggle that arose from the co-presence of two different modes of legitimate authority. What Marx – and before him the other political economists and sociologists – had suggested, was that beyond church and state there was something else that organized or determined people's lives. For Marx, this something else was the mode of production: in the contemporary world, capitalism. For others, it was the ethos of the times, the cultures of civilization, the basic features of human nature, or whatever one's imagination could suggest. Weber sensed that 'the city' was fundamental to whatever rivalled the formative influence of church and state. To use Marxist language, the city was from a Weberian perspective the material base for the economy, culture, and everyday social life.[6] As Weber noted, European cities had attained a unique autonomy in relation to church and state in medieval times. The growth and development of these cities – their power over their inhabitants and their dependencies – could not be explained simply in terms of governmental or religious initiatives. Kings might create capitals and bishops might raise cathedrals, but in the end 'the economy' – or was it the city? – had relative autonomy. The market system – local, regional, continental, and ultimately global – had a life of its own, and the kings and bishops discovered at their peril the cost of defying its logic. Perhaps this had always been so, but the relative autonomy of the city as a nexus of expansive economic activity became especially apparent from the fifteenth century onward. In that context, one could hardly deny the formative influence of what Lewis Mumford later called 'the culture of cities.'

The American urban sociologists who attempted in the early part of this century to build on the work of Weber, Durkheim, Tonnies, and Simmel were quick to point out that the Marxist identification of the city with capital (or with the class relation of capital and labour) was too simplistic.[7] Louis Wirth noted that 'urbanism' could be conceived as a distinctive 'way of life'[8] – what others might call a culture or form of society. This way of life was not contained within the boundaries established by political, religious, or other authorities. On the contrary, it constantly spilled over those boundaries, colonized the surrounding rural areas, and pulled people out of their former modes of existence, be they agrarian, pastoral, or otherwise. Many medieval cities had been walled; modern cities were unwalled, and their outer limits were increasingly difficult to define. From the earliest years of the modern era, there was a global network of cities linked by post roads and sailing vessels. Railways, steamships, and telegraph lines tightened these connections in the nineteenth century, and in Wirth's time automotive transport, air travel, and telecommunications were hastening integration. By the 1920s it was already difficult to distinguish one city from the next in densely urbanized parts of the world such as southern England;[9] by the 1950s this was a common condition in 'advanced' industrial countries; by the 1970s it was being recognized as a nearly universal phenomenon; and by the 1990s one could begin to talk meaningfully to a popular audience about a 'global city' whose presence was felt almost everywhere.

Those who followed Wirth in his analysis resisted the Marxist and neo-Marxist identification of world order with capitalism. They thus avoided the economic reductionism to which Marxism was so often subject, especially in the Stalinist era. On the other hand, they had a tendency to 'naturalize' the process of urban development, and so to depoliticize their conception of urbanism. This was a major theoretical error, which has elicited much neo-Marxist criticism.[10] However, the urbanist approach did have value in that it suggested that there was a 'beyond' to the city – a 'surplus' – that could not easily be theorized in Marxist or statist terms. The city was not just an effect of state organization, although its development might well be governed in important ways by state policy. To approach the city as mode of cultural organization was useful, but not entirely satisfactory, since cultures were not free-floating entities. It was clear that the form of urban life changed dramatically with new technologies; yet it was also clear that the city was more than a technological outcome. It was also more than a mode of capitalist organization. One could read much off the logic of capital, but not the national, religious, and other identities that were formed in and through the urban experience. Thoughtful urbanists were thus driven toward interpretations that defied every form of reductionism. It seemed that the city as a way of life, or form of world order, had to be understood in its own terms.

This insight has been extended in various ways by the analysts of urban social movements. The study of social movements as an urban phenomenon predates the interest in 'new social movements' among critical scholars in the 1980s.[11] The work of Manuel Castells was critical in this respect, because he attempted to come to terms with both the American tradition of urban analysis derived from Weber, and the European tradition of political economy derived from Marx.[12] The result was a sustained effort, on the part of Castells and those whom he had influenced, to theorize the city as a site of complex political struggles – struggles that were conditioned by the logic of the market but were not simply effects of that logic. Out of this effort has emerged an intellectual field, urban political economy, that is in many ways the complement to international political economy.[13] Contemporary urbanists and urban political economists are struggling to understand the impact of globalization on the contemporary city, to take account of the new patterns of migration and acculturation, to make sense of new problems of human security, and to come to terms with forms of political struggle that are not neatly contained within the routines of well-ordered states. Urbanists bring to this a sensitivity to place-based issues of housing, transportation, public services, cultural expression, environmental quality, and so on. Ethnic and racial conflict, organized violence, pervasive threats to order and security – these are part of the familiar stuff of urban politics as it can be observed in major cities.

Viewed from an urbanist's perspective, city life is where the principles of state sovereignty – and the complementary principles of individual sovereignty – fall apart in the face of the complexities of human existence.[14] There is a wildness and danger to the city that reminds one, quite properly, of the 'anarchy' of international relations. IR theorists see themselves as working at the boundary where the niceties of domestic politics no longer apply. Urbanists have the same sense of themselves, because they are confronted with a kind of raw politics – especially in the major cities – that has little to do with the formalities of democratic elections, impartial adjudication, and bureaucratic administration. These niceties may be present in some form, but there is a disorder to urban life and urban politics that cannot be comprehended without recognizing that a sort of anarchy prevails. Of course, this anarchy – like the supposed anarchy of the international system – is more apparent than real. Urban life is ordered and in many respects orderly, but this orderliness cannot be understood as a simple effect of state action or market relations. The sources of order (and disorder) are various, and must be understood in relation to one another. Thus, the study of urban politics drives one away from the tidy routines of constitutional government, in search of the processes that give form and structure to urban life. In the end, these processes can hardly be distinguished from the ones that create world order.

We tend to be deceived about the relationship between the urban and the global, because the global is normally identified with inter-state relations and the urban with local government. Local government appears to be just an administrative matter well within the bounds of the state. One thinks in terms of levels of government, from the immediate community to the district or province and on up to the country as a whole. The state encompasses the widest area, and it is broken into intermediate units responsible for smaller territories. Local governments deal with cities or communities within these smaller territories. Years ago, Robert Dahl suggested that we might think of this in terms of a set of Chinese boxes or Russian dolls.[15] The biggest and most important doll is the state, which contains the lesser dolls within it, and bumps up against the other big dolls in a complex system of international relations. IR and IPE theorists tend to assume that they can ignore the little dolls, because they are neatly tucked away inside the big ones. Unfortunately, the imagery is simply not accurate. New York is not just a locality within the United States; nor is it merely part of a larger geographic unit. On the contrary, it is a major node in an international urban system, the spatial organization of which differs in character from, and ultimately transcends the spatial organization of, the state system. In terms of urbanism as a way of life, the state system is just an element in the complex that produces order in the global city.

One interpretation of Thatcherism is that it was an effort to reorganize the British state to suit the new requirements of the City of London.[16] From this perspective, recent British politics has been mainly about the struggle by the City's leaders – few of whom are crowned with formal political office – to protect London's position as the financial centre of Europe and as one of the three great financial centres of the world. This is a sign of the primacy of urban politics, broadly conceived. Similarly, one might analyse the contemporary question of China, not in terms of inter-state relations, but in terms of the challenge to Beijing from the tri-city megalopolis of Hong Kong–Singapore–Taipei. Equally, one might approach the question of Palestine or South Africa in terms of relations between different urban diasporas: Jewish and Arab, African and European. If we moved beyond the Eurocentric analyses with which we are familiar, we might see both the 'old' social movements (labour/socialist, nationalist) and the new ones (feminist, environmentalist, and so on) as political formations within the global city. And the question of culture could be understood in terms of the struggle between Hollywood and its various urban competitors. In fact, there are few questions in world politics that could not be approached from a city-centred rather than a state-centred perspective. When this new approach is taken, the assumed hierarchy is reversed, and inter-state or international relations are seen as subsidiary or local effects of a world politics constituted by urban struggles.

However, there is little point in simply inverting the old analytical hierarchy. The advantage of a city-centred perspective is that it forces us to think simultaneously of the local and the global, the universal and the particular. On the one hand, the city is an expression of a universalizing urbanism – a type of world system. On the other hand, it is also a particular settlement with its own physical, social, economic, and political structure. This ambiguity leads us away from the spatial hierarchies that have usually been invoked for the analysis of international relations. One must think again about the spatial order of contemporary life. Capitalism, statism, and other social movements appear to produce the forms of urbanism that we confront. Thus, they seem like movements within the city as a global order. That order can be comprehended politically if we recognize that none of these movements is simply natural, and that the interaction between them constitutes world government. To the extent that there is a world politics, it seems to be within and at the edge of urbanism, where the conditions of our lives are being created – or resisted.

**The Global City as World Order**

One of the distinctive features of the city as a mode of order and domination is that it is *not* governed from a single centre. The principle of sovereignty does not work effectively within the civic domain. Of course, sovereigns often try to exercise control *over* cities, but they can rarely if ever work *through* cities. A city is in large degree a self-organizing system produced by a variety of cultural, social, and economic enterprises. It is where people come to do things outside the domain of sovereignty, in relative freedom from the dictates of church and state. The medieval proverb that 'city air makes free' refers to more than the liberation of serfs, who could gain the status of free persons after a year and a day. It also alludes to the possibility for new enterprises that escape the dead hand of established authority. Such enterprises are not, in principle, contained within the territory of a particular city: they reach out to the surrounding countryside and to other cities in the world beyond. Urbanity in its fullest sense implies deterritorialized relations between people in different parts of the world. In this sense, the city is not fixed to a particular place the way a village is. Urbanity implies a kind of nomadism: a presence within a space of flows that connect and reconnect different places in the world.[17] Obviously, the market structures many of these flows, and the logic of the market tends to determine which cities will expand and which will contract. However, the social and cultural flows that occur within urban space are not reducible to the logic of the market. They have more complex origins and many autonomous effects.

Present-day municipalities are lineal descendants of the early medieval corporations that were designed to contain and control urban development. Whether constituted by Royal Charter or formed from below by civic insurgents, the municipal corporations were intended to fix economic activity in particular places and to give urban life the form that people believed would be most rational. However, the municipal corporations were generally unable to contain what they were supposed to manage. This was partly because they lacked sovereignty, but more fundamentally because the activities that typified a city burst the bounds of any particular place. London could not be kept in its square mile, Paris could not be confined to the Île de la Cité, and even Manhattan was not big enough for New York. This physical overflow was a sign of economic, social, and cultural spillage of a much more profound character. By the seventeenth century the whole world was in London's domain, and, although London ultimately became the leading world-city, it was by no means the only city that could boast of a global or near-global reach.[18] Moreover, the leading cities were all linked to one another in patterns of dizzying complexity. None was 'independent' of the others, nor sought to be. Although there were governments of a sort in particular cities – sometimes even national governments with ostensibly sovereign authority – these governments exercised only a shadow control over their urban domains. Urbanism itself – the system of cities – was under no one's direct control, followed no one's orders in its development, and could not be managed from any single centre. On the contrary, as Braudel and others have reminded us, sovereigns of one sort or another have always depended heavily on the urban system that they pretend to govern. A productive and dynamic urbanism will produce the surpluses necessary to pay soldiers and make arms. It will also generate the ideas and the functionaries necessary for effective government or imperial expansion. Sovereignties will be sustained or overwhelmed by urban dynamism.

Arguably, the true heirs of the medieval cities are not the municipalities but the multinational corporations of the contemporary world. The corporate form as exemplified by IBM and ICI is a late mutation of the municipal corporation of medieval times, and is not connected (except nominally) to a particular place. It is slimmed down for the pursuit of profit, and projected into a truly global space. As organizations for economic enterprise, municipalities are largely anachronistic, because they are tied to particular territories and burdened with tasks of government. The free corporations of the present day occupy deterritorialized spaces that cannot be mapped onto the world like countries or provinces. Increasingly, they function within a cyberspace that is characterized by instantaneous electronic communication. This cyberspace is not stable, and in fact the major actors within it are constantly changing the systems of communication and control for their own purposes. Thus, the space within which these organizations act is largely the product of their own activities. To keep up with the most innovative actors is enormously difficult, and the evolution of cyberspace is not governed from any single centre. In this respect, the emergent cyberspace is typical of the spaces created by urban activity.

There is, of course, more to urban space than cyberspace. Urbanism is characterized by the continual production and reproduction of spaces of habitation, work, recreation, cultural expression, and so on. There is a dynamism to these processes that again defies any static representation. A building is simply a momentary expression of people's ideas about the way their activities need to be spatialized. Fixed as it is, a building is reformed in use until it becomes almost unrecognizable to its original founders. The physical form of the city as a whole is even more plastic. Once we take into account the city's relationship to the countryside and to other cities, it becomes apparent that urban space is a dynamic presence in the world as a whole. People are within urban space in their airplanes going from airport to airport, and in their cars speeding along the motorways. The airport cafe in Honolulu, which serves passengers on their way from San Francisco to Sydney, is a part of the space of all three cities – and many others. Similarly, the restaurants in the Black Forest, the beaches of Mauritius, and the mountains of British Columbia are extensions of the recreational space of urbanites in many parts of the world. Thanks to the means of transportation and communication that have been developed over the last thirty to thirty-five years, prosperous urbanites can inhabit any and all parts of the world in the routine course of their lives. It is a sign of parochialism – or poverty – if one fails to inhabit the whole world.

We might think of the wider habitat as a global 'hyperspace,' within which the 'cyberspace' of the computer nets is a particular but important domain.[19] Airports, motorways, offices, hotels, and boutiques are other elements in the most privileged domain of this hyperspace. Access to that domain is carefully controlled. In fact, cities are marked by exceedingly complicated strategies of territorialization.[20] Among the obvious signs of this are the urban fortresses of the sort that were first established in the late medieval Italian cities and later replicated in many forms. These are not the fortresses of kings and bishops, but of burghers who seek security within the turbulent, expansive and absorptive space of the city. When people venture out from these fortresses, they carry with them their personal security systems. Much public and private enterprise is directed toward securing privileged people's routes and places of work, recreation, shopping, and cultural expression.

Whole cities (for example, Paris) and whole regions of the tropics are being re-formed to make them comfortable spaces for the public life of the prosperous. Beside, beneath, and often co-present with these spaces are other, more constricted spaces that provide for the less prosperous. Homeless people live in every crack and cranny, having been swept from the places of privilege with ruthless efficiency. The zones of exclusion and inclusion are subtly layered and dynamically articulated, so that they register in the consciousness only in the enactment (and often not even then). Nevertheless, these half-understood urban zones are generally of much greater significance in people's lives than the boundaries between states.

Although the world functions as a single city, it is not a 'global village,' as Marshall McLuhan once suggested.[21] It lacks the fixity, community, and intimacy that is part of the image of the village. In fact, the global city is inherently complex, dynamic, and socially differentiated. It is at once expansive and inclusive, and it is more obviously marked by separations and exclusions than by the intimate relations of communal solidarity. The world as a city has many ethnic enclaves, rich neighbourhoods and poor, a multinucleated central business district, suburban office centres, shopping precincts, and recreational complexes, overcrowded systems of public transportation, and vast slums on its fringes that flow over and through the better-ordered and more prosperous districts. The government of this whole is ineffective at best and nonexistent at worst – just as it is within particular metropolitan areas. And, just as in particular cities, there is intense competition among the different jurisdictions, intermittent co-operation among them, and a vague sense that the whole could be much better ordered. If it is held together as a whole, it is mainly by economic transactions, facilitated by a common physical infrastructure. There is some sense that there is a common environment to be maintained, and that violence has to be curbed; and there is something of a shared culture that is dependent on common media of communication. However, there is no effective sovereignty, and it is by no means clear that people would want such a mode of political organization if they could have it.

To assert their sovereignty over municipal authorities, states have had to strip those authorities of most of the powers they would need for effective governance. A self-governing city would have the power to regulate its own economy and determine its own foreign trade policy. It would have to control the flow of arms in and out of its domain, and break the power of the armed gangs that defy its authority. Even to deal with questions of public health, it would have to project its authority far beyond its immediate boundaries. In a sense, it would have to follow its particular connections throughout the world. Thus, a municipal government that was determined to protect the interests of its own citizens would need a kind of world reach and freedom of action that is clearly inconsistent with state sovereignty. On the other hand, without such powers, municipal governments are condemned to a sort of observer status within the cities they are supposed to govern. Ironically, this is the status to which most if not all national governments are presently being reduced.[22] With respect to economic organization, public health, social services, and even 'security,' sovereignty seems increasingly like a 'show' that offers a comforting illusion of national control over national destinies.

**Social Movements as Political Space**

At least in its realist guise, international relations theory interprets world order as arising from the balance of power between self-subsistent states. This is an image that conforms to a particular conception of political space, one that Walker has described as Galilean.[23] In this conception, the behaviour of states is to be understood in terms of the principles of Newtonian mechanics: satellites orbit around stars (here, read 'great powers'); every body (state) continues in the same direction unless it is disturbed by a greater force; disaster strikes when two bodies (states) collide; order is achieved when everything (every state) is in its proper gravitational orbit; and so on. To spin out the implications of this model is a pleasant enough fantasy. However, as anyone knows who has had to represent the international system realistically, trying to produce an empirical account of the world order with this model is like trying to make Ptolemaic astronomy work: one gets lost in the revolving spheres. It is in response to this theoretical inadequacy that we are driven to conceptualize world order in an entirely different way.

This does *not* mean conceiving of an imaginary civil society as the reality that constitutes the state system. Such an approach replicates the assumptions of a state-centric analysis, because 'society' is defined as what is not the state.[24] That is why the shift to the city is such a crucial step: it enables us to move away from the state/society distinction, as well as from the other distinctions (such as politics/economics, and business/culture) that seem to flow from it. Conceived as the whole that we seek to understand, the global city appears as a panoply of movements. Although these are 'social' movements, in the end they are *political*. As Aristotle indicated, 'politics' refers to the activities by which a way of life is constituted or maintained.[25] Thus, the crucial politics of the moment are to be found in and between the social movements that constitute, maintain, or challenge the global city in which we live. These movements produce political spaces that cannot be modelled using Newtonian mechanics. What is 'here' is not distinct from what is 'there,' no place can be mapped without locating it temporally, and every domain of activity is relative to the others.

Since the 1920s, there has been increasing interest in 'movements' as political phenomena. It is obvious to any historical observer that the sea changes in political life are usually the result of movements that begin far from the established centres of political authority, build gradually in strength, and then wash over the landscape. Sometimes the floods leave most things intact; other times they alter the political landscape profoundly. To understand why and how these things happen is obviously important. However, the literature – which is mostly sociological and historical – has an odd bias in that it tends to define as a social movement only what appears outside the realms of the state system and the market economy.[26] That the institutions of the state and the market themselves arose from social movements, and that these social movements are by no means exhausted, are facts that tend to be obscured by conventional modes of analysis. It is much more realistic to say that the threefold separation of state, society, and economy (should we add culture?) is a product of social movements, and that these movements have to be understood as logically prior to the structures that they create. The failure to recognize this has led to the analytical neglect of the most powerful social movement of our times: capitalism.

That capitalism is powerful no one doubts. That its power is to be understood as the result of a social movement is rarely recognized. Yet the signs are there. Capitalism has its ideology, its exponents, its true believers. It rouses millions of people in its support, generates hundreds of political parties, and inspires the most incredible personal sacrifices. It is a way of life that attracts fierce loyalty and appears to offer people a means of solving all their problems. It generates countless books, movies, television programs, ad campaigns, and other items of propaganda every year. In terms of sustained activity, it is hard to think of anything that rivals this effort. More significant still is the day-by-day effort by which people prove the truth of capitalism as a way of living. They go off to work, provide their labour, take money in exchange, spend that money on the goods they want, and so extend the realm of capitalist activity. This realm has the feel of necessity to it: it seems like the inevitable product of normal behaviour. So powerful is the movement that during the communist era, people in Eastern Europe began to feel isolated from normal life, because they could not live in the proper, capitalist way. For hundreds of millions of other people in the world, proper capitalist life – what seems like proper *modern* life – is a distant ideal to be achieved by enormous personal and political struggles. Thus, these people are engaged in a widespread movement of social transformation.

Socialist theorists have tended to think of capitalism as a structure, rather than to understand that structure as a result of the capitalist movement.[27] The movement of and for capitalism is primary: its structural effects come and go. Thus, a form like the Keynesian welfare state – and perhaps even the system of representative government – is temporary: something liable to be superseded in the course of the movement. That movement is obviously global, and it can be traced back to fifteenth-century Europe if not earlier. It is associated with other movements such as secular rationalism, scientism, and liberalism, but it is by no means identical with them. Moreover, it has an intimate relationship to that other great movement of modern times: statism.

To think of statism as a social movement is even more eccentric than conceiving of capitalism in these terms. However, the sense of this analytical position ought to be apparent. The modern state did not emerge from the hand of God – indeed, God's representatives on earth were more than a little dubious about this new form of political organization – and it certainly was not always already there. It had to be created and subsequently sustained by continuous political activity. That activity has been so successful that many people cannot imagine that any other form of political life is possible. Hence, we have the anachronistic identification of statehood with organized government even in otherwise respectable scholarly analyses. Such effacement of the past is not a sign of *lack* of movement, but rather of the overwhelming *success* of the statist movement. Like capitalism, the state just seems like a part of normal life, and people enact its routines – and hence re-create the state – day by day. When fused with nationalism, statism generates fierce loyalties marked by a willingness to run at machine-gun nests, smother grenades, and annihilate other people's families. In this form, it seems immensely potent.

To speak of capitalism, statism, and nationalism is not to exhaust the list of governing social movements. Feminists would want to talk about patriarchy as a system of rule – one that can be traced back at least to Sumerian times[28] and that is now well established in the world as a whole. Environmentalists would want to explore the movement to dominate nature. Others would want to analyse the movement toward European hegemony, which was sustained in part by doctrines of white supremacy. In theory, this list of governing movements could be extended indefinitely. We certainly would not want to ignore religion, tribalism, clan and family systems, or modes of organizing sexual identity. Nor would we want to neglect the social movements that have become bearers of the Enlightenment dream of universal emancipation. However, this proliferation of politically significant movements leaves us in a condition of uncertainty, for it seems that each of these movements produces its own, distinctive political space. Is there no space where these movements come together and interact with one another? Is there no 'hyperspace' in which the different domains of political activity can be related?

As it is used in contemporary physics, 'hyperspace' refers to the multidimensional space in which the four visible dimensions appear.[29] (Since Einstein, time has been understood as the fourth dimension of space.) According to the most popular current theory, the universe is actually constituted in ten-dimensional space; however, the invisible six are curled up into a tiny ball. Only on the assumption that these other six dimensions exist can physicists make sense of the relationship between the four 'fundamental forces' of the universe (gravity, the weak and strong nuclear forces, and the electromagnetic force) and so explain what happens in the visible world. Although it would be wrong to suppose that a simple analogy can be made between the space of physics and the space of politics, the speculations of theoretical physicists may help us think more clearly about political space. There is no need to suppose that the space – that is to say, the space-time – within which we act is the same in every domain of our existence. As we have noted, every social movement seems to create its own space, and to be governed by forces that are peculiar to it. At the same time, however, these forces are not independent of the ones that operate in other domains. Each movement is *sui generis* but is nonetheless relative to the others. Whether the relations between the different domains of political space can be explained by some sort of general formula – some theory of the political hyperspace – remains an open question. However, it seems clear that we will not make much sense of these relations until we adopt an analytic model that is more complex and sophisticated than the one that to date has informed international relations theory in particular and the social sciences in general.

It is in this context that the concept of the global city becomes especially helpful. Difficult as it is to conceptualize urbanism, the experience of the city is in some sense always with us. We live urban lives and enact urban dreams, and our politics comes out of the urban experience. The city is here and now: where we live, how we live, when we live. Its presence is local and global, particular and universal, and its politics connects us to a particular time and place, while carrying us into the world where problems are created and occasionally resolved. As Wirth, Mumford, Jacobs, and others have insisted, urbanism is a definite mode of life with characteristic spatial relations, an intelligible momentum, and typical forms of politics. To argue that urbanism itself is simply another movement *within* modernity or postmodernity would be to mistake the ideology of urbanism for the phenomenon itself. The hyperspace of the urban constitutes the domain in which debates about modernity occur, and these debates are by no means the most important aspect of the processes of world government and politics that occur on this complex terrain.

If the argument so far is correct, the claims that identify world politics with inter-state relations must be understood as ideological gestures that support the statist movement. There is no need to doubt that this movement is powerful, or to deny that it will be with us for the foreseeable future. On the contrary, statism, like capitalism, appears to be one of the most powerful movements within the ensemble of the global city. What we must doubt are its assertions of sovereignty, which amount to little more than the claim that states control what they control. This claim, however tenuous, has an ideological force sufficiently great that it has been a major obstacle to the creative understanding of world politics. Many of the governing movements, like capitalism, have been complicit in this claim, because it helps to secure them from political challenge. At the same time, it is by no means clear that the mystification of world politics as inter-state relations can survive the ongoing integration of the global city.

## World Politics as Urban Politics

At the beginning, we suggested that world politics could be conceived as urban politics. The sense of that claim may be clearer now. If the global city constitutes the hyperspace in which the major governing movements interact, the former is evidently the domain of world politics in its most meaningful sense. World politics is urban politics in that it occurs within the hyperspace of the global city and ultimately produces the city in new forms. If qualitatively different domains are to be identified, this can be done in terms of the particular spaces produced by social movements. Thus, there is a space of statism that constitutes its own 'domestic' and 'international' politics. However, in relation to world or urban politics, the politics of statism (including inter-state relations) appears as a domestic politics that must be understood in relation to the domestic politics of other movements like capitalism. The domestic politics of capitalism includes the internal politics of business enterprises, intercorporate relations, labour relations, customer relations, and so on. Since the political space constituted by any movement is unique, it is impossible to apply any single formula in analysing them all.[30] Moreover, these various movements are constituted in relation to one another, and so cannot be analysed in sovereign independence. The simplifications of IR theory are misleading even within the restricted domain of inter-state relations.

Perhaps this can be illustrated with reference to the nexus of state and nation. State-centric analysts have made particular claims with respect to their ability to make sense of nationalism. The fusion of statism and nationalism in the form of the nation-state seems like the most potent of the world's political realities. However, this fusion is not automatic: nationalism does not simply fall into a space of states given from eternity. On the contrary, nationalism, tribalism, ethnic chauvinism, and racism are part of a family of responses to social and political conditions. That a response along this continuum should result in a demand for a state is contingent. It is the power of statism that shifts nationalism onto a particular political ground, where it becomes intelligible as the ideological support for a state. However, we know that there are innumerable nations in the world, and that the recognition of all their claims would lead to the dissolution of the state system in many parts of the world. Some nations are so large that they can only be empires or 'civilizations,' and others are so small that they can be little more than extended families. Thus, the demands of statism and the demands of nationalism, although they may cohere, are in fundamental tension. This has been painfully evident in places such as Bosnia and Rwanda, but it is also apparent in the Celestial Empire and on 'Turtle Island.' Urban analysis enables us to explore these realities afresh.

The Celestial Empire is, of course, China, which long resisted incorporation into the European state system. Even now, to regard it as a state is misleading, because to do so would imply that China can be identified with the People's Republic. China's national identity and civilizational presence extend far beyond the republic's boundaries, into an overseas community that is not subject to direct control by the Chinese state. Only gradually are analysts coming to recognize the enormous importance of this extension of China: a country of its own with 55 million people and one of the largest and most rapidly growing economies in the world.[31] In its mode of organization, this other China is more reminiscent of the urban networks of late medieval and early modern Europe than of the nation-states of the industrial era.[32] Aside from rural Taiwan, it consists of an archipelago of cities, of which Hong Kong, Taipei, and Singapore are the most important, along with a chain of ethnic enclaves in cities without Chinese majorities. The wider network extends across Southeast Asia, over the Pacific, and well beyond. This other China is now recolonizing the East Asian mainland, where Overseas Chinese investors have become the dominant capitalists.[33] The ultimate effect of this on the People's Republic is difficult to predict, but it seems likely that 'China' will continue to exist in two forms: as a *state*, and as a *network* of cities and urban enclaves extending across the boundaries of states and civilizations. Which of these forms will be more significant for international relations is a nice question.

'Turtle Island' – the mythical expression of the Amerindian homeland – is equally at odds with an easy identification of states and nations. The island signifies the idea that before the European conquest, the people of the Americas inhabited a world of their own, a world with distinctive civilizations and national identities. This idea is connected to the recent development of a Pan-Indian movement that expresses the shared identity of the indigenous peoples of North and South America. This movement opened out as the 'first nations' of the Americas made contact with Australian aborigines, Maoris in New Zealand, Pacific Islanders, Saamis, Inuit across the Arctic, and many others. The World Council of Indigenous Peoples, formed in the 1970s, gave one institutional expression to this enlarged identity.[34] It is claimed that all the peoples who have been overwhelmed by colonizing powers and made into minorities in their own homelands have had a common political experience. Generally, what is demanded by these peoples is not statehood, but a qualitatively different form of self-government that takes account of their extreme cultural vulnerability. For them, this means being inside/outside the states that assert sovereignty over them. In Canada, for instance, the powerful demands for aboriginal self-government, which have disturbed the Canadian state almost as much as the move for Quebec independence, have rarely been articulated as claims for independent statehood. On the contrary, the 'sovereignty' of the First Nations is conceived as qualitatively different from and thus compatible with the 'sovereignty' of the Canadian state. According to some views, the latter form of sovereignty, modified by the sovereignty of the United Nations, is actually essential to the sovereignty of the first peoples. Obviously, different sorts of sovereignty are at issue, and the contemplated order is more complex than the usual theory of international relations allows.

Ironically, the world movement of indigenous peoples, most of whom are identified with pre-urban modes of existence, has developed within *urban* space – the space of the global city. Indigenous leaders have made efforts to influence the United Nations in New York and tap into its resources; they have sent delegations from all over the world to the U.S. Congress; they have established links with international environmental groups, academic organizations, and foreign aid agencies; they have organized conferences to bring people together across the Arctic and Pacific; they have waged transnational campaigns to save aboriginal hunting and gathering grounds in the tropical and arboreal forests; and so on. Even (perhaps most especially) the groups that have been attempting to maintain traditional modes of life, dependent on gathering and hunting, have had to send their leaders into the urban world, and enter into the complex political discourse of the global city. These groups have had to function in a world of faxes, computer nets, airports, and luxury hotels.[35] Moreover, they have had to capitalize on their position as an exotic exterior to familiar urbanity, and appeal to environmentalists and others who want to preserve the 'unspoiled' from the depredations of civilization. This has involved indigenous peoples in self-positioning as guardians of a lost naturalness, spirituality, and wilderness. It is testimony to the power of urbanism as a way of life that these claims can be so easily integrated with a specifically urban vision of multiculturalism, postmaterialism, and ecological sensitivity, which is usually presented as a 'green' vision.

Incorporation of the critical discourse of indigenous peoples into the politics of the postmodern city is one sign of ongoing integration. The other and more important sign is the flow of indigenous peoples into the cities established by foreign civilizations. This is part of a larger flow of the rural into the urban – a flow which suggests that the millennia of autonomous rural life are drawing to a close as rapidly as the era of hunting and gathering. The rural has already been urbanized in most of the advanced countries, and its demise is foreshadowed elsewhere. Thus, the global city has become the site at which rural and 'natural' modes of existence are refigured as options for urbanites who have the resources to buy such privileges or who can make a claim to cultural entitlement. For most peasant and tribal peoples, proletarianization or worse is on offer. The conditions for this vary according to the civilizational forms of capitalism, as well as the policies of states. These civilizational forms affect the modes in which the rural and the natural are preserved, as well as the possibilities for family structure, tribal life, and ethnic recognition. Indigenous peoples must not only negotiate the patterns of statism and capitalism, but also come to terms with the hegemonic forms of family organization, national identity, and religious devotion.

This is where Europe, China, and the indigenous peoples come together, not just on the mainland of Asia but in every city around the Pacific Rim that has a Chinatown, an aboriginal community, and a Western presence. Africa, India, and Islam also meet in these cities, in varying ensembles. In recent years, the old assumption that European or Euro-American forms of urbanism would necessarily predominate has been profoundly shaken, and the tensions arising from the meeting of civilizations are readily apparent in many settings. This is not to say that these tensions are at the root of disorder. On the contrary, the conflicts we see are over-determined by the progress of capitalism, the crisis of statism, the disruption of patriarchy, the threat of ecological collapse, the recrudescence of old forms of violence and corruption, and so on. There is no doubt that much of what has been occurring around the Pacific and elsewhere has been a disappointment, especially in terms of modernist visions of human emancipation, and despite the hopes raised by urban rebellions in Beijing, Manila, and Bangkok (to say nothing of Warsaw, Prague, and Berlin). The successes of capitalism in East Asia and its failures elsewhere raise the prospect of new political horrors. In this context, it is not hard to imagine that a globalized urbanism will bring endless *stasis*, like the cycles of war and peace in the conventional models of international relations.

However, to imagine the world as ceaseless repetition is to retreat into the simplicities of traditional thought. Whatever else we may say of the global city, it is not a fixed order governed by linear equations of power, which we can use to foretell our future. On the contrary, the civic mode of political organization is akin to one of those physical systems that scientists have been modelling with chaos theory.[36] Although such systems are intelligible, they are not fully predictable, because of the nonlinearity of the key relationships. This reminds us of the inevitable complexity of the political hyperspace that constitutes the terrain for world politics. That terrain has no topography that can be modelled in three-dimensional space. To act on such a complex terrain is to be confronted with conditions of radical uncertainty. The governing movements are not neatly confined within the spaces of states, except insofar as statism itself succeeds as a movement. Even nationalism tends to break out of these state-spaces. Each movement is characterized by its own politics, as is each juncture between movements. No single movement governs the whole. And yet, the movements come together to produce urbanism as a way of life.

We, as political actors and analysts, have to respond creatively to this odd ensemble. We may look to the unity that emerges – to the nascent discursive community within the global city, which enables us to talk about preserving indigenous cultures, or recognizing different modes of civilization, or protecting human rights[37] – but we are liable to find that this unity is only a momentary sensation. We may retreat from this disappointment into our own particularities, only to discover that these too are momentary. It is an easy shift from there to despair, but that would be to repeat the odd nihilism of international relations theory. We can take heart instead from the reality of a global city in which only change is permanent. In that context, we should certainly be able to see that our politics is necessarily a politics of social movements. Perhaps that is what Thucydides, the archetypal realist, wanted to say in the first place.

# Conclusion:

# Toward a Postmodern Politics?

We began this inquiry with a nod toward Hannah Arendt, the refugee theorist of political freedom. For Arendt, the question of political space – or 'public space,' as she called it – was central. As she understood it, there was a fundamental tension between politics and the state, or between freedom and sovereignty. She followed Aristotle in thinking that politics proper only arose between equals, and that the mastery we associate with sovereignty was akin to slavery.

Arendt's insightful analysis was still keyed to the idea that a space of political freedom had to be one of enclosure. This is the idea that I have been attempting to challenge. In each of the preceding essays, I have approached the sovereignty solution with scepticism and tried to show that it is a false solution to the problem of political freedom. Whether or not my arguments are convincing, I hope that I have succeeded in raising pertinent questions about political space. These questions are implicit in the activities of people who have been trying to use the political spaces offered to them in the liberal democracies. My own analytic focus has been on efforts to reclaim the municipality as a space of political freedom. To understand this space, I have been forced to look at the politics of social movements. These movements claim spaces of freedom that connect localities to one another and redefine the relationship between past, present, and future. Gradually, I have come to see the politics of municipalities, the politics of social movements, and the politics of states in relation to a wider politics of the global city – a world politics of urbanism. How these various politics relate to one another is difficult to articulate, but I want to conclude with a formulation that might serve as a starting point for further analysis.

As I have argued (most explicitly in Chapter 4), the municipality is an especially significant political space. This is because of its ambiguity or liminality. The municipality is at the boundary between the state and civil society, the centre and the locality, social disciplines and everyday life. Because of its constitutional and other disabilities, the municipality can never provide to the people in a particular place the sovereignty in relation to their own affairs that is supposed to be necessary for political freedom. Thus, it seems to statist thinkers that sovereignty/freedom must be sought elsewhere, in the states that enclose municipalities. However, it does not take much analysis to confirm that nation-states reproduce the conditions of municipal politics within their own domains, despite the gift of sovereignty that is supposed to liberate them from dependency. In this era of globalized economics, globalized cultures, and globalized social movements, it is becoming ever more apparent that sovereignty is an illusion. If the municipality can be conceived as a ministate, it is because the state is a glorified municipality. Nevertheless, to look at the state in this way is not to devalue the politics that occurs within the spaces it provides: *re*valuation, not *de*valuation, is at issue. Revaluation takes us beyond the assumption that the space of political freedom must be self-enclosed ('sovereign') if it is to be adequate to human purposes. The decentred spaces in which we must act are never self-sufficient: they point beyond themselves; they constitute and are constituted by a myriad of relations with other spaces. This being so, it is not the political space of sovereignty that is paradigmatic. Rather, it is the municipality – archetypically limited in its authority and its command over popular loyalties, weak in relation to the global processes that form people's identities and shape their behaviour, and ambiguous in its position at the boundaries of human existence – that presents us with the most realistic political model.

If the political space of the municipality is paradigmatic – that is, if states are but municipalities writ large, rather than the other way around – then we had better learn to think about politics differently. Instead of seeking the enclosures that will make freedom possible, we will have to orient ourselves toward a politics of flows and connections, that takes us beyond where we are and decentres our own activities. This is the political world that analysts have been attempting to describe in the language of 'social movements.' Certainly, if we were to cast about now for the nearest equivalent to an Aristotelian polis in a great metropolitan area, we might well disdain any obvious territorial community and point at one of the networks associated with contemporary social movements. It is within the social movements, it seems, that people come closest to constituting their lives in political freedom. Although particular neighbourhoods are sometimes vested with hope, deterritorialized movements seem more akin to the spirit of modernity, which takes people out of particular places and into the world beyond. This being so, it would appear that the key political spaces – the ones in which ordinary people can enact their political freedom – have no inherent geographic limits. This is a misleading assumption, however. It would be more accurate to suggest – as I have tried to do, especially in Chapters 2 and 12 – that every social movement creates its own history and its own geography, within finite limits. A movement defines its political time and space in relation to its own objectives, and enacts its politics accordingly. However, in doing so it by no means 'fills up' all the available space and time. The unique space of each movement coexists with others, and there is no definite limit on the number of political spaces that can be created. These spaces are not independent of one another: the activity in each affects activity in the others. Again, we can see that the spaces of political freedom do not take the form of self-subsistent communities; rather, they are venues for action that relate to one another in infinitely complicated ways.

This suggests that the paradigmatic quality of the municipality as a political space arises from its character as a juncture between localities and movements. Territorially, a municipality is always an ensemble of localities. Its political space concentrates attention on the relationships between localities. At the same time, it poses movements in relation to one another as well as to the localities with which they connect. Since the municipality is never adequate politically, it points the localities and movements beyond themselves to the world outside. It is not the case that the municipality normally functions as we would like it to do: on the contrary, it always disappoints us. The vexations of municipal politics are nonetheless indicative of politics more generally. There is no escape 'there' from the frustrations 'here,' in the way that sovereignty-theorists would have us believe.

So, how are we to think about the obstacles that have been identified by critical social movements – obstacles such as capitalist exploitation, patriarchal domination, cultural imperialism, the degradation of nature, and the pattern of violence mediated by states and fundamentalist social movements? Is the sort of politics indicated in my analysis fundamentally conservative? Does that analysis suggest that basic changes can never be achieved politically? It should be obvious that I do not think so, but my reasoning may seem obscure to those who expect simplistic remedies. In fact, an enormous effort is required to begin thinking realistically about the possibilities for political change. A first step is to move away from the state-centric assumptions of 'modern' politics and from the sovereignty-thinking that informs those assumptions. A second step is to begin thinking in terms of movements and municipalities (rather than states and societies) as venues for political action. A third is to recognize that the architectonic political space – what I have called the 'hyperspace' of politics – is the 'global city' in which all of us live.

In the preceding essay, I have done little more than to bring out the rudiments of a theory of the global city in relation to political space. What I have tried to indicate is that the global city is the polis we have been creating willy-nilly for more than two thousand years. People did not have a good idea of what they were doing in this respect, but they were nonetheless acting politically. They were constituting a world for themselves and their descendants – one that they hoped would be more or less adequate to their purposes. This 'worlding' or humanization of the natural environment has been going on since time immemorial; but urbanism – which we can trace to ancient times – involves a qualitative shift in human interaction with nature, and hence in the interaction of human beings with one another. We might think of urbanism as a social movement stretching across the centuries, in which people more or less consciously attempt to create a world for themselves. There is a clear analogy between the sort of 'constitutive' activity that is implicit in urbanism as a social movement and the kind of activity that Aristotle (and Arendt) identified with the foundation and maintenance of the polis. Given what our ancestors have already done, and what people have become in the process, there is no longer a choice to be made about whether or not we will have a global city. We already live in such a city. The political problem we face is twofold: we hardly know what our own responsibilities are in relation to the city we are creating, and we lack the means for calling one another to account for the discharge of those responsibilities. As a result, we experience the global city as anarchic, even though we know it is 'governed' in many different ways.

The state system, through which we are supposed to practice our politics, tends to displace and conceal political responsibility. However, it is only one of a number of coexisting and largely complementary systems of government (in the broadest sense of that term). In these systems – especially capitalism, but also the relations of gender, race and ethnicity, and natural life – political responsibility is even more elusive. We are confronted with various systems of government that organize space and time and constitute us variously as individuals. All of us are agents of government in one way or another, and all of us are subjects of government. Thus, the move toward political responsibility has two dimensions: one involves recognizing and taking responsibility for one's own actions; the other involves calling upon others in that context to face up to their own responsibilities. Significantly, a good deal of the political activity of contemporary social movements revolves around *calls* to responsibility that are keyed to commitments that involve an *assumption* of responsibility. Not only others, but we ourselves, are asked in these contexts to recognize what we are doing as polluters or exploitative employers or cultural snobs or ethnocentric bigots, and to take responsibility for our own actions. Such a politics of personal responsibility depends not only on a recognition of our common human failings, but also on an understanding that in this infinitely complicated global city, the good cannot come from a sovereign centre. The best that is within us must be produced by the activities of millions of different people.

The political space of the global city has no centre from which it can be governed as a whole. This would not change if we had a formally elected 'world government.' Such a government would be like one of those weak metropolitan authorities with which urbanists are familiar – achieving a few things of significance, providing a forum for the discussion of some problems, but in no sense exercising the sovereignty of which many still dream. In the typical metropolis, public authority is fragmented in innumerable ways, that authority is weak and limited, ostensibly private bodies have enormous power, and the sites for effective political intervention are spread widely and are constantly changing. To the extent that a vital urban politics emerges, it spills over all the boundaries and challenges people to take responsibility for what is happening in their own city. All our experience of modern cities suggests that urban politics is sapped of its vitality when it is forced into the molds of the sovereign state. Thus, it appears that a creative politics on a global scale must be one that takes the limits of particular political spaces as challenges to be overcome. In this context, the hierarchies that establish global politics at one level, national politics at another, and local politics at a third come to seem like obstacles. To urbanize our conception of political space is to move beyond these hierarchies into a complex domain of interconnected movements, where the distinctions of above and below, within and without, start to lose meaning. It is in such a domain that we can begin to think about politics afresh.

I began working on this book before the Soviet Union dissolved and the Cold War ended. When I look at my earliest writings on this theme, they seem to come out of another time and place. To experience such distance, and to know that it represents but a few years, is to be reminded that the fixtures of politics come and go very quickly. As I write this conclusion in the late summer of 1995, the civil war continues in the former Yugoslavia, and the prospect of more massacres in Rwanda and Burundi seems very real. The hopes associated with 1989 have come and gone, and the commentators in the media are all focused on the barbarism of the new ethnic conflicts. Like most people, I share in the general dismay and wonder where hope for the future lies. If I am reassured, it is not because I have definite ideas about *What Is To Be Done* (to quote Lenin), but because I remember the experiences to which I have been referring throughout this book. Those experiences of innovation and political invention were not the result of a blind confidence in the future. On the contrary, the people who have risked so much in municipal politics – and been so little rewarded – were generally inspired by a hope born of despair. That was the tenor of the politics of the New Left and of the new social movements of the 1970s and 1980s. The fact that there were no guarantees of the sort that the classical Marxists had earlier promised gave to the activists concerned a sense of freedom, which enabled them to explore a wide range of political possibilities.

It may be that we have come to the end of a political cycle, and that the innovations of the next few decades will take a form unrecognizable to the activists of the 1980s. If so, the experiences to which I have alluded here will be of interest more for their spirit than for their substance. As I understand it, that spirit is one of exploration and innovation, and – if I am right – that is the spirit that must inform the search for political space in the coming years. Although there are signs of people retreating to the certainties of sovereignty-thinking, there are as many indications that people find the verities of fundamentalism unsatisfying. Out of their dissatisfaction will come the explorations that help us make sense of the space of the global city.

# Notes

**Introduction: Elusive Spaces**

1 Hannah Arendt, *Between Past and Future* (London: Faber, 1961), 164–5.
2 Compare Elisabeth Young-Bruehl, *Hannah Arendt: For Love of the World* (New Haven: Yale University Press, 1972), and Phillip Hansen, *Hannah Arendt: Politics, History, Citizenship* (Cambridge: Polity Press, 1993).
3 See especially her *On Revolution* (New York: Vintage Books, 1963).
4 Rob Walker develops this theme with particular insight in *Inside/Outside: International Relations as Political Theory* (Cambridge: Cambridge University Press, 1993). Compare Henri Lefebvre, *The Production of Space* (Oxford: Basil Blackwell, 1991), and Barbara Adam, *Time and Social Theory* (Cambridge: Polity Press, 1990).
5 See, for instance, J.T. Fraser, ed., *The Voices of Time* (Amherst: University of Massachusetts Press, 1981), and John Bender and David E. Wellberg, eds., *Chronotypes: The Construction of Time* (Stanford: Stanford University Press, 1991). Compare E.E. Evans-Pritchard, *The Nuer* (Oxford: Oxford University Press, 1940), and B.L. Whorf, *Language, Thought and Reality* (Cambridge, MA: MIT Press, 1956).
6 See, for instance, Edward J. Soja, *Postmodern Geographies: The Reassertion of Space in Critical Social Theory* (London: Verso, 1989), and Doreen Massey, *Space, Place and Gender* (Cambridge: Polity Press, 1994).
7 Compare Anthony Giddens, *A Contemporary Critique of Historical Materialism*, 3 vols. (London: Macmillan, 1981–), and Michael Mann, *The Sources of Social Power*, 3 vols. (Cambridge: Cambridge University Press, 1986–) for recent efforts to overcome this abstraction.
8 Doreen Massey, 'Politics and Space/Time,' *New Left Review*, no. 196 (1992), 65–84 (reprinted in *Space, Place and Gender*, Chapter 11).

9 Adam, *Time and Social Theory,* Chapter 2.

10 Tom Stoppard explores this idea with his usual wit in *Arcadia* (London: Faber and Faber, 1993). Compare Ilya Prigogine and Isabelle Stengers, *Order out of Chaos: Man's New Dialogue with Nature* (London: Heinemann, 1984).

11 For an introduction to this literature, see Michael Ryan, *Marxism and Deconstruction: A Critical Articulation* (Baltimore: Johns Hopkins University Press, 1982); Mark Poster, *Critical Theory and Poststructuralism: In Search of a Context* (Ithaca, NY: Cornell University Press, 1989); and Stephen K. White, *Political Theory and Postmodernism* (Cambridge: Cambridge University Press, 1991). Among the influential texts out of Paris were Michel Foucault, *Power/ Knowledge: Selected Interviews and Other Writings, 1972–1977,* ed. Colin Gordon (New York: Random House, 1980); Jacques Derrida, *Writing and Difference* (Chicago: University of Chicago Press, 1978); and Jean-François Lyotard, *The Postmodern Condition: A Report on Knowledge,* trans. Geoff Bennington and Brian Massumi (Minneapolis: University of Minnesota Press, 1984).

12 On the philosophical trends see, for instance, Richard Bernstein, *The Restructuring of Social and Political Theory* (London: Methuen, 1976), and Richard Rorty, *Philosophy and the Mirror of Nature* (Princeton: Princeton University Press, 1979). Nervous attacks on postmodernism are various: see, for example, Alex Callinicos, *Against Postmodernism: A Marxist Critique* (Cambridge: Cambridge University Press, 1989); Somer Brodribb, *Nothing Ma(t)ters* (Sydney: Spinifex Press, 1991); and Thomas L. Pangle, *The Ennobling of Democracy: The Challenge of the Postmodern Age* (Baltimore: Johns Hopkins University Press, 1992).

13 For a thoughtful commentary on this terror, see John G. Gunnell, 'Relativism: The Return of the Repressed,' *Political Theory* 21, no. 4 (1993), 563–84.

14 Compare R.B.J. Walker, *One World, Many Worlds* (Boulder, CO: Lynne Rienner, 1988), and Magnusson and Walker, 'Decentring the State: Political Theory and Canadian Political Economy,' *Studies in Political Economy: A Socialist Review,* no. 27 (1988), 37–71.

15 In a recent book, Sidney Tarrow defines social movements as 'collective challenges by people with common purposes and solidarity in sustained interaction with elites, opponents and authorities.' Tarrow, *Power in Movement: Social Movements, Collective Action and Politics* (Cambridge: Cambridge University Press, 1994), 4. Alain Touraine defines social movements even more broadly as challenges to 'the logic of order.' *Critique of Modernity* (Oxford: Blackwell, 1995), 235.

16 On liminality, see Anne Norton, *Reflections on Political Identity* (Baltimore: Johns Hopkins University Press, 1988).

17 For an example, see Allan Bloom's interpretive essay in his edition of *The Republic of Plato* (New York: Basic Books, 1970).

18 'In fact, I have especially wanted to question politics, and to bring to light in the political field, as in the field of historical and philosophical interrogation, some problems that had not been recognized there before.' Michel Foucault, 'Politics and Ethics: An Interview,' in Paul Rabinow, ed., *The Foucault Reader* (New York: Pantheon Books, 1984), 375.

19 See Chapter 1, note 4 below. Compare Andrew Vincent, *Theories of the State* (Oxford: Basil Blackwell, 1987), and R.B.J. Walker and Saul H. Mendlovitz, eds., *Contending Sovereignties: Redefining Political Community* (Boulder, CO: Lynne Rienner, 1990).

20 Weber defined the state in this way: 'A compulsory political organization will be called a "state" insofar as its administrative staff successfully upholds the claim to the monopoly of the legitimate use of physical force in the enforcement of its order. Social action, especially organized action, will be spoken of as "politically oriented" if it aims at exerting influence on the government of a political organization; especially at the appropriation, expropriation, redistribution or allocation of the powers of government.' *Economy and Society*, ed. Guenther Roth and Claus Wittich (Berkeley: University of California Press, 1978), 1:54.

21 For what I take to be the classic nineteenth-century expressions of this ideal, see *Hegel's Philosophy of Right*, trans. T.M. Knox (Oxford: Oxford University Press, 1952), and John Stuart Mill, *Utilitarianism, On Liberty* and *Considerations on Representative Government*, ed. H.B. Acton (London: Dent, 1972). John Rawls – see especially *A Theory of Justice* (Cambridge, MA: Harvard University Press, 1971) – and his many imitators have continued this tradition.

22 Immanuel Kant is routinely associated with this hope, because of his plan for 'perpetual peace'; see H.S. Reiss, ed., *Kant's Political Writings* (Cambridge: Cambridge University Press, 1977). There are anarchist, socialist, and liberal idealist versions of the same aspiration. See, for instance, David Held, 'Democracy, the Nation-State and the Global System,' in Held, ed., *Political Theory Today* (Stanford: Stanford University Press, 1991).

23 See, for instance, Reinhold Niebuhr, *Christian Realism and Political Problems* (New York: Scribner's, 1953). Compare Charles Taylor, *Sources of the Self: The Making of Modern Identity* (Cambridge: Harvard University Press, 1989), and William E. Connolly, *Identity/Difference: Democratic Negotiations of Political Paradox* (Ithaca, NY: Cornell University Press, 1991), and *The Augustinian Imperative: A Reflection on the Politics of Morality* (Newbury Park, CA: SAGE, 1993). See also Walker, *Inside/Outside*; Jim George, *Discourses of Global Politics: A Critical (Re)Introduction to International Relations* (Boulder, CO: Lynne Rienner, 1994); and Magnusson and Walker, 'Socialism and Monotheism: A Response

to Jenson and Keyman,' *Studies in Political Economy: A Socialist Review*, no. 34 (1991), 235–9.

24 Walker, 'The Prince and "The Pauper",' *Inside/Outside*, Chapter 2.

25 Arguably, most of the works identified as 'classics' of political thought (and taught as such in the universities) put the space for politics at issue. However, the answers offered by a few of these writers – especially Aristotle, Hobbes, Locke, and Mill – are usually taken to have settled the question in a way that confirms the logic of state sovereignty. See John G. Gunnell, *Political Philosophy and Time: Plato and the Origins of Political Vision*, 2nd ed. (Chicago: University of Chicago Press, 1987), and *Between Philosophy and Politics: The Alienation of Political Theory* (Amherst: University of Massachusetts Press, 1986), for thoughtful reflections on both the spatialization of political thought and the reification of the classics. Among recent theorists, Hannah Arendt raised the question of the 'space' for public life most explicitly: see especially *On Revolution*. Compare Richard Sennett, *The Fall of Public Man: On the Social Psychology of Capitalism* (New York: Vintage, 1978), and Murray Bookchin, *Urbanization without Cities: The Rise and Decline of Citizenship* (Montreal: Black Rose Books, 1992).

26 See Robert D. Kaplan, 'The Coming Anarchy,' *The Atlantic Monthly*, no. 273 (February 1994), 44–76, for an influential journalistic view of the consequences. Compare Nicholas Xenos, 'Refugees: The Modern Political Condition,' and Daniel Warner, 'An Ethic of Responsibility in International Relations and the Limits of Responsibility/Community,' *Alternatives: Social Transformation and Humane Governance* 18, no. 4 (1993), 419–52; Manfried Bienefeld, 'Capitalism and the Nation State in the Dog Days of the Twentieth Century,' in Ralph Miliband and Leo Panitch, eds., *Between Globalism and Nationalism, Socialist Register 1994* (London: Merlin Press, 1994), 94–129.

27 For recent commentary, see Bob Jessop, 'The Schumpeterian Workfare State,' *Studies in Political Economy: A Socialist Review*, no. 40 (1993), 7–39. Compare James O'Connor, *The Fiscal Crisis of the State* (New York: St. Martin's, 1973); Michel Aglietta, *A Theory of Capitalist Regulation* (London: New Left Books, 1979); Michael Piore and Charles Sabel, *The Second Industrial Divide* (New York: Basic Books, 1984); Claus Offe, *Disorganized Capitalism* (Cambridge: Polity, 1985); Scott Lash and John Urry, *The End of Organized Capitalism* (Cambridge: Polity, 1987); Andre Lipietz, *Mirages and Miracles: The Crisis of Global Fordism* (London: Verso, 1987); Steven Gill and David Law, *The Global Political Economy* (Baltimore: Johns Hopkins University Press, 1988); Gosta Esping-Anderson, *The Three Worlds of Welfare Capitalism* (Princeton, NJ: Princeton University Press, 1990); Robert B. Reich, *The Work of Nations* (New York: Vintage, 1992); Ralph Miliband and Leo Panitch, eds., *New World Order? Socialist Register 1992* (London: Merlin Press, 1992).

28 On the experience of postmodernity, see Marshall Berman, *All That Is Solid Melts Into Air: The Experience of Modernity* (New York: Simon and Schuster, 1982); David Harvey, *The Condition of Postmodernity: An Enquiry into the Origins of Cultural Change* (Oxford: Basil Blackwell, 1989); Scott Lash, *Sociology of Postmodernism* (London: Routledge, 1990); Frederic Jameson, *Postmodernism, or, the Cultural Logic of Late Capitalism* (Durham, NC: Duke University Press, 1991); Jon Bird et al., eds., *Mapping the Futures: Local Cultures, Global Change* (London: Routledge, 1993); and Scott Lash and John Urry, *Economies of Signs and Space* (London: SAGE, 1994).

29 Max Weber, *The City* (New York: The Free Press, 1958). Compare Lewis Mumford, *The City in History* (New York: Harcourt Brace, 1961); Jane Jacobs, *The Economy of Cities* (New York: Random House, 1969); and R.J. Holton, *Cities, Capitalism and Civilization* (London: Allen & Unwin, 1986).

30 There are exceptions to this reticence. Among recent works, see Iris Marion Young, *Justice and the Politics of Difference* (Princeton: Princeton University Press, 1990), especially Chapter 8; Stephen L. Elkin, *City and Regime in the American Republic* (Chicago: University of Chicago Press, 1987); and Benjamin Barber, *Strong Democracy: Participatory Politics for a New Age* (Berkeley: University of California Press, 1984). See also Robert A. Dahl, 'The City in the Future of Democracy,' *American Political Science Review* 61, no. 4 (1967), 953–70.

31 I use this term loosely to refer to theorists who take the necessity of sovereignty for granted. For more explicit analysis (and defence) of the sovereignty principle, see F.H. Hinsley, *Sovereignty*, 2nd ed. (Cambridge: Cambridge University Press, 1986), and W.J. Stankiewicz, ed., *In Defence of Sovereignty* (Oxford: Oxford University Press, 1969).

32 Karen Offen, 'Defining Feminism: A Comparative Historical Approach,' *Signs: Journal of Women in Culture and Society* 14, no. 1 (1988), 119–57, cautions against an uncritical and anachronistic use of the term 'feminism' to describe this activity. The term 'feminist' was introduced in France in the 1880s and spread quite gradually to other countries.

33 See Robin Morgan, ed., *Sisterhood Is Powerful: An Anthology of Writing from the Women's Liberation Movement* (New York: Vintage, 1970). Compare Judith Grant, *Fundamental Feminism: Contesting the Core Concepts of Feminist Theory* (New York: Routledge, 1993).

34 This phrase is taken from Carole Pateman, *The Disorder of Women: Democracy, Feminism and Political Theory* (Cambridge: Polity Press, 1989). Compare Richard Sennett, *The Uses of Disorder: Personal Identity and City Life* (New York: Vintage Books, 1970).

35 For some of the more interesting recent contributions to the feminist debate,

see Denise Riley, *'Am I That Name?' Feminism and the Category of 'Women' in History* (Minneapolis: University of Minnesota Press, 1988); Judith Butler, *Gender Trouble: Feminism and the Subversion of Identity* (New York: Routledge, 1990); Linda Nicholson, ed., *Feminism/Postmodernism* (New York: Routledge, 1990); Judith Butler and Joan W. Scott, eds., *Feminists Theorize the Political* (New York: Routledge, 1992); and Kathy E. Ferguson, *The Man Question: Visions of Subjectivity in Feminist Theory* (Berkeley: University of California Press, 1993).

36 Compare Sara Evans, *Personal Politics: The Roots of Women's Liberation in the Civil Rights Movement and the New Left* (New York: Knopf, 1979), and Todd Gitlin, *The Sixties: Years of Hope, Days of Rage* (New York: Bantam, 1987), Chapter 16.

37 Alain Touraine, *The May Movement* (New York: Random House, 1971); Wini Breines, *Community Organization in the New Left, 1962–68*, 2nd ed. (New Brunswick, NJ: Rutgers University Press, 1989); James Miller, *Democracy Is in the Streets: From the Port Huron Statement to the Siege of Chicago* (New York: Simon and Schuster, 1987); Gitlin, *The Sixties.*

38 On these new social movements, see Alain Touraine, *The Voice and the Eye: An Analysis of Social Movements* (Cambridge: Cambridge University Press, 1981); Carl Boggs, *Social Movements and Political Power: Emerging Forms of Radicalism in the West* (Philadelphia: Temple University Press, 1986); Alberto Melucci, *Nomads of the Present* (Philadelphia: Temple University Press, 1989); Ron Eyerman and Andrew Jamison, *Social Movements: A Cognitive Approach* (Cambridge: Polity Press, 1991); William K. Carroll, ed., *Organizing Dissent: Contemporary Social Movements in Theory and Practice* (Toronto: Garamond Press, 1992); and Marcy Darnovsky, Barbara Epstein, and Richard Flacks, eds., *Cultural Politics and Social Movements* (Philadelphia: Temple University Press, 1995).

39 Compare Charles S. Maier, ed., *Changing Boundaries of the Political* (Cambridge: Cambridge University Press, 1987); John Keane, ed., *Civil Society and the State* (London: Verso, 1988); and Dick Howard, *Defining the Political* (London: Macmillan, 1989).

40 These struggles were reported in two early books: Martin Boddy and Colin Fudge, eds., *Local Socialism? Labour Councils and New Left Alternatives* (London: Macmillan, 1984), and John Gyford, *The Politics of Local Socialism* (London: George Allen & Unwin, 1985). David Blunkett and Keith Jackson, *Democracy in Crisis: The Town Halls Respond* (London: Hogarth Press, 1987), offer a later, positive view, and Stewart Lansley, Sue Goss, and Christian Wolmar, *Councils in Conflict: The Rise and Fall of the Municipal Left* (London: Macmillan, 1989), take a more critical perspective at the end of this cycle of

radicalism. See also Simon Duncan and Mark Goodwin, *The Local State and Uneven Development* (Cambridge: Polity Press, 1988).

41 This is my term. Compare Pierre Clavel, *The Progressive City: Planning and Participation, 1969–1984* (New Brunswick, NJ: Rutgers University Press, 1986).

42 Warren Magnusson, William K. Carroll, Charles Doyle, Monika Langer, and R.B.J. Walker, eds., *The New Reality: The Politics of Restraint in British Columbia* (Vancouver: New Star Books, 1984), and Magnusson, John DeMarco, Charles Doyle, and R.B.J. Walker, eds., *After Bennett: A New Politics for British Columbia* (Vancouver: New Star Books, 1986).

43 See my 'Progressive Politics and Canadian Cities,' in Desmond S. King and Jon Pierre, eds., *Challenges to Local Government* (London: SAGE, 1990), 173–94.

44 'Community Organization and Local Self-Government,' in Lionel D. Feldman, ed., *Politics and Government of Urban Canada*, 4th ed. (Toronto: Methuen, 1981), 61–86; 'Metropolitan Reform in the Capitalist City,' *Canadian Journal of Political Science* 14, no. 3 (1981), 557–85; and 'Bourgeois Theories of Local Government,' *Political Studies* 34, no. 1 (1986), 1–18.

45 On this theme, see Warren Magnusson and Andrew Sancton, eds., *City Politics in Canada* (Toronto: University of Toronto Press, 1983); John Logan and Harvey Molotch, *Urban Fortunes: The Political Economy of Place* (Berkeley: University of California Press, 1987); and Sidney Plotkin, *Keep Out: The Struggle for Land Use Control* (Berkeley: University of California Press, 1987).

46 Magnusson and Walker, 'Decentring the State.'

**1: Decentring the State**

1 From an interview with John Meredith, 8 March 1989. The Sierra Club of Western Canada has since been divided into separate clubs for the Prairies and British Columbia.

2 Bernard Crick, *In Defence of Politics*, 4th ed. (Chicago: University of Chicago Press, 1993).

3 This is not to suggest that either the Sierra Club or the Raging Grannies – a loosely organized social protest group that began in Victoria, B.C., and that has been imitated elsewhere – are without value; on the contrary. For a positive assessment of the Grannies, see my 'Critical Social Movements,' in Alain-G. Gagnon and James P. Bickerton, *Canadian Politics: An Introduction to the Discipline* (Peterborough, ON: Broadview Press, 1990), 525–41.

4 On this theme, see Chapters 3 and 4 below. Compare Herbert Marcuse, *One Dimensional Man* (London: Routledge and Kegan Paul, 1964), and Alain Touraine, *Critique of Modernity* (Oxford: Blackwell, 1995).

5 Watkins, *The State as a Concept of Political Science* (New York: Harper &

Brothers, 1934), 1. Compare Woodrow Wilson, *The State: Elements of Historical and Practical Politics* (Boston: D.C. Heath & Co., 1918) – a book first published in 1898, but distributed in this edition (revised by Edward Elliott) to American troops near the end of the First World War.

6 See especially *The Political System* (Chicago: University of Chicago Press, 1953).

7 There are now many accounts of this process. Compare Perry Anderson, *Lineages of the Absolutist State* (London: New Left Books, 1974); Charles Tilly, ed., *The Formation of National States in Western Europe* (Princeton: Princeton University Press, 1975); Quentin Skinner, *The Foundations of Modern Political Thought*, 2 vols. (Cambridge: Cambridge University Press, 1979); David Held, ed., *States and Societies* (Oxford: Martin Robertson, 1983); James Anderson, ed., *The Rise of the Modern State* (Brighton: Wheatsheaf, 1986); Andrew Vincent, *Theories of the State* (Oxford: Basil Blackwell, 1987); and Jens Bartelson, *A Genealogy of Sovereignty* (Cambridge: Cambridge University Press, 1995).

8 Jean Bodin, *On Sovereignty*, ed. Julian H. Franklin (Cambridge: Cambridge University Press, 1992).

9 Jean-Jacques Rousseau gave classic expression to the idea that sovereignty had to be popular in his *On the Social Contract*, trans. and ed. Donald A. Cress (Indianapolis: Hackett, 1983).

10 Thomas Hobbes, *Leviathan*, ed. Michael Oakeshott (New York: Collier Books, 1962).

11 Karl Marx, 'On the Jewish Question' [1843], in David McLellan, ed., *Karl Marx: Selected Writings* (Oxford: Oxford University Press, 1977).

12 For a recent discussion, see Lawrence Wilde, *Modern European Socialism* (Aldershot: Dartmouth, 1994).

13 Compare Robert W. Cox, *Production, Power, and World Order* (New York: Columbia University Press, 1987); Stephen Gill and David Law, *The Global Political Economy: Perspectives, Problems and Policies* (Baltimore: The Johns Hopkins University Press, 1988); and Julian Rosenberg, *The Empire of Civil Society: A Critique of the Realist Theory of International Relations* (London: Verso, 1994).

14 Theodor Adorno, *Negative Dialectics* (New York: Continuum, 1973).

15 Iris Marion Young, *Justice and the Politics of Difference* (Princeton, NJ: Princeton University Press, 1990).

16 For subtler views of these issues, see Edward Said, *Orientalism* (London: Routledge and Kegan Paul, 1978); and Homi K. Bhabha, *The Location of Culture* (London: Routledge, 1994).

17 See especially 'The German Ideology,' in McLellan, ed., *Marx*, 159–91.

18 In recent years, the most influential expression of proletarian 'standpoint'

theory has been Georg Lukacs, *History and Class Consciousness* (Cambridge, MA: The MIT Press, 1971), originally published in 1923.

19 Compare Nancy Hartsock, *Money, Sex and Power: Toward a Feminist Historical Materialism* (New York: Longman, 1983); and Dorothy E. Smith, *The Everyday World as Problematic* (Toronto: University of Toronto Press, 1987).

20 Compare Andrew Dobson, ed., *Green Political Thought* (London: Unwin Hyman, 1990); Robyn Eckersley, *Environmentalism and Political Theory: Toward an Ecocentric Approach* (Albany: State University of New York Press, 1992); and Robert E. Goodin, *Green Political Theory* (Cambridge: Polity Press, 1992).

21 Compare Ernest Gellner, *Nations and Nationalism* (Oxford: Basil Blackwell, 1983); Benedict Anderson, *Imagined Communities*, 2nd ed. (London: Verso, 1991); Partha Chatterjee, *The Nation and Its Fragments: Colonial and Postcolonial Histories* (Princeton: Princeton University Press, 1993); and Joseph A. Camilleri, Anthony P. Jarvis, and Albert J. Paolini, eds., *The State in Transition: Reimagining Political Space* (Boulder, CO: Lynne Rienner, 1995).

22 Compare R.B.J. Walker and S.H. Mendlovitz, eds., *Contending Sovereignties: Rethinking Political Community* (Boulder, CO: Lynne Rienner, 1990); Walker, *Inside/Outside: International Relations as Political Theory* (Cambridge: Cambridge University Press, 1993); and Jim George, *Discourses of Global Politics: A Critical (Re)Introduction to International Relations* (Boulder, CO: Lynne Rienner, 1994).

23 Compare James Tully, *Strange Multiplicity: Constitutionalism in an Age of Diversity* (Cambridge: Cambridge University Press, 1995).

24 See, most notoriously, Francis Fukuyama, 'The End of History?' *The National Interest* 16 (1989), 3–18. Robert Heilbroner offers some more sobering reflections in 'The Triumph of Capitalism,' *The New Yorker* 64 (23 January 1989), 98–109, and 'After Communism,' *The New Yorker* 66 (10 September 1990), 91–100.

25 On the question of origins, see especially Gerder Lerner, *The Creation of Patriarchy* (New York: Oxford University Press, 1986). She continues the story in *The Creation of Feminist Consciousness: From the Middle Ages to Eighteen-Seventy* (Oxford: Oxford University Press, 1993).

**2: The Reification of Liberal Community**

1 On this point, see especially John G. Gunnell, *Political Philosophy and Time: Plato and the Origins of Political Vision*, 2nd ed. (Chicago: University of Chicago Press, 1987).

2 See, for instance, Susan Moller Okin, *Women in Western Political Thought* (Princeton: Princeton University Press, 1979); G.E.M. de Ste. Croix, *The Class Struggle in the Ancient Greek World* (London: Duckworth, 1981); and Jean

Bethke Elshtain, *Public Man Private Woman* (Princeton: Princeton University Press, 1981).

3 J.G.A. Pocock, *The Machiavellian Moment* (Princeton: Princeton University Press, 1975), offers a particularly subtle analysis of the transposition of classical ideals into a republican idiom.

4 C.B. Macpherson, *The Life and Times of Liberal Democracy* (Oxford: Oxford University Press, 1977), offers a succinct account of this process. Compare James Tully, *Strange Multiplicity: Constitutionalism in the Age of Diversity* (Cambridge: Cambridge University Press, 1995), especially Chapter 3.

5 See, for example, C.B. Macpherson, *Democratic Theory: Essays in Retrieval* (Oxford: Oxford University Press, 1973); Jack Lively, *Democracy* (Oxford: Basil Blackwell, 1975); J. Roland Pennock, *Democratic Political Theory* (Princeton: Princeton University Press, 1979); Graeme Duncan, ed., *Democratic Theory and Practice* (Cambridge: Cambridge University Press, 1983); Giovanni Sartori, *The Theory of Democracy Revisited* (Chatham, NJ: Chatham House, 1987); David Held, *Models of Democracy* (Cambridge: Polity, 1987); and Anthony H. Birch, *The Concepts and Theories of Modern Democracy* (London: Routledge, 1993).

6 The most notable is Robert A. Dahl. See his 'The City in the Future of Democracy,' *American Political Science Review* 61, no. 4 (1967), 953–70; *After the Revolution?* (New Haven: Yale University Press, 1970); and *Dilemmas of Pluralist Democracy: Autonomy vs. Control* (New Haven: Yale University Press, 1982). See also Norton E. Long, *The Unwalled City: Reconstituting the Urban Community* (New York: Basic Books, 1972); W. Harvey Cox, *Cities: The Public Dimension* (Harmondsworth: Penguin, 1976); and Stephen L. Elkin, *City and Regime in the American Republic* (Chicago: University of Chicago Press, 1987).

7 Alexis de Tocqueville, *Democracy in America*, 2 vols. (New York: Vintage Books, 1945); and John Stuart Mill, *Utilitarianism, On Liberty* and *Considerations on Representative Government*, ed. H.B. Acton (London: Dent, 1972). On the development of ideas about local government, see Sidney and Beatrice Webb, *The Development of English Local Government, 1689–1835* (London: Oxford University Press, 1963); Anwar H. Syed, *The Political Theory of American Local Government* (New York: Random House, 1966); W. Hardy Wickwar, *The Political Theory of Local Government* (Columbia: University of South Carolina Press, 1970); Jon C. Teaford, *The Municipal Revolution in America: Origins of Modern Urban Government, 1650–1825* (Chicago: University of Chicago Press, 1975); Gerald Frug, 'The City as a Legal Concept,' *Harvard Law Review* 93, no. 6 (1980), 1059–1154; and Nancy Burns, *The Formation of American Local Governments: Private Values in Public Institutions* (New York: Oxford University Press, 1994).

8 Compare Arthur Maass, ed., *Area and Power* (New York: The Free Press, 1959).

9 Plato and Aristotle, the most renowned of the ancient theorists, were, of course, strong critics of democracy. For a more sympathetic account of ancient practices, see M.I. Finley, *Democracy Ancient and Modern* (London: Hogarth Press, 1973).

10 Aristotle anticipated this argument. Indeed, it was he who insisted on 'self-sufficiency' as the criterion for political community. He denied, however, that self-sufficiency was a matter of military or economic necessity alone. See *The Politics of Aristotle*, trans. Ernest Barker (New York: Oxford University Press, 1962), especially Books 1 and 7.

11 Ernest Gellner, *Nations and Nationalism* (Oxford: Basil Blackwell, 1983), 5.

12 Ibid., p. 34.

13 Scott Lash and John Urry, *The End of Organized Capitalism* (Madison: University of Wisconsin Press, 1987); Robert W. Cox, 'Global *Perestroika*,' in Ralph Miliband and Leo Panitch, eds., *New World Order? Socialist Register 1992* (London: The Merlin Press, 1992), 26–43; and Joseph A. Camilleri, 'State, Civil Society, and Economy,' in Camilleri, Anthony P. Jarvis, and Albert J. Paolini, eds., *The State in Transition: Reimagining Political Space* (Boulder, CO: Lynne Rienner, 1995), 209–28.

14 The classic statement of this 'realist' position is in Kenneth A. Waltz, *Man, the State and War* (New York: Columbia University Press, 1959). On the unrealism of 'realism,' see especially R.B.J. Walker, *Inside/Outside: International Relations as Political Theory* (Cambridge: Cambridge University Press, 1993); and Jim George, *Discourses of Global Politics* (Boulder, CO: Lynne Rienner, 1994).

15 On the tradition, see John G. Gunnell, *Political Theory, Tradition and Interpretation* (Boston, MA: Little, Brown, 1979), and *Between Philosophy and Politics: The Alienation of Political Theory* (Amherst: University of Massachusetts Press, 1986). See also Sheldon Wolin, *Politics and Vision: Continuity and Innovation in Western Political Thought* (Boston: Little Brown, 1960).

16 It is in continental Europe that explicit theorization of the state as a hegemonic (or counterhegemonic) order has been most pronounced. See Kenneth Dyson, *The State Tradition in Western Europe* (Oxford: Martin Robertson, 1980). What Dyson misses is the silent presence of the state in Anglo-American political theory, which is revealed most dramatically in discussions of international relations.

17 More serious arguments are deployed, of course. Philip Resnick, *Letters to a Québécois Friend* (Kingston and Montreal: McGill-Queen's University Press, 1990), including a response from Daniel Latouche, offers a good insight into the issues that have been posed by progressive thinkers.

18 However, see Chapter 4 below.

19 Larry Pratt and Garth Stevenson, *Western Separatism: The Myths, Realities and Dangers* (Edmonton: Hurtig, 1981); and Gordon Gibson, *Plan B: The Future of the Rest of Canada* (Vancouver: Fraser Institute, 1994).
20 Classic treatments are in James W. Fesler, *Area and Administration* (Montgomery: University of Alabama Press, 1949); and Maass, *Area and Power.* For an overview and critical assessment of the relevant ideas, see Brian C. Smith, *Decentralization: The Territorial Dimension of the State* (London: Allen & Unwin, 1985). Compare Mark Gottdiener, *The Decline of Urban Politics: Political Theory and the Crisis of the Local State* (Beverly Hills, CA: SAGE, 1987).
21 Compare Suzanne Keller, *The Urban Neighborhood* (New York: Random House, 1968); and Robert L. Bish, The *Public Economy of Metropolitan Areas* (Chicago: Markham, 1971).
22 This problem is the subject of a vast literature on local government reorganization. See, for instance, Donald C. Rowat, ed., *International Handbook on Local Government Reorganization* (London: Aldwych Press, 1980); and Arthur B. Gunlicks, ed., *Local Government Reform and Reorganization: An International Perspective* (Port Washington, NY: Kennikat Press, 1981). Compare Alan Norton, *International Handbook of Local and Regional Government: A Comparative Analysis of Advanced Democracies* (London: Edward Elgar, 1994).
23 See, for example, Kirkpatrick Sale, *Dwellers in the Land: The Bioregional Vision* (San Francisco: Sierra Club Books, 1985).
24 The classic 'public choice' analysis is in Robert L. Bish and Vincent Ostrom, *Understanding Urban Government: Metropolitan Reform Reconsidered* (Washington: American Enterprise Institute, 1973). See Chapter 12, note 13, for further references.
25 This state-centred view has been developed with particular sophistication in Britain. See Jack Brand, *Local Government Reform in England, 1888–1974* (London: Croom Helm, 1974); John Dearlove, *The Reorganization of British Local Government* (Cambridge: Cambridge University Press, 1979); and L.J. Sharpe, 'The Failure of Local Government Modernization in Britain: A Critique of Functionalism,' in Feldman, *Urban Canada,* 321–57. See also Jon C. Teaford, *City and Suburbs* (Baltimore: Johns Hopkins University Press, 1979) and John C. Bollens and Henry Schmandt, *The Metropolis*, 3rd ed. (New York: Harper & Row, 1975). The interdependence of state-centred and market-centred views becomes apparent in works that purport to marry them. See Paul E. Peterson, *City Limits* (Chicago: University of Chicago Press, 1981) or, significantly, Sidney Webb and Beatrice Webb, *A Constitution for the Socialist Commonwealth of Great Britain* (Cambridge: Cambridge University Press, 1975).
26 Compare the articles in the Introduction, note 44.
27 Compare Milton Friedman, *Capitalism and Freedom* (Chicago: University of

Chicago Press, 1962); and Milton Friedman and Rose Friedman, *Free to Choose: A Personal Statement* (New York: Avon, 1980).

28 See Dennis F. Thompson, 'Bureaucracy and Democracy,' in Duncan, *Democratic Theory and Practice*, 235–50.

29 Milton Kotler, *Neighborhood Government* (Indianapolis: Bobbs-Merrill, 1969); David Morris and Karl Hess, *Neighborhood Power* (Boston: Beacon Press, 1975); Harry C. Boyte, *The Backyard Revolution* (Philadelphia: Temple University Press, 1980); and Shlomo Hasson and David Ley, *Neighbourhood Organizations and the Welfare State* (Toronto: University of Toronto Press, 1994).

30 See, for example, Seymour Martin Lipset, Martin A. Trow, and James S. Coleman, *Union Democracy* (Glencoe, IL: The Free Press, 1956); Paul Blumberg, *Industrial Democracy* (London: Constable, 1968); Tom Schuller, *Democracy at Work* (Oxford: Oxford University Press, 1985); and Carmen Sirianni, ed., *Worker Participation and the Politics of Reform* (Philadelphia: Temple University Press, 1987).

31 Carole Pateman, *Participation and Democratic Theory* (Cambridge: Cambridge University Press, 1970); and Jaroslav Vanek, *The General Theory of Labor-Managed Economies* (Ithaca, NY: Cornell University Press, 1970).

32 Harold Lydall, *Yugoslavia in Crisis* (New York: Oxford University Press, 1989); and James Simmie and Joze Dekleva, eds., *Yugoslavia in Turmoil: After Self-Management* (London: Pinter, 1991).

33 See Benjamin R. Barber, *Strong Democracy: Participatory Politics for a New Age* (Berkeley and Los Angeles: University of California Press, 1984), 273–8, for a thoughtful proposal that attempts to address such issues. Compare Iain McLean, 'Mechanisms for Democracy,' in David Held and Christopher Pollitt, eds., *New Forms of Democracy* (London: SAGE, 1986), 134–57. Jean Bethke Elshtain, *Democracy on Trial* (Concord, ON: Anansi, 1993), 27–9, expresses the more sceptical view indicated here.

34 See Macpherson, *The Life and Times of Liberal Democracy*, Chapter 4, for a comparatively optimistic assessment of the possibilities of *soviet* democracy. Compare Philip Resnick, *Parliament vs. People* (Vancouver: New Star Books, 1984).

35 See Gregory Albo, David Langille, and Leo Panitch, eds., *A Different Kind of State? Popular Power and Democratic Administration* (Toronto: Oxford University Press, 1993).

36 Arendt, *The Human Condition* (Chicago: University of Chicago Press, 1959), *Between Past and Future* (London: Faber, 1961), and *On Revolution* (New York: Viking Press, 1965).

37 For example, see Jean L. Cohen and Andrew Arato, *Civil Society and Political Theory* (Cambridge, MA: The MIT Press, 1992).

38 The neglect of the local is apparent even in works that emphasize the need for mass democratic participation. Compare Macpherson, *The Life and Times of Liberal Democracy;* Barber, *Strong Democracy;* John Burnheim, *Is Democracy Possible? The Alternative to Electoral Politics* (Cambridge: Polity Press, 1985); and Philip Green, *Retrieving Democracy: In Search of Civic Equality* (Totowa, NJ: Rowman and Allanheld, 1985).

39 Arthur F. Bentley, *The Process of Government*, ed. Peter H. Odegard (Cambridge, MA: Belknap Press, 1967). See also David B. Truman, *The Governmental Process: Political Interests and Public Opinion* (New York: Knopf, 1951); and David Easton, *The Political System* (Chicago: University of Chicago Press, 1953).

40 Peter B. Evans, Dietrich Rueschmeyer, and Theda Skocpol, eds., *Bringing the State Back In* (Cambridge: Cambridge University Press, 1985).

41 On the state-centric conception of 'society' among sociologists, see Anthony Giddens, *A Contemporary Critique of Historical Materialism* (London: Macmillan, 1981), and *The Nation-State and Violence* (Berkeley and Los Angeles: University of California Press, 1987).

42 See, for example, Neil Smelser, *The Theory of Collective Behavior* (New York: The Free Press, 1962); Mancur Olson, *The Logic of Collective Action* (Cambridge, MA: Harvard University Press, 1965); Anthony Oberschall, *Social Conflict and Social Movements* (Englewood Cliffs, NJ: Prentice-Hall, 1973); John Wilson, *Introduction to Social Movements* (New York: Basic Books, 1973); and Mayer D. Zald and John D. McCarthy, eds., *The Dynamics of Social Movements* (Cambridge, Mass.: Winthrop, 1979).

43 Hence, the fact that sociologists, not political scientists, have developed the concept and led the study of social movements. See J. Craig Jenkins, 'Resource Mobilization Theory and the Study of Social Movements,' *Annual Review of Sociology* 9 (1983), 527–53; and Ron Eyerman, 'Social Movements and Social Theory,' *Sociology* 18, no. 1 (1984), 71–82.

44 Compare Manuel Castells, *The City and the Grassroots: A Cross-Cultural Theory of Urban Social Movements* (Berkeley and Los Angeles: University of California Press, 1983); Jean Cohen, ed., 'Social Movements,' *Social Research* 52, no. 4 (1986); Sidney Tarrow, *Power in Movement* (Cambridge: Cambridge University Press, 1994); and Alain Touraine, *Critique of Modernity* (Oxford: Blackwell, 1995). For further references, see Introduction, note 37.

45 See Walker, *One World Many Worlds.*

46 Roberto Michels, *Political Parties* (New York: The Free Press, 1962).

47 Friedrich Engels, 'Socialism: Scientific and Utopian,' in Karl Marx and Friedrich Engels, *Selected Works* (London: Lawrence and Wishart, 1968), 430.

48 The great footnoter of the 1970s was John Rawls. See *A Theory of Justice*

(Cambridge: Harvard University Press, 1971). Compare Robert Nozick, *Anarchy State and Utopia* (New York: Basic Books, 1974); Michael Walzer, *Spheres of Justice* (New York: Basic Books, 1973); A. Bruce Ackerman, *Social Justice in the Liberal State* (New Haven: Yale University Press, 1980); Amy Gutmann, *Liberal Equality* (Cambridge: Cambridge University Press, 1980); and Michael Sandel, *Liberalism and the Limits of Justice* (Cambridge: Cambridge University Press, 1982).

49 I should emphasize that I would make this claim in relation to both 'liberals' and 'communitarians,' whose debates tend to conceal a common commitment to the state as the foundation for political life. See Robert A. Nisbet, *The Quest for Community* (New York: Oxford University Press, 1953, 1969); Richard Sennett, *The Fall of Public Man* (New York: Knopf, 1978); Glenn Tinder, *Community: Reflections on a Tragic Ideal* (Baton Rouge: Louisiana State University Press, 1980); Eugene Kamenka, ed., *Community as a Social Ideal* (New York: St. Martin's Press, 1982); Jurgen Habermas, *The Theory of Communicative Action* (Boston: Beacon Press, 1984); Iris Marion Young, *Justice and the Politics of Difference* (Princeton: Princeton University Press, 1990); and Charles Taylor, *Multiculturalism and the Politics of Recognition* (Princeton: Princeton University Press, 1992).

**3: Critical Social Movements**

1 *Victoria Times-Colonist*, October 14, 1993, 1.

2 M. Nichols, 'The Whole World is Watching,' *Maclean's*, 16 August 1993, 20–7. Compare 'Tree Mischief,' *The Economist*, 1 May 1993, 41.

3 S. Ward, 'Pressure mounting in Europe to stop clearcutting in B.C.,' *Victoria Times-Colonist*, 1 March 1994, A2; 'British supplier drops B.C. paper hankies,' *Vancouver Sun*, 1 March 1994, B1.

4 Glenn Bohn, 'Premier says Victoria's taking new tack of compromise on environmental issues,' *Vancouver Sun*, 14 April 1993, A3; Keith Baldrey, 'War of the woods vowed,' *Vancouver Sun*, 14 April 1993, A1. Continued pressure from the environmentalists has forced the government to put further restrictions on Clayoquot logging: see Patricia Lush, 'B.C. moves fast to save Clayoquot,' *The Globe and Mail, Report on Business*, 7 July 1995.

5 His decision is excerpted in 'The judge and the prisoner,' *Vancouver Sun*, 4 November 1993, A17.

6 C. Coull, M. Dyment, and C. Kleiman. 1993. 'The Women of Clayoquot,' *Focus on Women* [Victoria], November, 16–21; R. Hatch et al., *Clayoquot and Dissent* (Vancouver: Ronsdale, 1994); Ron MacIsaac, ed., *Mass Trials: Defending the Rainforests* (Philadelphia: New Society Publishers, 1994).

7 G. Hamilton, 'Environmentalists call for boycott: Clayoquot wood goods target in Europe,' *Vancouver Sun*, 11 May 1993, D1; Valerie Langer, 'Clayoquot International Campaign,' *British Columbia Environmental Report* (October 1993), 25.
8 Paul Tennant, *Aboriginal Peoples and Politics: The Indian Land Question in British Columbia*, 1849–1989 (Vancouver: University of British Columbia Press, 1990).
9 Menno Boldt and J.A. Long, 'Tribal Traditions and European-Western Political Ideologies,' *Canadian Journal of Political Science* 17 (1984), 537–53. Compare Don Monet and Skanu'u (Ardythe Wilson), *Colonialism on Trial: Indigenous Land Rights and the Gitksan and Wet'suwet'en Sovereignty Case* (Philadelphia: New Society Publishers, 1992). See also Chapter 4 below.
10 R.B.J. Walker, *Inside/Outside: International Relations as Political Theory* (Cambridge: Cambridge University Press, 1993).
11 Warren Magnusson and R.B.J. Walker, 'Decentring the State: Political Theory and Canadian Political Economy,' *Studies in Political Economy: A Socialist Review* 26 (1988), 37–81.
12 Shlomo Avineri, *Hegel's Theory of the Modern State* (Cambridge: Cambridge University Press, 1972).
13 David McLellan, ed., *Karl Marx: Selected Writings* (Oxford: Oxford University Press, 1977).
14 Perry Anderson, *Lineages of the Absolutist State* (London: New Left Books, 1974).
15 Wendy Brown, *Manhood and Politics: A Feminist Reading in Political Theory* (Totowa, NJ: Rowman and Littlefield, 1988); and Judith Butler and Joan W. Scott, eds., *Feminists Theorize the Political* (New York: Routledge, 1992).
16 Robyn Eckersley, *Environmentalism and Political Theory: Toward an Ecocentric Approach* (Albany: State University of New York Press, 1992).
17 Gregory Albo, David Langille, and Leo Panitch, *A Different Kind of State? Popular Power and Democratic Administration*. (Toronto: Oxford University Press, 1993).
18 Desmond S. King, *The New Right: Politics, Markets and Citizenship* (Chicago: The Dorsey Press, 1987); and Kenneth Hoover and Raymond Plant, *Conservative Capitalism in Britain and the United States* (London: Routledge, 1989).
19 Kies Van der Pijl, *The Making of an Atlantic Ruling Class* (London: Verso, 1984); David Langille, 'The Business Council on National Issues,' *Studies in Political Economy*, no. 24 (Autumn 1987), 41–85; Stephen Gill, *American Hegemony and the Trilateral Commission* (Cambridge: Cambridge University Press, 1990).
20 Joyce Kolko, *Restructuring the World Economy* (New York: Pantheon, 1988); Stephen Gill and David Law, *The Global Political Economy: Perspectives, Problems, and Policies* (Baltimore: The Johns Hopkins University Press, 1988).

21 Timothy Luke, 'Discourse of Disintegration, Texts of Transformation: Re-reading Realism in the New World Order,' *Alternatives: Social Transformation and Humane Governance* 18 (1993), 229–58.
22 Mike Davis, *City of Quartz: Excavating the Future in Los Angeles* (London: Verso, 1990).
23 See chapter 10 below.
24 R.B.J. Walker, *One World, Many Worlds: Struggles for a Just World Peace* (Boulder, CO: Lynne Rienner, 1988).
25 Michel Foucault, *Discipline and Punish: The Birth of the Prison* (New York: Vintage Books, 1979); and Graham Burchell, Colin Gordon, and Peter Miller, eds., *The Foucault Effect: Studies in Governmentality* (Chicago: University of Chicago Press, 1991).
26 For further discussion, see my 'Critical Social Movements,' in Alain-G. Gagnon and James P. Bickerton, eds., *Canadian Politics: An Introduction to the Discipline* (Peterborough, ON: Broadview Press, 1990), 529–32. Compare Martin Ennals, 'Amnesty International and Human Rights,' in Peter Willetts, ed., *Pressure Groups in the Global System* (London: Frances Pinter, 1982), 63–83.
27 M. Brown and J. May, *The Greenpeace Story* (Scarborough, ON: Prentice-Hall, 1989); and F. Pearse, *Green Warriors* (London: The Bodley Head, 1991).
28 For critical commentary and analysis of Greenpeace, see M. Harwood, 'Daredevils for the Environment,' *New York Times Magazine*, 2 October 1988, 72–5; T. Horton, 'The Green Giant,' *Rolling Stone*, no. 612 (5 September 1991), 42–8, 108–12; B. Ostertag, 'Greenpeace Takes Over the World,' *Mother Jones* 16, no. 2 (March/April 1991), 32–7, 84–7; L. Spencer with J. Bollwerk and R.C. Morris, 'The Not So Peaceful World of Greenpeace,' *Forbes Magazine*, 11 November 1991, 174–80; and B. Livesey, 'Greenpeace Exposed,' *Canadian Dimension* 28, no. 4 (August-September 1994), 7–12.
29 Magnusson, 'Critical Social Movements,' 532–6.

**4: Radical Municipalism**

1 'Is It Really a Global Village?' University of Victoria Distinguished Lectures, 17 January 1992. Compare Ivan Head and Pierre Elliott Trudeau, *The Canadian Way: Shaping Canada's Foreign Policy* (Toronto: McClelland & Stewart, 1995).
2 For background, see Sean McCutcheon, *Electric Rivers: The Story of the James Bay Project* (Montreal: Black Rose Books, 1992); *The Globe and Mail*, 13–19 April 1990; and Northeast Alliance to Protect James Bay, *No Thank You Hydro-Quebec: There Are Alternatives* (Undated tabloid [1991?], available from Earthroots, 307–19 Mercer St., Toronto M5V 1H2).
3 Andre Picard, 'Cree leader hails result of referendum, *The Globe and Mail*,

10 October 1991. See Chapter 8, note 6, below for references on progressive politics in Burlington.

4 'Musicians jam to "ban the dam": concerts and rallies aim to stop James Bay II project,' *The Globe and Mail*, 9 October, C1–2. See also 'Dinkins urges delay in Quebec hydro deal,' *Toronto Star*, 6 August 1991, A10. The Clayoquot protesters, discussed in Chapter 3, had a similar impact on American municipal politicians, this time using the Rain Forest Alliance to secure a supportive resolution from the San Francisco Board of Supervisors. 'Clear-cut row escalates,' *The Globe and Mail*, 1 May 1995, B2; Wendy Tanaka, 'Pulp fiction,' *San Francisco Examiner*, 4 May 1995.

5 Geoffrey York, 'Great Whale project suffers blow,' *The Globe and Mail*, 17 March 1992. Eventually the Quebec government was forced to put the project on hold. Philip Authier and Graeme Hamilton, 'Quebec shelves Great Whale,' *The Gazette* (Montreal), 19 November 1994, A1, A8.

6 For a comprehensive account of the events at Oka and the internal politics of the Mohawks, see Geoffrey York and Loreen Pindera, *People of the Pines: The Warriors and the Legacy of Oka* (Toronto: Little Brown, 1991). Compare 'Beyond Oka: Dimensions of Mohawk Sovereignty: Interview with Kahn-Tineta Horn,' *Studies in Political Economy*, no. 35 (Summer 1991), 29–41; and Gerald R. Alfred, *Heeding the Voices of Our Ancestors: Kahnawake Mohawk Politics and the Rise of Native Nationalism* (Toronto: Oxford University Press, 1995).

7 Most famously, as workers on the high steel. See York and Pindera, *People of the Pines*, Chapter 6.

8 Paul Tennant, *Aboriginal Peoples and Politics: The Indian Land Question in British Columbia, 1849–1989* (Vancouver: University of British Columbia Press, 1990), and Frank Cassidy and Norman Dale, *After Native Claims? The Implications of Comprehensive Claims Settlements for Natural Resources in British Columbia* (Lantzville, BC, and Halifax, NS: Oolichan Books and the Institute for Research on Public Policy, 1988).

9 The literature on this has been expanding rapidly. See, for instance, Menno Boldt and J. Anthony Long, eds., *The Quest for Justice: Aboriginal Peoples and Aboriginal Rights* (Toronto: University of Toronto Press, 1985); Frank Cassidy and Robert L. Bish, *Indian Government: Its Meaning in Practice* (Lantzville, BC, and Halifax, NS: Oolichan Books and the Institute for Research on Public Policy, 1989); Bruce Clark, *Native Liberty, Crown Sovereignty: The Existing Aboriginal Right of Self-Government in Canada* (Montreal and Kingston: McGill-Queen's University Press, 1990); Diane Englestad and John Bird, eds., *Nation to Nation: Aboriginal Sovereignty and the Future of Canada* (Concord, ON: Anansi, 1992); Menno Boldt, *Surviving as Indians: The Challenge of Self-Government* (Toronto: University of Toronto Press, 1993); and Alfred, *Heeding the Voices of Our Ancestors*.

10 Ironically, one of the effects of this is to put the authority of the Indian leaders themselves into question. The inherent right of self-government extends to women and men who are not privileged under existing arrangements, and who demand a democratic dispersal of power within Indian nations. Compare Frank Cunningham, 'Community, Democracy, and Socialism,' in *The Real World of Democracy Revisited* (Atlantic Highlands, NJ: Humanities Press, 1994), 95–114; Ron George, 'Becoming Visible: Aboriginal Urban Self-Government,' in Henri Lustiger-Thaler, ed., *Political Arrangements: Power and the City* (Montreal: Black Rose Books, 1992), 196–201; and J. Anthony Long, 'Political Revitalization in Canadian Native Societies,' *Canadian Journal of Political Science* 23, no. 4 (December 1990), 751–73.

11 There has been practically no discussion of the right of refuge in recent debates on the Canadian Constitution. This contrasts with the situation in Germany, where the rights of refugees have been promoted in the face of powerful neofascist forces. Jurgen Fijalkowski, 'Aggressive Nationalism, Immigration Pressure and Asylum Policy Disputes in Contemporary Germany,' *International Migration Review*, no. 27 (Winter 1993), 850–69.

12 Compare Jane Jacobs, *Canadian Cities and Sovereignty Association* (Toronto: CBC, 1980), and *Cities and the Wealth of Nations* (New York: Random House, 1984).

13 Compare Kirkpatrick Sale, *Dwellers in the Land: The Bioregional Vision* (San Francisco: Sierra Club Books, 1985); Murray Bookchin, *The Limits of the City* (Montreal: Black Rose Books, 1986); and Bookchin, *Urbanization without Cities: The Rise and Decline of Citizenship* (Montreal: Black Rose Books, 1992).

14 On this subject, see especially Iris Marion Young, *Justice and the Politics of Difference* (Princeton: Princeton University Press, 1990).

15 Perhaps not surprisingly, these ideals seem to be particularly attractive to planners.

16 It is significant that the Sechelt Band in British Columbia – the first in Canada to agree to a new arrangement for self-government – has seen its own future in terms of condominium development on the coast north of Vancouver. Such are the shades of Hong Kong.

17 Compare Patrick Neal and David Paris, 'Liberalism and the Communitarian Critique: A Guide for the Perplexed,' *Canadian Journal of Political Science* 23 (September 1990); and Shlomo Avineri and Avner de-Shalit, eds., *Communitarianism and Liberalism* (Oxford: Oxford University Press, 1992).

18 Seen from another perspective, the market itself can be understood as a fixation occasionally unfixed by the operations of the state. I defer to Marx's analysis in this respect.

19 George Ross, Stanley Hoffmann, and Sylvia Malzacher, eds., *The Mitterrand Experiment* (Cambridge: Polity Press, 1987).

20 Paul Rauber, 'U.S. Cities Starting to Act on the International Stage,' *In These Times* 13, no. 33 (6–12 September 1989).
21 See Chapter 11 below for more on this subject.
22 *The New Abolitionist* 8, no. 1 (March 1990). More generally, see Gordon C. Bennett, *The New Abolitionists: The Story of Nuclear Free Zones* (Elgin, IL: Brethren Press, 1987).
23 Shannon Selin, *Canada as a Nuclear Weapon-Free Zone: A Critical Analysis* (Ottawa: Canadian Centre for Arms Control and Disarmament, 1988), 8.
24 Compare Maureen Mackintosh and Hilary Wainwright, eds., *A Taste of Power: The Politics of Local Economics* (London: Verso, 1987); and Stewart Lansley, Sue Goss, and Christian Wolmar, *Councils in Conflict: The Rise and Fall of the Municipal Left* (London: Macmillan, 1989). See also Chapters 6 and 8 below.
25 'Local Initiatives: Can They Meet the Environmental Crisis?' *Bulletin of Municipal Foreign Policy* 5, no. 1 (Winter 1990–1), 12–14.
26 Lansley, et al., *Councils in Conflict*, Chapter 8. Lest we misconstrue the significance of this, it is well to recognize that Canada's Women's Bureau – a federal agency – pioneered this sort of activity. Compare Sue Findlay, 'Facing the State: The Politics of the Women's Movement Reconsidered,' in Heather Jon Maroney and Meg Luxton, eds., *Feminism and Political Economy: Women's Work, Women's Struggles* (Toronto: Methuen, 1987), 31–50. Compare Chapter 10 below.

**5: Beyond the Metropolis**

1 Kenneth Fox, *Better City Government: Innovation in American Urban Politics, 1850–1937* (Philadelphia: Temple University Press, 1977), Chapter 7.
2 I discuss this subject at greater length in 'Victoria *Regina*: Social Movements and Political Space,' in Jon Caulfield and Linda Peake, eds., *Critical Perspectives to Canadian Urbanism* (Toronto: University of Toronto Press, forthcoming). On Victoria's history, see especially Peter Baskerville, *Beyond the Island: An Illustrated History of Victoria* (Burlington, ON: Windsor Publications, 1986).
3 Norbert MacDonald, *Distant Neighbors: A Comparative History of Seattle and Vancouver* (Lincoln: University of Nebraska Press, 1987). See also Theodore H. Cohn, David E. Merrifield, and Patrick J. Smith, 'North American Cities in an Interdependent World: Vancouver and Seattle as International Cities,' in Earl Fry, Lee Radebaugh, and Panayotis Soldatos, eds., *The International Cities Era: The Global Activities of North American Municipal Governments* (Provo, UT: Brigham Young University, 1989), 73–117; Donald Gutstein, *The New Landlords: Asian Investment in Canadian Real Estate* (Victoria: Porcepic Books, 1990); and Paul Delany, ed., *Vancouver: Representing the Postmodern City* (Vancouver: Arsenal Pulp Press, 1994).

4 See Chapter 2, notes 7 and 18–24, for references on the theme of local government consolidation.

5 See Chapter 4, notes 12 and 13.

6 Thoughtful comparative analysis of the three countries is comparatively rare, but see Michael Keating, *Comparative Urban Politics: Power and the City in the United States, Canada, Britain and France* (Aldershot, Hants: Edward Elgar, 1991). On the United States and Britain, see also Ted Robert Gurr and Desmond King, *The State and the City* (London: Macmillan, 1987); Timothy Barnekov, Robin Boyle, and Daniel Rich, *Privatisation and Urban Policy in Britain and the US* (Oxford: Oxford University Press, 1989); Michael Goldsmith and Harold Wolman, *Urban Politics and Policy* (Oxford: Basil Blackwell, 1992); and Susan S. Fainstein, *The City Builders: Property, Politics, & Planning in London and New York* (Oxford: Basil Blackwell, 1994). For Canadian-American comparisons, see Donald N. Rothblatt and Andrew Sancton, eds., *Metropolitan Governance: American/Canadian Intergovernmental Perspectives* (Berkeley: Institute of Governmental Studies Press, 1993).

7 John Calvert, *Government Limited: The Corporate Takeover of the Public Sector in Canada* (Ottawa: Canadian Centre for Policy Alternatives, 1984).

8 Donald J.H. Higgins, *Local and Urban Politics in Canada* (Toronto: Gage, 1986), Chapter 5.

9 This is one of the reasons why the Canadian school system has been more egalitarian than the American. Stephen Lawton, 'Political Values in Educational Finance in Canada and the United States,' *Journal of Educational Finance* 5 (1979), 1–8.

10 Richard A. Loreto and Trevor Price, *Urban Policy Issues: Canadian Perspectives* (Toronto: McClelland & Stewart, 1990); and C. Richard Tindal and Susan Nobes Tindal, *Local Government in Canada*, 4th ed. (Toronto: McGraw-Hill Ryerson, 1995).

11 James Lorimer, *A Citizens' Guide to City Politics* (Toronto: James Lewis and Samuel, 1972); Larry S. Bourne, *Urban Systems, Strategies for Regulation: A Comparison of Policies in Britain, Sweden, Australia and Canada* (Oxford: Oxford University Press, 1975); Warren Magnusson and Andrew Sancton, eds., *City Politics in Canada* (Toronto: University of Toronto Press, 1983); J. Barry Cullingworth, *Urban and Regional Planning in Canada* (New Brunswick, NJ: Transaction Books, 1987); and Gerald Hodge, *Planning Canadian Communities: An Introduction to the Principles, Practice, and Participants*, 2nd ed. (Scarborough, ON: Nelson, 1991).

12 On this and related themes, see also Trudi Bunting and Pierre Filion, eds., *Canadian Cities in Transition* (Toronto: Oxford University Press, 1991); Frances Frisken, ed., *The Changing Canadian Metropolis: A Public Policy Perspective*, 2 vols. (Berkeley: Institute of Governmental Studies, University of California,

1994); and James Lightbody, ed., *Canadian Metropolitics: Governing Our Cities* (Toronto: Copp Clark, 1995).

13 Michael Goldsmith and Ed Page, eds., *Central and Local Government Relations: A Comparative Analysis of West European States* (London: SAGE, 1987).

14 It was during the 1930s that American municipal politicians learned to turn to Washington: Mark I. Gelfand, *A Nation of Cities: The Federal Government and Urban America, 1933–1965* (New York: Oxford University Press, 1975). Compare Donald H. Haider, *When Governments Come to Washington: Governors, Mayors, and Intergovernmental Lobbying* (New York: The Free Press, 1974); and Dennis R. Judd, *The Politics of American Cities: Private Power and Public Policy*, 3rd ed. (Glenview, IL: Scott, Foresman, 1988). Lionel D. Feldman and Katherine Graham, in *Bargaining for Cities* (Montreal: Institute for Research on Public Policy, 1979), discuss the Canadian experience.

15 Rufus Browning, Dale R. Marshall, and David H. Tabb, eds., *Racial Politics in American Cities* (New York: Longman, 1990).

16 Michael A. Goldberg and John Mercer, *The Myth of the North American City* (Vancouver: University of British Columbia Press, 1986).

17 On the Canadian New Left, see Margaret Daly, *The Revolution Game: The Short Unhappy Life of the Company of Young Canadians* (Toronto: New Press, 1970); James Draper, ed., *Citizen Participation: Canada* (Toronto: New Press, 1971); Gerry Hunnius, ed., *Participatory Democracy for Canada: Workers' Control and Community Control* (Montreal: Black Rose Books, 1971); and Richard Harris, *Democracy in Kingston: A Social Movement in Urban Politics, 1965–1970* (Montreal and Kingston: McGill-Queen's University Press, 1988).

18 Stuart Lowe, *Urban Social Movements* (London: Macmillan, 1986).

19 James Lorimer and Caroline MacGregor, eds., *After the Developers* (Toronto: James Lorimer, 1981); Richard Harris, 'A Social Movement in Urban Politics: A Reinterpretation of Urban Reform in Canada,' *International Journal of Urban and Regional Research* 11 (1987), 363–79; Jon C. Caulfield, 'Canadian Urban "Reform" and Local Conditions: An Alternative to Harris's "Reinterpretation",' *International Journal of Urban and Regional Research* 12 (1988), 477–84; and Warren Magnusson, 'Progressive Politics and Canadian Cities,' in Desmond King and Jon Pierre, eds., *Challenges to Local Government* (London: SAGE, 1990), 173–94.

20 John Sewell, *The Shape of the City: Toronto Struggles with Modern Planning* (Toronto: University of Toronto Press, 1993), 135–98, recounts the shift of sensibilities in that city. Compare Edmund P. Fowler, *Building Cities That Work* (Montreal and Kingston: McGill-Queen's University Press, 1992).

21 Trevor Price, 'The Environment,' in Loreto and Price, *Urban Policy Issues*, 124–44; and Robert Paehlke, 'Possibilities for and Limitations on Environ-

mental Protection in the Changing Metropolis,' in Frisken, *The Changing Canadian Metropolis*, 1:105–22;

22 City of Toronto, *Equal Opportunity Program: Policy and Guidelines for the Toronto Civic Service* (1977), and *The Safe City: Municipal Strategies for Preventing Public Violence Against Women* (1988). Compare Gerda R. Wekerle, Rebecca Peterson, and David Morley, eds., *New Spaces for Women* (Boulder, CO: Westview Press, 1980); and Regula Modlich, 'Planning Implications of Women Plan Toronto,' *Plan Canada* 28, no. 4 (1988), 120–31.

23 Patrick J. Smith, 'International Cities and Municipal Paradiplomacy: A Typology for Assessing the Changing Vancouver Metropolis,' in Frisken, *The Changing Canadian Metropolis*, 2:613–49.

24 Jon Caulfield, *The Tiny Perfect Mayor: David Crombie and Toronto's Reform Aldermen* (Toronto: James Lorimer, 1974); and Dimitrios Roussoupoulos, ed., *The City and Radical Social Change* (Montreal: Black Rose Books, 1982).

25 Marc V. Levine, et al., *The State and Democracy: Revitalizing America's Government* (New York: Routledge, 1988), 123. See also Chapter 6, note 7.

26 See Chapter 3, note 18.

27 James O'Connor, *The Fiscal Crisis of the State* (New York: St. Martin's Press, 1973).

28 Albert Rose, *Canadian Housing Policies, 1935–1980* (Toronto: Butterworth, 1980).

29 John Bacher, *Keeping to the Marketplace: The Evolution of Canadian Housing Policy* (Montreal and Kingston: McGill-Queen's University Press, 1993); and John Sewell, *Houses and Homes: Housing for Canadians* (Toronto: James Lorimer, 1994). See also Gerald Daly, 'The State's Response to Homelessness: A View of Three Countries,' in Frisken, *The Changing Canadian Metropolis*, 2:391–426; and Peter Dreier and J. David Hulchanski, 'The Role of Nonprofit Housing in Canada and the United States: Some Comparisons,' *Housing Policy Debate* 4, no. 1 (1993), 43–80, for comparative analysis.

30 On this theme, see Chapter 10 below.

31 Clarence Lo, *Small Property versus Big Government: Social Origins of the Tax Revolt* (Berkeley: University of California Press, 1990), offers a particularly interesting account of the California experience.

32 Dennis Judd and Michael Parkinson, eds., *Leadership and Urban Regeneration: Cities in North America and Europe*, Urban Affairs Annual Review 37 (Newbury Park, CA: SAGE, 1990), 152–87.

**6: Flexible Specialization**

1 See Janice Caulfield and John Wanna, eds., *Power and Politics in the City: Brisbane in Transition* (South Melbourne: Macmillan, 1995).

2 Paul E. Peterson, *City Limits* (Chicago: University of Chicago Press, 1980). Peterson's rather pessimistic analysis of the American situation has attracted much criticism. See, for instance, John R. Logan and Todd Swanstrom, eds., *Beyond the City Limits: Urban Policy and Economic Restructuring in Comparative Perspective* (Philadelphia: Temple University Press, 1990).
3 Karl Marx and Friedrich Engels, 'The Communist Manifesto,' in David McLellan, ed., *Karl Marx: Selected Writings* (Oxford: Oxford University Press, 1977), 224.
4 See, for instance, C. Johnson, *MITI and the Japanese Miracle* (Stanford: Stanford University Press, 1982); D. Friedman, *The Misunderstood Miracle: Industrial Development and Political Change in Japan* (Ithaca, NY: Cornell University Press, 1988); and P.Q. Hirst and J. Zeitlin, eds., *Reversing Industrial Decline? Industrial Structure and Industrial Policy in Britain and Her Competitors* (Oxford: Berg, 1989).
5 Steven Gill and David Law, *The Global Political Economy: Perspectives, Problems and Policies* (Baltimore: The Johns Hopkins University Press, 1988); Stephen Gill, 'Economic Globalisation and the Internationalisation of Authority: Limits and Contradictions,' Fourth International Karl Polanyi Conference, Concordia University, Montreal, 11 November 1992.
6 In the United States, this goes under the name of a 'public-private partnership.' For celebratory views, see the National Council on Urban Economic Development, *Coordinated Urban Economic Development: Public/Private Development Institutions* (Washington, DC: NCUED, 1978); Committee for Economic Development, *Public-Private Partnership: An Opportunity for Urban Communities* (New York: CED, 1982); R. Scott Fosler and Renée Berger, eds., *Public-Private Partnership in American Cities* (Lexington, MA: D.C. Heath, 1982); and Rachelle Levitt, ed., *Cities Reborn* (Washington, DC: Urban Land Institute, 1987). For more critical perspectives, compare Gregory D. Squires, ed., *Unequal Partnerships: The Political Economy of Urban Redevelopment in Postwar America* (New Brunswick, NJ: Rutgers University Press, 1989); and Dennis Judd and Michael Parkinson, eds., *Leadership and Urban Regeneration: Cities in North America and Europe*, Urban Affairs Annual Review 37 (Newbury Park, CA: SAGE, 1990). In Britain, American practice has been taken as a model: see Brian D. Jacobs, 'Business Leadership in Urban Regeneration: Towards a Shared Vision?' in Desmond S. King and Jon Pierre, eds., *Challenges to Local Government* (London: SAGE, 1990), 195–211; and Chris Moore and J.J. Richardson, *Local Partnership and the Unemployment Crisis in Britain* (London: Unwin Hyman, 1989). Compare Timothy Barnekov, Robin Boyle, and Daniel Rich, *Privatism and Urban Policy in Britain and the United States* (New York: Oxford University Press, 1989); Frank Gaffikin and Barney Warf,

'Urban Policy and the Post-Keynesian State in the United Kingdom and the United States,' *International Journal of Urban and Regional Research* 17, no. 1 (1993), 67–84; and Michael Keating, 'Political Change and Local Development Policies in the United States, Britain, and France,' *Urban Affairs Quarterly* 28, no. 3 (1993), 373–96.

7 On the Italian case, see N. Jaggi, et al., *Red Bologna* (London: Writers and Readers' Cooperative, 1977); and Stephen Gundle, 'Urban Dreams and Metropolitan Nightmares: Models and Crises of Communist Local Government in Italy,' in Bogdan Szajkowski, ed., *Marxist Local Governments in Western Europe and Japan* (London: Frances Pinter, 1986), 66–95. More generally, see Michael Piore and Charles Sabel, *The Second Industrial Divide: Possibilities for Prosperity* (New York: Basic Books, 1984); Allen J. Scott, *New Industrial Spaces: Flexible Production Organization and Regional Development in North America and Western Europe* (London: Pion, 1988); and Hirst and Zeitlin, *Reversing Industrial Decline*.

8 See Marc V. Levine, 'The Politics of Partnership: Urban Redevelopment Since 1945,' in Squires, *Unequal Partnerships*, 12–34. On Pittsburgh, see below, note 24. On Atlanta, see Clarence N. Stone, *Regime Politics: Governing Atlanta, 1946–1988* (Lawrence: University Press of Kansas, 1989). On Baltimore, compare B.L. Berkowitz, 'Economic Development Really Works: Baltimore, Maryland,' in R.D. Bingham and J.P. Blair, eds., *Urban Economic Development*, SAGE Urban Affairs Annual Review 27 (Beverly Hills, CA: SAGE, 1984), 201–21; Robert P. Stoker, 'Baltimore: The Self-Evaluating City?' in Stone and Sanders, *The Politics of Urban Development*, 244–66; Marc Levine, 'Downtown Redevelopment as an Urban Growth Strategy: A Critical Appraisal of the Baltimore Renaissance,' *Journal of Urban Affairs* 9 (1987), 103–23; and Richard C. Hula, 'The Two Baltimores,' in Judd and Parkinson, *Leadership and Urban Regeneration*, 191–215.

9 I take this to be one of the themes of Jane Jacobs, *Cities and the Wealth of Nations* (New York: Random House, 1984).

10 Henri Pirenne, *Medieval Cities* (Princeton: Princeton University Press, 1925); Max Weber, *The City* (New York: The Free Press, 1958); and Lewis Mumford, *The City in History* (New York: Harcourt Brace, 1961), offer classic expositions of the relationship between urban autonomy and the rise of capitalism. For more recent views, see R.J. Holton, *Cities, Capitalism and Civilization* (London: Allen & Unwin, 1986); and Engin F. Isin, *Cities Without Citizens: The Modernity of the City as a Corporation* (Montreal: Black Rose Books, 1992).

11 Richard Batley, 'London Docklands: An Analysis of Power Relations between UDCs and Local Government,' *Public Administration* 67 (1989), 167–87; Tim Brindley, Yvonne Rydin, and Gerry Stoker, *Remaking Planning: The Politics of Urban Change in the Thatcher Years* (London: Unwin Hyman, 1989), 96–120;

and Susan S. Fainstein, *The City Builders: Property, Politics, & Planning in London and New York* (Oxford: Blackwell, 1994), 189–217.

12 Sidney Webb and Beatrice Webb, *The Development of English Local Government, 1689–1935* (London: Oxford University Press, 1963).

13 Gerald E. Frug, 'The City as a Legal Concept,' *Harvard Law Review* 93 (1980), 1059–1154.

14 Compare Robert Fogelson, *The Fragmented Metropolis: Los Angeles, 1850–1930* (Cambridge: Harvard University Press, 1967); Charles Hoch, 'City Limits: Municipal Boundary Formation and Class Segregation,' in William K. Tabb and Larry Sawers, eds., *Marxism and the Metropolis*, 2nd ed. (New York: Oxford University Press, 1984), 101–19; and Mike Davis, *City of Quartz: Excavating the Future in Los Angeles* (London: Verso, 1990).

15 Edward W. Soja, 'Economic Restructuring and the Industrialization of the Los Angeles Region,' in Michael Peter Smith and Joe R. Feagin, *The Capitalist City: Global Restructuring and Community Politics* (Oxford: Basil Blackwell, 1987), 178–98.

16 See, for instance, Michael A. Goldberg, ed., *Zoning* (Vancouver: Fraser Institute, 1980).

17 Joe R. Feagin, John I. Gilderbloom, and Nestor Rodriguez, 'The Houston Experience: Private-Public Partnerships,' in Squires, *Unequal Partnerships*, 240–59; Robert E. Parker and Joe R. Feagin, 'A Better Business Climate in Houston,' in Judd and Parkinson, *Leadership and Urban Regeneration*, 216–38; and Joe R. Feagin, *The Free Enterprise City: Houston in Political-Economic Perspective* (New Brunswick, NJ: Rutgers University Press, 1988).

18 Shelby Stewman and Joel A. Tarr, 'Four Decades of Public-Private Partnerships in Pittsburgh,' in Fosler and Berger, *Public-Private Partnerships in American Cities*; Alberta Sbragia, 'The Pittsburgh Model of Economic Development: Partnership, Responsiveness, and Indifference,' in Squires, *Unequal Partnerships*, 103–20; and Sbragia, 'Pittsburgh's "Third Way": The Nonprofit Sector as a Key to Urban Regeneration,' in Judd and Parkinson, *Leadership and Urban Regeneration*, 51–68.

19 See, for instance, David Perry, 'The Politics of Dependency in Deindustrializing America: The Case of Buffalo, New York,' in Smith and Feagin, *The Capitalist City*, 113–37; and 'Recasting Urban Leadership in Buffalo,' in Judd and Parkinson, *Leadership and Urban Regeneration*, 258–76.

20 Simon Duncan and Mark Goodwin, *The Local State and Uneven Development: Behind the Local Government Crisis* (Cambridge: Polity Press, 1988).

21 Geoff Green, 'The New Municipal Socialism,' in Martin Loney, ed., *The State or the Market: Politics and Welfare in Contemporary Britain* (London: SAGE, 1987), 203–21, offers a succinct exposition of this.

22 Warren Magnusson, 'Regeneration and Quality of Life in Vancouver,' in Judd and Parkinson, *Leadership and Urban Regeneration*, 171–87. Compare Christopher Leo, 'The Urban Economy and the Power of the Local State,' in Frances Frisken, ed., *The Changing Canadian Metropolis*, vol. 2 (Berkeley: Institute of Governmental Studies Press, 1994), 657–98.

23 This was most obvious in Sheffield, where the metal-working industry was devastated by disinvestment. David Blunkett and Keith Jackson, in *Democracy in Crisis: The Town Halls Respond* (London: The Hogarth Press, 1987), Chapter 6, offer a positive account of the Sheffield experience. For more critical views, see Paul Lawless, 'Regeneration in Sheffield: From Radical Intervention to Partnership,' in Judd and Parkinson, *Leadership and Urban Regeneration*, 133–51; and Patrick Seyd, 'Radical Sheffield: From Socialism to Entrepreneurialism,' *Political Studies* 38 (1990), 335–44. The Greater London Council was responsible for the most radical economic initiatives: see Greater London Council, *The London Industrial Strategy* (London: GLC, 1985); and Maureen Mackintosh and Hilary Wainwright, eds., *A Taste of Power: The Politics of Local Economics* (London: Verso, 1987). Among the critical reviews, see especially Aram Eisenschitz and David North, 'The London Industrial Strategy: Socialist Transformation or Modernising Capitalism?' *International Journal of Urban and Regional Research* 10 (1986), 419–39; Peter Totterdill, 'Local Economic Strategies as Industrial Policy: A Critical Review of British Developments in the 1980s,' *Economy and Society* 18 (1989), 478–526; Allan Cochrane and Alan Clarke, 'Local Enterprise Boards: The Short History of a Radical Initiative,' *Public Administration* 68 (1990), 315–36; and Alan Harding, 'Local Autonomy and Urban Economic Development Policies: The Recent UK Experience in Perspective,' in King, *Challenges to Local Government*, 79–100.

24 Jon G. Davies, 'From Municipal Socialism to ... Municipal Capitalism?' *Local Government Studies* 14 (1988), 19–22; Cochrane and Clarke, 'Local Enterprise Boards'; and Lawless, 'Regeneration in Sheffield.' More generally, see David Harvey, 'From Managerialism to Entrepreneurialism: The Transformation in Urban Governance in Late Capitalism,' *Geografiska Annaler*, 71B (1989), 3–17.

25 I have explored this idea in a limited way in 'Can Local Governments Engage in "Redistribution"?' presented at the 12th World Congress of Sociology of the International Sociological Association, Madrid, 1990.

**7: Municipal Socialism and Social Democracy**

1 James A. Fairlie, *Municipal Administration* (New York: Macmillan, 1901); Ernest S. Griffith, *The Modern Development of City Government in the United Kingdom and the United States* (London: Oxford University Press, 1927); Harold J. Laski,

et al., eds., *A Century of Municipal Progress* (London: George Allen & Unwin, 1935); and Jon C. Teaford, *The Unheralded Triumph: City Government in America, 1870–1900* (Baltimore: The Johns Hopkins University Press, 1984).

2 Fabian Society, *The Fabian Municipal Program*, First Series (London: Fabian Society, 1891) and Second Series (London: Fabian Society, 1899–1901). See also A.M. McBriar, *Fabian Socialism and English Politics, 1884–1918* (Cambridge: Cambridge University Press, 1966).

3 This is not to say that these regimes originated in the nineteenth century. Michel Foucault, *Discipline and Punish: The Birth of the Prison* (New York: Vintage Books, 1979); and Gordon C. Burchell and P. Miller, *The Foucault Effect: Studies in Governmentality* (Chicago: University of Chicago Press, 1991).

4 Compare Michael Katz, *Class, Bureaucracy and Schools* (New York: Praeger, 1971); Michael Ignatieff, *A Just Measure of Pain: The Penitentiary in the Industrial Revolution, 1750–1850* (New York: Random House, 1978); and David Harvey, *The Urbanization of Capital* (Oxford: Blackwell, 1985) and *Consciousness and the Urban Experience* (Oxford: Blackwell, 1985).

5 For contemporary arguments to this effect, see Joshua Toulmin Smith, *Local Self-Government and Centralisation* (London: John Chapman, 1851) and *The Parish*, 2nd ed. (London: H. Sweet, 1857); and George E. Howard, *An Introduction to the Local Constitutional History of the United States* (Baltimore: Johns Hopkins University, 1889). Compare Amasa M. Eaton, 'The Right to Local Self-Government,' *Harvard Law Review* 13 (1900), 441–54, 570–88, 638–58, and 14 (1900–1) 20–38, 116–38; Eugene McQuillan, *A Treatise on the Law of Municipal Corporations* (Chicago: Callaghan and Company, 1911); W. Ivor Jennings, 'The Municipal Revolution,' in Laski et al., eds., *A Century of Municipal Progress*, 55–65; and Jennings, 'Central Control,' 417–54.

6 For general references, see Chapter 2, note 7. The legal issues are discussed in more detail in the standard texts on the law of municipal corporations.

7 Compare L.J. Sharpe, 'Theories and Values of Local Government,' *Political Studies* 18 (1971), 153–74.

8 See, for instance, S.T. Glass, *The Responsible Society* (London: Longmans, Green and Co., 1966); and James T. Kloppenberg, *Uncertain Victory: Social Democracy and Progressivism in European and American Thought, 1870–1920* (New York: Oxford University Press, 1986), Chapters 7 and 9.

9 Andrew Sancton reviews some of the relevant ideas in 'British Socialist Theories of the Division of Power by Area, *Political Studies* 24 (1976), 158–70. Compare Sidney Webb and Beatrice Webb, *A Constitution for the Socialist Commonwealth of Great Britain* (Cambridge: Cambridge University Press, 1975 [1920]); G.D.H. Cole, *The Future of Local Government* (London: Cassell and Company, 1921) and *Local and Regional Government* (London: Cassell and

Company, 1947); and Harold J. Laski, *A Grammar of Politics*, 5th ed. (London: George Allen & Unwin, 1967), Chapter 8.

10 Hannah Arendt, *On Revolution* (New York: Viking Press, 1965), Chapter 6.

11 Asa Briggs, *Victorian Cities* (London: Penguin Books, 1968).

12 David Owen, *English Philanthropy, 1660–1960* (Cambridge: Harvard University Press, 1964); Samuel Haber, *Efficiency and Uplift: Scientific Management in the Progressive Era, 1890–1920* (Chicago: University of Chicago Press, 1964); Allen F. Davis, *Spearheads for Reform: The Social Settlements and the Progressive Movement, 1890–1914* (New York: Oxford University Press, 1967); and Paul Boyer, *Urban Masses and Moral Order in the America, 1820–1920* (Cambridge: Harvard University Press, 1978).

13 E.P. Thompson, *The Making of the English Working Class* (London: Penguin Books, 1968), offers a classic account of the prehistory of this activity. See also note 34 below.

14 Jill Lewis, 'Red Vienna: Socialism in One City, 1918–1927,' *European Studies Review* 13, no. 3 (July 1983), 335–55; and Anson Rabinbach, ed., 'Red Vienna: Municipal Socialism and Cultural Politics,' *The Austrian Socialist Experiment: Social Democracy and Austromarxism 1918–1934* (Boulder and London: Westview Press, 1985), Part 4. On the earlier American experience, which brought socialists to office in Milwaukee and other cities before the First World War, see Michael Bassett, 'Municipal Reform and the Socialist Party 1910–1914,' *Australian Journal of Politics and History* 19, no. 2 (August 1973), 179–87; Bruce M. Stave, ed., *Socialism and the Cities* (Port Washington, NY: Kennikat Press, 1975); Donald T. Critchlow, ed., *Socialism in the Heartland: The Midwestern Experience, 1900–1925* (Notre Dame, IN: University of Notre Dame Press, 1986); and Richard W. Judd, *Socialist Cities: Municipal Politics and the Grass Roots of American Socialism* (Albany: State University of New York Press, 1989).

15 Sheffield District Labour Party, *Six Years of Labour Rule in Sheffield, 1926–1932* (Sheffield: Sheffield District Labour Party, 1932).

16 Compare William A. Robson, *The Development of Local Government* (London: George Allen & Unwin, 1931); Cole, *Local and Regional Government*; and Sue Goss, *Local Labour and Local Government* (Edinburgh: Edinburgh University Press, 1988).

17 David Stafford, *From Anarchism to Reformism: A Study of the Political Activities of Paul Brousse within the First International and the French Socialist Movement, 1870–90* (London: Weidenfeld and Nicolson, 1971).

18 Ibid., 6.

19 Karl Marx, 'The Civil War in France,' in David McClellan, ed., *Karl Marx: Selected Writings* (Oxford: Oxford University Press, 1977), 539–58.

20 Stafford, *From Anarchism to Reformism*, 40–1.

21 Sidney Webb, 'Historic,' in George Bernard Shaw, ed., *Fabian Essays* (London: George Allen & Unwin, 1948), 30, 47.
22 Paul Thompson, *Socialists, Liberals, and Labour: The Struggle for London, 1885–1914* (London: Routledge and Kegan Paul, 1967), 117.
23 Ibid., 133.
24 Eduard Bernstein, *Evolutionary Socialism: A Criticism and Affirmation*, trans. E.C. Harvey (London: Independent Labour Party, 1909), 159.
25 Frederic C. Howe, *European Cities at Work* (New York: Scribner's Sons, 1913), 37. Compare Howe, *The City: The Hope of Democracy* (Seattle: University of Washington Press, 1967 [1905]).
26 As Howe also noted, German municipalities were free from the constrictions of the *ultra vires* rule, which kept their American and British counterparts under tight legislative and judicial control. Like a private individual or a private corporation, a German municipality could do whatever it was not specifically forbidden to do. 'The city is assumed to have all the power necessary for its local life' (Howe, *European Cities*, 254). This meant that German municipalities could acquire land, engage in businesses, regulate the use of private property, raise new taxes, invent new services, and so on, without requiring specific authority. This latitude meant innovation and expansiveness – especially when combined with the professionalism of German local government. Compare William Harbut Dawson, *Municipal Life and Government in Germany* (London: Longmans, Green and Co., 1914).
27 Friedrich Engels to F.A. Sorge, 18 January 1893, in *Marx-Engels Selected Correspondence* [italics in original].
28 V. I. Lenin, *Collected Works* 13 (1962), 336.
29 Ibid., 339 (italics in original).
30 Ibid., 340 (italics in original).
31 Ibid., 359 (italics in original).
32 Ibid., 360 (italics in original).
33 Ibid.
34 John Foster, *Class Struggle and the Industrial Revolution* (London: Methuen, 1974). Compare Derek Fraser, *Urban Politics in Victorian England* (Leicester: Leicester University Press, 1976) and *Power and Authority in the Victorian City* (Oxford: Basil Blackwell, 1979).
35 Noreen Branson, *Poplarism, 1919–1925: George Lansbury and the Councillors' Revolt* (London: Lawrence and Wishart, 1979); George W. Jones, 'Herbert Morrison and Poplarism,' *Public Law* (1973), 11–31; Bryan Keith-Lucas, 'Poplarism,' *Public Law* (1962), 52–80; and Stuart Macintyre, *Little Moscows: Communism and Working-Class Militancy in Inter-War Britain* (London: Croom Helm, 1980).

36 Bernard Donoughue and George W. Jones, *Herbert Morrison: Portrait of a Politician* (London: Weidenfeld and Nicolson, 1973), 196–7.
37 Anson Rabinbach, *The Crisis of Austrian Socialism: From Red Vienna to Civil War, 1927–1934* (Chicago: University of Chicago Press, 1983).
38 Ibid., 27.
39 Ibid., 27–8.
40 Compare Rabinbach, *The Austrian Socialist Experiment;* Charles A. Gulick, *Austria: From Habsburg to Hitler,* 2 vols. (Berkeley and Los Angeles: University of California Press, 1948); Carl E. Schorske, *German Social Democracy, 1905–1917: The Development of the Great Schism* (Cambridge: Harvard University Press, 1955); and Tom Bottomore and Patrick Goode, eds., *Austro-Marxism* (Oxford: Oxford University Press, 1978).
41 Rabinbach, *The Crisis of Austrian Socialism,* 28.
42 Helmut Gruber, 'Socialist Party Culture and the Realities of Working-Class Life in Red Vienna,' in Rabinbach, *The Austrian Socialist Experiment,* 223–46.
43 Ibid., 237.
44 Ibid., 230–1.
45 On Communism and local government in Europe, see Bogdan Szajkowski, ed., *Marxist Local Governments in Western Europe and Japan* (London: Frances Pinter, 1986); and Martin A. Schain, *French Communism and Local Power: Urban Politics and Political Change* (London: Frances Pinter, 1985). Compare Martin Mowbray, 'The Red Shire of Kearsley, 1944–1947: Communists in Local Government,' *Labour History* 51 (November 1986), 83–94.
46 Compare Ralph Miliband, *Marxism and Politics* (Oxford: Oxford University Press, 1977), and Nicos Poulantzas, *State, Power, Socialism* (London: Verso, 1978).
47 See, for instance, Robert W. Campbell, 2nd ed., *Soviet Economic Power* (New York: Houghton Mifflin, 1966).
48 Compare James Weinstein, *Ambiguous Legacy: The Left in American Politics* (New York: New Viewpoints, 1975); Mark E. Kann, *The American Left: Failures and Fortunes* (New York: Praeger, 1982); and Mike Davis, *Prisoners of the American Dream* (London: Verso, 1986).

**8: Radical Municipalism and Local Socialism**

1 Dick Flacks, 'What Happened to the New Left?' *Socialist Review* 19, no. 1 (1989), 91.
2 Jack Whalen and Richard Flacks, *Beyond the Barricades: The Sixties Generation Grows Up* (Philadelphia: Temple University Press, 1989); and Marcia Darnovsky, Barbara Epstein, and Richard Flacks, eds., *Cultural Politics and Social*

*Movements* (Philadelphia: Temple University Press, 1995). See Introduction, note 37, for further references. Contemporary views are expressed in Carl Oglesby, ed., *The New Left Reader* (New York: Grove Press, 1969); Priscilla Long, ed., *The New Left* (Boston: Porter Sargent, 1969); and Alexander Cockburn and Robin Blackburn, eds., *Student Power: Problems, Diagnosis, Action* (London: Penguin Books, 1969).

3 Alan Altshuler, *Community Control* (New York: Pegasus, 1970); and Douglas Yates, *Neighborhood Democracy* (Lexington, MA: D.C. Heath, 1973).

4 Harriet Nathan and S. Scott, *Experiment and Change in Berkeley: Essays on City Politics, 1950–1975* (Berkeley: University of California Institute of Governmental Studies, 1978).

5 Berkeley activists have been flattered with hostile criticism from the right. See, for instance, Joseph P. Lyford, *The Berkeley Archipelago* (Chicago: Regnery Gateway, 1982); and Peter Collier and David Horowitz, 'Slouching towards Berkeley: Socialism in One City,' *The Public Interest*, no. 94 (Winter 1989), 47–68. From a different perspective, see Gus Newport, 'Berkeley: From the April Coalition to the Clean Underwear Gang,' in *Fire in the Hearth: The Radical Politics of Place in America*, ed. Mike Davis et al., *The Year Left* 4 (London: Verso, 1990), 83–94. Newport was mayor of Berkeley.

6 Murray Bookchin and Benjamin R. Higgins, 'Socialism in One City?' *Socialist Review*, no. 90 (1986), 51–70; Bernard Sanders, 'Reflections from Vermont,' *Monthly Review* 41, no. 7 (December 1989), 13–21; Greg Guma, *The People's Republic: Vermont and the Sanders Revolution* (Shelburne, VT: The New England Press, 1989); and William J. Conroy, *Challenging the Boundaries of Reform: Socialism in Burlington* (Philadelphia: Temple University Press, 1990).

7 Allan David Heskin, *Tenants and the American Dream: Ideology and the Tenant Movement* (New York: Praeger, 1983), Chapters 3 and 8; Mark E. Kann, *Middle Class Radicalism in Santa Monica* (Philadelphia: Temple University Press, 1986); David S. Daykin, 'The Limits to Neighborhood Power: Progressive Politics and Local Control in Santa Monica,' in Scott Cummings, ed., *Business Elites and Urban Development* (Albany: State University of New York Press, 1988), 357–87; and Stella M. Capek and John I. Gilderbloom, *Community vs Commodity: Tenants and the American City* (Albany: State University of New York Press, 1992).

8 Pierre Clavel, *The Progressive City: Planning and Participation, 1969–1984* (New Brunswick, NJ: Rutgers University Press, 1986); Carl Boggs, *Social Movements and Political Power: Emerging Forms of Radicalism in the West* (Philadelphia: Temple University Press, 1986); Joseph M. Kling and Prudence S. Posner, eds., *Dilemmas of Activism: Class, Community, and the Politics of Local Mobilization* (Philadelphia: Temple University Press, 1990); Mike Davis, Steven Hiatt,

Marie Kennedy, Susan Ruddick and Michael Sprinker, *Fire in the Hearth: The Radical Politics of Place in America* (London: Verso, 1990); Donald L. Rosdil, 'The Context of Radical Populism in U.S. Cities: A Comparative Analysis,' *Journal of Urban Affairs* 13 (1991), 77–96; and Robert Fisher and Joseph Kling, eds. *Mobilizing the Community: Local Politics in the Global Era*, Urban Affairs Annual Review 41 (Newbury Park, CA: SAGE Publications, 1993).

9 Bruce B. Brugman, ed., *The Ultimate Highrise* (San Francisco: San Francisco Bay Guardian Books, 1971); Manuel Castells, *The City and the Grassroots* (Berkeley and Los Angeles: University of California Press, 1983); Chester Hartman, *The Transformation of San Francisco* (Totowa, NJ: Rowman and Allanheld, 1984); and Richard E. DeLeon, *Left Coast City: Progressive Politics in San Francisco, 1975–1991* (Lawrence: University Press of Kansas, 1992).

10 Boston Urban Study Group, *Who Rules Boston? A Citizen's Guide to Reclaiming the City* (Boston: Institute for Democratic Socialism, 1984); Barbara Ferman, *Governing the Ungovernable City* (Philadelphia: Temple University Press, 1985); J. Anthony Lukas, *Common Ground* (New York: Vintage Books, 1986); James Jennings and Mel King, eds., *From Access to Power: Black Politics in Boston* (Cambridge, MA: Schenkman, 1986); Peter Dreier, 'Economic Growth and Economic Justice in Boston: Populist Housing and Jobs Policies,' in Gregory D. Squires, ed., *Unequal Partnerships: The Political Economy of Urban Development in Postwar America* (New Brunswick, NJ: Rutgers University Press, 1989), 35–58; Peter Dreier and W. Dennis Keating, 'The Limits of Localism: Progressive Housing Policies in Boston, 1984–1989,' *Urban Affairs Quarterly* 26 (1990), 191–216; and Peter Dreier and Bruce Ehrlich, 'Downtown Development and Urban Reform: The Politics of Boston's Linkage Policy,' *Urban Affairs Quarterly* 26, no. 3 (1991), 354–75.

11 Larry Bennett, Kathleen McCourt, Philip Nyden, and Gregory Squires, *Chicago: Race, Class and Response to Urban Decline* (Philadelphia: Temple University Press, 1987); Melvin G. Holli and Paul M. Green, *Bashing Chicago Traditions: Harold Washington's Last Campaign* (Grand Rapids, MI: William B. Eerdmans, 1989); Robert P. Giloth and Robert Mier, 'Spatial Change and Social Justice: Alternative Economic Development in Chicago,' in Robert A. Beauregard, ed., *Economic Restructuring and Political Response* (Newbury Park, CA: SAGE, 1989), 181–208; Pierre Clavel and Wim Wiewel, eds., *Harold Washington and the Neighborhoods: Progressive City Government in Chicago, 1983–1987* (New Brunswick, NJ: Rutgers University Press, 1991); and Larry Bennett, 'Harold Washington and the Black Urban Regime,' *Urban Affairs Quarterly* 28, no. 3 (March 1993), 423–40.

12 John Mollenkopf, *A Phoenix in the Ashes: The Rise and Fall of the Koch Coalition in New York* (Princeton: University Press, 1992).

13 Ian Loveland, 'Local Government Responses to Homelessness – A Californian Case Study,' *Local Government Studies* 17, no. 1 (1991), 13–44.

14 S.D. Soifer, 'The Burlington Land Trust: A Socialist Approach to Affordable Housing?' *Journal of Urban Affairs* 12 (1990), 237–52; and Mt. Auburn Associates, *Jobs and People II: Furthering Burlington's Economic Progress, A Report to the Community and Economic Development Office, City of Burlington, Vermont* (January 1989).

15 Martin Carnoy, Derek Shearer, and Russell Rumberger, *A New Social Contract* (New York: Harper & Row, 1983); Susan S. Fainstein, 'Local Mobilization and Economic Discontent,' in Michael Peter Smith and Joe R. Feagin, eds., *The Capitalist City* (Oxford: Basil Blackwell, 1987), 323–42; Derek Shearer, 'In Search of Equal Partnerships: Prospects for Progressive Urban Policy in the 1990s,' in Gregory D. Squires, ed., *Unequal Partnerships* (New Brunswick, NJ: Rutgers University Press, 1989), 289–307; and Pierre Clavel and Nancy Kleniewski, 'Space for Progressive Local Policy: Examples from the United States and the United Kingdom,' in John R. Logan and Todd Swanstrom, eds., *Beyond the City Limits* (Philadelphia: Temple University Press, 1990), 199–234.

16 David McLellan, ed., *Karl Marx: Selected Writings* (Oxford: Oxford University Press, 1977), 300.

17 For general discussions, see Martin Boddy and Colin Fudge, eds., *Local Socialism? Labour Councils and New Left Alternatives* (London: Macmillan, 1984); John Gyford, *The Politics of Local Socialism* (London: George Allen & Unwin, 1985); Simon Duncan and Mark Goodwin, *The Local State and Uneven Development: Behind the Local Government Crisis* (Cambridge: Polity Press, 1988); and Stewart Lansley, Sue Goss, and Christian Wolmar, *Councils in Conflict: The Rise and Fall of the Municipal Left* (London: Macmillan, 1989).

18 Lin Chun, *The British New Left* (Edinburgh: Edinburgh University Press, 1993) brings out the distinctive origins of the New Left in Britain. I use the term New Left more loosely than he does.

19 Martin Loney, *Community against Government: The British Community Development Project, 1968–78* (London: Heinemann, 1983).

20 Stuart Hall and Martin Jacques, eds., *The Politics of Thatcherism* (London: Lawrence & Wishart, 1983); and Andrew Gamble, *The Free Economy and the Strong State* (London: Pluto, 1987).

21 Patrick Seyd, *The Rise and Fall of the Labour Left* (London: Macmillan, 1987); and Hilary Wainwright, *Labour: A Tale of Two Parties* (London: The Hogarth Press, 1987).

22 John Carvel, *Citizen Ken*, 2nd ed. (London: Hogarth Press, 1987); and Ken Livingstone, *If Voting Changed Anything, They'd Abolish It* (London: Collins, 1987).

23 Andrew Forrester, Stewart Lansley, and Robin Pauley, *Beyond Our Ken: A*

*Guide to the Battle for London* (London: Fourth Estate, 1985); N. Flynn, Steve Leach, and C. Vieba, *Abolition or Reform? The GLC and the Metropolitan County Councils* (London: George Allen & Unwin, 1985); Brendan O'Leary, 'Why Was the GLC Abolished?' *International Journal of Urban and Regional Research* 11, no. 3 (1987), 192–217; and Desmond S. King, 'Political Centralization and State Interests in Britain: The 1986 Abolition of the GLC and MCCs,' *Comparative Political Studies* 21, no. 4 (1989), 467–94.

24 David Blunkett and G. Green, *Building from the Bottom: The Sheffield Experience*, Fabian Tract no. 491 (London: Fabian Society, 1983); Blunkett and Keith Jackson, *Democracy in Crisis: The Town Halls Respond* (London: Hogarth Press, 1987); and Patrick Seyd, 'Radical Sheffield: From Socialism to Entrepreneurialism,' *Political Studies* 38 (1990), 335–44.

25 Michael Parkinson, *Liverpool on the Brink* (Hermitage, Berks.: Policy Journals, 1985); Michael Crick, *The March of Militant* (London: Faber and Faber, 1986); Liverpool Black Caucus, *The Racial Politics of Militant in Liverpool* (Liverpool: Merseyside Area Profile Group, 1986); Derek Hatton, *Inside Left* (London: Bloomsbury, 1988); and Peter Taaffe and Tony Mulhearn, *Liverpool: A City That Dared to Fight* (London: Fortress Books, 1988).

26 Compare John Benington, 'Local Economic Strategies: Paradigms for a Planned Economy?' *Local Economy: The Journal of the London Economic Policy Unit* 1, no. 1 (1986), 7–24; Blunkett and Jackson, *Democracy in Crisis*, 108–42; and Maureen Mackintosh and Hilary Wainwright, eds., *A Taste of Power: The Politics of Local Economics* (London: Verso, 1987).

27 Aram Eisenschitz and Jamie Gough, *The Politics of Local Economic Policy: The Problems and Possibilities of Local Initiative* (London: Macmillan, 1993). See also Chapter 6, notes 23 and 24.

28 Greater London Council, *London Industrial Strategy* (London: GLC, 1985), *London Labour Plan* (London: GLC, 1986), and *London Financial Strategy* (London: GLC, 1986).

29 However, see Community Ownership Organizing Project, *The Cities Wealth: Programs for Community Economic Control in Berkeley, California* (Washington: Conference on Alternative State and Local Policies, 1976); Boston Urban Study Group, *Who Rules Boston? A Citizen's Guide to Reclaiming the City* (Boston: Institute for Democratic Socialism, 1984); Marc V. Levine, 'Economic Development in States and Cities: Toward Democratic and Strategic Planning in State and Local Government,' in Levine, et al., *The State and Democracy: Revitalizing America's Government* (New York: Routledge, 1988), 111–46; Jack Layton, *Reclaiming the City: An Alternative Economic Strategy* (Toronto: Jack Layton for Mayor Campaign, 16 October 1991); Christopher Gunn and Hazel D. Gunn, *Reclaiming Capital: Democratic Initiatives and Community Development*

(Ithaca, NY: Cornell University Press, 1991); and Eric Shragge, *Community Economic Development: In Search of Empowerment* (Montreal: Black Rose Books, 1993).

30 Danny Burns, Robin Hambleton, and Paul Hoggett, *The Politics of Decentralisation: Revitalising Local Democracy* (London: Macmillan, 1994).

31 We will be discussing this at greater length in Chapter 9. Compare Duncan and Goodwin, *The Local State and Uneven Development*.

32 Sue Goss, 'Women's Initiatives in Local Government,' in Martin Boddy and Colin Fudge, eds., *Local Socialism? Labour Councils and New Left Alternatives* (London: Macmillan, 1984), 109–32; Frankie Ashton and Gill Whitting, eds., *Feminist Theory and Practical Politics: Shifting the Agenda in the 1980's* (Bristol: School of Advanced Urban Studies, University of Bristol, 1987); and Lansley, et al., *Councils in Conflict*, 142–59; and Kathryn Riley, 'Equality for Women – The Role of Local Authorities,' *Local Government Studies* 16, no. 1 (1990), 49–68. See also Liz Bondi and Linda Peake, 'Gender and the City: Urban Politics Revisited,' in Jo Little, Linda Peake, and Pat Richardson, eds., *Women in Cities: Gender and the Urban Environment* (London: Macmillan, 1988), 21–40; and Jane Foulsham, 'Women's Needs and Planning – A Critical Evaluation of Recent Local Authority Practice,' in John Montgomery and Andy Thornley, eds., *Radical Planning Initiatives: New Directions for Urban Planning in the 1990s* (Aldershot: Gower, 1990), 244–58. Compare Greater London Council in Co-operation with the GLC Gay Working Party, *Changing the World: A London Charter for Gay and Lesbian Rights* (London: GLC, 1985); and Greater London Council, *A Right to Equality: A London Charter for People with Disabilities* (London: GLC, 1984).

33 Compare Herman Ouseley, 'Local Authority Race Initiatives,' in Boddy and Fudge, *Local Socialism?* 133–59; and Shamit Saggar, 'The Changing Agenda of Race Issues in Local Government: The Case of a London Borough,' *Political Studies* 39, no. 1 (1991), 100–21.

34 Some of these initiatives are discussed Chapter 11.

35 John Gyford, *The Changing Politics of Local Government* (London: Unwin Hyman, 1989), 310–12; and Kann, *Middle Class Radicalism*, 12–17.

36 Margit Mayer, 'Restructuring and Popular Opposition in West German Cities,' in Michael P. Smith and Joseph R. Feagin, eds., *The Capitalist City: Global Restructuring and Community Politics* (Oxford: Basil Blackwell, 1987), 343–63; Werner Hulsberg, *The German Greens: A Social and Political Profile* (London: Verso, 1988); Roland Roth, 'Local Green Politics in West German Cities,' *International Journal of Urban and Regional Research* 15 (1991), 75–89; Margit Mayer, 'The Career of Urban Social Movements in West Germany,' in Fisher and Kling, *Mobilizing the Community*, 149–70; and R. Ronneberger and Roger Keil,

'Riding the Tiger of Modernization: Red Green Municipal Reform Politics in Frankfurt am Main,' *Capitalism Nature Socialism* 4, no. 2 (1993), 19–50.

37 Richard Harris, 'A Social Movement in Urban Politics: A Reinterpretation of Urban Reform in Canada,' *International Journal of Urban and Regional Research* 11 (1987), 363–79; and Jon C. Caulfield, 'Canadian Urban "Reform" and Local Conditions: An Alternative to Harris's "Reinterpretation",' *International Journal of Urban and Regional Research* 12 (1988), 477–84.

38 Shlomo Hasson and David Ley, *Neighbourhood Organizations and the Welfare State* (Toronto: University of Toronto Press, 1994), 172–204.

39 Stephen Schecter, *The Politics of Urban Liberation* (Montreal: Black Rose Books, 1978); and Dimitrios Roussopoulos, ed., *The City and Radical Social Change* (Montreal: Black Rose Books, 1982).

40 Guy Bourassa and Jacques Léveillée, eds., *Le système politique de Montréal*, Cahiers de l'AFCS, no. 43 (Montréal: L'association canadienne-française pour l'avancement des sciences, 1986); Jean-François Léonard and Jacques Léveillée, *After Drapeau* (Montreal: Black Rose Books, 1986); Susan Ruddick, 'The Montreal Citizens' Movement: The Realpolitik of the 1990s?' in Davis et al., *Fire in the Hearth*, 287–316; Henri Lustiger-Thaler, 'New Social Movement Discourse: The Unsolved Democracy,' in William K. Carroll, ed., *Organizing Dissent: Contemporary Social Movements in Theory and Practice* (Toronto: Garamond Press, 1992), 174–99; Harold Chorney and Andrew Molloy, 'Boss Politics and Quebec Nationalism, Jean Drapeau to Jean Doré: The Pre-Modern to the Post-Modern,' in Alain-G. Gagnon, ed., *Quebec: State and Society*, 2nd ed. (Toronto: Nelson, 1993); and Timothy Thomas, 'New Forms of Political Representation: European Ecological Politics and the Montreal Citizen's Movement,' *Canadian Journal of Political Science* 28, no. 3 (September 1995), 509–31.

41 Metro Toronto NDP, The Committee for '88, *Toronto: A New Vision* (unpublished pamphlet, 1988). Compare Layton, *Reclaiming the City.*

42 See Chapter 7, note 14.

43 James Weinstein, *The Decline of American Socialism, 1912–1925* (New York: Monthly Review Press, 1967).

**9: Fiscal Struggles and Municipal Autonomy**

1 Desmond S. King, *The New Right: Politics, Markets and Citizenship* (Chicago: The Dorsey Press, 1987).

2 Robert Nozick, *Anarchy, State and Utopia* (New York: Basic Books, 1974); James M. Buchanan, *The Limits of Liberty: Between Anarchy and Leviathan* (Chicago: University of Chicago Press, 1975); and Friedrich A. von Hayek, *Law,*

*Legislation and Liberty*, 3 vols. (London: Routledge & Kegan Paul, 1976–79).

3 Clarence Lo, *Small Property versus Big Government: Social Origins of the Tax Revolt* (Berkeley: University of California Press, 1990).

4 Crawford Kilian, *School Wars: The Assault on B.C. Education* (Vancouver: New Star Books, 1985), 180–207.

5 Tony Travers, *The Politics of Local Government Finance* (London: George Allen & Unwin, 1986), 150–91; Simon Duncan and Mark Goodwin, *The Local State and Uneven Development* (Cambridge: Polity Press, 1988), 168–249; and Stewart Lansley, Sue Goss, and Christian Wolmar, *Councils in Conflict: The Rise and Fall of the Municipal Left* (London: Macmillan, 1989), 34–46.

6 George W. Jones and John Stewart, *The Case for Local Government* (London: George Allen & Unwin, 1985). Compare Dilys M. Hill, *Citizens and Cities: Urban Policy in the 1990s* (Hemel Hempstead: Harvester Wheatsheaf, 1994).

7 John Stewart and Gerry Stoker, eds., *The Future of Local Government* (London: Macmillan, 1989) and *Local Government in the 1990s* (London: Macmillan, 1995).

8 Travers, *The Politics of Local Government Finance*, 51–78.

9 David Blunkett and Keith Jackson, *Democracy in Crisis: The Town Halls Respond* (London: The Hogarth Press, 1987), 149.

10 *Local Government Finance: Report of the Committee of Inquiry* (London: HMSO, 1976).

11 R.A.W. Rhodes, 'Continuity and Change in British Central-Local Relations: "The Conservative Threat",' *British Journal of Political Science* 14, no. 3 (1984), 261–83, and 'Intergovernmental Relations in the Post-war Period,' *Local Government Studies* 11, no. 6 (1985), 35–57; and Travers, *The Politics of Local Government Finance*, 79–149.

12 Michael Ward, *Municipal Monetarism* (London: Greater London Labour Party, 1987).

13 David Clapham, *Goodbye Council Housing?* (London: Unwin Hyman, 1989); and Ian Cole and Robert Furbey, *The Eclipse of Council Housing* (London: Routledge, 1994).

14 Travers, *The Politics of Local Government Finance*, 150–64.

15 Arthur Midwinter, Michael Keating, and Peter Taylor, 'Excessive and Unreasonable: The Politics of the Scottish Hit List,' *Political Studies* 21, no. 3 (1983), 394–417. On subsequent Scottish developments, see Peter John, *Introduction of the Community Charge in Scotland* (London: Policy Studies Institute, 1989); and Arthur Midwinter and Claire Monaghan, *From Rates to the Poll Tax* (Edinburgh: Edinburgh University Press, 1993).

16 Michael Parkinson, *Liverpool on the Brink* (Hermitage, Berks.: Policy Journals, 1985).

17 On Poplar, see Chapter 7. Compare Dennis Skinner and D. Langdon, *The Story of Clay Cross* (Nottingham: Spokesman Books, 1974).

18 Michael Crick, *The March of Militant* (London: Faber and Faber, 1986), 215–63.

19 Derek Hatton, *Inside Left* (London: Bloomsbury, 1988); and Peter Taaffe and Tony Mulhearn, *Liverpool: A City That Dared to Fight* (London: Fortress Books, 1988).

20 For the views of key participants, see Mark Page, 'Ratecap Resistance: Interview with David Blunkett,' *Marxism Today* (March 1985), 7–12; Blunkett and Jackson, *Democracy in Crisis*, 166–98; and Ken Livingstone, *If Voting Changed Anything, They'd Abolish It* (London: Collins, 1987), 308–36.

21 John Carvel, *Citizen Ken*, 2nd ed. (London: The Hogarth Press, 1987), 238–51.

22 Blunkett and Jackson, *Democracy in Crisis*, 181.

23 Crick, *The March of Militant*, 264–98.

24 Gerry Stoker, *The Politics of Local Government*, 2nd ed. (London: Macmillan, 1991).

25 David Butler, Andrew Adonis, and Tony Travers, *Failure in British Government: The Politics of the Poll Tax* (Oxford: Oxford University Press, 1994).

26 Robert C. Allen and Gideon Rosenbluth, *Restraining the Economy: Social Credit Economic Policies for B.C. in the Eighties* (Vancouver: New Star Books, 1987).

27 J. Terence Morley, Neil Swainson, R. Jeremy Wilson, and Walter D. Young, *The Reins of Power* (Vancouver: Douglas & McIntyre, 1984); and Donald Blake and David Elkins, *Two Political Worlds* (Vancouver: University of British Columbia Press, 1985).

28 Paul Tennant, 'Vancouver Civic Politics: 1929–80,' in Lionel D. Feldman, ed., *Politics and Government of Urban Canada*, 4th ed. (Toronto: Methuen, 1981), 126–47; and Donald Gutstein, 'Vancouver,' in Warren Magnusson and Andrew Sancton, eds., *City Politics in Canada* (Toronto: University of Toronto Press, 1983), 189–221.

29 Michael Howlett and Keith Brownsey, 'The Old Reality and the New Reality: Party Politics and Public Policy in British Columbia, 1941–1987,' *Studies in Political Economy: A Socialist Review*, no. 25 (1988), 141–76.

30 Warren Magnusson, William K. Carroll, Charles Doyle, Monika Langer, and R.B.J. Walker, *The New Reality: The Politics of Restraint in British Columbia* (Vancouver: New Star Books, 1984).

31 William K. Carroll, 'The Solidarity Coalition,' in Magnusson et al., *The New Reality*, 94–113; Kilian, *School Wars*, 84–97.

32 Bryan D. Palmer, *Solidarity: The Rise and Fall of an Opposition in British Columbia* (Vancouver: New Star Books, 1987).

33 See Chapter 10.

34 Magnusson and Monika Langer, 'The New Reality in Education,' in Magnus-

son et al., *The New Reality*, 242–57. Compare *Four Years of Restraint and Four Years to Recover* (Vancouver: Vancouver School Board, September 1986).

35 Kilian, 188–96.

36 *Weinstein v. Ministry of Education* (SCBC 1985), 20 D.L.R. (4th) 609.

37 Referendum provisions were retained when the school financing system was overhauled in 1990. British Columbia, Ministry of Education, *School Finance '90: Changes to the School Finance System* (Victoria: Ministry of Education, 1990). The new NDP government kept these limitations when it came to power in 1991.

38 Lee Bridges et al., *Legality and Local Politics* (Aldershot: Gower, 1987); and Peter John, *Recent Trends in Central-Local Government Relations* (London: Policy Studies Institute, 1990).

39 See notes 5 and 6, Chapter 7.

**10: Women in Transition**

1 Del Martin, *Battered Wives* (San Francisco: Glide Publications, 1976); Linda Macleod, *Wife Battering in Canada: The Vicious Cycle* (Ottawa: Canadian Advisory Council on the Status of Women, 1980); Jan Barnsley, Helga E. Jacobson, Jean McIntosh, and M. Jane Wintemute, *'Battered and Blamed': A Report of Wife Assault from the Perspective of Battered Women* (Vancouver: Women's Research Centre, 1980); Susan Schecter, *Women and Male Violence: The Vision and Struggles of the Women's Movement* (Boston: South End Press, 1982); Linda Gordon, 'Family Violence, Feminism, and Social Control,' *Feminist Studies* 12, no. 3 (1986), 453–78, and *Heroes of Their Own Lives: The Politics and History of Family Violence* (New York: Penguin Books, 1988); and Kersti Yllo and Michele Bograd, eds., *Feminist Perspectives on Wife Abuse* (Newbury Park, CA: SAGE Publications, 1990).

2 Megan Ellis, The Vancouver Transition House: A Case Study (unpublished manuscript, 1984), 7. See also Valerie MacDermot, 'An Account of the History and Operation of Vancouver Transition House,' in Jan Barnsley, *Battered and Blamed: A Report on Wife Assault from the Perspective of Battered Women* (Vancouver: Women's Research Centre, 1980), Appendix IV; and Jillian Ridington, 'The Transition House Process: A Feminist Environment as Reconstitutive Milieu,' *Victimology: An International Journal* 2, no. 3/4 (1977/8), 563–75.

3 Sue Findlay, 'Facing the State: The Politics of the Women's Movement Reconsidered,' in Heather Jon Maroney and Meg Luxton, eds., *Feminism and Political Economy: Women's Work, Women's Struggles* (Toronto: Methuen, 1987), 31–50; and Findlay, 'Feminist Struggles with the Canadian State: 1966–1988,' *Resources for Feminist Research* 17, no. 3 (1988), 5–9.

4 Michael Clague, Robert Dill, Brian Wharf, and Roop Sebaran, *Reforming Human Services: The Experience of the Community Resource Boards in B.C.* (Vancouver: University of British Columbia Press, 1985).

5 Heather Jon Maroney, 'Feminism at Work,' in Maroney and Luxton, *Feminism and Political Economy*, 85–108; Jackie Ainsworth et al., 'Getting Organized: In the Feminist Unions,' in Maureen FitzGerald, Connie Guberman, and Margie Wolfe, eds., *Still Ain't Satisfied* (Toronto: Women's Press, 1982); Linda Briskin and Linda Yanz, eds., *Union Sisters: Women in the Labour Movement* (Toronto: Women's Press, 1983).

6 See Jan Barnsley's critique of the symposium in *Feminist Action, Institutional Reaction: Responses to Wife Assault* (Vancouver: Women's Research Centre, 1985). Compare Gene Errington, 'Family Violence: Is it a Women's Problem?' in Patricia D. Ross, *Proceedings from Symposium on Family Violence, March 9, 10, 11, 1977* (Vancouver: United Way of Greater Vancouver, 1977); and Flora MacLeod, *Report of the Task Force on Family Violence* (Vancouver: United Way of the Lower Mainland, 1979).

7 Jean Grossholtz, 'Battered Women's Shelters and the Political Economy of Sexual Violence,' in Irene Diamond, ed., *Families, Politics, and Public Policy: A Feminist Dialogue on Women and the State* (New York: Longman, 1983), 59–69; Micheline Beaudry, *Battered Women* (Montreal: Black Rose Books, 1985); Somer Brodribb, 'Winonah's: In the Spirit of the Place,' *Resources for Feminist Research* 7, no. 13 (1988), 49–55; Gillian Walker, *Family Violence and the Women's Movement: The Conceptual Politics of Struggle* (Toronto: University of Toronto Press, 1990); and British Columbia Task Force on Family Violence, *Is Anyone Listening?* (Victoria: Queen's Printer, February 1992).

8 Jillian Ridington, 'Providing Services the Feminist Way,' in Fitzgerald et al., *Still Ain't Satisfied*, 93–107.

9 *Kinesis* (May 1982).

10 Warren Magnusson, William K. Carroll, Charles Doyle, Monika Langer, and R.B.J. Walker, eds., *The New Reality: The Politics of Restraint in British Columbia* (Vancouver: New Star Books, 1984).

11 Vancouver City Council, *Minutes* (23 May 1985).

12 Megan Ellis for the Women's House Saving Action, press release, 28 June 1985.

13 'B.C. Ignores Battered Women,' *Kinesis* (July 1985), 1.

14 See *Kinesis*, April and May 1986.

15 Sharlene Frank, *Family Violence in Aboriginal Communities: A First Nations Report* (Victoria: Queen's Printer, 1992); Ontario Native Women's Association, *Breaking Free – A Proposal for Change to Aboriginal Family Violence* (Thunder Bay, ON: Ontario Native Women's Association, 1991).

16 Linda MacLeod and Maria Shin, *Isolated, Afraid and Forgotten: The Service Delivery Needs and Realities of Immigrant and Refugee Women Who Are Battered* (Ottawa: National Clearinghouse on Family Violence, Health and Welfare Canada, 1990); Enashki Dua, 'Racism or Gender? Understanding Oppression of South-Asian Canadian Women,' *Canadian Woman Studies* 13, no. 1 (1992), 6–10; and U. Thaker, 'Combatting Family Violence: the South Asian Experience in Canada,' *Canadian Woman Studies* 13, no. 1 (1992), 30–2.

17 *Feminist Manifesto* (1985).

18 See, for example, Roxanne Ng, *The Politics of Community Services: Immigrant Women, Class and the State* (Toronto: Garamond Press, 1988); Eric Shragge and Linda Davies, eds., *Bureaucracy and Community: Essays on the Politics of Social Work Practice* (Montreal: Black Rose Books, 1990); and Roxanne Ng, Gillian Walker, and Jacob Muller, eds., *Community Organization and the Canadian State* (Toronto: Garamond Press, 1990).

**11: Municipal Foreign Policy**

1 Earl H. Fry, Lee H. Radebaugh, and Panyotis Soldatos, eds., *The New International Cities Era: The Global Activities of North American Municipal Governments* (Provo, UT: David M. Kennedy Center for International Studies, Brigham Young University, 1989).

2 However, see Chadwick F. Alger, 'The World Relations of Cities: Closing the Gap Between Social Science Paradigms and Everyday Human Experience,' *International Studies Quarterly* 34 (1990), 493–518; and Heidi Hobbs, *City Hall Goes Abroad: The Foreign Policy of Local Politics* (Thousand Oaks, CA: SAGE, 1994). The best source of information on American municipal initiatives in the latter part of this period is *The Bulletin of Municipal Foreign Policy* (1987–91), published by the Center for Innovative Diplomacy (then located at 17931 Sky Park Circle, Suite F, Irvine, California 92714 and subsequently relocated to the Institute for Policy Studies in Washington, D.C.). See also *The New Abolitionist*, Newsletter of Nuclear Free America, 325 East 25th Street, Baltimore, MD 21218, and *News from MCLI*, Meiklejohn Civil Liberties Institute, Box 673, Berkeley, CA 94701.

3 The first five American congregations to declare sanctuaries for Central American refugees made their announcements on 24 March 1982, the anniversary of Archbishop Romero's assassination. These included the Southside Presbyterian Church in Tucson, Arizona, and the First Lutheran Church in Berkeley, California. My thanks to the Reverend Gus Schultz of First Lutheran for this information.

4 My thanks to Penny Deleray, Administrator of the National Sanctuary

Defense Fund, 942 Market Street, Room 708, San Francisco, CA 9412–4008, for supplying this information. Compare the weaker resolution adopted in Takoma Park, MD, reprinted in Michael H. Shuman, *Building Municipal Foreign Policies: An Action Handbook for Citizens and Local Elected Officials* (Irvine, CA: Center for Innovative Diplomacy, n.d.), 52–3.

5 '29 U.S. Cities Declare Themselves Sanctuaries,' *Bulletin of Municipal Foreign Policy* 3, no. 4 (Autumn 1989), 18.

6 Victor Merina, 'Council votes 8–6 for L.A. sanctuary,' *Los Angeles Times*, 28 November 1985. Compare Mayor Tom Bradley's address to the National League of Cities (10 December 1985), reprinted in Shuman, *Building Municipal Foreign Policies*, 4–6. On the ambiguous role of the local diocese of the Roman Catholic Church, see Mike Davis, *City of Quartz: Excavating the Future in Los Angeles* (London: Verso, 1990), 350–6.

7 'San Francisco Backs Plan to Safeguard Refugees,' *New York Times*, 25 December 1985, 7. On 9 May 1988, the Board of Supervisors declared San Francisco a city of refuge from South Africa and Namibia as well. *Bulletin of Municipal Foreign Policy* 2, no. 3 (Summer 1988), 42.

8 E.P. Thompson and Dan Smith, eds., *Protest and Survive* (Harmondsworth: Penguin, 1980); and E. Thompson, *Zero Option* (London: The Merlin Press, 1980).

9 Pam Solo, *From Protest to Policy: Beyond the Freeze to Common Security* (Cambridge, MA: Ballinger, 1988).

10 Gordon C. Bennett, *The New Abolitionists: The Story of Nuclear Free Zones* (Elgin, IL: The Brethren Press, 1987), 80, 82–3.

11 Manchester City Council, *Manchester: A Nuclear Free City* (July 1987).

12 Compare Solo, *From Protest to Policy*, and John Trinkl, 'Struggles for Disarmament in the USA,' in Mike Davis and Michael Sprinker, eds., *Reshaping the US Left: Popular Struggles in the 1980s, The Year Left* 3 (London: Verso, 1988), 51–62. Attracting less media attention was the Jobs with Peace campaign that began in San Francisco in 1978, and led to ballot initiatives in eighty-five cities on the redirection of military spending. 'Jobs with Peace: Mayors Should be "Mad as Hell",' *Bulletin of Municipal Foreign Policy* 3, no. 2 (Spring 1989), 18.

13 See Bennett, *The New Abolitionists*, Appendix D, for a chronological listing. This listing is updated periodically in *The New Abolitionist*.

14 Bennett, *The New Abolitionists*, 7.

15 See, for example, Proposed Ordinance Designating Washington County, Indiana, a Nuclear Weapons-Free Zone, 1984, in 'Nuclear Free Zone Legislation,' mimeo. (Baltimore, MD: Nuclear Free America, n.d.). For the most part, penalties for violating such NFZ regulations in the United States are minor; Berkeley is exceptional in imposing a thirty-day jail term and a $500 fine for each violation (with each day being considered a separate violation).

16 'Sample Legislation on Nuclear Free Investments and Contracts,' in 'Nuclear Free Zone Legislation,' 33–4. Takoma Park, MD, was in 1983 the first community to adopt a divestment policy with respect to nuclear weaponry, although its initial measure was looser than this. The ordinance is reproduced in Bennett, Appendix E, 257–63. A dozen communities had adopted such measures by 1989. *The New Abolitionist* (June/July 1989), 4.

17 'Sample Legislation on Nuclear Investments,' 34. Takoma Park also led the way on purchasing and contracting. The borough of Southwark, England, resolved in December 1982 not to employ any of the firms involved at the Cruise missile site at Greenham Common. Peterborough and Haringey councils took similar stands with respect to Cruise missile work in 1985. In 1984–5 Hackney and Camden adopted more general resolutions with respect to arms contractors. However, there was little progress in carrying these resolutions into effect before the central government reacted with legislation to curb 'contract compliance' policies at the local level. National Steering Committee, Nuclear Free Zone Authorities, 'Nuclear Free Zones and Contractor Policies,' *NSC Briefing No. 8* (July 1986). In contrast, American municipalities gradually made their boycotts more effective, by insisting on 'nuclear-free' declarations from suppliers and checking them against information supplied by Nuclear Free America and other national research organizations.

18 See the Model Ordinance on Transportation of Hazardous (including radioactive) Materials and Waste, developed by the Environmental Policy Institute, 218 D Street S.E., Washington 20003. ('It is based on similar ordinances in large cities, perhaps most closely on Boston's, and is designed primarily for a densely populated city or county.' Dr. Fred Millar, EPI, covering letter.) However, such regulatory activity may be ultra vires: Sachnoff, Weaver & Rubenstein, Ltd., *Opinion for Chicago Clergy and Laity Concerned, February 25, 1986*, 21.

19 The most brilliant examples of this come from Britain, especially Manchester and London. See *London under Attack*: The Report of the Greater London Area War Risk Study Commission (Oxford: Basil Blackwell, 1986), and Manchester City Council, *Manchester: A Nuclear Free City* (July 1987). However, American cities have not been inactive: 'New York and Milwaukee high schools teach "peace studies" courses. San Francisco, Cambridge, Massachusetts, and Boulder, Colorado, have produced and disseminated pamphlets describing the effects of nuclear war and arguing for a nuclear freeze.' Michael H. Shuman, 'Dateline Main Street: Local Foreign Policies,' *Foreign Policy* 65 (Winter 1986–7), 160.

20 'The Nuclear Weapon Free Chicago Ordinance,' City of Chicago, *Municipal Code*, c. 202 [1986]. Compare 'A Sample Ordinance to Study the Local Eco-

nomic Impacts of Military Spending,' *Bulletin of Municipal Foreign Policy* 2, no. 4 (Autumn 1988), 3; and 'As It Lay Dying,' ibid., 28–30. See also 'Chicago: Peace in the Midst of Controversy,' *Bulletin* 3, no. 2 (Spring 1989), 40–1. The Chicago Commission received a budget of only $12,000 – obviously not enough to do a great deal of work. See Cheryl Devall, 'Seeking a nuclear-free economy,' *Chicago Tribune*, 10 August 1988, 1,9. Compare 'Dealing with Reality: Baltimore Commission Brings the Peace Movement to City Hall,' *Bulletin of Municipal Foreign Policy* 3, no. 1 (Winter 1988–9), 30–2.

21 Nancy Skinner, 'Making Energy Policy, Not War,' *Bulletin of Municipal Foreign Policy* 5, no. 2 (Spring 1991), 14–15.

22 Janice Love, *The U.S. Anti-Apartheid Movement: Local Activism in Global Politics* (New York: Praeger, 1985).

23 Nuclear Free America, 'Nuclear Free Zones and the Law,' 40.

24 Sachnoff, Weaver & Rubenstein, Ltd., for Chicago Clergy and Laity Concerned, 25 February 1986. The ordinance itself is reprinted in Shuman, *Building Municipal Foreign Policies*, 53–4.

25 Meiklejohn Civil Liberties Institute, Peace Law & Education Project, 'Memorandum: Using Peace Law in Local Government Work' (Meiklejohn Civil Liberties Institute, Box 673, Berkeley, CA 94701, January 1986), 4. This is part of the 'Peace Law Packet' available from the Meiklejohn Institute. My thanks to Ann Fagan Ginger for these materials. See Bennett, *The New Abolitionists*, 163–84, for similar arguments.

26 See Berkeley Ordinance No. 5784–N.S., adopted by initiative in 1986. Available in the Meiklejohn Civil Liberties Institute, 'Peace Law Packet.'

27 Shuman, *Building Municipal Foreign Policies*, 31.

28 Larry Agran, 'There They Go Again,' *Bulletin of Municipal Foreign Policy* 3, no. 3 (Summer 1989), 5. See Shuman, *Building Municipal Foreign Policies*, 31–6, for a fuller analysis.

29 Nuclear Free America, 'Nuclear Free Zones and the Law,' 15–26. Compare Bennett, *The New Abolitionists*, 164–7.

30 Michael Shuman, 'Dateline Main Street: Courts vs. Local Foreign Policies,' *Foreign Policy* 86 (April 1992), 160.

31 'FEMA's problems began in 1982, when it tried implementing "crisis relocation planning," which called for the evacuation of two-thirds of the U.S. population from cities to rural areas in the event of mounting international tensions and an imminent nuclear war. The $4.2 billion scheme slid off the drawing boards when more than 120 jurisdictions (representing some 90 million people) officially refused to participate, calling the program unworkable, chaotic, and dangerous.' 'FEMA Runs for Shelter,' *Bulletin of Municipal Foreign Policy* 1, no. 3 (Summer/Autumn 1987), 29. The same article reports that

Congress had recently refused funding for a new network of bomb shelters. 'Congressional action also forced FEMA to back down from its threats in recent months to cut off funds for all emergency planning (including for fires, floods, and earthquakes) from any state refusing to participate in its so-called "regional communications exercises," designed to test civil defense responses after a nuclear strike.' Ibid.

32 United Kingdom, Home Office, *Protect and Survive* (London: HMSO, 1980).

33 Thompson and Smith, *Protest and Survive.*

34 *Manchester: A Nuclear Free City,* 43–5.

35 NFZ NSC, 'Conventional War Planning in a Nuclear Weapon State,' *NSC Briefing No. 6* (January 1986).

36 NFZ NSC, 'Planning Assumptions Study: The Basic Guide,' ibid.

37 *London under Attack.*

38 Nuclear Free Zones National Steering Committee (NFZ NSC), 'The Hazards of Promoting Civil Defence: An Examination of the Home Office's "Civil Protection" Policy,' *NSC Briefing No. 12 (a)* (June 1987).

39 NFZ NSC, 'A Briefing Document for Fire and Civil Defence Authority Members on the NFZ Approach to Civil Defence,' *NSC Briefing No. 10* (October 1986).

40 NFZ NSC, 'A 'Planned Program for Implementation (PPI) for the 1983 Civil Defence Regulations,' *NSC Briefings No. 13 (a)–(h)* (January 1987 – December 1988).

41 *Local Government Act 1986* s 2 and *Local Government Act 1988* s 27.

42 NFZ NSC, 'Nuclear Issues, Local Authorities and Publicity: The Legal Framework,' *NSC Briefing No. 28* (November 1988).

43 The Secretary, National Conference of Nuclear Free Zone Authorities, *Report for Resolution* (27 March 1987), 6.

44 'The move to make nuclear free mean exactly that, opposition to the total nuclear fuel cycle, came at the A.G.M. of the NFZ movement at Dundee in September. From now on the terms of reference of the local authorities' National Steering Committee will include a commitment to the phasing out of nuclear power, combined with an equally strong policy to promote alternative energy sources and employment opportunities for displaced nuclear power workers.' Campaign for Nuclear Disarmament, *Nuclear Free Zone Bulletin,* no. 12 (December 1986), 1. Compare NFZ NSC, 'Taking NFZ Initiatives into the Mainstream,' A.G.M. Report 1987, *NSC Briefing No. 15* (1987); 'NFZ National Priorities and NSC Work Programme Report,' *NSC Briefing No. 14* (March 1987).

45 NFZ NSC, 'Local Authority Radiation Monitoring Conference Documents,' *NSC Briefing No. 17* (April 1987).

46 NFZ NSC, 'The Road Transport of Nuclear Warheads,' *NSC Briefing No. 7* (revised April 1987).
47 Humberside County Council for the NFZ NSC, 'Radioactive Waste Disposal in the UK: Current Position,' *NSC Briefing No. 27* (November 1988).
48 And, of course, educate them about nuclear war. See Fiona Cooper for the NFZ NSC, 'Peace Education – One Day Local Authority Conference,' *NSC Briefing No. 16* (January 1987), and NFZ NSC, 'Ministry of Defence Video – 'Keeping the Peace,' *NSC Briefings 22 (a)–(d)* (November 1987 – June 1988).
49 NFZ NSC 'Disaster Planning and Preparedness for Major Nuclear Accidents,' *NSC Briefing No. 32* (November 1988); 'Nuclear Facilities and Emergency Planning in the UK,' *NSC Briefing No. 34* (February 1989).
50 NFZ NSC, 'Alternatives to Nuclear Power: Promoting Energy Efficiency and Energy Conservation,' *NSC Briefing No. 24* (June 1988).
51 Susan Willett for the NFZ NSC, 'The Feasibility of a National Diversification Unit,' *NSC Briefing No. 31* (September 1988).
52 'Local Initiatives: Can They Meet the Environmental Crisis?' *Bulletin of Municipal Foreign Policy* 5, no. 1 (Winter 1990–1), 13.
53 'Cambridge: Winning the Middle Ground,' *Bulletin of Municipal Foreign Policy* 3, no. 2 (Spring 1989), 31–3. The ordinance establishing Cambridge's Peace Commission is reproduced in Shuman, *Building Municipal Foreign Policies*, 51–2.
54 Eric Bailey, 'Civic Leaders Launch Effort to Save Ozone: Inability of Nations to Stem Growing Crisis Spurs Action by Delegates at Irvine Conference,' *Los Angeles Times*, 22 July 1989. See also *Bulletin of Municipal Foreign Policy* 3, no. 4 (Autumn 1989), 8–12; and Cheryl Downey, 'Officials gather in Irvine to find local solutions to global problems,' *The Orange County Register*, 22 July 1989.
55 Maureen Law and Jean Larivière, 'Canada and WHO: Giving and Receiving,' *Health Promotion* 26, no. 4 (Spring 1988), 4.
56 This is WHO's code word for social inequality and economic exploitation.
57 Quotations in this paragraph are from 'Cologne Appeal: Joint Action of NGOs and Local Communities for North-South Development Co-operation: "From Charity to Justice",' in *Bulletin of Municipal Foreign Policy* 2, no. 4 (Autumn 1988), 58–9.
58 Trevor Hancock, Bernard Pouliot, and Pierre Duplessis, 'Public Health,' in Richard A. Loreto and Trevor Price, eds., *Urban Policy Issues: Canadian Perspectives* (Toronto: McClelland & Stewart, 1990), 193. See also Trevor Hancock, 'Public Health Planning in the City of Toronto – Part 1. Conceptual Planning,' and Diana Baxter, 'Public Health Planning in the City of Toronto – Part 2. Turning Concepts into Programs,' *Canadian Journal of Public Health* 77 (May/June 1986), 180–9; also Heather MacDougall, *Activists and Advocates: Toronto's Health Department, 1883–1983* (Toronto: Dundurn Press, 1990), 283–9.

59 Barbara J. Lane, 'Healthy Cities in the U.K.: Implications for Canadian Healthy Communities Projects,' *Plan Canada* 29, no. 4 (July 1989), 5–12.
60 United Kingdom, Department of Health and Social Security, *Inequalities in Health: Report of a Research Working Group* (London: DOHSS, 1980).
61 Although coded in other terms, the socialist slant of the WHO Project comes through clearly enough in an early working paper: [Trevor Hancock and Leonard Duhl] WHO Healthy Cities Project, *Promoting Health in the Urban Context*, WHO Healthy Cities Papers, No. 1 (Copenhagen: FADL, 1988), 41. Hancock was Associate Medical Officer of Health in Toronto, Duhl a professor at Berkeley. For further analysis, see John Ashton, ed., *Healthy Cities* (Milton Keynes: Open University Press, 1992), and John K. Davies and Michael P. Kelly, eds., *Healthy Cities: Research & Practice* (London: Routledge, 1993).
62 Lane, 'Healthy Cities in the U.K.,' 7.
63 Geoff Green, 'Health and Social Policy in Sheffield' (A Sheffield District Labour Party Education Paper/Conference of Socialist Economists Discussion Paper, 31 October 1988). Compare Sheffield City Council, *Good Health for All: The Sheffield Plan* (1987).
64 The Canadian Project is jointly sponsored by the Canadian Institute of Planners, the Canadian Public Health Association, and the Federation of Canadian Municipalities, with a grant from the federal government. See Trevor Hancock, 'Healthy Cities: The Canadian Project,' *Health Promotion* 26, no. 1 (Summer 1987), 2–4, 27; and Susan Berlin, 'The Canadian Healthy Community Project: Shapes of the Reality,' *Plan Canada* 29, no. 4 (July 1989), 13–15. There is a parallel project in Quebec: Réal Lacombe et Louis Poirier, 'Villes et villages en santé,' *Plan Canada* 29, no. 4 (July 1989), 16–21. In *Achieving Health for All: A Framework for Health Promotion* (Ottawa: Health and Welfare Canada, 1986), the federal government had advanced a new health promotion strategy based on fostering public participation, strengthening community health services, and co-ordinating healthy public policy. This fit with WHO's new emphases, expressed in the *Ottawa Charter for Health Promotion* (Geneva: WHO, 1986), named after a WHO conference in that city.
65 See, for instance, Ann Goldblatt, 'Edmonton's Healthy Communities Initiative,' and R. W. Kendal, 'The Healthy Communities Project: Healthy Capital Regional District 2000,' Plan Canada 29, no. 4 (July 1989), 22–7. However, see Barbara J. Lane, *Canadian Healthy Communities Project: A Conceptual Model for Winnipeg* (Winnipeg: Institute of Urban Studies, University of Winnipeg, 1989), for a more innovative, participatory strategy. Compare Brijesh Mathur, 'Community Planning and the New Public Health,' *Plan Canada* 29, no. 4 (July 1989), 35–44.
66 *Healthy Toronto 2000* (Toronto: Board of Health, City of Toronto, September 1988).

67 Sheffield's health plan also contemplates development of a food policy. Sheffield City Council, *Good Health for All*, 20.
68 Prompted especially by women's concerns.
69 'City Council [should] develop a Community Development Policy and facilitate community empowerment through its grants, through purchase of service agreements with community groups, where appropriate, and by ensuring that all City departments use community development approaches.' *Healthy Toronto 2000*, 12.
70 The strategy was 'to include targets for resource and energy conservation, pollution control, recycling and waste management and the incorporation of sustainability criteria in the Official Plan.' *Healthy Toronto 2000*, 12.
71 Preface to David Regan, *The New City Republics: Municipal Intervention in Defence* (London: Institute for European Defence and Strategic Studies, 1987).
72 Regan, 57. Compare 'Sanity Disarmament,' *Wall Street Journal*, 8 May 1989: 'Unless reined in such actions could create a foreign-policy Tower of Babel that would weaken the federal government's ability to further American interests. With members of Congress such as Jim Wright already trying to usurp the role of Secretary of State, the United States has enough trouble developing one foreign policy. It cannot tolerate cities and states developing hundreds of their own.'

**12: Social Movements and the Global City**

1 Compare Eric R. Wolf, *Europe and the People without History* (Berkeley: University of California Press, 1982), Chapter 1; and John A. Agnew and Stuart Corbridge, *Mastering Space: Hegemony, Territory and International Political Economy* (London: Routledge, 1995).
2 To create a political space is to establish a domain for public action in which various positions and, hence, various relationships and identities become possible, and others are implicitly excluded. Thus, to establish the state as the predominant political space is to create the relation of citizens and noncitizens, and to open a range of political possibilities for those who enjoy the status of citizenship. A social movement may establish a relationship – as between worker and worker or woman and woman, for instance – that challenges the divisions between citizens in different states and in the process posits a new political space in which, say, workers of the world struggle against capitalism or women of the world unite against patriarchy. Needless to say, it takes more than a brave proclamation to make such an alternative space effective politically.
3 For a brilliant – and still relevant – opening to the discourse of the global city,

see John Friedmann and Goetz Wolff, 'World City Formation: An Agenda for Research and Action,' *International Journal of Urban and Regional Research* 6 (1982), 309–44. Like those who follow them, they tend to speak of world cities or global cities as distinct entities – which is not the approach suggested here. Compare Michael Timberlake, ed., *Urbanization in the World-Economy* (Orlando, Florida: Academic Press, 1985). For more recent writing, see Michael Peter Smith and Joe R. Feagin, *The Capitalist City: Global Restructuring and Community Politics* (Oxford: Basil Blackwell, 1987); Hank V. Savitch, *Post-Industrial Cities: Politics and Planning in New York, Paris and London* (Princeton, NJ: Princeton University Press, 1988); Anthony D. King, *Global Cities* (New York: Routledge and Kegan Paul, 1990); Saskia Sassen, *The Global City: New York, London, Tokyo* (Princeton, NJ: Princeton University Press, 1991); and Susan S. Fainstein, *The City Builders: Property, Politics, and Planning in London and New York* (Oxford: Blackwell, 1994). Compare Roland Robertson, *Globalization: Social Theory and Global Culture* (London: SAGE, 1992); Mike Featherstone, Scott Lash, and Roland Robertson, eds., *Global Modernities* (London: SAGE, 1995); and Malcolm Waters, *Globalization* (London: Routledge, 1995).

4 On this issue, see especially David Harvey, *The Condition of Postmodernity* (Oxford: Basil Blackwell, 1989); and Fredric Jameson, *Postmodernism: Or, the Cultural Logic of Late Capitalism* (Durham, NC: Duke University Press, 1991).

5 See Max Weber, *Economy and Society* 2, ed. Guenther Roth and Claus Wittich, (Berkeley, CA: University of California Press, 1978), Chapter 16. This section of Weber's work has also been translated in Weber, *The City*, ed. Don Martindale and Gertrud Neuwirth (New York: The Free Press, 1958).

6 This is not to suggest that Weber would have agreed with this formulation – on the contrary. See Brian Elliott and David McCrone, *The City: Patterns of Domination and Conflict* (London: Macmillan, 1982), for a careful discussion of Weber's urban sociology. More generally, compare Lewis Mumford, *The Culture of Cities* (New York: Harcourt Brace Jovanovich, 1970) and *The City in History* (New York: Harcourt, Brace, 1961); Jane Jacobs, *The Economy of Cities* (New York: Random House, 1969); and R.J. Holton, *Cities, Capitalism and Civilization* (London: George Allen & Unwin, 1986).

7 The new urban sociology was dominated by the Chicago School of 'human ecology.' See Robert E. Park, Ernest W. Burgess, and Roderick D. McKenzie, *The City* (Chicago: University of Chicago Press, 1925); and Amos Hawley, *Human Ecology: A Theory of Community Structure* (New York: Ronald Press, 1950). Richard Sennett, ed., *Classic Essays on the Culture of Cities* (New York: Appleton-Century-Crofts, 1969), brings a number of the interesting contributions together with earlier German work.

8 Louis Wirth, 'Urbanism as a Way of Life,' *American Journal of Sociology* 44

(1938), 1–24, reprinted in Wirth, *On Cities and Social Life*, ed. Albert J. Reiss (Chicago: University of Chicago Press, 1964).

9 The dates here are meant to be suggestive rather than exact. In fact, there was already a widespread recognition of the implications of urban spread in the 1880s. V.D. Lipman, *Local Government Areas, 1834–1945* (Oxford: Basil Blackwell, 1949).

10 See especially Michael Peter Smith, *The City and Social Theory* (New York: St. Martin's Press, 1979), 1–48. For more general critical discussions, see Manuel Castells, *The Urban Question* (London: Edward Arnold, 1977); Peter Saunders, *Social Theory and the Urban Question*, 2nd ed. (London: Hutchinson, 1986); and Harold Chorney, *City of Dreams: Social Theory and the Urban Experience* (Toronto: Nelson, 1990).

11 See Chris Pickvance, ed., *Urban Sociology: Critical Essays* (London: Tavistock, 1976); and Stuart Lowe, *Urban Social Movements* (London: Macmillan, 1986). Compare Frances Fox Piven and Richard A. Cloward, *Poor People's Movements* (New York: Vintage Books, 1979).

12 As well as *The Urban Question*, see Castells, *City, Class and Power* (London: Macmillan, 1978), *The City and the Grassroots* (Berkeley and Los Angeles: University of California Press, 1983), and *The Informational City* (Oxford: Basil Blackwell, 1989).

13 The public-choice approach to urban political economy was first adumbrated in the 1950s. Two articles were especially influential: Charles Tiebout, 'A Pure Theory of Local Expenditures,' *Journal of Political Economy* 44 (1956), 416–24; and Vincent Ostrom, Charles Tiebout, and Robert Warren, 'The Organization of Government in Metropolitan Areas,' *American Political Science Review* 55 (1961), 831–42. The analysis by Ostrom and his colleagues ought to be of particular interest to scholars of international relations because it gives an account of the conditions under which a beneficial order may emerge when there is competition and conflict between autonomous governments. The public-choice approach was further developed in works such as Robert L. Bish and Vincent Ostrom, *Understanding Urban Government: Metropolitan Reform Reconsidered* (Washington: American Enterprise Institute, 1973); and Paul E. Peterson, *City Limits* (Chicago: University of Chicago Press, 1981). A radical alternative, influenced by the revival of Marxist theory in the late 1960s, began to emerge with the publication of works such as David Harvey, *Social Justice and the City* (Baltimore: Johns Hopkins University Press, 1973); Harvey Molotch, 'The City as Growth Machine: Toward a Political Economy of Place,' *American Journal of Sociology* 82 (1976), 309–32; Michael Harloe, ed., *Captive Cities: Studies in the Political Economy of Cities and Regions* (London: Wiley, 1977); William K. Tabb and Larry Sawers, eds., *Marxism and the Metrop-*

*olis* (New York: Oxford University Press, 1978); and Kevin Cox, ed., *Urbanization and Conflict in Market Societies* (Chicago: Maaroufa, 1978). Among the later work of particular interest, see David Harvey, *The Urbanization of Capital* (Baltimore: Johns Hopkins University Press, 1985) and *Consciousness and the Urban Experience* (Baltimore; Johns Hopkins University Press, 1985); John R. Logan and Harvey L Molotch, *Urban Fortunes: The Political Economy of Place* (Berkeley and Los Angeles: University of California Press, 1987); Edward W. Soja, *Postmodern Geographies* (London: Verso, 1989); Sharon Zukin, *Landscapes of Power: From Detroit to Disneyworld* (Berkeley: University of California Press, 1991); and Scott Lash and John Urry, *Economies of Signs and Space* (London: SAGE, 1994).

14 This is one way of interpreting the phenomenon of the 'postmodern.' For early appreciations of the disorder of the city (and implicit critiques of sovereignty), see Jane Jacobs, *The Death and Life of Great American Cities* (New York: Random House, 1961); Richard Sennett, *The Uses of Disorder: Personal Identity and City Life* (New York: Vintage Books, 1970); Jonathan Raban, *Soft City* (London: Hamish Hamilton, 1974); and Sennett, *The Fall of Public Man: On the Social Psychology of Capitalism* (New York: Vintage, 1978). Compare the later, bleaker reflections in Mike Davis, *City of Quartz: Excavating the Future in Los Angeles* (London: Verso, 1990); and Timothy Luke, 'Discourse of Disintegration, Texts of Transformation: Re-Reading Realism in the New World Order,' *Alternatives: Social Transformation and Humane Governance* 18 (1993), 229–58.

15 Robert A. Dahl, 'The City in the Future of Democracy,' *American Political Science Review* 61, no. 4 (1967), 953–70.

16 Compare Bob Rowthorn, 'The Past Strikes Back,' in Stuart Hall and Martin Jaques, eds., *The Politics of Thatcherism* (London: Lawrence and Wishart, 1983), 63–78; and Nicolas Costello, Jonathan Michie, and Seumas Milne, *Beyond the Casino Economy: Planning for the 1990s* (London: Verso, 1989), 115–45. See also Richard Minns, *Take Over the City* (London: Pluto Press, 1982); Jerry Coakley and Laurence Harris, *The City of Capital* (Oxford: Basil Blackwell, 1983); and Greater London Council, *The London Financial Strategy* (1986).

17 Compare Michael J. Shapiro, 'Spatiality and Policy Discourse: Reading the Global City,' *Reading the Postmodern Polity: Political Theory as Textual Practice* (Minneapolis: University of Minnesota Press, 1992), 86–103. The concept of a 'space of flows' is from Manuel Castells. See his 'European Cities, the Informational Society, and the Global Economy,' *New Left Review*, no. 204 (March/April 1994), 18–32; and more generally *The Informational City*. On nomad identities, see Melucci, *Nomads of the Present*; and Gilles Deleuze and Felix Guatarri, *Anti-Oedipus: Capitalism and Schizophrenia* (New York: Viking Press, 1977). Compare Jon Bird, Barry Curtis, Tim Putnam, George Robertson, and

Lisa Tickner, eds., *Mapping the Futures: Local Cultures, Global Change* (London: Routledge, 1993).

18 Fernand Braudel, *Civilization and Capitalism, 15th-18th Century,* 3 vols. (London: Collins, 1981–4). See also Braudel, *The Mediterranean and the Mediterranean World in the Age of Philip II,* 2 vols. (London: Collins, 1972).

19 William Gibson is normally credited with inventing the concept of cyberspace. On hyperspace as it is understood by physicists, see Michio Kaku, *Hyperspace: A Scientific Odyssey through Parallel Universes, Time Warps, and the Tenth Dimension* (New York: Oxford University Press, 1994). Compare Baudrillard's account of 'hyperreality' in Mark Poster, ed., *Jean Baudrillard: Selected Writings* (Stanford, CA: Stanford University Press, 1988); and the more conventionally materialist interpretations in Erik A. Swyngedouw, 'The Heart of the Place: The Resurrection of Locality in an Age of Hyperspace,' *Geografiska Annaler* 71B (1989), 31–42; and Sharon Zukin, 'Socio-Spatial Prototypes of a New Organization of Consumption: The Role of Real Cultural Capital,' *Sociology* 24, no. 1 (1990), 37–56. I use the concept loosely here, to refer to the architectonic domain of the global city, within which various spatializations appear. One can think of each spatialization as a region of hyperspace in which some dimensions of reality are apparent and others are concealed. On this, more below.

20 On this subject, see especially Harvey, *The Condition of Postmodernity,* Jameson, *Postmodernism,* Zukin, *Landscapes of Power,* and Doreen Massey, *Space, Place and Gender* (Cambridge: Polity Press, 1994).

21 *Understanding Media: The Extensions of Man* (New York: Signet, 1964).

22 Students of international relations will be familiar with analyses such as Stephen Gill and David Law, *The Global Political Economy* (Baltimore: Johns Hopkins University Press, 1988). Compare Peter K. Eisinger, *The Rise of the Entrepreneurial State: State and Local Economic Development Policy in the United States* (Madison, WI: University of Wisconsin Press, 1988); Gregory D. Squires, ed., *Unequal Partnerships: The Political Economy of Urban Development in Postwar America* (New Brunswick, NJ: Rutgers University Press, 1989); and Mark Schneider, *The Competitive City: The Political Economy of Suburbia* (Pittsburgh: University of Pittsburgh Press, 1989).

23 Walker, *Inside/Outside,* Chapter 6.

24 Alternatively, 'society' may be identified with social relations in general, so that all forms of politics come to be understood as forms of social activity, to be interpreted sociologically. This is a nice move for sociologists to make, since it reduces the study of politics to a branch of sociology. However, it does not explain the nature of politics. The perspective here is that society must be understood as a political construct, and not the other way around.

25 Aristotle, *The Politics*, especially Books 3 and 4.

26 Until the 1970s, most of the literature on social movements reflected a social control perspective, from which movements appeared as a threat to good order. See Eyerman and Jamison, *Social Movements*, Chapter 1.

27 This is not a criticism I would apply to Marx.

28 Gerder Lerner, *The Creation of Patriarchy* (New York: Oxford University Press, 1986).

29 Kaku, *Hyperspace*.

30 For instance, the environmental movement defines the world as an ecosystem with naturally determined regions. Its political organization must reflect this perception, and that means struggling against the forms of government and politics that make it difficult to address environmental issues. As it gains in strength, the movement begins to impose its understanding of natural regions on other actors, and forces them to address issues within that spatial framework. Neither the global nor the regional ecosystem is a natural unit of organization for other social movements, including ones like the traditional labour movement or the contemporary women's movement, which claim affinities. Marxists long thought that the factory was the natural site of workers' organization. Industries were their regions. Similarly, feminists have had to address themselves to women's distinctive experiences and autonomous activities, and this has involved different forms of localization and regionalization. Although there are similarities in the modalities of organization and repertoires of action of all the contemporary social movements, each movement is obliged to organize a political space appropriate to its own objectives. These spatializations do not conform to any single pattern.

31 See John Kao, 'The Worldwide Web of Chinese Business,' *Harvard Business Review* 71, no. 2 (1993), 24–7, 30–4, 36; Dudley L. Poston, Jr., and Mei-Yu Yu, 'The Distribution of the Overseas Chinese in the Contemporary World,' *International Migration Review* 24 (1990), 480–508; and 'China's Diaspora Turns Homeward,' *The Economist* 329 (27 November 1993), 21–2, 24. Compare Peter Nemetz, ed., *The Pacific Rim: Investment, Development and Trade* (Vancouver: University of British Columbia Press, 1990).

32 Compare Louis Kraar, 'A New China Without Borders, *Fortune* 126, no. 7 (5 October 1992), 124–6, 128; Louise de Rosario, 'Network Capitalism,' *Far Eastern Economic Review* (2 December 1993), 17; and Philippe Le Corré, 'Canada's Hong Kong,' *Far Eastern Economic Review* (10 February 1994), 36–7. More generally, see Peter Kwong, *The New Chinatown* (New York: Hill and Wang, 1987); Bernard Wong, *Partnership, Brokerage, Entrepreneurship and the Chinese Community of New York* (New York: AMS Press, 1988); Richard H. Thompson, *Toronto's Chinatown: The Changing Social Organization of an Ethnic*

*Community* (New York: AMS Press, 1989); Donald Gutstein, *The New Landlords: Asian Investment in Canadian Real Estate* (Victoria, BC: Porcepic Books, 1990); and Phillippe Regnier, *Singapore: The City State in Southeast Asia* (London: Hurst, 1991).

33 'Overseas Chinese sources probably account for nearly 80 percent of total foreign investments. Investment from 'real' foreigners, especially from large multinational corporations, has in fact been very low. In China's four special economic zones, the majority of foreign investment has also come from overseas Chinese. This will continue for some time.' Zongli Tang, 'Is China Returning to Semi-Colonial Status?' *Monthly Review* 45, no. 3 (1993), 77–87.

34 On the origins of the Council, see Peter McFarlane, *Brotherhood to Nation: George Manuel and the Making of the Modern Indian Movement* (Toronto: Between the Lines, 1994). See also Augie Fleras and Jean Leonard Elliott, *The Nations Within: Aboriginal-State Relations in Canada, the United States and New Zealand* (Toronto: Oxford University Press, 1992).

35 For a poignant example, see Joe Kane, 'Moi Goes to Washington,' *The New Yorker* 77, no. 11 (2 May 1994), 74–81.

36 James Gleick, *Chaos: Making a New Science* (London: Penguin Books, 1987); and Nina Hall, ed., *Exploring Chaos: A Guide to the New Science of Disorder* (New York: W.W. Norton, 1991).

37 For useful reflections on some of the issues, see Mike Featherstone, ed., *Global Culture: Nationalism, Globalization and Modernity* (London: SAGE, 1990).

# Index